Branislav Dimitrijević
& Jelena Vesić
The Yugoslav Art Space:
Ješa Denegri in the First Person

JRP|EDITIONS & LES PRESSES DU RÉEL

Branislav Dimitrijević
& Jelena Vesić
The Yugoslav Art Space:
Ješa Denegri in the First Person

Table of Contents

INTRODUCTIONS

Learning from Denegri:
Introductory Notes
Branislav Dimitrijević

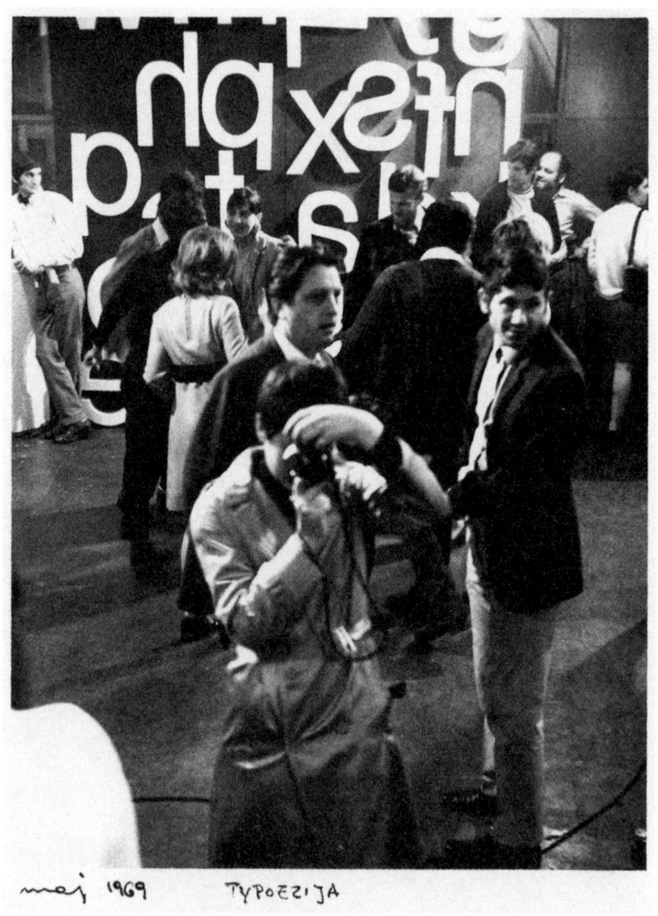

Ješa Denegri (right) at the opening of the exhibition *Typoezija* (*Typoetry*) organised in the context
of *Nove Tendencije 4. Kompjutori i vizuelna istraživanja* (*New Tendencies 4. Computer and Visual Research*),
Galerija suvremene umjetnosti (Gallery of Contemporary Arts), Zagreb, 1969

Ješa Denegri's contribution to and impact on the Yugoslav and post-Yugoslav art space can hardly be overestimated. As the main critical voice behind the term after which this book takes its title – *The Yugoslav Art Space* – his work continues to attract attention, and has for decades served as the point of departure for scholars and artists belonging to or interested in Yugoslav art of the 20th century. However, today 'Yugoslav Art Space' not only signifies the art scene of a vanished country that existed throughout most of the 20th century, but also a real environment of continuously interrelated practices and encounters that stem from a shared historical, social and cultural background, and particularly from shared language(s). By the same token, this shared space cannot simply be boiled down to a space of common identity, as it is also a space of common production as well as a space of politics – and, in fact, a space for the production of politics. The Yugoslav 'socialist experiment' still provokes highly contrasting attitudes and has not been resolved as a completed historical phenomenon. Socialist Yugoslavia remains undead, lingering among the living who cannot simply erase it because this historical entity was, in its day, already an (avant-garde) alternative to the current strains of ideology that operate through a synergetic mix of global capitalism and local nationalisms. The Yugoslav model, for its part, pursued quite the opposite – a fusion of socialism and internationalism – and was an active, revolutionary-driven construction of social *becoming* interwoven with numerous internal contradictions and ultimately overshadowed by the counter-revolutionary act of a civil war that terminated its historical reality, without however preventing it from having an afterlife. This afterlife of Yugoslavia has primarily been developed in the cultural field; and when it comes to practices of visual art this legacy has come to us through, among other sources, the meticulous writings and curatorial work of Ješa Denegri (b. 1936, Split).

This book of conversations may be taken both as the historical testimony of an insider on the social and artistic developments in socialist Yugoslavia, and also as a diachronic map of the artistic activities and collaborations that developed not only before and during the time the country with that name was created and violently destroyed, but afterwards as well. The book focuses on Denegri as an informed witness, a productive protagonist and an insightful interpreter of a highly dynamic period in art – from the late 1950s to the early 1980s – and it also offers researchers of Yugoslavia an important document of an *oral history*, accompanied by a comprehensive index of protagonists. This oral history is here interleaved with translations of some of Denegri's key texts – so that the more flexible tone characteristic of a live conversation is balanced with the rigorous quality of his critical and theoretical writings.

The book is divided into two parts: the first largely consists of discussions about the situation in the 1960s, while the second part dwells on the 1970s, with brief references to and comments on the final decade of socialist Yugoslavia. Given the impressive volume of Denegri's writings, the texts that have been selected for this volume primarily refer to some crucial moments in our transcribed conversations; and this transcription represents just a fraction of the more than 40 hours of audio recorded over the period 2016–2019. The majority of these conversations were held in the Montenegran coastal town of Budva, in the house of the late painter Filo Filipović and his wife Dušanka (to whom we are especially grateful) and continued on several occasions in Belgrade. Making a selection of these recordings proved the biggest challenge for me and my co-editor Jelena Vesić, and the whole process took far longer than originally expected. However, what was invaluable in the process was the time spent together, getting to know Ješa Denegri much better personally and gaining so much from his knowledge, his way of thinking and his takes on art, together with his overwhelming personal charm.

This book arrives in a time of particularly heightened interest in the Yugoslav culture, art and architecture that somehow 'survived' its post-1989 inclusion in the larger overall category of 'Central and Eastern European Art'. For many ex-Yugoslav scholars (Denegri included) the geo-political operation of what has been called East Art[1] – for which the radical art practices in socialism have largely been perceived as a 'dissident' challenge to the constraints of the 'official' socialist realist, or even 'totalitarian' culture – was primarily a post-1989 tactical move that did not, however, fully observe various implications of the Yugoslav political and cultural specificity within the imposed division between official and dissident cultures and politics. According to Denegri's understanding, the 'Yugoslav Art Space' is an operative, non-identitarian notion that refers to 'a really existing social and political environment' of socialist Yugoslavia and to a variety of artistic practices and discourses, and primarily to the situation of flux, of constant communication and collaboration between artists and other protagonists of the scene. Thus this notion does not speak about a fixed identity, but about a process of *building*, a process in which a backward country devastated during the Second World War achieved extremely rapid modernisation and social emancipation based on promises of economic and social equality that were never fulfilled.

In one of his earliest texts, written in 1965 and entitled 'For an Art of Building', Denegri claims that only 'the ideal of building can prevent art from becoming a part of some new destruction', and argues for an art that will stop being merely the 'refuge of an individual's wounded psyche' and become an 'active and sober construction' finding 'purpose and meaning before a shared contemporaneity and our open future'.[2] From that time on, Denegri's mission was to identify and argue for taking a perspective like this on art, in a variety of manifestations – and to do it not in a reductive manner but by paying full attention to the specificities of individual approaches within the concrete social and political conditions. Out of this emerges another crucial notion in Denegri's vocabulary – that of the 'Art of the Constructive Approach',[3] the notion that emphasises art that transcends the primacy of expressive artistic singularity and enters the social arena as a proposition arguing for art to instigate new social relations beyond its traditional confinement to individuality, singularity and dependence on ceremonial power. But what needs immediate clarification here is the fact that Denegri is no 'dissident' in the socialist realm, but is able to accept that the socialist relations of production and distribution offered a basic 'civilisational level'[4] for Yugoslav society, a level in which that society's art production could realise its full potential.

Denegri was neither a passive observer nor a distanced interpreter of art; rather he played a part in broadening notions of artistic innovation and its challenge to the dominant local traditions. He considered not only those art practices that fitted into his theoretical scheme, but also the entire field of artistic production in Yugoslavia, and he argued not only for its importance in the local art context but also for its contribution to global art history. As a curator at the Museum of Contemporary Art in Belgrade, from its inauguration in 1965 until he took a professorship at the Department of Art History at the University of Belgrade in 1991, Denegri was dedicated both to *being with* the art community and to formulating a historical and theoretical account that would preserve and organise the practices he witnessed or took part in. Every researcher of post-war Yugoslav art knows well that such research could hardly be undertaken without recognising that Denegri had provided the initial interpretation, or at least had identified and kept record of important art events and specific works. Beyond the fact that he served as an institutional curator for 25 years, his role in the artistic development of an era also prefigured the notion of the contemporary curator, of one expected to be continuously curious and abreast of developments and breaks with and within art. In the early 1960s Denegri emerged as a modernist critic *par excellence*, yet he immediately embraced the changes that came with the late 1960s to become one of the main proponents of the New Art Practices. Even by the end of the 1970s, and unlike most of his peers, he embraced rather than rejected the changes in art that emerged after 'Modernism's nervous breakdown'.[5] And most importantly, in the midst of embracing these changes and flows, he meticulously contributed to art history with volumes of books, exhibition catalogues and articles in journals and periodicals, all of which serve to form and constitute a huge map with and by which we understand the term Yugoslav Art Space.

Unlike most other Yugoslav art historians who were studying modern art in order to adapt it to the narratives of national traditions and lineages, Denegri treated the entire operational space of art in Yugoslavia as *heterogenous* and *de-centred*. He articulated real connections rather than assumed differences between 'local traditions'. But again, these connections were not directed or informed by an identitarian logic of bringing the various national cultures under a single umbrella, but were led by the artistic logic of productive, mutual and free cross-fertilisation. This is why it was important for us to present Denegri 'in the first person',[6] through his own words and through direct speech that goes beyond and beneath the rigorously structured theoretical language of his texts. We have taken the opportunity to revisit the history of Yugoslav art as seen through his own experience and theoretical understanding, and also occasionally to contest it with our interventions and friendly provocations. We therefore wish to express our deepest gratitude to Professor Denegri for accepting the challenge of such an open and sweeping dialogue with the intention of presenting the striking relevance that his work still has today – and not only in the specific context of Yugoslav art, but also as a remarkable contribution to art history more generally.

Today, many international exhibitions, major museums and art collections feature and document works and events in which Denegri features as a witness, as an initial interpreter and indeed also frequently as a protagonist. These range in style from the New Tendencies and Gorgona in the 1960s to the emerging New Art Practices in Yugoslavia in the 1970s, whose protagonists included Marina Abramović, Raša Todosijević, Tomislav Gotovac, Braco Dimitrijević, Goran Trbuljak and others Denegri initially wrote about; through the work of the OHO, KÔD and Bosch+Bosch groups and Denegri's participation in the seminal *Oktobar 75* event (1975) at the Student Cultural Centre in Belgrade; and finally to his co-initiating and setting up the last major contemporary art exhibition in Yugoslavia, the second *Yugoslav Documents* in 1989. Today, all these events have for the most part become 'canonised', yet there is a clear need to listen more carefully to the voice that was always present at these events yet never distinctly articulated and internationally acknowledged. Although the topics of our conversations are here limited largely to the 1960s and 1970s, Denegri remains as active as ever, and he is still closely involved in the contemporary art scenes in all of the post-Yugoslav countries.[7]

In his accounts of the history of 20th century art in Yugoslavia, Denegri formulated two main operational terms. The Yugoslav Art Space is the overarching term that encompasses a loose but concretely structured network of professional protagonists, institutions, artworks and academic discourses, and within it a polemical distinction is made between the *main line* in the art produced within this system, and the Other Line in the art that was systematically defined by its own walk on the margins of the professional art system. The Other Line is by no means a replacement for the notion of 'dissident art', as dissidence here does not imply a dissent in relation to the idea of a socialist or communist social structure, or any dissent in relation to the Yugoslav federationist idea. If it was a 'dissident art' of sorts, the Other Line posited it in relation to more deeply embedded national-bourgeois traditions and their modes of institutionalisation. And these modes did in fact inform and channel the main line of post-war modernist art in Yugoslavia. Denegri introduces this term in the late 1970s,[8] and then develops it

in the 1980s;[9] and for our purposes here he sums it up
as follows:

> This term refers to the avant-garde, the neo-avant-
> garde and the radical modernist models of artistic
> language and forms of behaviour articulated in
> the Yugoslav Art Space from the early 1920s to the
> early 1980s. Precisely because of its temporal range,
> the Other Line is not an idea that encompasses
> linguistically-related artistic phenomena intercon-
> nected by a strong stylistic coherence, nor is it a
> term that depends on a strict theoretical foundation.
> It is rather an operational, critical and polemical
> procedure that seeks to emphasise differentiation,
> deviation, parallel existence, separation and even the
> opposition to artistic phenomena that are recognised,
> valued and accepted as mainstream and major ten-
> dencies, and which as a rule are concentrated within
> the mindset of a moderate form of modernism
> with its varying linguistic species and sub-species.[10]

The Other Line is a diachronic structure but not a linear
sequence; rather it is structured as a network that grows
both synchronically and diachronically. For Denegri, the
phenomenon that was the avant-garde groups of the 1920s
in Yugoslavia, like Zenit and Yugo-Dada, is not only a
remarkable historical reference that demonstrates that
Yugoslav groups were part of the international avant-garde
network, but it is also a model of an artistic and intellectual affiliation with the material practices built on differentiation, deviation and opposition that he recognises in
a sequence of artistic events that unfolded in Yugoslavia
in the course of the 20th century. The Yugoslav avant-garde
was thus neither simply a Western-induced phenomenon,
nor an 'authentic' local event within the national cultural
history. Culturally, it was both, but as a material practice
that operated on the margins of the cultural hierarchy it
represented a concrete proposal for an artistic rupture that
created its own urgency and its own time-space. The Other
Line emerged from this founding moment, but it was not
in any sense claiming or establishing a continuity in any *style*,
or in any *school*, or in any *type*, but rather a continuity of

the rupture with both the bourgeois-modernist and the identitarian-folkloric cultural poles in Yugoslavia. Finally, the Other Line concept anticipates a distinction that was introduced by Thierry de Duve in order to oppose the operational logic of 'aesthetic modernism' with what he named 'generic modernism'.[11] From such a perspective, modernist art is to be studied as historical-ontological rather than as aesthetic. In *generic art*, instead of the medium-specific critical judgment of the quality of a painting or a sculpture, there is a critical judgment of the recognition of *art* itself and of the *artistic*. The definition of the Other Line lies precisely in observing the historical ontology of art rather than in observing its aesthetic development, and Denegri thus very early establishes an 'alternative tradition' of modernist art.

And here is one of the main reasons for making this book of conversations with Denegri. His theoretical perspective was most definitely tuned with (Western) modern art history, but as a critical practice it was primarily based on studying peripheral artistic environments, the modes in which they produce their own operational logic and also the modes through which they reproduce their Western influences. If there was a significant Western influence on Yugoslav post-war art, it was most noticeably the influence of media-specific aesthetic modernism – as in the famous example of the influential exhibition and series of lectures that Henry Moore gave in Yugoslavia in 1955,[12] or in more general terms the academic standardisation of the post-Cézannian model of modern painting. Denegri recognised very early on that another kind of art history writing is required to go beyond this legacy that in fact prevents attributing significant critical meaning to the concept of art itself. As a modernist, he remained faithful to the formal analysis of an artwork, something he calls an investigation of the 'operational procedure', which implies the entire process of production of the work of art in its concrete socio-economic context. His analysis transcends the limitations of the aesthetic evaluation of medium-specific works, and engages in the challenge of formulating a historical map of artistic activities that demands something else from a critic or an art historian. The Other Line presents this 'alternative tradition' which is, as we know, and as summed up by

Peter Osborne, 'now the main tradition of artistic modernism in the 20th century, running from Duchamp, Dada, Surrealism and the Russian avant-gardes through to Fluxus, Conceptual art, a certain minimalism … and beyond'.[13] Emerging from and working within the social and artistic contexts of socialist Yugoslavia, i.e. in the Yugoslav Art Space itself, with the term the Other Line Denegri became one of the first art historians to develop a version of this 'alternative tradition' that is today decisive for and integral to our contemporary perspectives on the art of this period and beyond.

[1] An influential example of this tactical intervention of including Eastern European Art in (Western) art history is IRWIN (eds.), *East Art Map: Contemporary Art and Eastern Europe*, MIT Press, Cambridge (MA) 2006. The term 'East Art' is specific to IRWIN who coin it in this publication as their designation for Eastern Europe Art.

[2] Ješa Denegri, 'Za jednu umetnost građenja' ('For an Art of Building'), *Anale mladih* (*Annals of Youth*), no. 1, Galerija Dom Omladine, Belgrade 1965.

[3] Ješa Denegri, *Art of the Constructive Approach – EXAT 51 and New Tendencies*, Horetzky, Zagreb 2004.

[4] During our conversations, one of the most frequently quoted names with which Denegri identified was that of the artist and architect Vjenceslav Richter (1917–2002), who is one of the main protagonists in his historical account. Denegri paraphrases Richter, saying: 'Socialism is not a matter of taking power, nor is it a matter of one party or its leader, rather it is the matter of a *civilisational level*'. 'For us, life under socialism was not a matter of the one-party system nor of the figure of Josip Broz Tito, rather it involved a social ascent that enabled our entire generation to become educated, to live a decent quality of life, and that was also demonstrated through the fact that we understood something of the times we lived in.' As quoted from the conversation below on p. 61–62.

[5] To quote the famous definition of Conceptual art by the collective Art & Language.

[6] The 'Artist in the First Person' is an expression first used by Denegri on the occasion of the exhibition of that name at the Salon of the Museum of Contemporary Art in Belgrade in October 1975, which was composed of a photographic documentation of the artistic actions and forms of behaviour that constitute the linguistic range of Happenings, Fluxus, Nouveau Réalisme, Body art, performance and other means of personal artistic intervention that have been voided of any mediation via the material object. In the catalogue of the first retrospective survey of the New Art Practices in Serbia (*Nova umetnost u Srbiji – pojedinci, grupe, pojave*, Museum of Contemporary Art, Belgrade 1983, p. 7–13), Denegri published a text entitled 'Speech in the First Person – Emphasising the Individuality of the Artist in the New Art Practices of the 1970s', in which he discusses the radical positions of some of the artists of the New Art Practices in Serbia, including Marina Abramović, Zoran Popović, Neša Paripović, Era Milivojević, Slavko Matković, Raša Todosijević and others.

[7] It is important to note that Denegri's work is published, and he holds lectures in academic and cultural institutions, not only in Serbia where he lives, but also in Slovenia, Croatia, Montenegro, Macedonia and Bosnia and Herzegovina. It is hardly possible to mention any other member of his generation that still has such a broad influence and exposure.

[8] Although yet not coined as a discrete term, the concept of the Other Line emerged from the essay 'Three Historical Periods – Related Models of Artistic Behaviour' that Denegri published in the Belgrade journal *Umetnost* (*Art*) in 1979 (no. 65, May–June 1979). This text refers to various exhibitions of the Yugoslav avant-garde art vis-à-vis the exhibitions of radical Informel, Gorgona and the New Art Practices, and discusses the critical aspects in which these practices are related.

[9] Denegri sums up his thesis in the essay 'The Reason for the Other Line' published originally in the catalogue of the exhibition *Jugoslovenska dokumenta '89* held in Sarajevo in 1989, which we include in the selection of his essays in this book. See p. 266–275.

[10] See below, p. 265.

[11] See Thierry de Duve, *Kant after Duchamp*, MIT Press, Cambridge (MA) 1996.

[12] Želimir Koščević, 'Henry Moore's exhibition in Yugoslavia, 1955', *British Art Studie*s, no. 3, Summer 2016, www.britishartstudies.ac.uk/issues/issue-index/issue-3/ moore-belgrade.

[13] Peter Osborne, *Anywhere or Not at All: Philosophy of Contemporary Art*, Verso, London 2013, p. 81.

Art History with the Sounds of its own Making: Dialogues with Denegri
Jelena Vesić

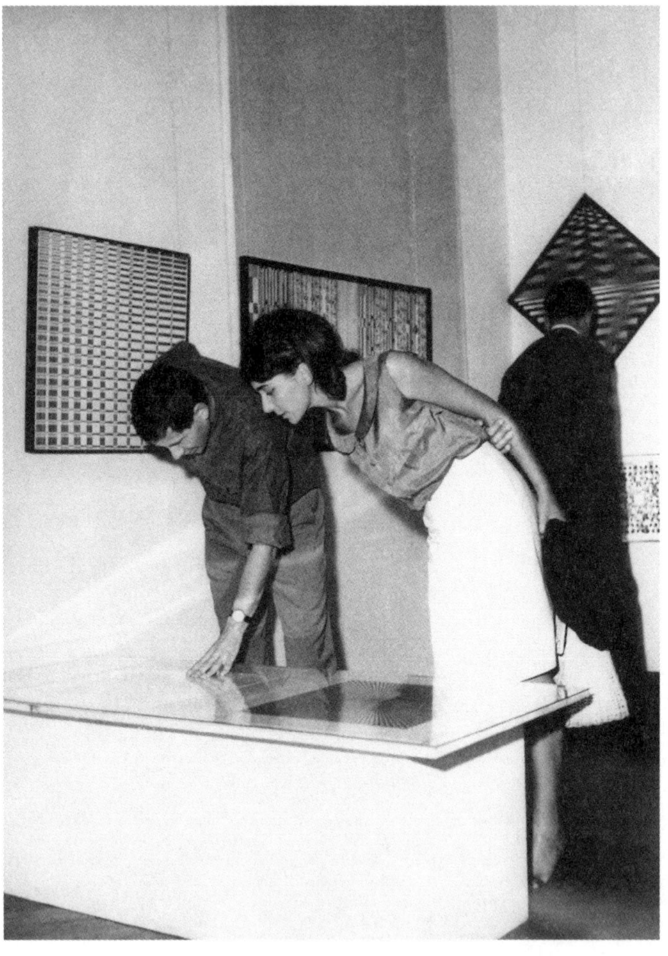

Ješa Denegri and Biljana Tomić visiting the exhibition *Nove Tendencije 4* (*New Tendencies 4*), Centar za kulturu i informacije (Centre for Culture and Information), Zagreb, 1969

This book investigates the multiplicity of ideas and practices behind the designation Yugoslav art. Structured as a discussion between Ješa Denegri, Branislav Dimitrijević and me, it unfolds as a dialogue about modernist historical claims and contemporary revisionisms, both critical and reactionary. Denegri appears in the roles of witness, protagonist and producer of art historical narratives. Branislav and I act as interpreters, translators, moderators and provocateurs. The dialogical format employed here is neither random nor accidental. It presents Denegri's historical choices and art historical narratives in a critical and polemical spirit, within a concrete, thematically structured form.

The art phenomena identified by Denegri's concept of the Other Line in Yugoslav art became an important part of the global art history of the 20th century.[1] Today, Denegri is a figure and a resource to whom many generations of art historians turn in their various fields of research. He serves as a living archive, a walking database of Yugoslav art after the Second World War, with a rich wealth of details and anecdotal information. As Branislav Dimitrijević comments in his introductory text, there is little if any research of art in this field that has not been preceded by Denegri's writings and his highly personal yet authoritative accounts – he stands as the generous witness behind countless investigations by younger generations of like-minded colleagues.

Denegri also happened to be our favourite teacher: Branislav and I originally met him at the Faculty of Philosophy of the University of Belgrade, and found him to have a very deep and detailed understanding of modern art that he talked about with passion and commitment. As good students we went on to apply all of his concepts to our object of investigation – Denegri himself. His thesis on the artist's 'Speech in the First Person', originally referring to performance art and other artistic activities in the 1970s, is now used in this volume to re-examine his own art historical speech. His concept of the Constructivist Approach or the Art of Building is applied to the process that shows how art histories were made, and to deconstructing the fixed art historical narratives of the 20th century. Our more than 40 hours of dialogue together, edited for the purposes of this book (in many takes), evolved into a durational performance composed of multiple similar research-driven conversations that Branislav and I conducted with Denegri over the years, even decades.

Our dialogues unfold on a shared platform, on the basis of an inter-generational engagement in the reading of Yugoslav art histories in an international context.[2] Known for his evocative accounts of past events, Denegri provides an inexhaustible source of testimony. Branislav and I, on the other hand, belong to those later generations characterised by differently structured memory and views of history mediated by contemporary technology and revisionist historical sentiments. We well know and have personally experienced ('in the flesh') the way that global post-socialism has changed the path of historical memory, and how all the attributes of 'art exceptionalism' have been comfortably incorporated into creative businesses. Denegri is firmly

rooted in the experience of the 20th century. He still insists
on the absolute connection between art and the public.
After the wars of the 1990s, as a result of which Yugoslavia
disappeared, after the fall of socialist systems and values,
neither art nor humanism have retained much of their former
attributes; but Denegri has somehow managed to preserve
those very attributes in his life and work. He still believes
that 'the whole of art should be embraced'.[3] And he supports
this claim in his behaviour and in his attitude towards
people and life. For Denegri, art still constitutes the primary
cognitive instrument.

In the specific institutional framework of a single socialist
country – in post-Second World War Yugoslavia – Denegri
operated both as an art historian involved in the work and
activities of the state's principal institutions and as the
main critic behind the larger articulation of countercultural
artistic movements, acting across and beyond all the national
and formal/linguistic borders of art. He was a curator at the
Museum of Contemporary Art in Belgrade (Muzej savremene
umetnosti, Beograd, MSUB) – one of the most important
official structures in the country – where he worked on
exhibitions and inter-state cooperation projects carried out
through the Federal Committee for Foreign Cultural
Relations; and he was simultaneously active as a freelance
critic associated with the most radical art phenomena
in Yugoslav art. In the spirit of a cultural reading of the Cold
War epoch characterised by binary thinking and paranoid
obsessions with power and espionage, Denegri would have
been the ideal candidate for a spy or double agent. Neither
of these, obviously, was his role, although this imaginative,
provocative setup would have been (and still is) worthy of
an action-packed movie plot. For his part, Denegri was led
by a less instrumentalising force – by his strong sense of
curiosity and his spirit of inquiry. He was deeply interested
in exploring the wide terrain of artistic practice, from centre-
stage to the hidden corners of authority and visibility across
the entire social and institutional spectrum. According to
his way of thinking – and sometimes his experience – art
provided the great opportunity of achieving (political)
autonomy and autonomous development if it was approached
as the *project*.[4]

Denegri participated in what can be called 'Yugoslav pluralism', a phenomenon and a way of thinking that was characteristic of Socialist Yugoslavia. The pluralism of self-managed interests and the concept of *associated labour* were key phrases of the system of socialist self-management,[5] and Denegri's understanding of his (own) institutional engagement reflects these conditions in the best sense; he would say that he 'associated his labour with the Museum'.

The designation Yugoslav art — as it is used in our dialogues — takes different political-aesthetic forms during two decades between the First and Second World Wars, in the period following the Second World War and then after the ethno-nationalist wars of the 1990s when, for some actors on the contemporary art scene, the space remained virtually unified through various cultural actions and through its new and in many ways problematic prefix of 'post'. Interestingly, Denegri decisively revived his much used concept of the Yugoslav Art Space at the exhibition of the permanent collection of the Belgrade Museum of Contemporary Art in the early 2000s.[6] Furthermore such an act of naming and articulating the modern art of the region carried political weight and had a certain canonizing dimension, in opposition to the 'novel' revisionist writing of national art histories unfolding on the substrate of the post-Yugoslav wars and through the decomposition of the space into the successor states that followed.

In the first chapter of our conversations, the concepts and practices of 'Yugoslavness' and Yugoslav art are discussed around three different yet mutually interconnected cultural-political tendencies. One is derived from decolonial theories and practices, where 'Yugoslavness' signifies the culture of small nations struggling to liberate themselves and self-determine vis-à-vis the canons of the imperial cultures (most notably, the West). This tendency we could call Krležian-Fanonian,[7] which we discuss with the example of the exhibition *Medieval Art in Yugoslavia* shown in Paris in 1950. The year and context of this exhibition are not contingent — they point to diversification and the achievement of 'another socialism' after the expulsion of Yugoslavia from Cominform in 1948. The search for authenticity and singularity, as the primary goal of this tendency, is manifested through resistance to both the West and the USSR, laying the ground for a 'third position' and the formation of the Non-Aligned Movement.

Another thread of Yugoslavness is based on the sensitive cultural construction of the Yugoslav socialist state and propagated via representative art institutions and an extensive exhibition practice within the country and abroad. Such major cultural institutions as the Museum of Modern Art (Moderna galerija) Ljubljana with its exhibition project the International Biennial of Graphic Arts (established in 1955), or the Museum of Contemporary Art in Belgrade with its series of decennial exhibitions *Yugoslav Art of the 20th Century* (1967–1980) and the representative exhibition *Tendencies in Yugoslav Art Today* (1978–1980, curated by Denegri himself), were some of the state's most important cultural projects. Museum directors like Zoran Kržišnik and Miodrag Protić opened the season of exhibitions of Yugoslav art in grand style – Yugoslavia was launched out into the world, and the world was launched into Yugoslavia. These actions were driven by both professional and diplomatic logic.

The third approach to Yugoslavness – and the one we discuss most here – could be called an operative approach, since the processes, circumstances and links between people played such a major role. In contrast to the other two larger cultural approaches, this model is 'small' and reflected in something that is, as Denegri would say, *lateral* and *marginal* in relation to the major stories and grand narratives most often derived from literature and philosophy. The whole of Krležian logic and the logic of the major institutions fully subscribed to this spectacular school of rhetoric. Denegri followed a different logic, one that opposed great art, great traditions and great literary narratives; and one that established a different form of continuity that he would come to call the Other Line.

Denegri's development as an art historian and a critic coincided spatially and temporally with both the beginning and the end of socialist Yugoslavia, in which he was active as both a thinker and concept maker, and also as a body in motion. Denegri had strong material attachments to this space and time, and travelled tirelessly, everywhere, to see new exhibitions and art events, large and small, mainstream

and alternative. This makes him an authentic protagonist
of Yugoslav art who connected this space and time with his
own movement, and the movement of art, and encompassed
it within his work and social dealings. Denegri was simply
present, and to be present means to be 'next to' and 'in
solidarity with' the conditions, the people and the events
that surround one. Our dialogues trace that dynamic, that
material practice. When we look closely at the details, we see
that relatively few art historians in socialist Yugoslavia
– perhaps not as many as we might expect from today's
perspective – were dealing with the notion of Yugoslav art.
Here the history of art is, as James Clifford writes, 'a story
of movements and meetings, of *routes rather than roots*'.[8]
Or, as Denegri's terminology would have it, a story of
movements and exchange rather than *local traditions*.

Denegri and his concept of the Other Line in Yugoslav
art are the main heroes of the conversations that play out
in this book, and also the protagonists who share the ways
their 'superhero' costumes are made and how they work.
Speaking in three voices Denegri, Dimitrijević and I examine
artistic and art historical forms 'as freed', as John Berger
proposed, 'from the mystique that is attached to them as
property objects'.[9] The critique of the idea of art-as-property
assumes, according to Berger, replacing the collector's
question *what is this?* with the question *what went into the
making of this?*[10] The making of narrative in the contested
field of Yugoslav art histories *then* and *now*, and Denegri's
first-hand insights into the occurrence of certain art
phenomena of the 1960s and 1970s and into the debates
and divisions in the Yugoslav and international art scenes
of the time, are testimonial entries that fill this book with
the sounds of their own making. In our dialogical unpacking
of the events behind the scenes, art historical concepts
are taken from their enclosed and abstract forms and
re-associated with the body, subjectivity and life – with the
processes of reasoning and sensing in specific circumstances. We are trying here to bring to the surface
the knowledge that demystifies a dry condensate of 'pure
meaning' and reveals itself as a *process of production*. How do
the concepts come into being? How do they relate to – or
break with – the previous state of affairs? The dialogues
insist on a materialist analysis of art history; here we zoom

in and get deeper into the fragments and details of existing art historical narratives.

Denegri elaborates his concept of the Other Line for the first time in the journal *Umetnost* (*Art*) in 1979, and later re-writes it for the catalogue of the exhibition *Yugoslav Documents* in Sarajevo in 1989. Intersecting with the dialogues, the second version is included in the selection of essays republished in this book. Denegri's description of the term the Other Line summarises almost all the highlights of artistic thought of the 1960s and 1970s: it *radicalises* the notions of art and *artistic behaviour*; its meaning is derived from the concepts of *process* or *decision* rather than a finished product; it experiments with *negation* and researches the *new fields*; it thinks and acts *constructively* and *projectively*. The Other Line is characterised by a demand for the demystification of the notion of creation by breaking with the logic of the market and its speculative dialectic through which art appears both as myth and as commodity.

Denegri's art historical narrative is a synthesis of the ideas shared by many cultural producers, thinkers, curators, artists and groups with whom he collaborated and was in close exchange. It corresponds with the ideas of Vjenceslav Richter, EXAT 51, New Tendencies with Matko Meštrović as its main ideologue, then Radoslav Putar, Vera Horvat Pintarić, Želimir Koščević, Giulio Carlo Argan and many others. In the dialogues we focus on the scene that presents Denegri as a young critic in the throes of professional confusion, whose knowledge systems are collapsing before the *Achromes* by Piero Manzoni exhibited at the exhibition *New Tendencies* in Zagreb in 1961. But we also watch him restoring himself by opening up to a deeper process of sensing and cognition – the exact moment in which Denegri breaks (in himself) with the language of socialist modernist painting dominating institutional education and shaping (the knowledge of) art history.

But Denegri also makes a break with himself, with his own postulates. As the 1960s come to a close he abandons the idea of 'scientification as the principle of humanisation'[11] advocated by the New Tendencies and turns to the critique of technological and social utopias, then corrupted by the Soviet intervention in Prague and the new waves of socialist bureaucratisation in the wider world. During these years, Denegri internalises the cultural and political critique of students' and workers' protests in 1968; he follows the new theses on art criticism (such as *critica acritica* – uncritical criticism – by Germano Celant), and witnesses the early exhibitions of Arte Povera in Rome and Turin. But he learns the most – and most immediately – about the New Art Practices from his life partner, the curator Biljana Tomić, who was close to the circles of artists engaged in concrete poetry, performance and Conceptual art. In the early 1970s at the Museum of Contemporary Art in Belgrade Denegri exhibits groups of artists who were active in Student Cultural Centres, Tribunes of Youth and other independent alternative spaces throughout Yugoslavia. The intentionally 'poor', visually reduced exhibition entitled *Examples of Conceptual Art in Yugoslavia* (1971) was the first exhibition of the New Art Practices in the context of Belgrade; it was, paradoxically enough, presented just a few months before the succession of Conceptual art shows that followed in the Belgrade Student Cultural Centre (Studentski Kulturni Centar, SKC) as the original stage-source of the New Art Practices.[12] Here we trace the processes of historicisation of the New Art Practices through exhibition in the chapters dedicated to the art of the 1970s. In the same chapters we discuss the two editions of the Biennale Internationale des Jeunes Artistes de Paris, or the Paris Biennial, for which Denegri served as a selector in 1971 and 1977. He talks about the artistic atmosphere in Paris of the late 1960s and about the way the Paris Biennial intervened in the shift of paradigms from the model of the artist embodied in Picasso to the model of artist embodied in Duchamp and the protagonists of Nouveau Réalisme.

The dialogues return, persistently, to questions related to the Other Line, since it is not a 'pure' and totalizing homogenous phenomenon. It cannot be explained using the epistemologies of Eastern European art; it does not fit the binary oppositions represented by *official art* versus *alternative art,* or the totalitarianism of state art versus the freedom of underground currents. The logic of the Other Line, as Denegri emphasises, is not predetermined by a singular artistic language, 'but rather [by] a mentality and a reaction of certain artists and artist groups to cultural and social circumstances'.[13] For Denegri, the Other Line in Yugoslav art breaks the conceptual ties with *moderate modernism* entrenched in the forms of associative abstraction and bourgeois local tradition and signals 'the possibility of establishing another continuity – one with a legacy of historical avant-gardes'.[14] The Other Line unfolds as a thread of art historical narrative that connects the *moments of rupture* in the smooth development of the mainstream traditions in art. Or, as I defined it in the project *Political Practices of (Post-)Yugoslav Art*, it is a 'continuum of breaks with some of the ever dominant "bourgeois" artistic tendencies' both national and global.[15]

Denegri's original term in our (Serbian-Croatian) language is *Druga linija*, which may be translated as the Other Line, the Second Line or even Another Line. In our dialogues he explains his choice by drawing a comparison with the term *un art autre* (art of another kind), introduced by the French critic Michel Tapié (1909–1987), and used as the title of his well-known book of 1952.[16] But *Druga linija* is more complex and divergent in itself. 'Other' in our translation of *druga* indicates a kind of otherness in relation to the 'professionalist' logic in art that has today become the dominant matrix of production, through which the figure of the artist is turned into a model of a creative businessman. Denegri himself states that the Other Line is characterised by '*understanding art as an ethical vocation* rather than dealing with art as a mere profession, a source of material benefits and social status'. It acts in accordance with the principles of *necessity*, not *success*. With his description of the Other Line Denegri indirectly claims that serious and responsible art thinking always happens on the margins of the art system.[17] And this is one of the reasons for his appreciation of the fragility of the artistic position. The Other Line creates the ground for an inter-generational grouping of dedicated, sometimes visionary, uncompromising art figures – those artists who always strive for more than the circumstances offer, and reject conformity to the expected patterns and the given structures of thought and action.

Denegri does not talk much about Yugoslavia's political links with the Third World embodied in the ideas and political practices of the Non-Aligned Movement, which has today been re-actualised as a timely and relevant idea in discussions on alternative approaches to globalisation and living together.[18] His comments on the Ljubljana International Biennial of Graphic Arts – established in 1955 with the aim of representing the cultural links between Yugoslav Non-Alignment and the country's openness to the entire world – are not particularly extensive. But, as we read in the dialogues, this policy was pursued only nominally, in large cultural-political brushstrokes, and not discursively, in the language of display. Although Denegri's art historical thinking falls out of line with the contemporary postcolonial turn in art history, he does offer his own modest contribution to the material practice of decolonising art with his choice of *the margins* and marginal artistic figures. According to Denegri, being on the margins does not mean living on the edge of life and events, but taking a position that is firmly grounded in ideas and attitudes – a position of a certain *inviolability* – beyond those of mainstream narratives.

The anti-heroic heroes of Denegri's story of art are particular 'anti-art art believers' who consciously manifest a certain kind of naivety. And I would argue that it is precisely *that naivety* that is used *as an artistic strategy of the critique of hegemony* of whatever might be the case in the specific circumstances: Western art, state art, market-driven art, or instrumental reason in art. Naivety is not an ahistorical designation. The category of *Naive Art* in Socialist Yugoslavia shares many features with today's postcolonial readings of folk and indigenous art. Many critics and artists active in the field of the New Art Practices were at the same time interested in naive art, and actively contributed to the understanding and promotion of it.[19] But, the 'official' *Naive* is a very distant reference from the political and aesthetic positioning in art advocated by the protagonists of the Other Line – those artists who thought and lived clearly urban lives and used the city, the gallery, the square and open spaces as their field of action. They were knowledgeable art thinkers familiar with the art histories of the avant-gardes, Western modernism and the experimental art practices of the 1960s and 1970s.

Our dialogues follow all the complexities and contradictions of Denegri's thesis on the art of the Other Line. We discuss the fact that he escapes inclusion within the Belgrade Surrealist circle, although all the other historical avant-gardes are gathered around and within it. His 'official' explanation is that the group was more involved in poetry and literature and less active in the visual arts, so their work was rather the subject of literary theory than art history. But reading through our passionate exchanges we discover that the actual problem resides in the fact that the majority of surrealists became the cultural officials of the post-Second World War era, serving as ambassadors, ministers and members of the Federal Committee for Foreign Cultural Relations, so that their life circumstances and artistic function could not be part of the same story as that of the autonomous and often singular 'Other Liners'.

In our dialogues with Denegri we encounter a number of artistic characters using what we called 'strategies of self-marginalisation' – and we used this formula for the title of one of the chapters in this book. We discuss the case of Bogoljub Jovanović, who paints a single visionary painting, *K-55* (1955), that is shown at almost all the exhibitions of the permanent collection at the Museum of Contemporary Art in Belgrade, but then decides to spend the rest of his life in anonymity as a taxi driver in New York. We come across the story of the neo-avant-garde artist Miroslav Mandić, who argues with the curator who has invited him to exhibit at the Paris Biennial about whether it makes more sense to help people carry coal to their cellars in the neighbourhoods of Novi Sad or to exhibit at the biennial. We also read how the Paris Biennial becomes a central symbolic point for the group of Yugoslav artists who experience a sense of funda-mental disappointment in Conceptual art as they stand before an 'aestheticised' work of Joseph Kosuth.[20] And how the Belgrade-based conceptualist Neša Paripović forgets about a scheduled meeting with an important curator and goes hiking in the mountains with a friend instead.

We conclude our conversations with a return to the *Yugoslav Documents* exhibitions in Sarajevo, an exhibition that has been extensively analysed on several occasions and was re-staged at the Ljubljana Museum of Modern Art in 2017.[21] Denegri's emotional account relates the organisational

details of the second version of the *Yugoslav Documents*
exhibition, which was interrupted by the opening salvos of
the ethno-nationalist wars that were soon to follow.
He describes the mood and atmosphere of the telephone
call that he receives from Enver (Enjo) Hadžiomerspahić,
one of the organisers in Sarajevo, who continues with
his work on the grand Yugoslav show against the background
of falling bombs and the reality of yet new chapters in
history being written. Enjo's 'strategic naivity' is also one
of the small acts that speak volumes of the passion of the
art-friendships, ideas and actions that were driven by the
20th century's belief in the possibility of achieving political
autonomy through art.

[1] Denegri's texts are included in some of the major overviews of global art after the Second World War, such as Okwui Enwezor, Katy Siegel, Ulrich Wilmes (eds.), *Postwar: Art between the Pacific and the Atlantic 1945–1965*, exh. cat., Haus der Kunst, Munich 2016. His reading of the art of the 1960s was included in such important surveys as Margit Rosen (ed.), *A Little-Known Story about a Movement, a Magazine, and the Computer's Arrival in Art: New Tendencies and Bit International, 1961–1973*, MIT Press, Cambridge (MA) 2011.

[2] I am referring here to the long history of collaborations between Dimitrijević, Denegri and me on a number of projects related to Yugoslav heritage that we initiated over the last two decades. Dimitrijević co-founded the School of History and Theory of Images, Centre for Contemporary Art, Belgrade in 1999; he initiated the Yugoslav Studies programme, Museum of Contemporary Art, Belgrade, 2011; he co-edited the reader *Yugoslavia, Why and How?*, Museum of History of Yugoslavia, Belgrade 2019; and more. I co-edited *Prelom, a journal for images and politics* in 2001; I curated the exhibition and its catalogue *Political Practices of (Post-)Yugoslav Art: Retrospective 01*, Museum of History of Yugoslavia, Belgrade 2009; I initiated and wrote for the publishing project *Non-Aligned Modernisms*, Museum of Contemporary Art, Belgrade 2015.

[3] Denegri's reply to the question: 'Shall we then embrace all art?' See the chapter 'Anti-Modernism in the Age of the Project' in this book, p. 120–128.

[4] The concept of art that Denegri inherited from Giulio Carlo Argan and his famous essay *Progetto e destino* (*Project and Destiny*, 1965) that was printed, translated from the Italian, in the journal *Život Umjetnosti* (*Life of Art*), no. 9, 1969, p. 85–110.

[5] Edvard Kardelj linked Yugoslav socialist self-management to the politicisation of the individual and society at large through a democratic system of pluralism that involved self-managing local interests, emphasising that it was a system that had truly overcome having to choose between multi-party pluralism and the one-party system, which alienated society from people and from individual citizens. See Edvard Kardelj, *Pravci razvoja političkog sistema socijalističkog samoupravljanja* (*Directions of Development in the Political System of Socialist Self-Management*), Komunist, Belgrade 1978, p. 108–132.

[6] See the catalogue/exhibition guide: Ješa Denegri, *Yugoslav Art Space*, Museum of Contemporary Art, Belgrade 2005.

[7] The term was first used by Stanko Lasić in his *Sukob na književnoj ljevici 1928–1952* (*Clashes within the Literary Left 1928–1952*), Liber-Izdanja Instituta za znanstvo o knjizevnosti, Zagreb 1970, and was recently elaborated by the art historian Ivana Bago in 'Yugoslav Fanonism and a Failed Exit from the (Cultural) Cold War', in Anselm Franke, Nida Ghouse, Paz Guevara, Antonia Majaca (eds.), *Parapolitics: Cultural Freedom and the Cold War*, Sternberg Press, Berlin 2021, p. 285–293.

[8] James Clifford, *Routes: Travel and Translation in the Late Twentieth Century*, Harvard University Press, Cambridge (MA) 1997.

[9] John Berger, 'The Historical Function of the Museum', first published in 1966 and collected in John Berger, *The Moment of Cubism and Other Essays*, Pantheon Books, New York 1969, p. 35–40.

[10] *Ibid.*

[11] The catalogue text by Matko Meštrović for the 1963 exhibition of the New Tendencies demanded the 'scientification' of art, while at the same time warning about the dangers of an alienated and instrumentalised science. According to the New Tendencies science could only realise its full potential if it became the common property of society as a whole.

[12] More has been written about Denegri's historicisation of the New Art Practices through exhibitions in Jelena Vesić, 'The Three Exhibitions: Simultaneity of Promotion and Historization of New Art Practices – From Alternative Spaces to the Museum and Back', *Parallel Chronologies*, tranzit.hu, 2014, see http://tranzit.org/exhibitionarchive/the-three-exhibitions-simultaneity-of-promotion-and-historization-of-new-art-practices-from-an-alternative-spaces-to-the-museum-and-back (last accessed May 2024).

[13] See below p. 267.

[14] *Ibid.*

[15] Prelom kolektiv (Jelena Vesić and Dušan Grlja), 'Two Times of One Wall: The Case of the Student Cultural Centre in the 1970s', in Zorana Dojić and Jelena Vesić (eds.), *Political Practices of (Post-)Yugoslav Art*, p. 128.

[16] Tapié identified a tendency in post-war European painting that he saw as a radical break with all traditional notions of order and composition. In describing this work, he used the term *art informel* (from the French *informe*, meaning unformed or formless).

[17] Denegri's reflections on the art system and ideology are summarised in his short essay 'The Language of Art and the System of Art' originally written for *Oktobar 75*, Student Cultural Centre, Belgrade 1975. See below p. 196–202.

[18] For example the seven volumes of *Non-Aligned Modernisms*, Zoran Erić (ed.), with contributions by Ana Sladojević, Dubravka Sekulić, Vladimir Kulić, Dominique Malaquais and Cédric Vincent, Olivier Hadouchi, Stevan Vuković, Jelena Vesić, Rachel O'Reilly, Vladimir Jerić Vlidi, Museum of Contemporary Art, Belgrade 2014–2017; the *Travelling Communiqué* project, initiated by Doreen Mende, Armin Linke and Milica Tomić in 2014; the Non-Aligned Museum conference programme organised in 2016 by Ana Sladojević, Museum of Yugoslavia, Belgrade; Naeem Mohaiemen's multi-channel video installation, *Two Meetings and a Funeral*, 2017; the exhibition *Southern Constellations: The Poetics of the Non-Aligned*, curated by Bojana Piškur, Museum of Contemporary Art Metelkova, Ljubljana, 2019; Bojana Videkanić's book *Nonaligned Modernism: Socialist Postcolonial Aesthetics in Yugoslavia, 1845–1985*, McGill Queen's University Press, Montreal 2019; the conferences Non-Aligned Movement and Socialist Yugoslavia, RLS, 2021, and Models and Practices of Global Cultural Exchange and Non-Aligned Movement. Research in Spatio-Temporal Cultural Dynamics, ALUO, Ljubljana and Institute of Art History, Zagreb, 2021.

[19] For example, Dimitrije Bašičević Mangelos and Goran Trbuljak to name but a few.

[20] See our chapter 'Before the Work of Joseph Kosuth', p. 233–237.

[21] *The Heritage of 1989. Case Study: The Second Yugoslav Documents Exhibition*, curated by Zdenka Badovinac and Bojana Piškur, Museum of Modern Art, Ljubljana, 2017.

PROLOGUE
Ješa Denegri in Conversation with Branislav Dimitrijević and Jelena Vesić

JELENA VESIĆ   Let's start from the beginning, from your beginnings, from your decision to get involved in art.

JEŠA DENEGRI   When I was in secondary school, I had to repeat a year because of mathematics – there was no way I could pass the course. After my traumatic experiences with maths I enrolled at the Advanced School of Pedagogy in Split. This was an extraordinary school, a college of three-year courses that was only one year shy of fulfilling the criteria for a philosophical faculty. We had very good professors, especially in history. Our chosen courses were archaeology and art history. The school educated teachers for lower secondary schools. However, the seminars and open discussions between professors and students were very much like university, firstly because we really had to read a lot. I have continued with this at the university in Belgrade.

I never studied the textbooks, rather the many volumes of literature – various books and articles – instead. I learned how to read books and how to connect different sources, so I never learned definitions by heart like most other students. What was also interesting during the debates among the students themselves was the two standpoints expressed regarding the way historical science should be articulated in socialist Yugoslavia. The main reason for this was a two-volume book entitled *History of the Peoples of Yugoslavia*: the first volume covered history up until the 16th century, and the second covered it up until the 19th century.[1] The authors were from all the Yugoslav republics. It was a large historiographic project, initiated with the aim of establishing, on the basis of historical materialism, a new perspective on historical science. One group of the students was inclined to accept this idea, which was encapsulated in the phrase 'history is the history of class struggle'. But since we were studying the available research literature, a bourgeois historiography was still in place in which history was defined or delineated according to great historical personalities and rulers. So from the Middle Ages in Croatia you have a sequence that runs from King Tomislav and onwards to Krešimir the Fourth and so on.

So these discussions among the students resulted in the emergence of two major groups – one that claimed history as an issue of class struggle, and the other that thought history in terms of great historical figures. The question that confronted these two groups was is the French Revolution more important, or is perhaps Charlemagne? I myself couldn't take a stance on this question, but as a result of those chosen courses in archaeology and art history I became aware of the material role of concrete artefacts and their meaning. Our professors often took us to museums, as most of them worked in museums as their regular full-time job and merely lectured on a part-time basis. I was particularly impressed by Kruno Prijatelj, who worked as the director of the Museum of Fine Arts (Galerija umjetnina) in Split from 1950 to 1979. He took us through the collection of the museum, which was relatively good. When someone takes you through the Archaeological Museum in Split and you see all those historical remains, and when you come to learn what a certain stone relief represents, what kind of

meaning is inscribed in its materiality, you come to realise
that there is a third option, and that you do not have to
struggle with yourself to decide – to choose between history
as a class struggle and the history of great individuals as
carriers of historical processes. Instead of all this, someone
shows you some artefacts and tells you: this object means
this and that and somebody produced it in such and such a
way. This is where my love for art was born – a love, that is,
for the history of art.

BRANISLAV DIMITRIJEVIĆ   We may therefore conclude
that for you the history of art became a kind of escape from
the predominant options on the table, an escape from the
grindstone of two ideologies – on the one hand, from the
doctrine of dialectical materialism, and on the other hand
from national history?

JD   Yes, and I have managed to get out from under that
grindstone. Both of these options somehow made me
disoriented. Here it seemed I could come to some conclusion, that I could perceive something, that I could offer
some interpretation, that someone else could give me some
other interpretation … Then I realised that getting out of
this dilemma might mean that one day – since the school in
Split went through various transformations as it was reduced
to a two-year study programme – I could go to the university and graduate in art history. What I was learning there
was a kind of foundation, and that meant that I could teach
secondary school history or geography, somewhere on the
islands or in the provinces, because everyone started like
that. But after I served my military service – which was in
1959 – I had a chance to enrol in art history in Belgrade.
On the one hand, my wish to study was fulfilled, and on the
other, I had enough prior knowledge to finish these studies
rather easily. Unlike my colleagues who were learning in
rather a mechanical fashion, I already knew how to study –
which was enough for me to observe various processes, and
to study using research literature.

BD   How did your family react to your decision?

JD   Well, there is an anecdote for that. My relatives from my mother's side used to gather regularly in Split over the summer holidays. On one such occasion, when I went there after the first year of my studies, one of our cousins who was a hard-line communist asked me: 'So, Bariša,[2] what do you study there in Belgrade?' I told him: 'I study art history'. And he asked me again: 'What's that? Is it about old rocks?' (Because for him the history of art meant archaeology.) And I replied: 'Dale – his name was Dalibor – it is not just about old rocks, but also about old and modern paintings'. To which he said: 'That's good – one of us should learn this too. We won't leave anything to the bourgeoisie!'

JV   Your cousin's statement repeats the gesture of the socialist state's nationalisation or rather socialisation of private property – 'we won't leave anything to the bourgeoisie!' – the appropriation of ownership for the sake of re-distribution. Or, as one would say today, the appropriation of knowledge and aesthetics in the interests of egalitarianism.

JD   Yes. It is an anecdote, but it has some very serious connotations. Finally, this same cousin told me: 'Well … Bon voyage! And give my regards to Red Belgrade!' For him, Belgrade was the centre of Yugoslavia – Tito lived there, and he thought that at least one of us was lucky enough to live and work there.

[1]   *Istorija naroda Jugoslavije* (*History of the Peoples of Yugoslavia*), Prosveta, Belgrade 1953–1960.
[2]   Denegri's childhood nickname.

PART I

I. The Yugoslav Art Space and Reasons for the Other Line
Ješa Denegri in Conversation with Branislav Dimitrijević and Jelena Vesić

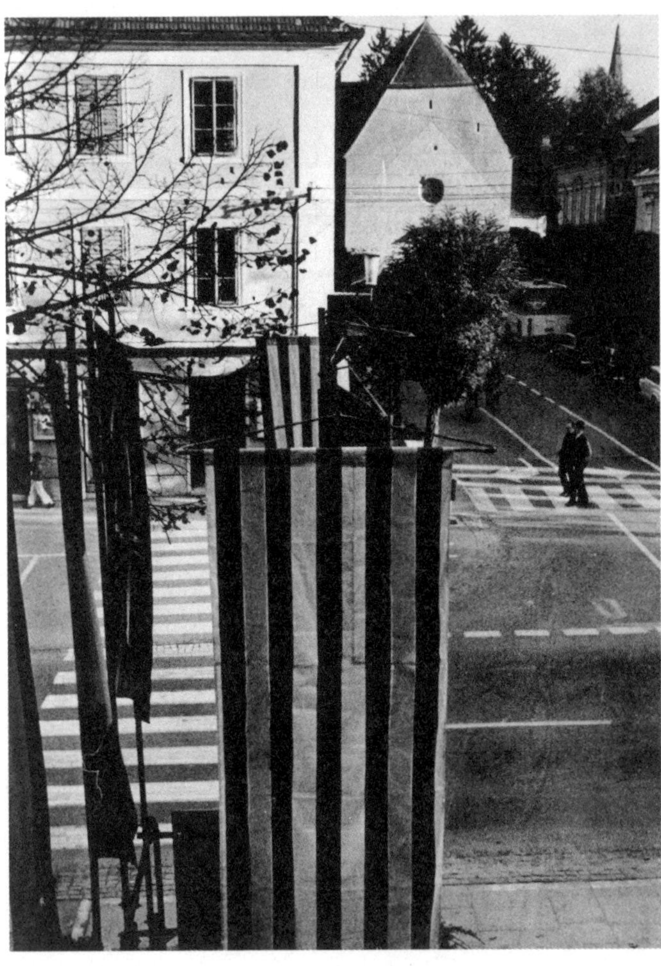

Daniel Buren, *Flags*, 1975, presented at the exhibition *Mir '75 (Peace '75)*, Slovenj Gradec, Slovenia, 1975

1. <u>Figurative Art, Engaged Art and Domestic Traditions</u>

JELENA VESIĆ   We have before us rather a large number of catalogues from international exhibitions in Yugoslavia, as well as catalogues from exhibitions representing Yugoslav art abroad. Many of them are examples of important international projects produced by modern cultural institutions in socialist Yugoslavia (the Socialist Federal Republic of Yugoslavia or SFRY). One such institution was the Museum of Contemporary Art in Belgrade, where you were employed as a curator.

BRANISLAV DIMITRIJEVIĆ   Ješa, you have already picked out one of these catalogues. What is the exhibition we are talking about?

JEŠA DENEGRI   This catalogue is not related to the projects of the Museum of Contemporary Art in which I took part as one of its curators. We're now talking about the exhibition *Mir '75* (*Peace '75*) which was held in Slovenj Gradec (Slovenia) from 19 October 1975 to 19 January 1976. The UN Secretary General Kurt Waldheim served as the patron of that exhibition, so you can imagine the level on which the whole thing was operating. It was an international exhibition of figurative art.[1]

BD   The subtitle of the exhibition was *Angažovana figurativna umetnost*, which was translated into English as *Committed Figurative Art*.

JV   This is a canonical assertion of the time – engaged art should be figurative!

JD   Yes. It was a mantra of that period in Yugoslavia and around the world. I remember I sent an objection to the organisers of the exhibition and to my colleagues, asserting that the essence of engaged art lies not in that mantra; rather it calls into question the system of art in one way or another. And then Aleksander Bassin and Irina Subotić suggested I should make my own selection as a critical contribution to the exhibition, so in this catalogue I published an essay entitled 'Critical Diagnoses'.[2] The artists in my selection were Braco Dimitrijević, Zoran Popović, Goran Trbuljak and Raša Todosijević. But the biggest thing was that we managed to bring Daniel Buren to that exhibition. He made his intervention at the entrance of the building in which the exhibition was held. There were flags of the various countries from which the participating artists and artworks came, and Buren put his canvases with stripes amongst those flags. The organizers accepted the gesture, although they did not quite understand it; nor did they like it, but they let it happen, so there were no problems. However, when I was there some fifteen years ago, I met the same director of the gallery and he told me that the gallery was very proud of Buren's flags, saying: 'You see, we had Buren here among the participants'. And I replied: 'You had Buren, but you wouldn't otherwise have invited him, nor would you have known who he was'.

JV   The point of this story about the exhibition *Mir '75* is the connection between the notion of 'engaged art' and engaged figurative art as an art practice. Can you tell us more about that?

JD   This issue was preoccupying some important art critics, like Irina Subotić in Serbia and Aleksander Bassin in Slovenia. Subotić, for example, valued the work of Vladimir Veličković very highly and saw it as engaged art. Yet the question 'What is engaged art?' is in fact a question of principle. And this question was crucial at the time. Is engaged art that which visualises or realizes the engaged theme – so that this representation will later be bought by gallerists and collectors – or is engaged art an art that in some way undermines the art system itself? This was a matter of constant debate. And the same question resonates in my text 'Jezik umetnosti i sistem umetnosti' ('The Language of Art and the System of Art'), written for the publication of the Student Cultural Centre in Belgrade, *Oktobar 75* (*October 75*), the same year.[3] For me it was completely clear that art does not and cannot initiate major political or social changes, but if it does anything at all it can denounce the art system and art institutions that are part of it. I maintained that critique of the art system was a form of engaged art, but I also claimed that engaged art could only operate within the system of art, and not within the system of politics. At the same time, I think that precisely within such operation, within the framework of such a function, it can also become a real political factor.[4] Now, such a way of thinking may be controversial, debatable, but that's how I was thinking at that moment.

BD   There was a conventional wisdom, particularly within the Belgrade art scene, that figurative art was art that carried some political weight and occupied some critical position in relation to the ruling ideological system. The notion of critical art was deeply linked to figurative representation. Perhaps the best-known painter in Belgrade working in this vein at the time was Mića Popović. Given your impressive textual production, it is noticeable that you wrote almost nothing about his paintings. Why?

JD   I did write something about Popović's work, but mostly about his earliest phase dating back to the 1940s while he was a member of the Zadar Group, the first painter's commune active in post-war Yugoslav art.[5]

BD   Later, most of the members of the Zadar Group emigrated from Yugoslavia, or were considered dissidents, like Popović. What is important for our discussion is to differentiate this position from yours. Figurative art was considered to be a sine qua non for 'engaged art' on the premise that its content addressed some social issue. This position was not one that was close to you. At the beginning of the 1970s Popović engaged with precisely that kind of social criticism, which he pursued through figurative art. His paintings from the early 1970s deal with the mass migrations of Yugoslav workers to Western Europe, where they became the so-called *Gastarbeiters* (guest workers). Popović was also linked with the Black Wave cinema of the 1960s, as the creator of such films as *Čovek iz hrastove šume* (1964, *The Man from the Oak Forest*) and *Delije* (1969, *Brave Men*). You haven't dealt with Mića Popović from that most celebrated phase of his. However, his early painting, *Autoportret sa maskom* (*Self-Portrait with a Mask*) dated 1948, was of crucial importance for you, wasn't it?

JD   This story begins with the Zadar Group. Popović and his partners, who at that time were students at the Belgrade Fine Arts Academy, went to the Dalmatian coastal town of Zadar in 1947 and established an art colony that is considered to be the first example of a self-organised and independent artistic effort after the war. During this period, three out-standing self-portraits appeared in Serbian art – this one by Mića Popović; a second one by Bata Mihailović, *Autoportret sa šeširom* (1947, *Self-Portrait with a Hat*); and a third one by Petar Omčikus, *Autoportret sa šajkačom* (1947–1948, *Self-Portrait with a šajkača*[6]). These three self-portraits connote, rather obviously, a certain political attitude. The face of the artist disguised by a smiling mask symbolises a particular critical position on the enforced collective ideological optimism that pasted over a troubled existence in the post-war era. In my book about Serbian art of the 1950s I point to Popović as a member of the Zadar Group, as one of the first artists of the group who had a solo exhibition at the ULUS Gallery in Belgrade in 1950,[7] and who also wrote the introductory text in the exhibition catalogue. This introduction is considered to be the first text that called into question certain assumptions of Socialist Realism, which still meant something.

BD   Yet your interest in the Zadar Group, and in the 1950s in general, was more or less based on the theses developed by Miodrag Protić, and his argument for a decisive split between dogmatic socialist realists and progressive modernists. You are relying on his interpretation here, since you were not a part of those developments.

JD   Our knowledge is drawn from texts by Miodrag Protić, because he was certainly a contemporary of those events. I wasn't interested in the Zadar Group in particular, but in what it meant in the larger context. I met Bata Mihailović and Petar Omčikus during my stays in Paris, because they were the first of the post-war generation artists who moved beyond our local context and went out into 'the big wide world' in search of affirmation. It wasn't so much a political gesture as it was a gesture of personal courage. The two of them showed great perseverance in establishing themselves in the French art scene. Initially they made a living by taking different jobs, mostly as house painters. At their exhibitions in Belgrade, at the beginning of the 1960s, they presented themselves with large gestural paintings. Popović was also a part of that story, but he didn't stay in Paris and became, during the same period, the main protagonist of Belgrade Informel. Then there followed his figurative art phase, which he called *slikarstvo prizora* (scene paintings). Texts about Popović were written by influential figures like the Serbian novelist Dobrica Ćosić.[8] And Lazar Trifunović later published a monograph about Popović.

BD   Is it true that one of Popović's exhibitions in Belgrade was banned?

JD   It was his exhibition at the Cultural Centre of Belgrade in 1974. The institution's board of managers decided the day before the opening that they weren't going to take any risks, in view of the fact that Tito appears in some of the

paintings, which were arranged provocatively in relation to
the other paintings in the show. Also, alongside his painting
career Popović pursued a career in film and literature.
He was certainly an exceptional figure within the framework
of the socio-political and cultural developments in Serbia,
because he operated in several places at the same time.
He wrote a number of literary works, among them a novel
entitled *The Picnic* (1957), which is considered to be a representative existentialist novel. However, I didn't have any
inclinations towards such a form of expression; I actually
think that Popović was not a particularly significant figure,
not even within the Belgrade Informel landscape. Branislav
Protić and Vera Božičković Popović were in my opinion
more important. As an art critic, for me Popović was not
the one to focus on; by the same token I can't deny that he
played an important role in Serbian art of the time.

BD   Here we are trying to begin our conversation about
the Yugoslav Art Space by approaching it from behind –
through consideration of an important artist who was not
overly relevant for you. We want to uncover and explore the
basic parameters of your critical position, bearing in mind
that you have written extensively about different artists and
different artistic positions, and not only about those closest
to your heart. We might say that for you Popović represents
a line of thought according to which there always needs to
be a certain dominant reference to narratives in the painting.

JD   Popović traverses a space from the expressive
language of painting to the language of literary symbolism,
which makes him interesting. But, on the other hand, what
makes his Art Informel from the beginning of the 1960s
rather weak is his over-aestheticisation, and his excessive
use of narratives with respect to the visual language he
employed. That's why he seemed to me to be less important
than the role that Serbian art history circles granted him.
In my essay in the book *Yugoslav Painting of the Sixth Decade,*
published by the Belgrade Museum of Contemporary Art in
1980 on the occasion of the exhibition of the same name,
I am of the opinion that in the Art Informel made in Belgrade
the essence of that type of art was missing: the amorphous,
formless state of matter that is beyond form, is beyond it.

With Mića Popović and the other protagonists of Belgrade
Informel everything remains within the sphere of the
traditionally understood model of painting and its aesthetic
intentions. Therefore such art does not represent a break
but rather a continuation of this traditional model.[9] In the
same text I choose instead to find some features of Informel
in the sculptures of Olga Jevrić produced in the late 1950s,
or in the paintings of Branislav Protić, who was only subsequently included in the narrative on the Belgrade Informel.
Previously, the critics thought that in those early exhibitions
he was not aware that what he was doing had something
of Art Informel in them, and that the Informel appears in
Belgrade only in the early 1960s, when it was recognised
as such. Then Popović appeared as a leading figure of the
movement even though, as we see now, this was only a
temporary phase in his work.

JV   Who, in your opinion, was crucial in positioning
Mića Popović as he was, who gave him the role of a leading
figure in the context of the Belgrade Informel artists?

JD   If we think today about the affinities between the
critic and his ideal artist, Mića Popović would be the ideal
artist for Lazar Trifunović. There is a monograph that was
published on the occasion of Popović's exhibition at the
Gallery of the Serbian Academy of Sciences and Arts
(Galerija SANU) not long before Trifunović's death, I think
in 1983.[10] This monograph was made in a well-coordinated
manner that brought together the positions of both the
critic and the artist. Popović is the ideal artist for
Trifunović, for his critical and political position, just as
Petar Lubarda was the ideal artist for Miodrag Protić. In this
monograph, Trifunović reacted to Protić's position and to
mine also: he believed that we wanted to devalue the place
of Art Informel in the history of modern art in Serbia.[11]

BD   We have been talking at length about Mića Popović
in order to get to the point, which in the case of Lazar
Trifunović is quite obvious: that there is a clearly defined
line that characterises and differentiates Serbian, Croatian
and Slovenian art. Trifunović was not interested in
approaching art as a single shared and common cultural

space – he wrote almost exclusively about Serbian artists. But which art critic other than you dealt with Yugoslav art as a whole? You – together with Miodrag Protić – were the main advocates of the notion of a Yugoslav Art Space.

JD   I don't think that other people weren't dealing with it; by the same token it is quite logical that they dealt largely with the milieu in which they were working and to which they were linked in existential and other ways. The conditions I was working in were somewhat different. Perhaps where I came from had something to do with it – the fact that I came from Split to Belgrade. Of course, much of my interest in modern and contemporary art was born of phenomena specific to Croatia that I had the opportunity to follow, but I was also travelling around various towns in Yugoslavia and abroad. All this can be explained by circumstances and different interests. I was really in touch with what was going on all over Yugoslavia. It seemed to me that what was happening in the Yugoslav Art Space should have been accessible to all of us. Then again, I understand that people were linked to their contexts, that they were personally connected with certain artists. Or, perhaps they understood the cultural processes at work in their milieus well and so were more attentive in interpreting them. I have always dealt with the entire Yugoslav Art Space – which can be seen from my book titles, and in the exhibition I curated in 2005 of works from the collections of the Museum of Contemporary Art in Belgrade entitled *The Yugoslav Art Space*. The exhibition followed the wars in the former Yugoslavia, when I was invited by the new managerial board of the Museum. I had been working in this museum before the wars began, and I was very familiar with its collections. The new director and the chief curator shared my view on the Yugoslav Art Space and the particular role of the museum in Belgrade in maintaining it, even after the breakup of the country.[12] Miodrag Protić was still alive then, in the early 2000s, and he was able to follow the way that his concept of museum collections was developing.

BD   You were a curator at the Belgrade Museum of Contemporary Art for over two decades, from the 1960s to the 1980s. How did you end up there?

JD   I was involved in the work of the museum from the very beginning – that is, even before the building itself was finished and opened in October 1965. I was very young then, and I had just graduated from the department of Art History at the Faculty of Philosophy, Belgrade. I had already published a couple of essays – the first was published in the Sarajevo-based journal *Izraz* (*Expression*) in 1962[13] – and in 1965 I became a member of the editorial board of the Belgrade journal *Umetnost* (*Art*). In those days there were only a few art historians in Belgrade dealing with modern art – even at the museum itself – and even fewer were writing about post-war art. So Protić, the museum's first director, invited me, which was a rather big gesture of trust. But right from the very beginning of my tenure at the museum we were confronted with the problem of defining the actual area we were dealing with. We were aware – especially people with some political experience like Protić and his generation of critics – that the question of naming the space was very important, and in some ways very problematic. And we were aware that using the term 'Yugoslav art' might give rise to certain misunderstandings within the profession itself, let alone the political sphere. We searched for a term that would designate the real, existing state of affairs in the art of our regions. In Yugoslavia there existed an art space that was both consistent and decentralised, and I felt that 'Yugoslav Art Space' was an appropriate term. It was a consistent space, because it was delineated as a single country, and decentralised because traditions in Slovenia, Croatia, Serbia and other republics really differed substantially.

BD   But, Ješa, did you consider Yugoslavism a particular national or supra-national identity?

JD   I belong to that group of people who felt a kinship with the entire space in which we lived. Although I had lived previously in Split, I had no problem with coming to Belgrade and thinking that I had only come to an other city, and not to an other culture. I even found many similarities, a certain affinity between people, so for me it really was one and the same milieu.

JV   The term 'affinity' is rather interesting and could be understood as the opposite of alienation, i.e. the feeling of cultural alienation. Other people also moved around and had the same feeling. This means that the Yugoslav space was born out of a common material experience and cannot simply be reduced to a question of identity. For you, it is a space that is built through exchange and contact with various places, through movement that unites this space and holds it together as a 'practical whole'. Contrary to the identity paradigm of getting to know the 'otherness', you're talking about establishing a closeness, about sharing what is common.

BD   We want to say that in the case of this concept of a Yugoslav Art Space of yours, and of Protić also, it is a matter of practice, not of identity. And here lies the difference in relation to, for example, Miroslav Krleža's 'Argument for Yugoslav art' and for the formation of a common Yugoslav identity in general, as he presented the concept at the exhibition *Medieval Art in Yugoslavia* at the Palais de Chaillot in Paris in 1950.[14] Krleža was searching for an authentic tradition and he saw it as a specific south-Slav dynamic which, to quote him, 'in itself, in its internal law of movement, was strong enough not to stop itself, and resistant enough not to submit passively to stronger civilisational forces around itself'.[15] This exhibition was the first example of an official presentation of Yugoslav art in a Western country after the Second World War, and the fact that it was conceived by Krleža imbues it with considerable importance. But such a concept of a Yugoslav identity seems to have been abandoned around the beginning of the 1960s – namely, the idea that it is possible to make, create, construct some common Yugoslav identitarian tradition that goes back deep into the past. What Jelena and I are trying to emphasise is that the issue of the Yugoslav Art Space need not necessarily be seen through a search for identity and by arriving at a cultural archetype, but rather in the way you propose – by looking to the practice, the movement, the communication, the exchange of opinions, publications, art projects, everything through which that space was actually created.

JD   Krleža's idea was epitomised in the concept of that exhibition in Paris, in 1950. It was intended to be the argument for the creation of some kind of Yugoslav cultural body vis-à-vis a form of Stalinist Socialist Realism together with the modernist abstraction of the Western canon. Krleža's representation of Yugoslavism stood on three pillars: medieval Bogomil gravestones from Bosnia with all their connotations of heretical independence from the two main religions;[16] sculptures from the portals of Dalmatian Roman cathedrals; and finally, frescoes from medieval Serbia that belong to the Byzantine cultural space. This meant that he couldn't bring this space together through a homogenous matrix of Yugoslav culture but had to create and build on a foundation composed of three specific cultural models, which are synthesised and united to form the base from which future Yugoslav art would emerge. In his considerations, therefore, Krleža retreated from a singular model of Yugoslav art and presented it as an assemblage of various cultural milieus.

JV   Shall we sum up these differences between Krleža's thesis, Protić's thesis and yours, when thinking about the Yugoslav Art Space? Within the context of the Clashes within the Left of the 1930s, Krleža chose Georg Grosz's line – the art of social critique that cannot be subsumed by a Socialist Realism canonised by socialist bureaucracies, nor by the current of modernist abstract art that dominated the Western art of the time,[17] the line he later developed from Krsto Hegedušić and his *Podravski motivi* (*Podravina Motifs*).[18] Krleža's resistance to modernism and abstraction was perceived as a conservative position by the art protagonists of the late 1950s and 1960s who favoured abstract art and constructive thinking. However, Krleža's position was not anti-modernist. Rather, it stemmed from his anti-colonial thinking, which follows from his personal and political uneasiness with the cultural domination of the West and the alleged second-ratedness of local cultures that simply blindly follow Western models.[19] Stanko Lasić explicitly labelled Krleža's view of art 'Fanonist', bearing in mind his double-sided rejection – on the one hand, following the Western canon of modernism and abstraction, and on the other the romanticising of 'authentic' local culture.[20]

Krleža found this pre-figuration of 'authenticity' in the Bogomils sect, and the Bogomils hadn't surrendered to Rome or to Constantinople, just as 'authentic' Yugoslav art in socialism was not supposed to submit either to the East or to the West. For him, abstract art was a self-colonizing form of transferring the Western canon, which is why he searched for 'authenticity' in the past. We can ask ourselves whether he succeeded in this aesthetic-political endeavour. The exhibition in Paris, about which Branislav was speaking, can also be explored through the politics of multiculturalism, which was in a way suggested by your interpretation of the exhibition as bringing together the three cultural models outside the single matrix. If Krleža's approach were to be critically examined from a certain historical distance one might even say that his exhibition in Paris presented the Yugoslav space through a multicultural cohabitation of small nations, through a folklorism of differences living together in some kind of 'peaceful co-existence'.

As opposed to Krleža, Protić acted from another position, on behalf of the new socialist cultural institutions. He approached the Yugoslav Art Space in the manner of real politics. He began from the perspective of Yugoslav statehood and socialism, and from the role of a new socialist institution in the new state politics. He was well aware that this space should be named, that it should be built through knowledge and run with a determined institutional politics. For him, the Yugoslav Art Space does not dwell in the past, but rather in the new and the modern, or in the contemporary, as the museum in Belgrade implied with its name – the Museum of Contemporary Art. And if we compare Protić's concept and your concept, Ješa, we can see the difference between the cultural-political nominalness of Protić's stand (which certainly had its material consequences) and your insistence on practice, on the sharing of the space in the sense of living together and on concrete material exchanges, through travel, joint institutional programmes and encounters with artists. The Yugoslav Art Space you're talking about is created through a network of life and the movement of people. Unlike Protić and Krleža, you approach the Yugoslav Art Space as material fact that comes to life through the process of becoming, through the art-life paradigm.

BD   Jelena and I are led to conclude that your position
is of key importance for understanding the difference
between what is simple historicism and what, by contrast,
is advocated by historical materialism. The historicist
position would be precisely the Krležanian attitude, meaning
that a flow is drawn from history, from ancient times in fact,
by a process which then develops and results in the possibility of establishing a direct connection between this fresco
and that gravestone from medieval times, all the way up to,
for instance, Lazar Vozarević or Lazar Vujaklija, or some
other artist embodying some such modern-folklore mix
characteristic of the 1950s. On the other hand, with you it
is always a matter of direct, immediate material practices,
and material practices actually produce this space in a way.
Of course, it is produced within an inherited context.

JV   Such as the institutional and socio-cultural public
space …

JD   I don't have the authority to speculate on suppositions about the way that the culture of a multinational
country should have looked. Everything I was trying to think
stems from the knowledge of art practices themselves –
both the historical and the contemporary – which by their
very nature are multifaceted because they are produced by
different people. And they have some particularities of their
own, which are established a posteriori, and not a priori.
This coincides in a way with an important statement Protić
made, which was related not to the Yugoslav Art Space
but to the question of art under socialism. He put forwards
a thesis that can be roughly summarised as follows: one
cannot tell a priori what art under socialism is, it can only
be established a posteriori. So, everything that possesses
a certain value in our multicultural community and within
the socialist political context is the art of socialism. That
was Protić's position, and it stood in opposition to the
model of Socialist Realism, according to which the nature
of socialist art should have been postulated in advance.

JV   The distinction you're talking about is crucial to
positioning Yugoslav socialism within a wider ideological
and real political sense – the idea that socialism is built

from below is crucial for the event of the National Liberation War (Narodno oslobodilačka borba, NOB), as well as for creating the model of socialist self-management and the politics of the Non-Aligned Movement. Such forms of social building presuppose a certain process. Thus, Protić says that we can see these processes and read them a posteriori, rather than being able to establish a priori a single dogma that is supposed to be followed by reality, and which would mean siding with a dogmatic version of socialism.

JD   Yes, such an understanding of processes is close to my way of thinking, especially if they are observed through the more specific questions of the history of art. It was only possible to establish a posteriori that in particular milieus there emerged and developed certain art practices that could be identified through important works of particular artists, or generations of artists – those who are today considered to be pioneers of modern art in the Yugoslav Art Space. For example, in Serbia the emblematic figure of a modern artist is Nadežda Petrović. She was a woman, an activist and a patriot who lost her life during the First World War as a nurse. Later, we discovered that she was a highly political person, and that she was driven by the Serbian politics of the time, for which she was a propagandist. The pioneers of modern art in Croatia include two artists who died very young – Josip Račić committed suicide, and the other artist, Miroslav Kraljević, died of tuberculosis when he was just 27. Thus, in Croatia the figure of a modern artist carried very different connotations. He is a loser, a sensitive being who instigates modernist art and destroys himself in the process. In Slovenia, we have this big story of Slovenian Impressionism, the story of the great figure of the artist Rihard Jakopič, who at the same time organised exhibitions and was crucial for building the art pavilion in Tivoli Park in Ljubljana at the beginning of the 20th century. The foundations of Jakopič's painting are linked to 'domestic landscapes' and everything that implies from the romantic tradition onwards. So, the history of art would be viewed with respect to local milieus – these three milieus in particular, as well as other milieus in Yugoslavia. We can identify key differences in the models of such artists as Petrović, Račić, Kraljević or the Slovenian impressionists.

Such models generate different lines of development.
On the other hand, we all lived in a single country that we
considered our homeland, and in those days it was incon-
ceivable to me that this country could fall apart, that we
would come into conflict both as nations and as individuals.

BD   But were nationalisms already apparent then, in the
art scene? What was your experience, as someone who was
travelling and meeting with people and who, as a Croat who
lived in Belgrade, had to consider all of that?

JD   Were there nationalisms? Above all there was a focus
on local cultures, on the fact that actors, important actors
on the scene, simply worked within their own milieus, and
within the scope of their milieus and, one might even say,
in the interest of their milieus. It was evident that these were
different contexts, that they could not have been brought
together through some homogenous cultural matrix, rather
that their richness consisted precisely in the fact that they
were different. But, were there nationalisms? Did historians,
artists, cultural workers insist on or impose their own
narrower national cultural interests? I can speak only from
personal experience. For example, when the Museum was
working on the decennial exhibitions – the project *Yugoslav
Art of the 20th Century* that Protić initiated[21] – we really
thought that we had provided a platform for each of these
milieus to express themselves adequately. Which is why
the contributing authors of texts were invited from various
milieus. Whether some of them thought that they had
been manipulated through this act, whether some of them
thought that they had been forced to enter the story of
the unitary Yugoslav project, that I wasn't aware of.

BD   Although the fear of an imposed Yugoslav unitarism
was present, especially in Croatia.

JD   In Croatia it existed. But it is also important where
it existed. It existed in the circles of the artists and critics
who cherished the concept of a national tradition.

JV   There's another interesting thing here, which is the
vocabulary. It seems that when nationalism or the affirmation

of national cultures was gaining real ground, it was channelled through the notion of tradition. To say 'tradition' and not 'national culture' was consistent with the state politics of the time. So the very word 'tradition' had a certain diplomatic function, so to speak.

JD   Yes, the phrase was 'domestic traditions'.

JV   On the other hand, we can also raise the issue of the metropolis hegemony. The entire platform you are talking about – the Yugoslav Art Space – as a proposition for discussing art in our regions came from the historical centre of Yugoslav unitarism, from Belgrade. And the largest institution that was dealing with the issue was the Belgrade Museum of Contemporary Art.

JD   This is an issue that could be raised. But only the Belgrade Museum of Contemporary Art had a comprehensive collection of Yugoslav art. Numerous exhibitions of Yugoslav art were held there. The fact is, and it shouldn't be avoided, that this was not to a great extent the case in institutions in Croatia and Slovenia. Although there were exchanges of exhibitions and artists from all milieus, the general opinion was 'these are our artists, and we will make exhibitions primarily of them and their work'.

BD   You and Protić seem to be the main actors who operated across the entire Yugoslav Art Space and produced the space through exhibitions and art historical discourse. Who was writing from Zagreb about Serbian artists, and who was writing from Belgrade about Croatians?

JD   Examples are sporadic. Even Protić wrote little about other milieus. These texts largely served as prefaces for exhibitions at the Salon of the Museum of Contemporary Art,[22] for artists who were indisputably significant, like Dušan Džamonja. In general, he wrote only about artists who were close to him. I have to say that I dealt with the Yugoslav Art Space systematically. Although now I don't know whether this is a positive or a negative thing.

JV   For us, it is certainly very positive. Among other things, that's why we're having this conversation.

JD   I'm also glad that I dealt with many of them. However, if we had to delve deeper into this issue, we would find that I largely related to and worked with Croatian art. I found my affinities there, but that has nothing to do with the identitarian notion of Croatian art and its domestic traditions.

BD   But what if you had studied art history in Zagreb? Who knows whether your life and work might have taken a similar path, and what it would all look like?

JD   Yes, who knows …

2.   <u>Socialism as a 'Civilisational Level' and Avant-garde Yugoslavism</u>

BD   You are from the island of Brač (which is part of Croatia). Logically, you moved to Split for further education, but then it would also be logical for you to have chosen to attend university in Zagreb, Croatia's capital. Your decision to move to Belgrade, the capital of Serbia, to study might have been perceived as an act of stepping out of the context of national culture.

JD   These are some personal stories, which are not so important. My interest in travelling, seeing and learning brought me to Belgrade. Most of the people in my circles went to Zagreb.

BD   What were the main domestic traditions during those years in Zagreb and generally in Croatia, when your interest in modern art emerged?

JD   I would say that broadly there existed two models of historical-artistic narrative. One had its source in Ljubo Babić, who was a painter but also a theoretician, an art historian and the first curator of the Modern Gallery (Moderna galerija) in Zagreb. Babić cultivated his views

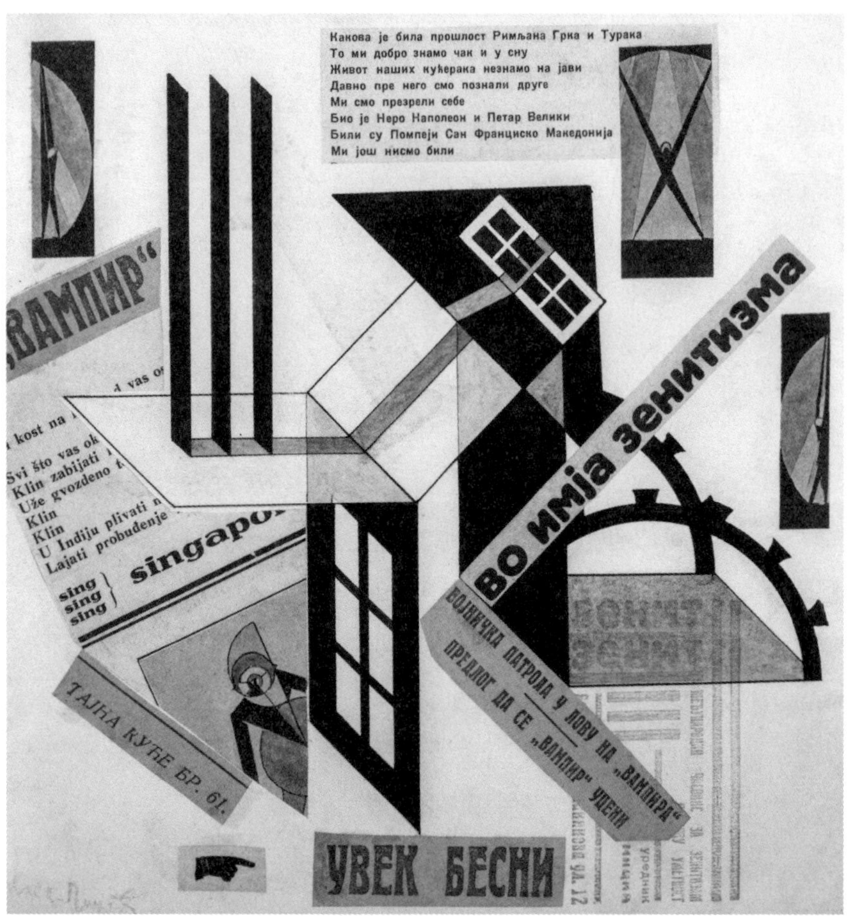

Jo Klek (Josip Seissel)
Vo imja zenitizma (*In the Name of Zenit*), 1925
Collage on paper, 16 × 20 cm

about art through phenomena linked with the Munich Circle,[23] and above all with Račić. Another narrative model was developed by the Dalmatian historians Grgo Gamulin and later Igor Zidić, who used the notion of the ancestor, which they found in the figure of Emanuel Vidović. It is a line that goes from Vidović, to Marino Tartalja and then to Ljubo Ivančić. It connotes an introverted artistic attitude, and also a Mediterranean identity, whatever one might understand by such a notion.

BD   But you became interested in some 'other line'?

JD   If I speak in those terms, I'd point to Jo Klek as my ancestor. Within Croatian art, which is close to me and interesting for me as a whole – and certainly not because it is signified as Croatian in nationalistic terms – the closest thing for me is Zenit, or more precisely the visual component of Zenit represented by Jo Klek. For me, he is the prototype of an enlightened marginal figure within a dominant cultural mainstream, and thus constitutes the founder of the Other Line.[24] Then, after the Second World War, this root branches out into two phenomena – EXAT 51 and Gorgona – which, however different they were, were also complementary in a certain way. These are the phenomena that are interesting for a debate related to culture under socialism, which is one of the themes of this conversation of ours. What I wanted to say is that the essence of my position – from art to politics – lies in this Zenit/Gorgona relationship. To a certain extent, this differs from the development of art in Serbia, since the first post-war generation of artists remained too far back in the shadow of the great figures of pre-war art who later determined so much thinking and practice.

BD   Post-war art discourse in Serbia is under the constant influence of local masters?

JD   Yes. And this has really blocked a more radical emergence of the post-war generation in the Serbian context. The leading figures in Croatia were either moved into the background or were not that present on the scene, so the younger generation of artists was able to take a stronger initiative. Why was EXAT 51 important to me? First of all, it continues another tradition, which is neither the tradition of the Munich Circle nor the one we just mentioned, the Dalmatian circle, but their sole point of origin is precisely Zenit and Jo Klek. When Želimir Koščević and I were working on the first historicisation of EXAT 51, when we were preparing and writing this lengthy book at Gallery Nova in Zagreb,[25] Ivan Picelj made a statement that was important, at least for me: 'We were constantly accused of not having roots in a domestic milieu. But it was disregarded, forgotten and neglected that it was in that milieu that the figures of the Zenit group were active – Ljubomir Micić, Jo Klek and also the post-cubist Sava Šumanović – and they are all an integral part of our culture.'

BD   So the Yugoslavism you are emerging from is the Yugoslavism of the avant-garde?

JD   Yes. In every case of avant-garde artists and movements one can find a mixture of several cultures and national identities. But today, paradoxically, we witness an absurd struggle for national cultural identities taking place particularly among literary historians, which should get to the root of the question as to whether Zenit belonged to Serbian or Croatian culture. Micić is a Serb in Croatia, and he can be considered a Serbian artist. On the other hand, Zenit originated in Zagreb and is a part of that cultural milieu. The same applies to Dragan Aleksić and Yugo-Dada, a short-lived movement without many followers, but in historical terms, it was certainly a timely and authentic episode.[26]

BD   The avant-gardes rejected national traditions, although not necessarily identitarianism in the broader regional sense – for Micić, this might be considered some kind of Balkanism. The figure of the 'barbarogenius' that he postulates is someone who 'smashes the bones of Western mammoths'.

        But is your concept of the Other Line a cultural-political intervention in an art history that is structured by national identities and local traditions? Here we can connect two crucial concepts of yours, one wider and the other narrower: the Yugoslav Art Space and the Other Line.

Through the phenomenon of the Yugoslav avant-garde,
with the participation of figures who were by nationality
Serbs, Croats or Slovenes, there begins to develop an
artistic course that is not interested in art as an expression
and as a continuity of national traditions. Therefore,
this would seem to be an epistemological break.

JD   This became evident to me when, during the 1970s,
Koščević and I were occupied with our book on EXAT 51.
I was not a contemporary of EXAT 51, so I could not have
followed it from the time of its emergence, but did so from
the first attempt to historicise it. The initiative came from
Ljerka Šibenik, who managed Gallery Nova from 1975, and
she invited Želimir Koščević and me to write, and Mladen
Galić to design the book. This initiative opened up an entire
platform of another kind of art for me. It is interesting
to mention the first reactions to EXAT 51 in Croatian art
criticism. They say that support for the abstract art of
EXAT 51 was considerably delayed, bearing in mind certain
affirmed sources of abstract art – Kandinsky, Mondrian,
Malevich – and assuming that EXAT 51's status is simply
a belated local response to these pioneers of abstraction.
However, it was immediately clear to me that something
else was at stake here. Since I was following the Italian and
the French cultural scenes to some degree, I knew that
groups of so-called 'concrete art' were active then, and had
almost identical programmes, such as the Movimento per
l'arte concreta (MAC) and Forma Uno in Italy, or the Groupe
Espace in France. These groups emerged after the Second
World War and advocated a constructive artistic renewal
after the terrible catastrophe. The art that was supposed to
contribute to such a renewal was not only opting for the
revival of art as such, but for transferring the notion of art
to the wider socio-architectural materiality. This is similar
to EXAT 51's connections with design and architecture.
The phenomenon of painting within EXAT 51 is therefore
not conceived as abstract painting per se, but as painting
that becomes an emblem of a constructive worldview.[27]
        And here's the reason why – let me put forwards
another thesis that is very important. Vjenceslav Richter had
written in one of his programmatic texts: 'Socialism is
not a matter of taking power, nor is it a matter of one party

or its leader, rather it is the matter of a civilisational level.' It is a statement to which I subscribe without hesitation even today, and it reflects very precisely my understanding of socialism. For us, life under socialism was not a matter of the one-party system nor of the figure of Josip Broz Tito, rather it involved a social ascent that enabled our entire generation to become educated, to live a decent quality of life, and that was also demonstrated through the fact that we understood something of the times we lived in, that we had travelled and had met other people. It is precisely this type of civilisational level that Richter was talking about. EXAT 51 created an important artistic and social platform in the period immediately after the Second World War, during which my generation (and I) were still children. But we were the children of the future, the children who got the opportunity, if nothing else, to be educated and to experience some joy in life. My inclination towards socialism comes from this aspect of it. Was it a one-party system, what was the relation between communism, authority and ideology? That's another question.

BD   So we can say that the idea of Yugoslav socialism was what should have replaced these particular identities; that in the Yugoslav space the notion of national identities should have been overcome with one greater idea – the idea of socialism.

JD   But with the concept of socialism as Richter defined it, as the concept of a civilisational level, not only as a political system.

BD   This new civilisational level overcomes the previous one, which is particular, national, traditional, and it includes the overcoming of national art schools and national cultural continuities?

JD   But overcoming local traditions was not enough. As Richter and Picelj said, we have followed Klek, Micić and so on. They were aware of the importance of establishing a different continuity in order to legitimise themselves. On the other hand, EXAT 51 was close to Denise René's gallery in Paris and was thus part of a broader international context.

This new civilisational level was based on the idea of internationalism, which meant that the art from the Yugoslav
space had to produce compatible relations with similar
phenomena in Europe – and not just be a local phenomenon.

JV   You wrote about this in your essay about art in
socialist countries that was published in the catalogue of the
Paris Biennial in 1977.[28] You maintained that the question
of art under socialism doesn't remain within the framework
of the narrative on the existence and destiny of an artistic
individual – as it was established by the western Cold War
discourse, and as it still persists today in post-socialism –
but that it is a question of a new framing of art in the spirit
of internationalism and through the concept of international
art. I want to suggest that you, through the paradigm of
the Other Line in Yugoslav art, were speaking about art that
is simultaneously Yugoslav and international. For you, the
concept of the Yugoslav Art Space did not imply the closing
down into a single identity or, what was an everyday political
question in those days, whether Yugoslavism can be viewed
as one nationality. Rather, you spoke about the opening up of
the Yugoslav Art Space in accordance with the international
character of art as it was conceived by the avant-garde.

BD   That is, the Yugoslavism here is an 'internationalism
on a small scale'; as an application of internationalism
within that concrete space?

JD   It has always been important to me, when looking at
a particular phenomenon, that I find, if possible, some wider
context that is not reducible to the nation and the state.

JV   Or we might say that the kind of art you're interested
in is the one that doesn't end with questions of the locality,
particularity and contextuality of the milieu itself, the kind
of art that cannot, in this or that version, be framed as
national and identitarian?

BD   Nowadays, identitarian politics dominates various
discourses, on different levels, from the colloquial to the
academic. This is in some way at odds with your view.
I'm returning to Yugoslavism, and to this idea of yours that

it can be viewed constructively, as an aspect of building socialism, and that it is not simply something that should replace particular national identities, but rather should take the place of national identitarianism as such. There is a similar thesis in the remarkable book by Dejan Jović, *Yugoslavia: A State That Withered Away*.[29] For Jović, the system gradually abandoned Yugoslavism as a supra-national identity, but the Yugoslav socialist project was itself aimed at overcoming identitarian politics by introducing the common denominator of a new socialist condition, if I may loosely paraphrase a far more complex argument in the book.

JD   Let's go back to Krleža. I think that he was constantly fighting the battle, and continued those Clashes within the Left before the Second World War that he was part of; and due to circumstances later in the 1950s he emerged triumphant. This can be seen after the War, through his positioning, through his works, through his closeness with Tito and, above all, through his role as the founder of the Yugoslav Lexicographical Institute in Zagreb in 1950. You can see that Krleža's speech at the Congress of the Communist Party in Ljubljana in 1952, when he practically eliminated the doctrine of Socialist Realism, at the same time announces the triumph of his ideas from the pre-war period (the Clashes within the Left of the 1930s). However, when speaking about the visual arts, he played a role that seemed problematic to many of the progressive artists we are talking about here. And now, after saying this, I should dissociate myself a bit from my own comments, because I do not regard myself to be worthy of standing next to as accomplished an intellectual figure as Krleža is, and my criticism may be merely an inappropriate simplification. But, in Krleža's speech from 1952, we come across his condemnation of abstract art. When I had the opportunity to speak about that with Picelj and other members of EXAT 51, they explicitly said that Krleža caused more damage to their art than anyone else; that his condemnations of abstract art and the line he drew of Yugoslav cultural specificity on the premises of old frescoes, gravestones and portals hadn't any benefit for post-war artistic practice or theory. There is no room for the ideas of EXAT 51 in the Krležian programme. For Krleža, this approach represented art that had no roots.

The clowns in a fine art circus of
abstract art before us pull dead
canaries out of their cockamamy
hats and bake abstract scrambled
eggs of their inspirations; and while
this show, in the era of Symbolism
and Art Nouveau at the end of the
last century, amidst the boredom
of bourgeois prosperity, could be
interesting for just a moment for
the curious crowd, today, when this
provincial black magic has grown
to international proportions, it is
time to determine that this fine art
and literary dolce far niente does
not speak of more than idealess
obeisance towards what is called
misery of the spirit. This 'revolution
of form' is closer to the fashion of
small-town misses who cackle about
Dior models, to whom the dernier
cri of fashion arrived with a delay of
several tasteless generations.

—Miroslav Krleža, Plenum of
the Union of Writers of Yugoslavia,
Belgrade, 1954[30]

And they were continuously attacked because of that. And then Picelj said what I have already mentioned: we had our roots in the magazines *Zenit* and *Dada Tank*, in Klek and Avgust Černigoj, even in the post-cubist Sava Šumanović, who was active in Zagreb in the 1920s. However, in the early 1950s, Krleža's argument was dominant, and for the most part other things were marginalised. Krleža's denouncement of abstract art was so intense that he negated both Kandinsky and Mondrian — we know that from his writings. He reduced the possibilities of a more robust development of such forms, but they nevertheless emerged and developed in spite of his power and regardless of his role — for his role was not totalitarian to the degree that he could have closed down all the channels.

BD   EXAT 51 was a prelude to the New Tendencies, which became the most important channel of communication for you.

JD   The exhibitions of the New Tendencies that were held in Zagreb from 1961 onwards made a great impression on me, primarily as encounters with an international scene to which the phenomenon of EXAT 51 itself belonged. I had the opportunity to see the first and second iterations while I was still a student, as I travelled between Belgrade and Split via Zagreb and always stopped there to see the exhibitions. The first exhibition of the New Tendencies (*Nove tendencije*, 1961) completely threw me out of the context of what we had learned or thought was art. What we knew was our limited local production, and through the New Tendencies we could come face to face — not even knowing what it was all about — with Piero Manzoni, with the group ZERO and numerous other phenomena. I intuitively suspected, without knowing what it was about, that some other typology of art was at stake. And already during the second exhibition, in 1963, it became clear to me that something big was happening. Ultimately it turned out that this shift of paradigms in international art, displayed and contextualised in a single Yugoslav city, was the product of deep strategic thinking on the part of the circle of art historians in Croatia and Zagreb, such as Božo Bek, Radoslav Putar, Matko Meštrović and others. Bek once said that the New Tendencies was actually the political platform made for those left-oriented artists and groups who broke with Stalinism and who wanted to continue thinking about a new art for new socialist societies. The idea was to make a new platform and to gather international constructivists in a socialist but also 'non-aligned' political space. This was an extraordinary vision, if you try to imagine the state of affairs in art at the beginning of the 1960s in Yugoslavia. Božo Bek was the first director of the Gallery of Contemporary Art in Zagreb. The year 1961 in Yugoslavia is marked by two big international events: one is the first World Summit of Non-Aligned Countries in Belgrade, and the other is the first exhibition of the New Tendencies in Zagreb.

BD   Yet within the Yugoslav context and especially today, after the dissolution of Yugoslavia, it turns out that the New Tendencies exhibitions were events that are exclusively related to the protagonists who emerged in the artistic and intellectual context of Zagreb. Through these events Zagreb became an internationally relevant artistic and intellectual hub. It seems that this phenomenon had very few if any connections with Belgrade.

JD   Yes, the New Tendencies didn't have much to do with other scenes.

JV   Or perhaps they did? The Yugoslav Art Space does not necessarily have to be viewed as a fixed geopolitical designation that has to be re-affirmed in every moment, in every place, in every city and in every art phenomenon. It can be read as a space-time in which we find a certain simultaneity and connectivity. If we say that the New Tendencies events introduced a certain new language into the Yugoslav Art Space, and a new attitude towards art through the node of Zagreb, then this attitude is transmitted, like a sporangium, via various protagonists and different channels into other milieus. Let's say, through you, Ješa, and later through Dunja Blaževic, these sporangia were brought into the Belgrade context and in some way initiated a thinking about a further radicalisation of art with the New Art Practices of the 1970s, or thinking about interwar avant-gardes through exhibitions at the Museum of Contemporary Art in Belgrade. EXAT 51 did actually originate in

Croatia, in Zagreb, but nevertheless it produced a certain flux of thinking within the Yugoslav space, and I'm not sure if we can speak about EXAT 51 as a phenomenon framed by the notion of Croatian art. Is EXAT 51 a phenomenon of Yugoslav socialism that originated in Croatia, or is it a Croatian phenomenon? Isn't saying that EXAT 51 is a Croatian phenomenon just another reflection of the contemporary politics of national revisionism?

JD   Yes, it is a complex question. EXAT 51 did originate in Croatia, but it also originated within Yugoslavia and within socialism.

3.   The Yugoslav Art Space and Identity Politics

BD   Such issues nowadays also shape various dominant views that create a particular geopolitics of art from the socialist era. There is, for example, a significant book by Piotr Piotrowski, *In the Shadow of Yalta,* one of the most influential books about the history of art in Eastern and Central Europe.[31] In this book, Yugoslavia is somehow already divided – from this space its Central-European identity is extracted. The book is very thorough when it comes to EXAT 51, the New Tendencies and Gorgona, while phenomena in Belgrade during the 1950s and 1960s are not mentioned at all, even when these phenomena are related to the themes discussed in the book – Art Informel, gestural painting, geometric tendencies. There is no mention of Olga Jevrić in the chapter on Informel, nor of Dušan Otašević in the context of the influences of Pop art. There's no mention of the painting of Miodrag Protić, nor of Ćelić, not even of Lubarda, so it seems that their work or their practices are seen as inferior. Piotrowski makes an effort to place a range of phenomena within the canon, but it seems that he does not take into consideration the material and spiritual specificities and differences in the concrete circumstances under which particular art phenomena also appear outside this Central European cultural matrix.

JV   Some of our conversations here deal with the issue of revisionism, a topic that Branislav just spoke about.

We are reading socialism in a post-socialist context, maintaining a critical distance towards post-socialism itself.
All these current re-appropriations of the art and the culture of Yugoslavia by and into the Central European framework repeat the gesture, on a symbolic level, of tearing apart Yugoslavia. Breaking Yugoslavia up into the Balkans and Central Europe implies bringing modernist art back into the bourgeois domain and discourse, as well as into the scheme of national culture and, finally, under the coat-tails of the Habsburg monarchy. Krleža would turn in his grave at the thought of such operations. For us, the whole idea of socialist Yugoslavia and all the many gestures of artists, intellectuals and art groups who tried to think socialist art for a socialist society represent an essential contextual frame for discussing the art of the 20th century in these areas. And it is a material fact, because this space, the way Ješa thinks about it, is materially determined by these connections, by this flux, by the movements through institutions, communities, individuals, through the entire public field of discussion. Thus, the point is to see this space as sharing the same problems with many contradictions, and not by focusing on cultural difference expressed as the division of the Balkans from Europe.

JD   These insights of yours seem very valuable to me, but I think that in all this I can be a listener rather than the speaker.

JV   You can be the speaker, too. If not 'in the first person' and in a live discussion, then through written documents. Here I have the catalogue for the Paris Biennial in 1977, in which there is a text of yours that can be seen not only as an elaborated counter-thesis to the concept of committed figurative art that we mentioned at the beginning of our conversation around the exhibition *Mir '75*, but also as an interesting counter-statement to these post-socialist art historical narratives about the art of Eastern Europe.

JD   There I participated as part of an international team of curators, but I was also invited to write about the state of art in socialist countries.

JV   Interestingly enough, the essay is entitled 'Some New Artistic Attitudes in Socialist Societies'.[32] Your insistence on the notion of society seems important here, since in today's post-socialist discourse there persists a strong contrast between the official sphere, which controlled art and the art institutions, and the alternative sphere, within which some kind of search for freedom was going on. There, the notion of the freedom of art – according to the canon of the global West, that is, according to the ideological key of the CIA's Congress for Cultural Freedom (1950–1967) – is introduced and reactivated. The concept of freedom within the Yugoslav context was constructed somewhat differently, outside a purely binary frame: individual self-realisation versus the totalitarianism of the State and the Party. Marko Ristić, in his letters to the renowned French intellectual Roger Caillois, the co-organiser of the Congress for Cultural Freedom in 1952, criticises the arbitrariness of the notion of totalitarianism in the context of socialist societies and the idea of the West as a universal guarantor of artistic freedoms; he refuses to participate in a conference titled as such, asserting that there is no freedom outside socialism.[33] What is crucial in your text for the 1977 Paris Biennial, and what can be seen as a counter-thesis to today's post-socialist mantra, is your insistence on the notion of society – namely, that you refer to socialist society, and not the authoritarian state or the socialist regime.

JD   Again, this is my internalisation of the EXAT 51 position, according to which the issue of socialism is not an issue of authority, but rather a civilisational issue.

JV   And you develop this way of thinking further on in the essay, while insisting on the concept of the new, which is an idea that went through various elaborations during the 20th century, particularly in the Clashes within the Left regarding the issue of new art for a new society and the very definition of such art. These discussions left a certain trace in the form of an autonomy of thinking and a freedom of critique that existed in the Yugoslav Art Space and were integrated within the art institutions.[34] You emphasise the concept of *the new* in the title and in the body of the text, and the same term will be reaffirmed later, with your colleagues

Marijan Susovski, Tomaž Brejc, Davor Matičević, Nena Baljković, Jasna Tijardović and Slavko Timotijević in a very important exhibition of the New Art Practices at the Gallery of Contemporary Art in Zagreb in 1978.

JD   It is interesting, I cannot recall the interpretation I provided in that essay. I haven't read it for a long time – but it sounds good to me, and I agree. [Laughs.]

JV   We might say that you introduced the identification of socialist societies with avant-garde art in the same essay. How much information did you have at that time about the historical avant-gardes in Yugoslavia of the 1920s? What kind of resources did you use to analyse the genesis of art in socialist societies by reflecting on the early positions of the historical avant-gardes?

JD   Well, we certainly knew a lot. It is an interesting fact – we mentioned Lazar Trifunović earlier – that he had written about the Russian avant-garde very early on, as early as the 1950s. He published a text in the Sarajevo-based journal *Izraz* (*Expression*) entitled 'The Left Wing of Russian Modern Painting in 1957'. This essay can be found in the collection of his theoretical essays that the Museum of Contemporary Art in Belgrade has published.[35] In general, essays about Malevich, Kandinsky and Constructivism were published in periodicals, and some Yugoslav art historians also began researching the local avant-gardes: in Belgrade it was Protić[36] and then Irina Subotić[37] who did major research on Zenit, and others. But the book by Camilla Gray, *The Russian Experiment in Art*, which was translated and edited by Branko Vučićević and published by a major publishing house, had greater widespread impact.[38] Gray's book was a source of basic knowledge about the Soviet avant-garde. And most of this knowledge came via the Western interpretations.

BD   However, by the end of the 1970s the Museum of Contemporary Art in Belgrade had also organised the exhibition of Polish Constructivism.[39] It was curated by Ryszard Stanislawski, and was the result of a specific institutional collaboration with Poland on the presentation of avant-garde heritage.

It seems inappropriate to me to
place totalitarianism and the West
in a priori opposition (as the many
organisers of all the conferences,
exhibitions and gatherings held
under the aegis of the Congress for
Cultural Freedom have done) by
equalising, also a priori, the West
and the freedom of creation. There
is no doubt that Stalinism is totalitarianism of the worst kind, and
that there is no significant creation
of art nor any creative freedom
whatsoever, regardless of whatever
Aragon may think, under the dictatorship of a single bureaucratic
cast. But in my opinion it is wrong
to propose the West as some metaphysical entity, as an incarnation
of freedom, as the opposite of
socialist totalitarianism, which in
this simplistic antinomy inevitably
includes, along with Stalinist
totalitarianism, everything that
the West is not, and I leave it to
you to imagine all that this implies.
Whether we want it to or not,
the notion of the West includes the

notion of Francoist Spain, as well
as the notion of colonialism;
and the concept of totalitarianism,
since its circumstances are in no
way specified in the language of
the Congress for Cultural Freedom,
inevitably also includes everything
that denies totalitarianism, that
fights it on the roughest, most
decisive terrain – Yugoslavia,
for example.

—Marko Ristić, letter to
Roger Caillois, 1952[40]

JD   After that exhibition I went on a study trip to Poland, to Łódź, which was part of our institutional cooperation with the Museum Sztuki, and there I developed some of my thinking. Before that I was in Prague in Czechoslovakia, at the National Gallery, within the framework of institutional collaboration and the exchange of curators. Interestingly enough, older colleagues – curators at the Belgrade Museum – didn't show much interest in travelling to Eastern European countries, so I applied alone when this professional exchange was initiated by Protić. I was able to follow different readings of historical avant-gardes in an international context.

4.   Ideology of Form: Moderate Modernism and Radical Formalism

BD   When we talk about the early relations that some post-war artists in Yugoslavia established with the historical avant-gardes, and primarily with the Soviet avant-garde, we should begin in the early 1950s with the group EXAT 51. At that time their work was mostly discussed as part of the debate about abstraction, and then a critical interpretation was formulated that EXAT 51 was simply a belated echo of abstract art. In contrast to this, your intervention lay in connecting their art with simultaneous phenomena in other European countries that manifested the post-war renewal of a constructive pole in modern and avant-garde art. Their path to abstraction was criticised as a shallow formalism without pictorial qualities. At the other pole of abstraction stood painters like Edo Murtić, as well as Protić, who pursued another type of abstract art – and we can't deny that these two artists were part of the highest artistic establishment in socialist Yugoslavia. Their abstraction was grounded in the poetic, painterly reduction of identifiable representations, and even when they turned to geometry, like Protić, this remained within the semantic parameters of representation and the fetishism of pictorial execution. EXAT 51's position was entirely outside this dominant view of abstraction.

JD   EXAT 51 is not formalism. It is rather an ideology.

BD   An ideology?

JD   EXAT 51 does not derive from what was understood as the intrinsic nature of painting. It presents a different ideology of art. With Protić, for example, the abstraction has to remain in collusion with an object that comes from the external world. These were essential ideological struggles.

BD   For you, this auto-referentiality in art seems crucial. You have continuously seen art exclusively as a concrete material practice. Hence your understanding of ideology through these concrete material practices. How very Althusserian!

JD   Ideology is certainly not only 'false consciousness' as Marx put it. I'm speaking here of direct clashes over the concept of art in Yugoslavia during the 1950s. Within these conflicts EXAT 51's abstraction couldn't cope with this form of soft abstraction that mitigates the language of art and makes compromises regarding its forms, for instance the abstraction of nature, the landscape, emotions, the type of brushstrokes used and so on. Formalism, which one might say is the art of pure form, is not simply formalism, but it is an ideology. My position is that socialist modernism, with its soft and moderate variants, is precisely this acceptable compromise in modern art within the political context of post-war Yugoslavia.[41] But for me, this art is structurally similar to the engaged art of Mića Popović, who belongs to the camp that in turn strongly opposes this type of socialist aestheticism. These two models were governing models, especially in the Serbian art milieu. The issues for EXAT 51 are the radicalisation of the form of art and the internationalisation of the language of art.

BD   Let's stick with the question of formalism. I think that it is one of those terms that produce permanent misunderstandings. I have formulated some of my views largely under the influence of the British social historians of art – particularly that of T. J. Clark – and their criticism of formalism that was related to the legacy of British formalists connected with the Bloomsbury group at the beginning of the 20th century, with Clive Bell and Roger Fry, and then to the American modernist critics like Clement Greenberg and Michael Fried. Now I think I used to have a somewhat simplified understanding of formalism, as some kind of reactionary act that blurs the question of the socio-economic context of art. However, over the course of time, first through reading the Russian formalists, as well as Mukarovsky, I have begun to think the notion differently and to connect it with the avant-garde *ostranenie* (defamil-iarisation) to the radical aspects of the form, and not only with bourgeois formalism. Thus, I came to the point where the question of formalism, and the examination of the art form in general, should be saved from this apolitical aestheticisation, which in practice resulted in 'modest modernism' as the main current of Yugoslav art. What you have been thinking all the time, Ješa, and what you have called the 'Art of the Constructive Approach',[42] and what in fact stems from the avant-gardes and from Soviet formalism in particular, is a demand for the radicalisation of the form. The juxtaposition of this notion of the constructive approach in art with what we might call the expressive approach as a dominant tendency in Yugoslav modern art seems crucial to me. Both approaches are formalist, in their own way, but there is a big difference. Within the practices of 'modest modernism' in Yugoslavia, formalism was linked to the art of expressing an artist's being through their individual personal gesture – what the Belgrade Fine Arts Academy has pursued as an affirmation of some kind of 'art from the gut'. Various types of associative abstraction, lyrical abstraction, symbolic abstraction and also gestural painting, as well as some iterations of Art Informel, correspond to this approach – the idea that the artist constantly expresses and invests their inner being within the forms of institu-tionalised art, which inevitably produces either aestheticisa-tion or existential breakdown. The opposite of this is the constructive approach, which is derived from the avant-garde, but also from the social-material conditions of the production of art as the production of new forms and new propositions that change, redistribute and even overcome the concept of art. I want to emphasise once more what you have yourself said – the opposite of this moderate socialist modernism is not Trifunović's idea of the engaged Mića Popović. It was only possible to oppose moderate modernism through radical interventions in the ways of understanding the art-matter and the art-form, and thus to oppose its

social role at the 'civilisational level' of socialism – just
to return to Richter once again. And this is what you have
insisted on all the time, and from which you have never
retreated.

JD   I should probably elaborate on the practices this
relates to. The formalism that would be a radical form
or an ideology of form would be exemplified by Picelj, when
he makes the painting *Homage to El Lissitzky* (1956). It is a
formalist painting – a composition of two forms, one strictly
geometrically angular, the other slightly curved like a sphere.
But the intention of the painting's title itself unequivocally
speaks of what it is about. Picelj finds his ideological and
aesthetic ancestor and dedicates the painting to him. The
title can be an ambiguous carrier of meaning when works
of art are named; but if we remove the title there remains
the pure fact that this painting is what it is. For me, it is
an ideological statement, whereby an artist from our context
clearly and unequivocally announces his paragon, in his
formation as an artist and in his work. If it is said in that way,
the fact of verbalisation and the fact of the visual are absolutely congruous and consequential; thus this painting is not
only formalism in the pejorative sense of the word, but is
in fact an extreme form of understanding the form, which
along with all the other connotations represents an explicit
ideological and culturological statement. This statement
tells us: I am someone who inherits the Russian avant-garde
and I try to incorporate this legacy within the circumstances
of Yugoslav post-war society and post-war socialism and
the cultural model in which I live. We can see geometric
tendencies in many other works, for example in the paintings
of Miodrag Protić, but it is a geometry of soft contours and
its origin is something completely different. It still dwells on
the associative vision. The question of form and formalism
has constantly created an insurmountable tension in our
milieus, because it seems that this type of 'dry geometry',
as in the work of Picelj and other artists who were close to
me, reveals a certain deficit of artistic imagination, of talent
even, and that this other soft geometry shows, in some way,
a flexibility of movement within visual features – through
colour, the treatment of the surface or the literary element,
etcetera. Here we see an explicit and not at all peaceful

Ivan Picelj
Omaž El Lisickom (Homage to El Lissitzky), 1956
Oil on canvas, 96 × 96 cm

debate within these circles and these generations of artists. The concept of formalism generated these sorts of debates, as you can see.

JV   In some way, you're saying that there's no need for a direct denouncement of formalism because formalism is not a single thing.

JD   Yes. It is not a single thing, and it is not a negative thing.

JV   There are different kinds of devotion to form and abstraction and you don't hesitate to say this. In the afore-mentioned essay for the 1977 Paris Biennial, you leave out Socialist Realism, engaged and figurative art, and remain in the domain of form and abstraction – where you actually make a break or a political division in art: you juxtapose the concepts of avant-garde internationalism and the language of mediocre abstractionism. You also emphasise the pre-vailing conformism in actual practice, in which mediocre artists enjoyed the benefits of the socialist state: institutional support, scholarships abroad, purchasing of works, state commissions, and so on. Some artists were getting more than others. The class struggle and the ideological struggle were always alive in the Yugoslav Art Space.

JD   Well, yes. I think so too.

JV   Indeed, this soft modernism was completely rooted in certain ideals of humanness, in universal human aspirations, in the vulnerability of the artistic subject, in the epic of the historical, and in fact it operates as a romanticised acad-emism of modern times. And now we have this art historians' truism repeated in many books on Yugoslav art: 'Tito broke with Stalin in 1948, and the doctrine of Socialist Realism was replaced by modernism.' But what does that mean? It doesn't mean anything. If we have art that is apologetic about the existing social reality, that is apologetic rather than constructive, if modernism and abstraction promote the epic and sentimental characteristics of art, then we have no break within art, and then this modernism is also nothing other than Socialist Realism by other means.

BD   And here we notice that this routine in the art historical narrative presents a false dichotomy. On the one hand there is socialist aestheticism and moderate modernism, which in practice capitalise on state grants and on acquisitions by state institutions, and on the other hand there is something proclaimed as engaged figurative art, which amounts to a form of structural dissidence within the system. Your answer, in turn, is *neither one nor the other*! Now, it is interesting that you introduced the term the 'Other Line', but in fact it might be the 'Third Line' in relation to this polarisation, which would be characteristic of Lazar Trifunović for instance. We think, in accordance with your formative orientation, that you are a dialectician and a historical materialist, and the Other Line actually represents a dialectical overcoming of an unproductive and even false antagonism that was particularly characteristic of the scene in Serbia. On the one hand, there is an official modernism that is seen as aestheticism and formalism, and on the other, there is engaged figurative art and the myth of 'dissidence'. You see these alleged opposites as one ideological body, as two sides of the same coin.

JD   There's no structural difference between these opposites, and it is a question whether they are opposites at all. I had the opportunity to spend time with those people, to listen to them and to watch them. There was no contradiction between, for example, Mića Popović and Stojan Ćelić. They are compatible. There's no opposition. Many of these artists are reconciliable, compatible, although their languages may not seem so. Together they are so close to success and so close in their interpersonal relations, that the fact that one is a figurative artist and another a soft abstractionist, that one is a dissident and the other a man of the system – this, in practice, was irrelevant. That's why I don't talk about the 'Third Line'. Because these so-called opposites are in fact compatible. It was a new mainstream that was a governing structure that had all the privileges – from grants and purchases to lecturing at academies and cultivating the next generations. Under socialism, it was very important to know who is allowed to work and who can work, and again who cannot, regardless of the absence of any direct prohibitions in the sense of any strong censorship. This is obvious in the case of Olga Jevrić who had the potential to be an extraordinary pedagogue and an internationally celebrated artist, but didn't have any infrastructure support.

JV   With her work and artistic consistency, Olga Jevrić would be on the same line as Picelj, in that very unrelenting position …

JD   She is that kind of a formalist, because when you talked with her, she would say: 'My concern is whether this rod will enter this mass at this angle, and this angle must not be greater than this nor less than that.' It is formalistic thinking par excellence, visible throughout the entirety of her work. With this attitude she also made proposals for large public monuments for the victims of war, but her projects were never realised.

BD   Recently, the Yugoslav memorial sculpture has received a lot of attention.[43] But we need to emphasise the fact that almost all the creators of these monuments were men. It is highly symptomatic that an accomplished sculptor like Olga Jevrić did not have the opportunity to see any of her proposals for monuments realised.

JD   Her position is similarly in line with Richter – defining socialism on or through the civilisational level. Defining it therefore not from a position of victory, not as people with power, but as individuals who build a new society, with all their capacities – new generations who live in this society and do everything to advance society, and not to degrade it.

JV   How was this actually manifested in her practice?

JD   In terms of her artistic language we could place her between Constructivism and Art Informel, which is in itself paradoxical. I had a polemic going with her because I thought that she was a protagonist of Art Informel. Contextualising her within the framework of Art Informel earned her an international reputation, as when she participated in the Venice Biennale in 1958.[44] For her part, she saw herself as an artist with constructivist foundations, but not by virtue of having similarities with Russian Constructivism, but by

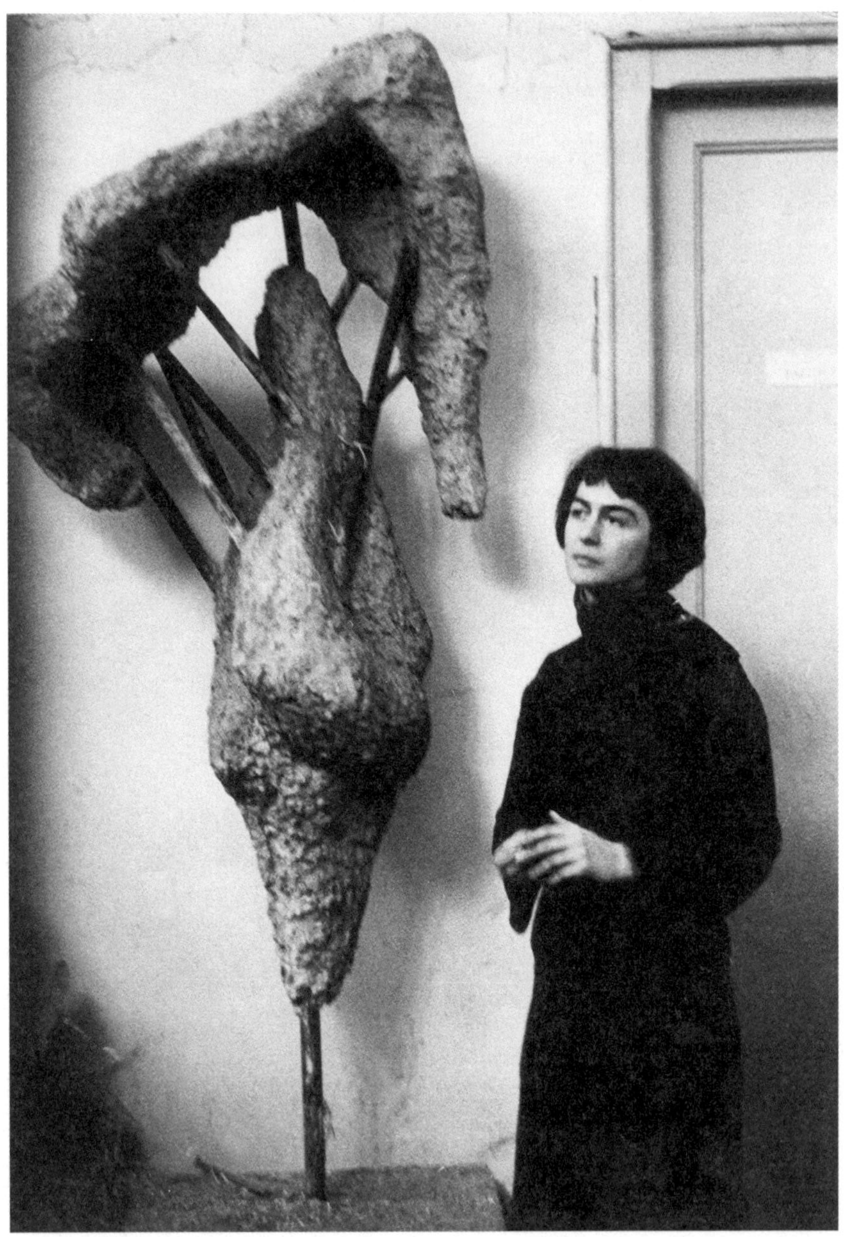

Olga Jevrić in her studio in Belgrade, 1959
With her sculpture *Vertikalna kompozicija 1a (Vertical composition 1a)*, 1956–1957
Cement, iron, 187 × 83 × 59 cm

building the principles of the post-war generation: namely, that form is a material fact that cannot be different from the way that it displays itself in a concrete realisation of a concrete sculpture. This means that between Olga Jevrić and Julije Knifer there is no crucial difference. And between Olga Jevrić and, for example, Olga Jančić, the difference is unbridgeable, even though, as Belgrade women artists, they were often compared. There is an absolute gap. And this was obvious to me early on, when I was probably not yet fully formed as an art historian. When I was looking at those things as a student, it was quite clear to me. And this also has political repercussions within the politics of form and as part of a broader socio-political constellation. Soft abstraction was indeed a style of art that ensured purchases, privileges, commissions, professorial sinecures and careers, and all those things together. I don't maintain that some of the artists who enjoyed this didn't deserve it. People were doing this, had their roles in all this, and I'm not the one to make any major moral differentiations, but it is also a matter of understanding and reading the language of art. That's why it is important to me. It is related to this notion of an art form that we had opened up, because the art form in itself does not have to include connotations of shallow formalism. It is a language of art in which everything is in its proper place and there are no structural errors present.

JV   In this entire mainstream of socialist aestheticism, of soft abstraction, the form appears as a kind of 'gate' that is supposed to be opened in order to see the reality of the expression of art, of the expressive articulation of the existing world. The form is not considered to be a product of the construction of the world, as an internal necessity.

JD   My approach is very reductive and very simple, but it is also based on experience that emphasises the importance of internationalisation. What's the problem? Šumanović goes to Paris and studies with André Lhote, because he cannot study with Picasso and Braque. This is the time of Analytical Cubism, and we see that even the pioneers like Lhote, whom we consider important because of his influence on 'our artists', did not really understand the radical model of Cubism of Picasso and Braque, and still influenced

Šumanović regardless. Neither Račić nor Kraljević managed to achieve what Klimt and Schiele did. It is a matter of certain geographies, power and knowledge, but also of the way of looking at things. On the other hand, the domain of art production I was interested in was both created within the local milieus and resonated with the language of art that transcends these localities. Today I have the satisfaction of seeing the importance of such a position – the position that I was part of from my art historical beginnings. How to explain the fact that today Mangelos is such an internationally recognised artist? For me, his validity and the validity of his work have been evident and clear the entire time, because in his concept there is no structural error. It is exciting to witness how relatively marginal phenomena are becoming important and real, how less visible practices are coming into focus. On the other hand, we can also consider the opposite currents: there is a structural, linguistic and formal inconsistency to be found in many of our artists who were active in the post-war period – from major figures like Lubarda onwards. What was it that blurred this understanding? For me, it was exactly this metaphysical projection of the way that art was interpreted. If art is placed within timeless coordinates, then this position of mine definitely fails, because it is not capable of grasping the elevated discourse of art that was used to explain, or rather to obscure, many of the very significant artistic positions both locally and internationally.

BD   But what you describe is precisely this discourse against which you opposed such notions as the Art of the Constructive Approach and the Other Line.

JD   Perhaps, because the possibility of crystallising one compact language that is evident in different aesthetic codes is very important to me. For example, I have an idea that the two closest artists within the Croatian scene are Gattin and Knifer. At first, one might think that they are incompatible, because one is an Informel ne plus ultra, and a very radical one, and the other could be called a geometric abstractionist. However, Knifer is very different from Picelj, who is also a geometric abstractionist, but very close to Gattin. How to convince anyone to see them this way? It is not that simple.

Any stylistic position would argue, 'well, you claim this, but you cannot convince me because they speak in different pictorial languages'. However, these are some parameters of mine that I have gathered and tried to explain under the notion of the Other Line. And they really appear contrary to everything that was around us artistically. Now, in this 'around' there were also worthy artists, I don't deny that.

BD   We do not want to imply in any way that you only focused on artists that you associated with the Other Line. It is difficult to name any important artist in the period we are talking about that you haven't written about (earlier in our talk, for this precise reason we discussed Mića Popović as an exception that proves the rule) or haven't collaborated with as a museum curator, even though in terms of ideas and form they were on the 'first' rather than on the 'other' line.

JD   That's right. But do you know why I insisted on the Other Line? First, in order to build an articulated critical position of my own – and in a certain sense a compact one. It was a proposition that was not concerned with artistic representatives of a particular tendency or style in art. Rather, it was a way of recognising and defining a historical trait that is equally connected to essential questions of the language of art, and to existential questions and social positions. More or less none of the representatives of the Other Line could be integrated into any system.

JV   National systems?

JD   Neither educational, nor national, nor institutional, though they were not really opponents of the regime. I mean, not explicitly. But they stood aside as far as the authorities were concerned. That's how they gained the status of persons of integrity, as people without any moral ambiguities.

JV   Some kind of uncompromising moral and artistic quality is therefore a characteristic of the artists of the Other Line. Let's clarify the following: for you, form is not a style but an attitude. And you have uncompromisingly built a critical attitude based on your radical inclination for

form, which owes a lot to the history of art forms seen as
a history of breaks with dominant paradigms and ideologies.

JD   You're right regarding these breaks. It was not at all
simple for me to be entrusted with the task of describing the
art of socialism for the catalogue of the 1977 Paris Biennial,
while bearing in mind the greatest part of Yugoslav art. It
also wasn't easy for me to designate this victorious modernism here, implicitly or explicitly, not only as a new mainstream, but also as a situation that would be unacceptable
from moral and political standpoints. It was clear to me
that many worthy and significant artists were active in the
field – after all, Miodrag Protić is also a proponent of this
discourse as the director of the Museum of Contemporary
Art in Belgrade. His virtues and merits are enormous,
but all that I'm saying in relation to the Other Line is about
another life situation and another art position. These were
people who chose isolation over immediate benefits, who
chose to stand aside for the sake of a sense of perseverance,
consistency and attitude, whose life and art implied a
particular endeavour. They would seize on something, they
would lose something, but they didn't want to behave in
socialism in the manner of a kitmān;[45] and they didn't think:
let's just adjust, anywhere and in any way we can, and in
all directions simply get along, gain from some material
benefits and live better. And that's how 90 percent of people
thought in those years. In this regard, the Other Line
represented a hard-core minority.

[1] *Mir '75 (Peace '75 – Committed Figurative Art)*, Art Gallery, Slovenj Gradec 1975.

[2] Ješa Denegri, 'Critical Diagnoses: Yugoslavia', *ibid.*, n. p.

[3] Ješa Denegri, 'Jezik umetnosti i sistem umetnosti' ('The Language of Art and the System of Art'), *Oktobar 75*, Student Cultural Centre, Belgrade 1975. See below p. 196–202.

[4] In his essay for the *Mir '75* catalogue Denegri writes: 'The position of art, which can be described as essentially critical, is that which proceeds from the assumption that the fine arts system is in a deep and chronic crisis, mainly because it is impacted by two extremely powerful factors that are, according to their nature, progressively directed towards the very nature of art. These are the market and [the cultural] ideology ... Any artistic practice that could overcome these obstacles would become not only a spiritual, but also a real political, factor of contests. Without being alienated from participation in solving the dilemmas of everyday life this practice would create a unique commitment.' In 'Critical Diagnoses: Yugoslavia'.

[5] Ješa Denegri, 'Zadarska grupa', *Pedesete: Teme srpske umetnosti*, Svetovi, Novi Sad 1993, p. 31–35.

[6] Traditional rural Serbian cap.

[7] Ješa Denegri, 'Izložba Miće Popovića 1950', *Pedesete: Teme srpske umetnosti* (*Themes of Serbian Art*), p. 36–43.

[8] Dobrica Ćosić (1921–2014) was a prominent novelist and an influential Serbian nationalist politician. He was the president of the Socialist Federal Republic of Yugoslavia (known as 'rump Yugoslavia') in 1992–1993.

[9] See Ješa Denegri, 'Kraj šeste decenije: Enformel u Jugoslaviji', in *Jugoslovensko slikarstvo šeste decenije* (*Yugoslav Painting of the Sixth Decade*), exh. cat., Museum of Contemporary Art, Belgrade 1980, p. 125–143. In this essay Denegri describes Popović's procedure as 'pictorial' and 'logically composed', which are not characteristics of Art Informel, which operates 'almost on the pre-morphological condition of the matter-in-itself'.

[10] Lazar Trifunović, *Slikarstvo Miće Popovića*, exh. cat., SANU, Belgrade 1983.

[11] See Lazar Trifunović, 'Enformel u Beogradu' (1982), in *Studije, ogledi, kritike*, exh. cat., Museum of Contemporary Art, Belgrade 1990, p. 111–149. In footnote 3 of this essay, Trifunović attacks Protić and Denegri and accuses the Museum of Contemporary Art of 'chronologically violating the development of art'.

[12] This refers to Branislava Anđelković, the director of the Belgrade Museum of Contemporary Art, and Dejan Sretenović, the chief curator, at the time when Denegri curated the new permanent museum display that opened in 2005 under the title *The Yugoslav Art Space*.

[13] Ješa Denegri, 'Pred jednim slikarstvom reda i mudrosti' ('Before One Painting of Order and Wisdom'), *Izraz* (*Expression*), no. 6, Sarajevo 1962, p. 620.

[14] *L'Art médiéval yougoslave*, Palais de Chaillot, Paris, 9 March –22 May 1950. The following year the exhibition was held in Zagreb at the Umjetnički paviljon, 11 March–30 April 1951.

[15] Miroslav Krleža, 'Izložba jugoslovenskog srednjevekovnog slikarstva i plastike – Plaidoyer pro domo' ('Exhibition of Yugoslavian Medieval Painting and Sculpture – Plaidoyer Pro Domo'), *Jugoslavija*, no. 2, winter 1950.

[16] Bogomilism was a Christian neo-Gnostic or dualist sect founded in the First Bulgarian Empire by the priest Bogomil in the 10th century. The Bogomils called for a return to what they considered to be early spiritual teaching, rejecting the ecclesiastical hierarchy, and their primary political tendencies were resistance to the state and church authorities. This helped the movement spread quickly in the Balkans. The Bogomils did not use the Christian cross, nor build churches, as they revered their gifted form and considered their body to be a temple. They were harshly persecuted within the Byzantine Empire and settled for some time in medieval Bosnia. (from the definition online: https://en.wikipedia.org/wiki/Bogomilism, last accessed May 2024)

[17] See Lovorka Magaš and Petar Prelog, 'Nekoliko aspekata utjecaja Georgea Grosza na hrvatsku umjetnost između dva svjetska rata' ('Some Aspects of George Grosz's Influence on Croatian Art During the Soviet Period'), *Radovi Instituta za povijest umjetnosti*, no. 33, Zagreb 2009, p. 227–240.

[18] Miroslav Krleža, 'Predgovor "Podravskim motivima" Krsto Hegedušića', first published in a collection of drawings in Krsto Hegedušić, *Podravski motivi* [Zagreb 1933] and later in *Hrvatska književna kritika VI*, Zagreb 1953; *Eseji III*, Zagreb 1963; *Eseji II*, Sarajevo 1973; and *Dijalektički antibarbarus*, Sarajevo 1983.

[19] See more on this topic in Ivana Bago, 'Yugoslav Fanonism and a Failed Exit from the Cultural Cold War', in Anselm Franke, Nida Ghouse, Paz Guevara, Antonia Majaca (eds.), *Parapolitics: Cultural Freedom and the Cold War*, Sternberg Press, Berlin 2021; and Ivana Bago, 'First as Yugoslav Revolution, then as Post-Yugoslav Art: History and A(na) estheticization around 1968 and Now', in *Mezosfera*, no. 8, 2020, see http://mezosfera.org/first-as-yugoslav-revolution-then-as-post-yugoslav-art-history-and-anaestheticization-around-1968-and-now1%EF%BB%BF/ (last accessed May 2024).

[20] Stanko Lasić, 'Sukob na književnoj ljevici 1928–1952', *Politička misao: časopis za politologiju*, vol. 8, no. 1, March 1971, p. 58.

[21] In the period between 1967 and 1980, Miodrag Protić and the curators of the Museum of Contemporary Art in Belgrade organised large-scale exhibitions and edited voluminous catalogues in the publication *Jugoslovenska umetnost XX veka* (*Yugoslav Art of the 20th Century*), which all presented surveys of different phenomena in Yugoslav art through decennial periodisation. Each catalogue was numbered according to the historical period it treats rather than the sequence of publishing by the Museum: *1. Počeci jugoslovenskog modernog slikarstva 1900–1920* (*The Beginnings of Yugoslav Modern Painting 1900–1920*), Belgrade 1972; *2. Treća decenija: Konstruktivno slikarstvo 1920–1930* (*The Third Decade: Constructive Painting 1920–1930*), Belgrade 1967; *3. Četvrta decenija: Ekspresionizam, Kolorizam, Poetski realizam, Intimizam, Koloristički realizam 1930–1940* (*The Fourth Decade: Expressionism, Colourism, Poetic Realism, Intimism, Colour Realism 1930–1940*), Belgrade 1971; *4. Nadrealizam i socijalna umetnost 1929–1950* (*Surrealism and Social Art 1929–1950*), Belgrade 1969; *5. Jugoslovensko slikarstvo šeste decenije 1950–1960* (*Yugoslav Painting of the Sixth Decade 1950–1960*), Belgrade 1980. There were special editions on sculpture and graphic art: *Jugoslovenska skulptura 1870–1950* (Yugoslav Sculpture 1870–1950), Belgrade 1975; and *Jugoslovenska grafika 1900–1950* (*Yugoslav Graphic Art 1900–1950*), Belgrade 1978.

[22] The Salon of the Museum of Contemporary Art has specialised in exhibiting contemporary art since the early 1960s.

[23] The Munich Circle refers to four Croatian painters – Miroslav Kraljević, Vladimir Becić, Josip Račić and Oskar Herman – who studied at the Royal Bavarian Academy of Art in Munich between 1905 and 1910.

[24] Ješa Denegri, 'Poglavlje povijesne avangarde: Josip Seissel/ Jo Klek', *Oko*, no. 13, Zagreb 1990.

[25] Ješa Denegri, Želimir Koščević, *EXAT 51 (1951–1956)*, Galerija Nova, Zagreb 1979.

[26] See Ješa Denegri, 'Dadaizam Dragana Aleksića', *Pogled*, no. 33, Belgrade 1977.

[27] For an abridged version in English and German of Denegri's text from his first monograph on EXAT 51, see Ješa Denegri, 'EXAT 51', in *EXAT 51 – Synthesis of the Arts in*

Post-War Yugoslavia, exh. cat., Kunstmuseen Krefeld, Krefeld 2017, p. 32–43.

[28] Ješa Denegri, 'Some New Artistic Attitudes in Socialist Societies', *10th Paris Biennial*, exh. cat, Paris 1977, p. 39–44. See p. 90–98.

[29] Dejan Jović, *Yugoslavia: A State That Withered Away*, Purdue University Press, West Lafayette, Indiana 2009.

[30] Quoted in translation from http://krlezijana.lzmk.hr/clanak.aspx?id=1773 (last accessed May 2024).

[31] Piotr Piotrowski, *In the Shadow of Yalta – Art and the Avant-garde in Eastern Europe 1945–1989*, Reaktion Books, London 2011.

[32] Ješa Denegri, 'Some New Artistic Attitudes in Socialist Societies', p. 39–44.

[33] The letter to Caillois is published in Marko Ristić, *Politička književnost (za ovu Jugoslaviju) 1944–1958 (Political Literature (For the Old Yugoslavia))*, Oslobođenje, Sarajevo 1977, p. 146–147. See also the lecture by Jelena Vesić and Antonia Majača, 'The Totalitarian Paradigm and the Making of Contemporary Art', Haus der Kulturen der Welt, 10 December, 2017, see https://www.hkw.de/en/programm/projekte/veranstaltung/p_136719.php. (last accessed May 2024)

[34] See Stanko Lasić, 'Sukob na književnoj ljevici 1928–1952', *Politička misao: časopis za politologiju*, vol. 8 no. 1, March 1971; and Predrag Matvejević, *Književnost i njezina društvena funkcija: od književne tendencije do sukoba na ljevici*, R. U. Radivoj Ćirpanov, Novi Sad 1977.

[35] Lazar Trifunović, 'Levo krilo ruskog modernog slikarstva' [1957], *Studije, ogledi, kritike*, no. 4, Museum of Contemporary Art, Belgrade 1990, p. 63–75.

[36] Miodrag Protić, 'Zenit, 1921-1926', *Treća decenija: Konstruktivno slikarstvo 1920–1930*, (*The Third Decade: Constructive Painting*), p. 14–17.

[37] Irina Subotić and Vida Golubović, *Zenit and the Avant-garde of the Twenties*, exh. cat., National Museum, Belgrade 1983.

[38] Kamila Grej, *Ruski umetnički eksperiment*, Jugoslavija, Belgrade 1978 (Camilla Gray, *The Russian Experiment in Art 1863–1922*, Thames & Hudson, London 1962).

[39] *Konstruktivizam u Poljskoj, 1923–1936 (Constructivism in Poland)*, exh. cat., Museum of Contemporary Art, Belgrade 1979.

[40] Marko Ristić from his letter to Roger Caillois, in which he expresses his dissent over the ideological assumptions of the influential Congress for Cultural Freedom founded in 1950 in Berlin, and disseminated internationally through a network of journals, discussions and exhibitions. Here Ristić shares the reasons behind his refusal to take part in this manifestation in 1952. See Marko Ristić, 'Sloboda kulture', in *Politička književnost (za ovu Jugoslaviju) 1944-1958*, p. 146–147.

[41] Ješa Denegri, 'Socijalistički estetizam', *Pedesete: Teme srpske umetnosti*.

[42] Ješo Denegri, *Art of the Constructive Approach – EXAT 51 and New Tendencies*, exh. cat., Horetzky, Zagreb 2004.

[43] Images of various Yugoslav monuments went viral on the internet in the 2010s. But they were affirmed on the institutional level, especially with the exhibition *Towards a Concrete Utopia: Architecture in Yugoslavia 1948–1980*, curated by Vladimir Kulić and Martino Stierli at The Museum of Modern Art, New York, 2018.

[44] See Ješa Denegri, *Olga Jevrić*, exh. cat., Topy, Belgrade 2005.

[45] *Kitman* derives from the Arabic *katama* meaning 'to conceal' or 'to hide', dissimulation by silence or omission, mostly used in the context of concealing beliefs in the face of persecution.

Some New Artistic Attitudes in Socialist Societies
Ješa Denegri

Published in the catalogue of the 10th Paris Biennial, which took place at the Palais de Tokyo and the Musée d'Art Moderne de la Ville de Paris from 17 September to 1 November 1977 (Paris, 1977, p. 39–44).

It should be noted, first of all, that it is extremely difficult to draw any firm and precise conclusions with respect to this extremely sensitive subject. Moreover, as all the experiments of avant-garde art since the October Revolution are relevant to the question, a careful historical examination would be required. Finally, this problem necessitates touching upon a great number of questions related to the theory and sociology of art such as they appear in Marxist philosophy. The following discussion is therefore restricted to the presentation of a few ideas based on some concrete experiences.

Today, in considering the question of the relation between the artistic avant-garde and the social context of socialist systems, the years following the October Revolution are taken as the specific point of departure. Although the opinions of the numerous representatives of Soviet avant-garde art of the 1920s were distinctively different, at a particular moment they were all confronted with a demand that was unacceptable to them – the requirement to make an instrument out of art and culture in general, the requirement to tie art directly to the needs of social strategy and realpolitik. Unable and unwilling to respond to these requirements, the protagonists of the avant-garde art movements were inescapably drawn into conflict with political power, which little by little imposed itself as the absolute arbitrator in the fields of art and culture. The accusation of 'formalism' leveled at the avant-garde in general (without making any differentiation between the principles inherent in the standpoint of some-one like Malevich as opposed to that of someone like Tatlin) tells us that the language of art attested to an apolitical position, and by virtue of this very attitude was antithetical to the general line describing the transformation of society. The outcome of these conflicts is well known – all the projects of the October Revolution avant-garde proved fragile in their confrontation with real political power and were more or less swiftly liquidated. Nevertheless, it is clear today that parallel to similar manifestations in literature, film and architecture, the concepts of the avant-garde artists represented the greatest contributions to the ideals of the October Revolution.

As was the case for those following it, this experience indicated that conflicts appeared when it became a question of the 'trend' and of the autonomy of artistic language. While dogmatic Marxism insisted on the 'trend' of art, requiring that it be strictly tied to the given social reality, a great number of thinkers and artists who rallied around the ideals of the revolution defended the autonomy of art – which is to say the need to create forms as well as meanings specific to the artistic language. The thesis that art is the reflection of concrete social conditions led to a Socialist Realism, characterised not only by certain stylistic attributes but, above all, by an intentionally apologetic stance in relation to the political system. It is this liaison with the structures of power that made these representatives of Socialist Realism privileged and protected members of the artistic profession. Those who pleaded for the autonomy of art motivated by the need to exteriorise their fundamental individual knowledge

rather than by adherence to some preconceived general
assumptions were viewed with suspicion under systems
whose political character was extremely homogeneous.
When art is treated as an element of ideology, artistic events
are read as signs of ideological confrontation. An essentially
political judgment determines whether or not a work has
artistic value, whether its qualities are positive or negative.

Contemporary Marxist theory includes two main approaches
to art. In the first, which can be called the gnoseological,
art is considered to represent a form of special knowledge
of the given reality. In the second, which we can call the
ontological, art is conceived as a specific application – the
construction of a world of new shapes and meanings. At
stake here is not an academic debate on the level of purely
theoretical problems, but rather two fundamentally different
concepts of social and ethical behaviour. For the gnoseological concept, art is in the final instance subjected to various
exterior pragmatisms. For the ontological concept, art is a
free and independent activity, subjected only to the requirements of discursive specifics and proper social functioning.

With these general considerations out of the way, let us
attempt to define the present state of new artistic manifestations in socialist societies. In countries where Socialist
Realism dominates (but which are nevertheless noticeably
different from each other) there is, on the one hand, a
practice that conforms to what is proclaimed by the dominant political and social forces and, on the other, there are
various forms of expression judged more or less negatively
according to the internal social possibility. In order to define
the acceptable forms of expression required or encouraged,
such terms as 'humanist', 'positive' and 'authenticity' are
employed, while the terms 'decadent', 'negative', 'nihilism'
and 'Western(ised)' are used to designate forms that are
neither acceptable nor desirable. However, it must be
emphasised that this phraseology, present mainly in official
and political communiqués, is not indicative of the way of
thinking found in artistic circles. It is indisputable that
certain of these milieus brought far-reaching contributions
to the historic body of contemporary art (alongside the
leading figures of the Soviet avant-garde are movements like

Czechoslovakian Cubism and Surrealism, the manifestations of Polish 'oneism' with Władysław Strzemiński, Katarzyna Kobro and Henryk Stażewski, Hungarian activism with Lajos Kassák, and so on).

The art of these movements still lives on today, providing a seed and a direction for new movements. In spite of all the efforts to channel these artistic movements ideologically, there was no diminishing of the conscious understanding of the fundamental nature of the language and the way of the avant-garde. This consciousness is alive today among those artists who seek new forms. Motivated by elevated – often idealised – feelings for the ethical purity of the vocation of the artist, and deprived of a market place for aesthetic objects, these artists work solely according to the subjective impulses that ensure the sincerity of their work, and which also provoke frequent interruptions and lead to the shrinking of the repertory of processes, which in turn hinders an ongoing thorough elaboration of the problems at hand. In the same way that they resisted the need for a heteronomy of the artistic language by refusing to adhere to the propagandistic messages of Socialist Realism and its derivatives, they try to resist the tendency towards militant art, since it is simply the other side of the coin – that is to say, it is another aspect of the same process of making art ideological. Radically refusing all ideological dimensions within the structure of the artistic language, refusing all apologetic and supportive art, they insist on the concept of the autonomy of their practice. However, it must not be concluded that this art, with its preoccupations with form and technique, is closed. On the contrary, in these works there is always a series of indirect messages embodying social situations or everyday data. Take for example the works of the circle of young Czechoslovakian artists who introduced two components of a general character into their work – the self and the very body of the artist, on the one hand, and nature as representing the broadest possible framework of existence on the other. Another example is the work of a group of young Poles – here sensory and sensual motivations play an important role, while contents linked to social factors are left in the background. This simultaneously possible and approximate transfer of significance is produced thanks

to certain techniques (film, photographs) which – while
maintaining an objectivity of representation – exclude
additional symbolic and metaphorical layers without,
however, restraining the contents and the scenes on the
level of documentary imitation. These two groups (and
others) would seem to be characteristic of the typology of
the expressive languages of the artistic avant-garde in
Czechoslovakia, Poland and Hungary. We can also identify
similarities, as well as differences, in relation to artistic
formulations both close and contemporary to them in
certain Western European countries.

More space is devoted to the situation in Yugoslavia since,
insofar as the theme treated here is concerned, the very
special situation of this country leads to revealing conclusions. The period in which Socialist Realism dominated was
relatively short in Yugoslavia (from around 1945 to 1949).
After the break with Stalinism, the opening of an independent path towards social development had inevitable repercussions in the domain of art and of culture. After 1950,
Yugoslav art followed the process of the internationalisation
of languages characteristic of other European countries,
and this is the way that specific stylistic forms like abstract
expressionism, hard-edge painting, Nouveau Réalisme,
Kinetic and Op art and more recently 'behaviour' art,
Conceptual art, the New painting and so on, appeared in
Yugoslavia. Nevertheless, the art network remained different
in Yugoslavia from that in Western Europe – the absence
of an art market was compensated for by various forms of
stimulation coming from the State and social institutions.
Artists received considerable support (study grants, purchase
of works, free healthcare and social security), and certain
critics rightly speak of 'a conjunction of the artistic profession' in Yugoslavia, a conjunction whose effect is to legitimise mediocrity, given the relative ease with which artistic
status is acquired (becoming a member of a professional
artist's association suffices). Even though there are no direct
interventions into the domain of fine arts by the State or
the Party in Yugoslavia, indirect arbitration has not completely disappeared. It reveals itself in the frequent appeals
to certain value-related parameters, expressed in very general
terms like 'humanitarian', 'sincerity', 'indigenous values'

and so on. It is not difficult to recognise the remains of the ideals of Socialist Realism in these terms. For the rest, the most important forms of support from social institutions went to individuals and exhibitions whose expressive language, independently from any stylistic attributes, was undeniably positive and sympathetic towards the social reality (memorial sculpture, folk art and various forms of abstract and figurative art with particularly aesthetic and sentimental qualities). Forms implying knowledge of a rigorous autonomy of the artistic language were certainly tolerated, but were never accepted with any confidence by the dominant forums overseeing the social validation of art (critics, commissions charged with purchasing works of art, councils, selection boards for major foreign exhibitions and so on). This situation changed around 1968 with the appearance of concepts based on the dematerialisation of the art object. The very fact that these concepts were, for the most part, being explored by young artists who, in keeping with the general orientation of the student population, maintained a critical stance in relation to a great number of concrete social and cultural situations, provoked the rejection of these concepts by the dominant artistic and critical bodies of the day. Only a few isolated exhibition spaces (those belonging to the student cultural centres) and some independent critics supported these artists. The dominant collective consciousness in this country, which had never known any real examples of artistic criticism or denigration (since Yugoslavia had almost no history of such avant-garde movements as Cubism, Futurism, Dada, etcetera) played an important role. Thus, the process of reduction or of exceding the fixed material status of the object of art led to a perception that devalued the work of these artists. They were placed in a paradoxical situation: on the one hand, they acted with complete freedom of expression in near total isolation; and on the other, they were called upon to represent the art of their country at such exhibitions as the Edinburgh Festival, the Paris Biennial and the Venice Biennale. (And on their own initiative they participated in such thematic exhibitions as *Information* in New York (1970), documenta in Kassel, *Contemporanea* in Rome (1973), *Projekt '74* in Cologne, *Attualità internationali 1972–1976* in the Venice Biennale and so on). Those artists who appear in books by such critics as Lucy Lippard, Gillo Dorfles, Achille Bonito Oliva and others, only barely succeeded in obtaining proper artistic and civil status within their own milieu. Acquiring this status, together with material and moral support, by contrast, did not pose any particular problems for a whole slew of reactionary and anachronistic artists.

All these considerations certainly require more detailed discussion but, for the moment, let it suffice to establish the fact that a series of clear and firm bonds exist between the language of the artistic avant-gardes and the social reality in socialist systems. The main problem is the question of determining how the two entities envisage the function and ends of art. At certain moments, history has produced a series of concrete responses: at certain moments there have been direct political or ideological interventions; at others, the creation of a more or less tolerant space where it was possible to elaborate a new expressive language. Coming into contact with the various stances of the social forum, artistic practice has continually characterised itself by its effort to withdraw art from all forms of paternalism, with the goal of laying the foundations for the possibility of an independent status for artists and for individuals. Nevertheless, as Theodor W. Adorno put it, 'a totally non-ideological art is hardly possible', and the tendency towards the extreme autonomy of art in socialist societies had a character implicitly critical of the overall system. Or as Adorno again affirms, 'because it crystallises in itself something special rather than accepting the existing social norms and thus being socially useful, art criticizes society by the simple fact that it exists as such'. In order to understand the behaviour of the new artists in socialist societies, it must be emphasised that they are not seeking to take action under the sign of what bourgeois culture traditionally thinks of as 'freedom'. For them, freedom signifies the right to have the social existence of the artist as a subject who is both critical and constructive recognised. Many obstacles arise along this path, which in its essence is socially positive, and the artist who has such a concept of freedom cannot avoid entering into a form of more or less visible conflict with society.

A spirit of activism and feelings of anguish and alienation
develop at the same time as a result of this state of conflict.
As in all the social constellations of both the past and the
present, the status of the artistic avant-garde in the socialist
countries is marked by various contradictions. It seems
that this form of art, whose very nature is to be critical,
cannot escape such a destiny in any socialist structure in
the near future.

II. Project and Destiny
Ješa Denegri in Conversation with Branislav Dimitrijević and Jelena Vesić

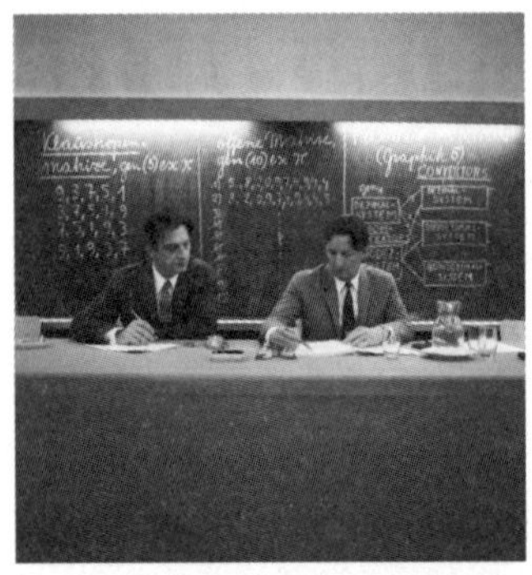

I

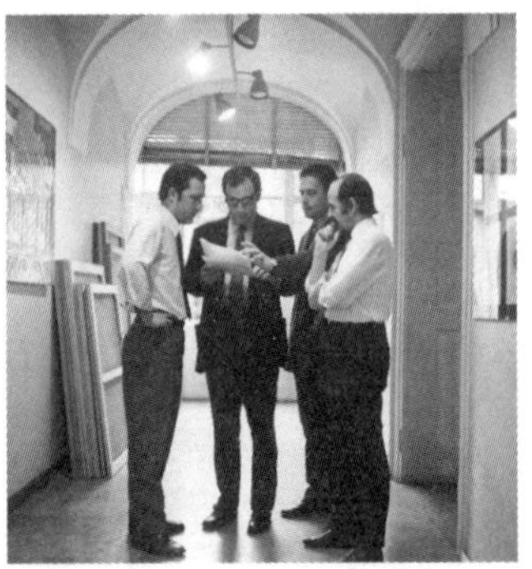

II

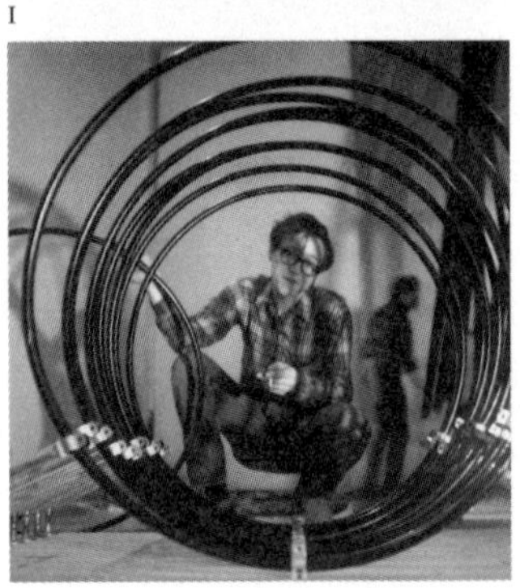

III

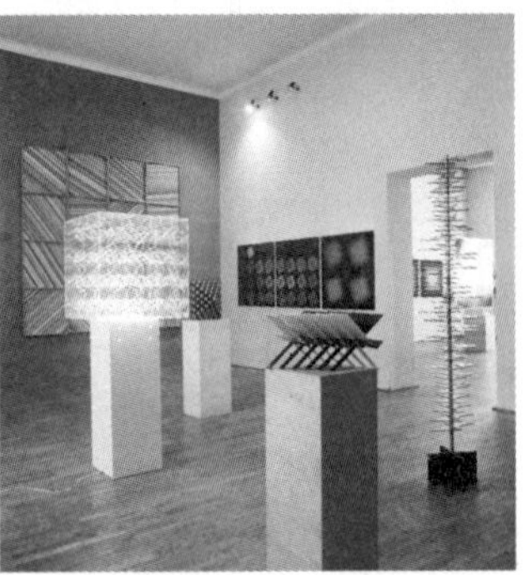

IV

I   Boris Kelemen and Vjenceslav Richter at the *Nove Tendencije 4* (*New Tendencies 4*) symposium organised at the Filmski Klub RANS Moše Pijade, Zagreb, 1969

II   Jury meeting of the *Nove Tendencije 4* (*New Tendencies 4*) exhibition, Galerija suvremene umjetnosti (Gallery of Contemporary Arts), Zagreb, 1969
From left to right: Matko Meštrović, Umberto Eco, Vladimir Bonačić, Martin Krampen

III   John F. Abbick installing his work for the *Nove Tendencije 4* (*New Tendencies 4*) exhibition, Muzej za umjetnost i obrt (Museum of Arts and Crafts), Zagreb, 1969

IV   View of the exhibition *Nove Tendencije 4* (*New Tendencies 4*), Galerija suvremene umjetnosti (Gallery of Contemporary Arts), Zagreb, 1969

I. <u>Towards an Art of Building</u>

BRANISLAV DIMITRIJEVIĆ Among your early texts from the 1960s there is an essay of 1968 in the second issue of the *Bit International* journal, which was published by the Galerije grada Zagreba (Zagreb City Galleries), from 1968 to 1972, as part of the New Tendencies project. This second issue accompanies the fourth exhibition of the New Tendencies, whose main topic was 'Computers and Visual Research'. There, among the essays by Herbert Franke, Georg Nees, A. Michael Noll and other theoreticians who were dealing with the relationship between cybernetics and aesthetics, and who were also the pioneering practitioners of computer art, you wrote the introductory text. This was probably, as far as Yugoslav art criticism is concerned, one of the first essays written on this topic by someone who is an art historian and an art critic. The case is also interesting

because – let's reveal to our readers an intimate detail
about you – you have never used a personal computer.
Instead, you have always written your essays on a typewriter.

JEŠA DENEGRI   Yes, that's true. [Laughs.]

BD   Your essay in *Bit International* is entitled 'A New
Perspective: Computers and Visual Research'.[1] In this text
there are two, let's say, preambles that are characteristic
not only for this essay but for other writing of yours as well.
You recognise in the art of that time, on the one hand,
a critical scepticism that has misgivings about the role of
computer technologies as a de-humanising force that is alien
to an 'artistic being', and on the other hand – a thesis that
is close to you – that the issue here is not some technological subjugation or refutation of the very 'being of art', but
rather, as you put it, a 'stabilisation of the positive spiritual
features of contemporaneity'. This means that an apocalyptic
view of the features of contemporaneity that appear through
technology is alien to you. Is this a preamble, a type of
basic starting point that can be seen as something that you
have pursued from then until now? Of course, back then you
couldn't have known where computer technology would …

JD   Yes, I couldn't have known where it would take us
today.

BD   This was the beginning of the Information revolution.
More than 50 years ago, when you wrote this essay, you
couldn't have known what everything would come to look
like, but here you have undoubtedly anticipated new times
regarding the relations between art and technology. These
questions began to be raised in the Yugoslav Art Space due,
above all, to the project of the New Tendencies.

JD   As I have already mentioned, I was a contemporary
of the New Tendencies from the first exhibition in 1961.
In contrast to the first exhibitions, when artists and artworks
were the focus of attention, the question of the relation
between art and science comes to the fore over the course
of time. In the seminars and conferences of the New
Tendencies there appeared people like the physicist and

philosopher Abraham Moles, the engineer of acoustics and electro-technology, one of the first researchers to analyse the relationship between aesthetics and cybernetic theories. There were others in Zagreb then, from whom I learned what *arte programmata* (programmed art) was. Questions about the difference between the notion of composition and the notion of structure in an artwork were discussed there. The essay of mine that you mention was the result of what I heard during these meetings.

BD   A few artists who were researching the relations between art and computer technologies also appeared in the Yugoslav Art Space at that time.

JD   Yes. First of all, there was Vladimir Bonačić, who was an engineer at the Ruđer Bošković Institute in Zagreb. He clearly showed that artists can be scientists, and that scientists can be artists. For example, he was visited at the Institute by Picelj, so this relation was established even earlier. For Bonačić, the computer was an amplifier of complexity, and he realised his works within the framework of the New Tendencies, and they are astonishing even today. There were also Zoran Radović with his oscillographs and Koloman Novak with his lumino-kinetic works.

BD   How did you relate to an artistic proposition of this kind?

JD   I could not have said then nor can I say today that it would have been possible for me to have developed a compact theoretical position – my education and knowledge were different. But from the beginning it was a matter of completely giving oneself up to artistic developments that simply carry you along like a river, like a whirlwind, and you have to manage all this somehow, find some ground, and see from these enormous possibilities what you can hold on to, and determine what is to be the leading idea that somehow defines you. It occurred by coincidence that I was the one who wrote this piece for the *Bit* journal and, now, this is supposed to fit into a complete and complex narrative about the New Tendencies movement. That was already 1968. So, many processes had already been launched, many practices that can be recorded today had changed since the first exhibition – which showed works by Piero Manzoni and the group ZERO – until the fourth or fifth exhibition in 1969 and 1973, when this entire chapter of thinking centred on the notion of construction came into question. For me, each of these phenomena was stimulating and interesting in a certain way. But if we are talking about whether there is some leading idea, some cornerstone in all this … Here, I'm holding a book of essays by Giulio Carlo Argan, which I had the opportunity of editing at the beginning of the 1980s. Here you can find the texts that during the 1960s perhaps most influenced me in the sense of articulating some theoretical position – above all his essay 'Art as Research' from 1965, as well as the essay 'Project and Destiny' from 1964 that opens the book.[2] This is Argan's seminal text, which was translated here very early on. I was really captivated by his ideas, and if anyone was ever a paragon, it was Argan; I really retained many things that I discovered in these texts.

BD   Tell us more about his influence on you.

JD   Look at this key phrase: 'project and destiny'. For Argan, this means something like the following: the project is something we do with a certain long-term orientation, when we are oriented towards a certain goal, when we build something towards that goal and in this building we participate with a desire to find a place in it. But when the guiding idea of the project is lost and when the individual, the society, the historical period are simply given up to the whirl of events, then we succumb to destiny. It was clear to me – and I think it was not a matter of a profession, but it can be a matter of any existential choice – that you as an individual have to project something over the long term: to work so as to accumulate knowledge, to accumulate the possibilities for doing the work and, finally, to provide for your existence. If you do not do this, you give yourself up to destiny, to circumstances that threaten you at every turn, in your profession, in your life, in politics, etcetera. Thus, this concept of the project was important to me, maybe through some instinct of mine. I can't say that I was philo-sophically oriented towards it either in life or in art. I had the possibility and the desire to project a situation of mine of some sort and, through this, to believe that the project is a frame of mind which, I think, should be immanent to every organised and relatively well-ordered and democratic socialist society ... These affinities of mine were demonstrated in my writings about EXAT 51 and the New Tendencies.

JELENA VESIĆ   Your research on EXAT 51 and the New Tendencies is part of your doctoral thesis.[3]

JD   That was when I began lecturing at the University in Belgrade in the late 1980s. The thesis was entitled 'Art of the Constructive Approach'. My earliest essay that tried to define this was entitled 'For an Art of Building', and was written on the occasion of the first Belgrade *Young Artists' Annual Exhibition* in 1965.[4] All this was an attempt to start a new initiative in the gallery of the Youth Centre in Belgrade, when Đorđe Kadijević was the curator. Kadijević was soon forced to resign because he got into a dispute with the Party cadres who expected the gallery to embrace a broader spectrum of artistic creativity, and amateur creativity, while Kadijević argued for more professional principles. So, this annual exhibition was never held, but there was a catalogue whose graphic design by Slobodan Mašić was very progressive for the times. Today, I am embarrassed by this text; it was so very pretentious.

BD   To us, it seems very valuable, it is almost a manifesto. You write about the need to make a persistent effort to build new forms of visual thinking and social consciousness – which in art have to oppose the secluding emphasis of personal tragedy, the alienation of individual existential dramas, and support a meaningful and constructive use of progress. The positions you have built from then on were already outlined in this text from 1965.

JD   Well, I did have some predisposition that emerged from my inclination towards the constructivist pole of the avant-garde and the neo-avant-garde. There are maybe more fascinating manifestations of the avant-garde that I also admire – like Duchamp, Dada and Fluxus – but in some way this idea about an 'Art of the Constructive Approach' – which implies the Arganian model of the *project* – is characteristic, perhaps, for me as a person.

BD   But let's go back to the juxtaposition we already introduced between expressive art and the 'Art of the Constructive Approach'. At first sight, one might conclude that this juxtaposition lies at the very heart of the modernist narrative, as it does for instance with Alfred Barr. In his famous diagram for the cover of the catalogue of the exhibition *Cubism and Abstract Art* in New York's MOMA in 1936, there are, as the ultimate distillation of the narrative of modern art, a non-geometric abstract art and a geometric one.[5] So, modern art is distilled down to these two poles, which we may identify as constructive and expressive.

JD   We are now entering the very broad field of the history of modern art. It really has this dichotomy – from phenomenon to phenomenon, from movement to movement, from individual to individual. For example, Dada in contrast to historical Constructivism. They are almost parallel time-wise, and I cannot take a definite stand regarding this and say 'I prefer Constructivism to Dada'. And if we go further, there is post-war art, where at one extreme you have Art Informel, and at the other you have this new geometrism, and both emerged almost simultaneously. Choosing between these two would lead us astray and prevent us from understanding modern art as an entirety, and we would fail to observe, perhaps, its most subtle and far-reaching consequences. For example, who could ever be against the ideas Dubuffet talks about – his Art Brut, his fondness of outsiders … It was also an extremely democratic idea, but it is not perhaps in line with the 'Art of the Constructive Approach', although it was in my opinion both very consistent and very persistent.

JV   So, it is also a project?

BD   Does this mean that the idea of the project is more extensive than the scope of the 'Art of the Constructive Approach'? Or that the notion of the project is not identified with the constructiveness of the approach? We've asked you to mark some parts here in Argan's text that stood out for you, so let me read one of the sentences you picked: 'Serious research into the evolution of technology cannot but take into account the question of art, because in the phase we have named historical, and which is congruous with the entire development of civilisation, art assumes part of the task of designating value models and operational conducts.'[6] Argan, it seems, avoids linking his thesis with the immediate practices of the times to which the concept of the project could be related, both with neo-constructivism in art and with the 'project of industrial production' as an outcome of the artist's participation in the production that for him is 'rather a precursory calculation than the project'. In contrast to this, Argan speaks about projecting as a 'historical construction', as a 'critical examination of historical situations' and even as 'the planning of existence'.[7]

JD   This is very important in Argan. The project is not identified with post-war neo-constructivism. Because while he writes this essay during that period, the project is a general category which is simply related to the existential conditions in which each individual lives, meaning that they project themselves into society, that they are an autonomous entity, that they are not manipulated. Argan says if we didn't project, we would be projected, which means that if we didn't take the initiative and refute our own destiny – if I'm allowed to use his term again – we would be giving ourselves up to everything that is happening around us, and thus lose our existence. This is a political statement.

JV   If I may sum up this political statement in the spirit of Argan's dichotomy and our previous conclusions, which relied on EXAT 51, Ristić and Krleža: the central project of the post-war generation in Yugoslavia was the building of socialism and thus attaining a certain 'civilisational level'. On the other hand, giving in to destiny and the spontaneity of human nature lead to an acceptance of capitalistic, free-market logic in which individuals, as basic agents of that system, do not acquire constructiveness and optimism, but on the contrary suffer. And this suffering in fact gives birth to expressive sentiments in art … I would understand it as such.

JD   We began with these two notions that we approached more generally, not only while interpreting Argan himself. We were of the opinion – and I think everyone has an opinion about this – that one is supposed to build one's life as a free individual, without allowing oneself to be outmanoeuvred, manipulated, exploited and so on. Art has the potential to become a space of guidance, to become something that is important in life.

BD   But what kind of art? The art projects we consider to be crucial for you – EXAT 51, Gorgona, the New Art Practices – were projects that were not the larger part of art, the art mainstream in Yugoslavia, which actually always displayed and even elaborated this idea of destiny. And this was the case with important artists, like Petar Lubarda. Lubarda is an ideal artist as the embodiment of the concept of destiny in a modern context – a destiny that connects an 'eternality' of the soil and the genus, and creates a fatalistic system that is continually regenerated; and this action of destiny could be achieved and made poetic by the artist. This is fatalism as a creative force. And there is a certain expectation of the ideal artist representing a specific epoch, who will embody such fatalism time and again. Lubarda is an outstanding artist, but in some way he affirms the immensity of destiny in his pictorial language.

JD   I wouldn't compare or juxtapose them; they are far too different. But Lubarda's opus, and he himself as a social being, may in fact be discussed within this framework.

BD   Historically speaking, EXAT 51 and Lubarda belong to the same period. I'm only comparing them here because, with regard to those early years of the 1950s, we have acquired formative, historically codified examples of the break with the doctrine of Socialist Realism, but with these entirely different propositions. I'm referring of course to Lubarda's exhibition at ULUS Gallery in Belgrade in 1951, on the one hand, and the exhibition of EXAT 51 at the Hall of Architects' Society of Croatia in Zagreb in 1953 on the other. The first represented a shift in the course that aspired towards some new compromise between 'domestic traditions' and modernity within the art system, while the second

wanted to make a complete reversal, both an aesthetic and
political about-turn.

JD   In a way, Lubarda incarnates various collective
mythologies that we inherited, archetypes, ancient traditions
and the like. I don't believe in this. Perhaps my life horizon
is not sufficiently developed for me to start believing in this.
If this served as his artistic motto, then I respect that. But
he was not the model for my own self-creation. Of course
this does not mean that I didn't try in my writing about
Lubarda to understand his significance in the history of
painting, which is certainly undeniable.[8]

BD   As a result, the project is something very specific and,
ultimately, very rare in the Yugoslav Art Space. EXAT 51
is a project. Gorgona is a project. Some aspects of the
New Art Practices are projects. These are more or less all
protagonists of the Other Line. What else is a project in
Yugoslav art?

JD   That's about it, more or less …

JV   And Surrealism? What about Belgrade Surrealism?
Now we've come to a contentious issue, which is the
question as to why Belgrade Surrealism is not included in
your narrative of the Other Line? Why doesn't it operate as
an ancestor to the neo-avant-garde tendencies in Belgrade,
similar to what members of EXAT 51 found in Jo Klek?

JD   It really is a contentious issue, and it was already held
against me by some connoisseurs of Belgrade Surrealism.
Branko Vučićević told me this in reference to one of my
essays from the 1990s entitled 'Belgrade Surrealism: Outside
or Inside the Other Line?'[9] I would say that there are two
main reasons why I do not equate Belgrade Surrealism with
the Other Line. First of all, because it was primarily a literary
movement, and the visual practice of Belgrade surrealists
was ephemeral and even the protagonists themselves didn't
make much of it. Also, in other writings of mine about
the avant-garde I single out the visual production, and I'm
not able to discuss their literary achievements. Belgrade
Surrealism is above all a literary phenomenon. Secondly,

for me they were not exemplary figures. First and foremost, Marko Ristić and Oskar Davičo occupied high structural and symbolic positions in the politics of post-Second World War Yugoslavia. They were not marginal figures like the Gorgonists and the conceptualists who were active on the scene precisely when these former surrealists occupied positions of power. And lastly, they manipulated the historicisation of Surrealism. There was a rumour that the first comprehensive book about the movement by Hanifa Kapidžić Osmanagić was written under the directions of Marko Ristić.[10] Also, the surrealists negated the avant-garde movements that came before them, for example Micić's Zenit and Aleksić's Yugo-Dada, when they were becoming politically institutionalised and were part of the functions and organs of the governing system. For me, it is at odds with the logic of an authentic avant-garde mentality.

BD   At the end of that essay you conclude quite unequivocally: 'Perceiving themselves probably as winners, not only as part of earlier aesthetic polarisations, but also in terms of political orientation, some of the members of Belgrade Surrealism, perhaps above all the donor of this valuable legacy,[11] did not persevere in commiting themselves to a position of permanent opposition to social power – they did not find within themselves sufficient reason to choose a position of permanent existence in the shadows, which necessarily stems from an exclusive dedication to their own intimate artistic preoccupations.'[12] Let's emphasise, therefore, what you call 'the position of permanent opposition' as a precondition for 'other-lining'. And yet, the objection that you haven't sufficiently acknowledged the practice of the Belgrade surrealists still stands. And since here we're speaking about the Arganian notion of the project, about opposing destiny with all means possible – artistic, political, military – we can certainly say that Belgrade Surrealism was very much the project in the Serbian cultural context of the late 1920s and early 1930s.[13]

2.   <u>Socialism, Dissidence and Appendages to
     the Other Line</u>

JV   In our conversations we have discussed, informally,
the art of the 1980s.[14] The art of the 1980s is certainly the
end of the project. In the art of the 1980s, which is highly
interesting in all of its manifestations and various practices
under the aegis of 'postmodernity', whatever such a notion
means today, we can see well that it marks the end of an
era which features precisely this progressive movement
towards a goal. In the art of the 1980s we see that all this
has eroded. Not only do I understand it this way myself, but
it is generally considered a historical fact. Therefore, it
seems to me that the end of the idea of the project coincides
with the end of the Other Line.

BD   So the time of the project and the time of the Other
Line coincide, after all?

JD   Yes, to some degree. Although, we could also say that
not everything in the Other Line is the idea of the project
as such. For example, to some extent, several developments
around Gorgona, around radical Art Informel, and also
Neo-Dada … Another matter we should mention here is
this: I'm from the generation who thought (and we all hoped
and in so many ways lived with the belief) that after those
horrible years of war and everything that had happened,
we expected that a time of healing, of social recovery,
was coming. And we did experience that. If nothing else,
no matter what kind of pupil you were, whether poor or
average, you still had a chance of getting a decent education,
to enrol at the faculty, to live in a space with your friends
and with your family. Our lives were moving towards positive
things in life.

JV   In fact, you have lived a project, the project of all
projects in the Yugoslav space after the Second World War:
the construction of self-managed socialism.

BD   We want to say, Ješa, that your starting points were
not purely apologetic in relation to the concrete socialist
project in Yugoslavia, nor did they adopt a critical-dissident

detachment in relation to the project. Your position was not confined to or representative of this simple dichotomy.

JD   Yes. I would not – and have no reason to – glorify the political system of post-war Yugoslavia. I happened to be there, and that system enabled me to be one of the participants, together with many others around me, who worked to make that situation as comfortable as possible, to make it better, more constructive, in order to realise our loves, our professions and everything else under such conditions.

BD   From an other perspective, from a perspective that has come to dominate with the emergence of the post-socialist condition, you could be criticised for not having been critical enough …

JD   That I have not been critical enough?

BD   … of the socialist system. And, what's most important for us, you stand by this socialist position in principle, even when many of your generation have revised their position in relation to it.

JD   On the contrary, it was clear to me that this political system carries within itself many things that were unacceptable to me. In the end, I didn't have any connection with concrete politics in that system. In other words, I was not a member of the Communist Party, nor did that interest me in the least. But again, that didn't prevent me from seeing what was positive in that system, from thinking that it should be shared as a way of life. Least of all did I think that I was entitled to or had any reason to take up a position of dissidence, because a dissident position always implied another kind of choice and another kind of seizing of power in another situation. I didn't deal with either of these positions. I didn't have the capacity for something like that.

BD   The notion of dissidence relates to the position of the critical and non-conformist intelligentsia in the Soviet bloc, and it is a question how much this notion can be applied in the case of Yugoslavia, even though the totalitarian paradigm, as a dominant norm in the academic research of the period, insists on this, and Jelena talked about it with respect to post-socialist discourses. Would you agree that dissidence in Yugoslav socialism was in fact an integral part of the system?

JD   Well, yes, if I ultimately had to say something so drastic …

JV   Dissidence was deeply rooted in the cultural establishment of the time – let's stay with drastic formulations – it was the ground on which those 'local greats' developed, those prominent figures of Yugoslav art whose works amalgamated soft modernism, bourgeois existential sentimentalism and epic old history painting. We have such protagonists among both the system-apologists and the dissident currents within the cultural establishment.

JD   Yes. I was not at all inclined towards these visible and invisible struggles within the establishment. There, I even agree that we have an enormous amount of examples, concrete examples, but let's not mention names now. I want to say that for me, this kind of dissident opposition was not a solution, nor did I have at any time in my life the ambition to be an apologist for the governing structure. Others were doing that. I was interested in art; I had a different position. Why did I deal with EXAT 51 long after it had stopped practising? It appeared manifest to me – and it was not just my reading – that there was something concealed in there that was exemplary. So, what was it all about? These were young people of the post-war generation who thought that they should build their own environment after the destruction of the war, and that they should, through art – and through other activities that were inherent to art education and orientation, such as design, architecture, urban planning/design – make an effort to rebuild society, a society that went through all the hardships in the social space that – let's not shy away from this – organised the Holocaust. EXAT 51 was about building a new argument for a progressive society. Their formation implied the construction of a new urban and natural environment in which people could live as human beings, and the practice in art and culture, in painting, sculpture, design and film,

that would exemplify this kind of worldview. Who would
not be inclined to such a worldview? It seems to me that,
in some way, it is very logical that such a view should be
accepted and endorsed as something positive and mobilising.

BD   How did what you're talking about happen? What
appears as an argument for socialist art, of which EXAT 51
is an example, as a programme for the project of socialist
art – why was it not … ?

JD   … not accepted?

BD   How did it not become a dominant model for art in
Yugoslavia? In his statement of protest on the occasion
of the rejection of his competition entry for the monument
to Lenin in Belgrade at the beginning of the 1970s,
Aleksandar Srnec, a former member of EXAT 51, says that
instead of taking Constructivism and the art after the
October Revolution as a guiding principle for the new art of
socialism, the authorities favoured an archetypal expression
of a petrified artistic symbol of the revolutionary ideal.
Srnec says: 'For them, for the authorities, Egypt is still
closer than October!'[15]

JD   This is how it happened. This was a position which,
from the very beginning – however reasonable it may have
been and, as it appears to us nowadays, a very clear and
compact position – in fact embodied numerous utopian
projections that were not fully related to actual reality.
Secondly, it didn't take into account rather complex artistic
traditions within its own milieu, which were regenerated
at the time that EXAT 51 was working, with their own
different starting points in relation to art and culture.
These are starting points that view the artist as an 'artistic
individual', as an alliance between the notion of the artist
as a strong, powerful subject, and his status as a privileged
social figure. EXAT 51 was not counting on that. They
counted on and looked to social egalitarianism in a society
that would be ready to embark on the project of renovation,
but didn't count on all of the recurrences that exist in such
a society – and one that was still burdened with numerous
contradictions and counterbalances of the recent closer

and more distant past. Among which are also sentiments that inhabit the world of art. The world of art consisted of very different ideals, and their proponents assumed leading positions in the Yugoslav art scenes. EXAT 51 could have been just one small group in the minority – and it really was in the minority. After all, it was located in one of the Yugoslav milieus. We don't have anything similar in other milieus, so their attitude could not have emerged as the pattern, the model. Today, and for some time past, it looks like a bright, shining light, a small star in a cosmos full of many other solutions.

BD   Does this mean that resistance to such a project within art came more from the artists themselves, and less from any of the higher political structures? Can we say that the majority of artists in Yugoslavia played a conservative and retrograde role, without seeing the socialist frameworks as a possible new way of thinking about art – that they still viewed art from a bourgeois-romantic perspective?

JD   Yes, totally. They were not ultimately raised that way. They were simply trained to be artists, artists who would adopt this exaggeratedly romantic understanding of art. And after some time, such an understanding of art simply turned out to be more lucrative for the artist as an individual in society than for an artist taking the other position, which is basically a highly altruistic one. Then it happened that this ideal not only became a reality, but it came to be ignored in a way, and by the very artists themselves. When there was a discussion about the monograph on EXAT 51, I remember Milan Prelog saying: 'Well, the main opponents of EXAT 51 were the artists, not the social or political system'.

BD   Do you mean the artists who, as part of society, maintained that they see much further, that they know how to get to the bottom of things; that they, for the most part, were some kind of guardians of an inherited cultural order, one that didn't want to allow a transformation and emancipation of art from those romantic, bourgeois foundations?

JD   EXAT 51 postulated something for which there was no substantial economic or cultural foundation, and no cultural heritage either. They were related to Russian Constructivism. The other artists were not raised on and formed by that. Petar Lubarda, as a great painter for example, was not formed by that; he was formed by something else. Not to mention all the generations that followed, both at the time and afterwards. And this created a situation consisting of a minority, which then had to endure certain marginalisation, and it survived on the scene, and existentially even, because those artists were – as architects, designers, scenographers – skilled enough to support themselves on the basis of these service jobs, and to integrate their internal artistic practices within this complex renewal of the social and cultural environment. That's how the entire matter ended. EXAT 51 could not have become a mass phenomenon, nor would it have been natural for it to be a mass phenomenon. But it could have been an exemplary model *post festum*, after many years, after it had been historicised. After all, we were also talking about Krleža and his theory – of the premise of the renewal of art after the Second World War based on the three matrices from medieval times, and on his rejection of abstract art. And we could hear the artists of the EXAT 51 circle saying: 'our biggest opponent was, in fact, Miroslav Krleža', even though he was absolutely instrumental in getting rid of the dogma of Socialist Realism.

BD   So we return to Krleža again. Although Krleža was probably the most important writer of the 20th century in Yugoslav languages, we have the impression that his role, when visual art is at stake, was experienced as regressive. Isn't that paradoxical? Because not only was he the greatest writer, but he is one of the most radical writers, and of course a great critic and a great polemicist. And we constantly return to him, to the fact that he had no understanding of more radical efforts within the visual arts. That impression has continued to exist, although lately studies have appeared that speak about certain connections he had with the main protagonists of the historical avant-gardes.

JV   These are interpretations emphasising that Krleža's position in the Clashes within the Left during the 1930s was closer to Brecht than to Lukacs;[16] for instance that at issue is some kind of avant-gardist position, and not the position of defending and advocating social art and realism. Krleža's avant-gardism is reflected, among other things, in his 'grand majestic letter' realised as papier collé, dated 2nd August 1936 and sent from Zagreb to Marko Ristić who was on vacation at Plitvice Lakes. This was written about in detail by Predrag Brebanović in his book *Avangarda Krležiana*,[17] which follows the lines of interpretation we have been discussing and which is interesting for the wider context of our discussion that is the Yugoslav Art Space. Brebanović sees the covering-up of the Krleža/Ristić relation as a veiling of the material existence of that space, as well as the connection between avant-gardism and Yugoslavism. This is supposed to mean that not only is Krleža's view on art not anti-modernist, but that it is also avant-gardist, regardless of the fact that he labelled the abstract painting an 'import' or 'cultural cretinism'. Thus the 'grand majestic letter' appears as an avant-gardist montage that begins with a complex rebus inspired by the Spanish Civil War, followed by other press cuttings and illustrations with comments. Actually, Brebanović, in the same spirit as Ješa's thesis, makes a difference between two types of montage, dadaist and constructivist, namely a montage of attractions and intellectual montage, and he considers the 'grand majestic letter' to be the constructivist-intellectual-fetishist type of montage. According to this reading, we could even label Krleža an 'artist of the Constructive Approach'.

BD   If we stay with the politics of art in Yugoslavia in the 1950s and 1960s, we must admit that Krleža preferred one particular thing in painting – the connection with 'domestic traditions' that the Zemlja (Earth) group advocated. There he saw a broader horizon for the development of socialist art, and could not understand that some non-representational art could have social effects.

JD   Well, it is obvious that he couldn't. It may be that such forms simply don't speak to his visual affinities, either. He has an overly developed literary imagination, so he couldn't identify with geometrically abstract paintings. For him, it may have been a shallow formal art, onto which he could not project those enormous visions of his. For me, it is not an entirely incomprehensible position. And secondly, his paragons are formulated, fostered and built on other premises.

BD   But can we say then that after EXAT 51 ceased to exist, its former members came to understand, in the widest sense of visual culture as it were, what some of the most prominent elements of their programme really were, and of the constructivist-productivist paradigm of the Soviet avant-garde – which was the active role of artists in the immediate construction of social and economic reality? They left an indelible mark on Yugoslav culture, in various fields – in graphic design, interior design, architecture, animation and experimental cinema, and so on.

JD   Picelj dealt with graphic design, as did Srnec. For a while, Srnec was also the art editor at *Svijet* (*World*) magazine, and that was the connection between the avant-garde origin of his design and the emerging Pop culture. Srnec was also interested in film – that quote you mentioned earlier is related to the competition for the monument to Lenin, for which he submitted a cinematographic proposal. Of course, that proposal was dismissed. As for film and film animation, Vlado Kristl was the central figure in that circle. Later on, he moved to Germany, but he remained a cult figure in Zagreb. He was an outstanding person. Božidar Rašica dealt with scenography, and was also an architect and an urbanist. And, of course, Richter, the architect of the famous Yugoslav pavilion (among others) at the Brussels *Expo 58*. Richter was a partisan combatant during the war, a diversionist, and took a bullet in the leg, so he suffered from a limp.

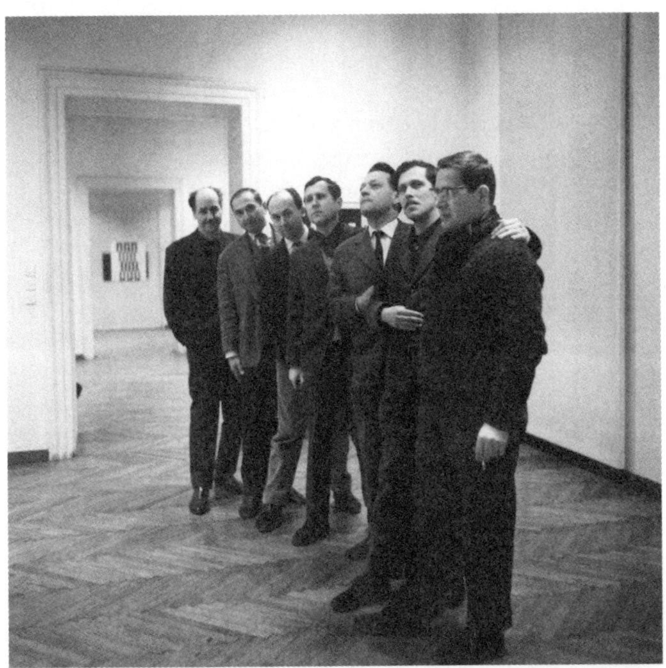

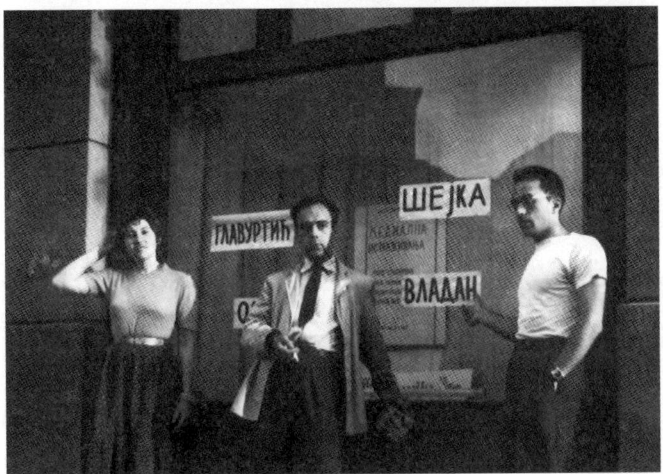

Gorgona, *A Step Forward (The Magnificent Seven)*, 1966
Photograph taken during the collective event *Adoration* organised during the opening of
Julije Knifer's solo exhibition, Galerija suvremene umjetnosti (Gallery of Contemporary Arts),
Zagreb, 1966

Members of the Mediala group in front of their first exhibition *Medijalna istraživanja*
(*Media Research*), Omladinska galerija (Youth Gallery), Obilićev venac, Belgrade, 1958
From left to right: Olja Ivanjicki, Leonid Šejka, Vladan Radovanović; missing: Miro Glavurtić

3.   Anti-Modernism in the Age of the Project:
       The Case of Mediala (A Hard Talk)

BD   Let's return to the opposition between project
and destiny, and to the notion of the Other Line. We have
concluded that the art phenomena you include in the
Other Line, such as EXAT 51 and Gorgona, were something
we might think through the Arganian notion of the project.
What about other phenomena in Yugoslav post-war art?
Let me ask you directly: is Mediala also a project?

JD   For me, Mediala is a complex and heterogenous
artistic community within which I cannot distinguish what
many in Serbia somehow readily identify as something
programmatic for that community.

BD   Is Mediala a modernist art phenomenon? Or, in
a narrower sense, even a neo-avant-garde phenomenon?

JD   Well, it is a modernist art phenomenon by its very
appearance within the historical corpus of modernism, post-
war modernism. It is not yet postmodernism, although some
manifestations of Mediala will be read as the announcement
and anticipation of it as such. So, in terms of art historical
labelling, Mediala would be a modernist phenomenon.
But within Mediala, it seemed to me that there were different individual solutions, which do not justify define this
phenomenon with a single concept. Therefore, if I were to
take a stance on the heritage of Mediala, I could make
my own distinctions within the phenomenon and say that
I prefer Leonid Šejka to the other members of the group.
Or I might prefer Vladan Radovanović, another artist among
the founders of the group, like Šejka, but who distanced
himself rather early on. Šejka declared himself to be an artist
whose artistic positions are contradictory: he was returning
to the perspectival painting of the Renaissance with his
concept of 'integral painting', while at the same time he also
considered himself to be an adherent of modernist views in
art. In this trajectory, there is a series of drawings and 'white
paintings' that he made in the last years of his life. At that
time he travelled throughout Europe a lot; he exhibited
his works and got to know the people from the Neo-Dada,

Pop art, and Nouveau Réalisme circles. Šejka's exhibition in Belgrade in 1966 entitled *Warehouses* reveals him to be sensitive to issues of his own contemporaneity as an artist.

BD   When in 1958 the exhibition *Medijalna istraživanja* (*Media Research*) was organised in Belgrade — which is considered to be the first public manifestation of the Mediala group, then still known as Balthasar — the members of the group were Leonid Šejka, Vladan Radovanović, Olja Ivanjicki and Miro Glavurtić. The other artists joined in the early 1960s. Mediala is, it seems, a completely heterogeneous phenomenon, which does not have, does not contain, any kind of concrete project. Its origins lie in some form of mysticism, esoterica …

JD   Yes, it seems so.

JV   If all these oppositions and contingencies are part of something — of some tensions, diversifications, wanderings, attempts at change and so on — then this can no longer be subsumed under the concept of the project.

JD   The project is not something that is, from beginning to end, under total control, nor is it something for which we can say 'now we are going to realize it'. The project is not something that would be assigned as a task. The project is something that occurs in the process of existence, in the process of historical circumstances and all possible controversies; the project is something one must fight for.

BD   So, is the project a kind of plan, as it were, through which destiny is overcome, through which destiny is controlled, or is the project some kind of dialectical formation within which one moves towards something that has no strictly controlled outcome?

JV   Or does the project relate to the internal coherence of the idea?

BD   Or is it some manifest formation? Does the project in art lead towards some predetermined destination, or does it imply precisely the uncertainty of the destination?

JD   I see … But this now opens the question up and requires some further interpretation. If we remain with the author from whom we borrowed the notion, Argan doesn't imply that the notion of the project should be identified with constructivist or geometric trends in art, but rather he inscribes it as some imminent quality of art. From that point of view, Mediala could be a project. Because, after all, we could say, like Argan, that every art is a project, it is a project in relation to the world which is, in some way, anti-projective in itself – if we consider it from the stand-points of war, the Holocaust, politics, intolerance and so on. Mediala doesn't hurt anyone.

BD   Does this mean we should embrace …

JD   Yes, the whole of art.

BD   But should we then also embrace Mediala as a neo-avant-garde project within the context of Belgrade and the Serbian art scene, which is equivalent to the other projects that appeared in other artistic environments in those days? That would mean Mediala and Gorgona, as near simultane-ous formations …

JD   … were compatible?

BD   In both cases we have this self-organisation of the group, and we also have the performative moment, which is one of the features of the neo-avant-gardes. The fact that none of the three of us has any ideological affinity with the Mediala project may simply be an expression of our disregard of the local circumstances in which there occurs one specific neo-avant-garde gesture.

JD   This is possible. After all, we have no reason to belittle any art phenomenon, nor to disrespect it now entirely within the limits of our ways of thinking. Mediala surely grew out of a resistance to socialist aestheticism, but also out of and against the tedium of everyday life, through a resistance that is profoundly existential, through a repudiation of norms and a search for alternative models of behaviour. This should not be neglected or ignored. But why am I not very inclined towards this art? Generally speaking, I understand and value it in a way, as an achievement in Serbian post-war art. But when I confront this heritage – and here I'm returning to the beginning of the story – I shift a little and accept with all my heart, with the greatest enthusiasm and respect, some of the things Leonid Šejka makes, and some of Vladan Radovanović's art, but I do not have faith in the work of Siniša Vuković or Olja Ivanjicki.

BD   But could you then talk about Gorgona the same way and say – well, I accept Knifer's and Vaništa's share in all that, I accept this and that, but I do not accept the whole group?

JD   They are more aligned in some of their features. There is no drastic difference in terms of quality and conceptual tendency, between Vaništa, Knifer, Kožarić, Seder or Jevšovar.

BD   Ok, now I will ask you to explain something to the foreign reader unfamiliar with the Mediala group, to those who are concerned with Yugoslav art in the era of socialism and who – we hope – will be readers of our book and will certainly know about Gorgona. A great number of texts were and continue to be published internationally on Gorgona, especially lately, and many exhibitions are being staged. I have in my hands one of the most recent publications, in which an essay of yours also appears. It is the catalogue for an exhibition at the Kunstmuseum in Liechtenstein, where your main theses related to this project are found.[18] But, to return to my question: how would you explain, to a foreign reader, who has never even heard of it, what Mediala actually is?

JD   I return to this dilemma yet again. As I see it, there are big differences within the artists' practices themselves, not only in terms of value, between what Šejka or Radovanović were doing, and what the painters inclined to mysticism and fantasy were doing. Where to put the early 'tactizons' of Radovanović, his tactile art from the 1950s?[19] Where does it belong? He himself would be very eager today to hear that it belongs to an extremely powerful anticipation of an international, European phenomena of the neo-avant-garde

– that it is proto-conceptualism sui generis. It is hard to explain this to someone unfamiliar with the local dynamics of art. But as you're now compelling me to articulate it, Mediala is somehow an artistic phenomenon that was opposed to various common, well-established views on art from the moment they appeared. It has features of reimagining alternative forms of living in and around art, but such expressions are located primarily in the domain of painting and are the result of cross-breeding different established models from the history of art: Leonardo, Bosch, Vermeer, de Chirico, Dali and so on. The question is whether this phenomenon can be viewed beyond its expansive local myth and how this 'translation' can be effected.

BD   You have written very unambiguously that one part of the Mediala output has the features of anti-modernism, while the other more important part has a progressive, positive artistic aspect. Then you state in a rather taxonomic way that 'this positive side of Mediala is reflected in a post-surrealist painting of fantasy spaces, of idealised Renaissance imagery, and in a Neo-Dada and Fluxus-like strategy of deconstructing the art object, then also in the poeticisation of everyday non-aesthetic objects and in broadening the strategy of the artist's activity from the production of works to ritual action'.[20] What you call the positive side of Mediala may be linked first of all to the work of Leonid Šejka, namely to his rather early Happenings from the 1950s, of which only a few photographs remain, and then to his Neo-Dada assemblages, as well as the 'white paintings' from the second half of the 1960s. You said that he saw himself as an artist who was working with something that was close to Neo-Dada and Pop art.[21]

JD   I knew Šejka very well, but not in the 1950s, so I don't know much about his early ritualistic actions. But where Šejka's work was closest to me was through his 'white paintings' and drawings – these 'warehouses' of his. I have labelled these works part of a new objectivity. There lies the key transition from this post-surrealist obsession with Renaissance painting, that is, 'integral painting' as he used to call it, into the whiteness of the paper and the canvas where there is no depth of space, no symbolic integration

of Renaissance perspective. This is the most important
thing that came from Mediala.

JV   I tend to see an epistemic-conceptual problem in
this, namely that something is called an art group and
is considered a group, and then there is a critic's selection
of certain moments from the entirety of the group's work.
So, if something is presented as an art group, then it is
a project, it is a community. This community can be non-
principled in terms of its unity; the Gorgonists actually
problematised the formality of an art group, but they
reflected this issue through, say, the concept of community
without the programme.[22] The members of Mediala didn't
reflect the specificities of their community, although there
existed clear differences within the group.

JD   You're actually asking whether it would be far easier
to interpret Mediala if we could place it within the contexts
we are dealing with here. Branislav mentioned Piotr
Piotrowski, and the fact that he omits Serbian art from the
context of Central and Eastern European art after the war
– precisely the kind of phenomena that emerged under less
collusion with Western European and American matrices,
and in some rather closed milieus. Because of that there is
no easy labelling.

BD   But Mediala still has some attributes of a single group
that has a considerable obvious interpretation. Now, Šejka
wrote a lot about art, Glavurtić was the ideologist of the
group. Olja Ivanjicki performed her first Happenings in
Belgrade when she returned from the USA in the early 1960s
– and, nota bene, was on a stipend from the Ford Foundation.
There is an enormous amount written in Serbia about
Mediala. But we cannot understand these writings as relevant
in the same way that we can, for instance, value the writings
on the Gorgonists. To sum up: does the problem of the
Belgrade art scene consist in the fact that only this scene has
the privilege of understanding itself, and that it is impossible,
or too complicated, to communicate it beyond this location?

JD   Well, yes, in a certain sense this problem arises.
It wasn't easy to present what you're asking from me,

nor was there anything that would evidence any frequent and adequate reception of this art from the outside. There are tensions, undistinguished relations.

BD   I think here we should return to the question of Belgrade Surrealism. Perhaps Mediala can be understood within this continuity, albeit distorted in many respects, with the position of the surrealists. However, a large number of the surrealists stood on the political left during the 1930s and some were close to the Communist Party, while many of the Mediala members identified with the Serbian nationalist right wing. Perhaps it is there that these tensions and undistinguished relations lie when we are trying to speak about Mediala. Mediala establishes a lineage in relation to Surrealism, but it doesn't do so with any particular insight into the character of local Surrealism. They understand Surrealism in a general way, as a continuation of a premodern fantastic painting, of Bosch, Arcimboldo or earlier, of the grotesques in the art of the Middle Ages.

JD   Mediala could have been linked to Surrealism, and it really was. Now, whether this linkage was direct or indirect in relation to Belgrade Surrealism as a phenomenon that emerged in this place, and which had its own position within European Surrealism, I cannot say. Would Mediala be some kind of post-war variant of Surrealism within Serbian art, one which has pre-war Surrealism as a prominent formative foundation?

BD   After the war, some Belgrade surrealists were directly involved in creating the cultural politics of the day and were, especially in the 1950s, in positions of decision-making. We think of Ristić, Vučo, Davičo among others. Koča Popović was the foreign minister. For Mediala, they could have been merely some socialist establishment, the elite against which they were creating an alternative. If we were to form an opinion according to Miro Glavurtić, the one who most commonly declares himself the founder of the group, Mediala was an anti-communist movement! It is interesting that, by nationality, Glavurtić is a Croatian, and declared himself a Catholic and an anti-communist. This in itself also says something about the Yugoslav Art Space.

JD   I would say that Mediala felt rather uncomfortable in socialism. It did not have the kind of integrative position that the December Group for instance had.[23] So there's some discomfort that can simply be read, if you will, even from the paintings of those less important members of Mediala. It is a density of feeling – something unpleasant haunts you while you are looking at them all. Aside from their integral value, one could say that Mediala primarily represented an opposition to the dominant modernism in painting as something integrated within the socialist system. They were not integrated in that way. They lived very difficult lives. Šejka was literally starving for days; he never had a job that would have enabled him to provide for his basic existence. That really was a special kind of artistic devotion.

JV   Speaking of the Yugoslav Art Space, there is something repetitive going on here. The Zagreb scene seems to be characterised by coherence and consistency, in the sense of being faithful to a certain project and to living the truth of that project unswervingly, which is a matter of a kind of continuity. By contrast, the Belgrade context is characterised by individual mythologies and swerving trajectories – if something happens on the art scene, it happens as a completely isolated occurrence; it flashes momentarily, and ends in a form of giving up, in a tragedy or an impossibility. If we return to Argan's dichotomy of project and destiny, it is almost exemplary here. The Gorgonists had an entirely anti-collectivist concept of collectiveness – a concept that stands in contrast to the socialist project of collectiveness, a concept that is rather neo-dadaist, more contingent, more ambivalent. But their life and work were in no way destined – the Gorgonists dealt with every detail of their own practice and pursued things to their utmost consequences. Whilst in Belgrade we have Mediala, which is almost a group and yet not fully a group. We stumble over their individuality and their destiny in the course of taking the first step. Neither they nor you as critic believe in their groupness, their collectiveness, in their project. There is no consistency, no insistence, no devotion to the project. The artist is here broken like a straw in the wind, in the whirlwinds of life and in their own inconsistency. A certain mysticism of the artistic act is central to this art, which also estranges us from the project. And it is a kind of artistic destiny, a sense of acute resignation.

JD   Yes. We could probably see it in that way.

4.   Models of Self-Marginalisation:
The Case of the Painting *K55*

BD   Let's introduce another example. When we speak about the differences between the Belgrade and Zagreb art contexts of the 1950s and 1960s, we speak about the fact that in contrast to the continuity of the Other Line in Zagreb, the historical avant-garde – EXAT 51, Gorgona – in Belgrade is characterised by occasional incidents, periodic flashes that happen without any ongoing articulation. One such case is the painting *K55* (1955) by Bogoljub Jovanović, which according to you has an important place as a superior yet solitary example of the first self-referential painting in the post-Second World War art scene in Serbia. You write about that painting on several occasions, and in the recently published monograph about him, you write that Jovanović is 'an artist who is honest to the point of idealism, for whom there is no space anywhere that is sufficiently appropriate for a decent existence, and in accordance with this awareness the only thing remaining for him is to aspire towards entirely limited individual freedom, which can only be realised by means of radical art'.[24]

JD   I found out about Bogoljub Jovanović from an essay written, to everyone's surprise, by Stojan Ćelić and published in the journal *Umetnost* (*Art*) at the end of the 1960s.[25] As an artist he had only two early exhibitions in Belgrade, in 1953, where he showed a series of gouaches with various enigmatic proverbs. But, lo and behold! – the introductory essay for the first exhibition was written by Zoran Mišić,[26] a literary critic who enjoyed a great reputation among the modernists; the text for the second one was written by Vasko Popa,[27] undoubtedly one of the greatest Yugoslav poets. There was even an essay on Jovanović by Stanislav Vinaver. This was in the newspaper *Republic* – the Party paper of the

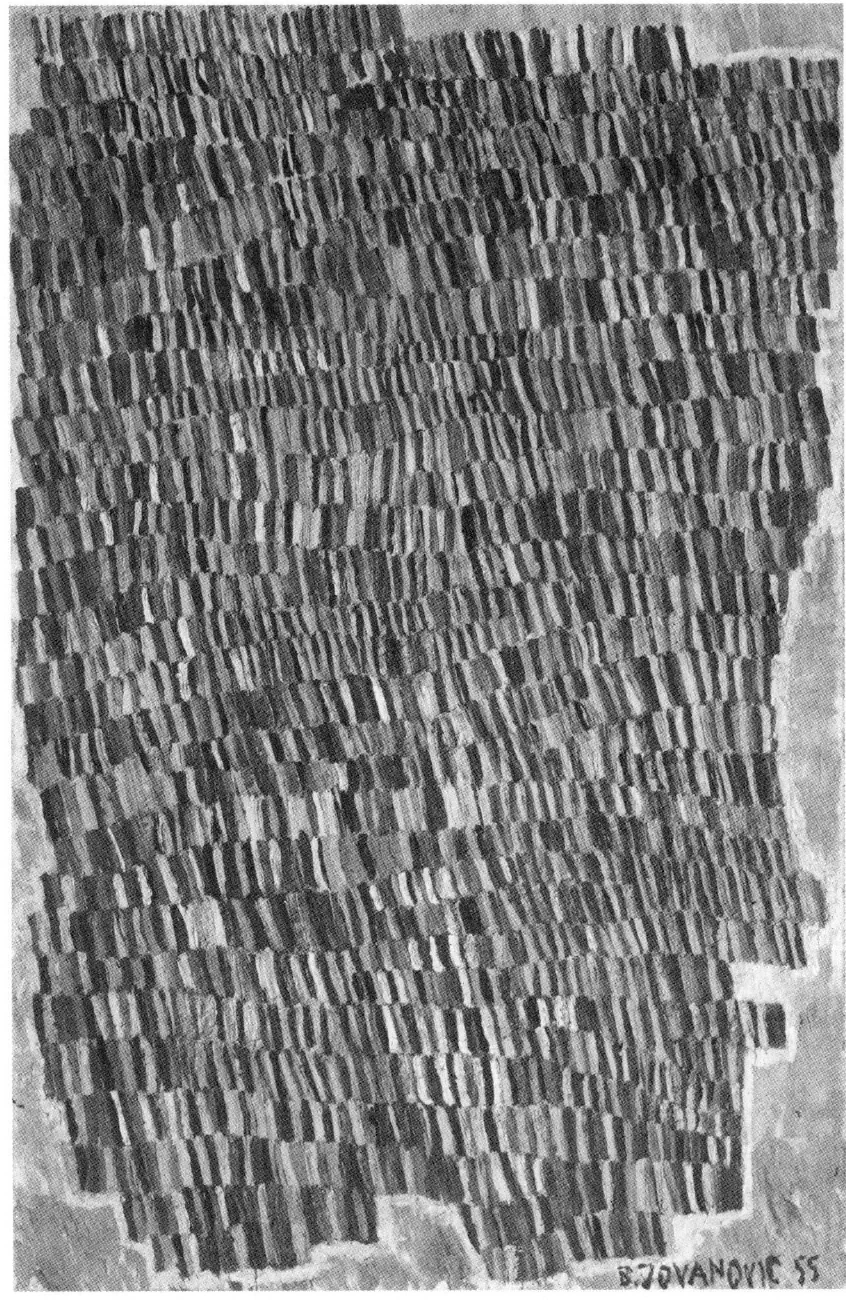

Bogoljub Jovanović
K55, 1955
Oil on canvas, 194.5 × 113 cm

Yugoslav Republican Party, which to my surprise actually existed in socialism.[28]

JV   And immediately after that he moved to Paris, where the painting *K55* was made – the only painting of that kind that he ever made.

JD   It was long believed that *K55* was his only painting from Paris that survived. Recently, a painting very similar to it turned up that somewhat spoils the impression. But regardless, had he only made *K55*, that would as far as I'm concerned be sufficient grounds for him to be considered an outstanding artist of his time. Production and overproduction are not important. After Paris, he moved to New York and nobody heard anything from or about him for a long time.

BD   What did he do for a living in New York?

JD   Vasa Mihić told me that he was a taxi driver, and a bell-boy, and that he made his living doing these jobs. He told Vasa that when he lived in Paris he didn't try to do anything, unlike his friends who 'worked their asses off' there – alluding to Peter Omčikus and Bata Mihailović – and that afterwards he went to New York, which is even bigger, in order to be even less visible. It is a form of self-marginalisation that was characteristic of Serbian art. Of course, he does not exist in American art. Allegedly, he once sold a drawing, but the buyer later expressed regret for ever having bought it. When the news reached him, he bought the drawing back.

BD   But, isn't this all a lot of myth and mystification? There is this radical painting, and everything else somehow looks like part of the myth around that painting.

JD   Nonsense! If something is conveyed in one painting, then it need not be conveyed in numerous other paintings! Isn't this also characteristic of Gorgona? If Vaništa drew one line – something is uttered there. Or Jevšovar's painting that he worked on for two years, from 1960 to 1962, scraping one surface, then adding to it, scraping and adding until at a certain point he stopped. That one painting is sufficient! There are forms of art that are amputated as the result of overproduction and quantity. We must not be captives of conventions that require us to view artists within the limits of their reputations and within a series of endless demands for productivity – that's like saying an artist should be productive all their life, stay fresh and produce fresh content, fuck in their seventies … We should instead support artists as exquisite beings, and not have anything to do with conventions like these. It was the two of you who told me just the other day how Neša Paripović dismissed Hans Ulrich Obrist – how he was not interested in meeting him when Obrist was in Belgrade, how he forgot about the meeting with the famous curator, about all the business arrangements involved in being an artist, and went for a walk instead.[29] With this gesture, he said: 'I don't give a shit about Obrist, or about anything that the art system means and ensures'. And this is not a myth. This is exactly what a project is. Make your life the way you have imagined it. Art provides the frame to that life.

JV   So, in the case of Jovanović, this kind of life represents an artistic decision, and thus its manifestation at the same time. Is this a project?

JD   Art presents the right of a human to realise their freedom through the medium of art. The project is a self-realisation, an evading of destiny, and it is a human matter. The majority of artists suffered enormously, and at the same time many good-for-nothings profited. That's why I long for just one Bogoljub Jovanović, one Koloman Novak, one Vladan Radovanović, or Neša Paripović, or Era Milivojević. The history of art has to adapt to various situations, figures and events.

JV   Yet each of them is legitimised by some of their work. Let's go back to the painting *K55*. Why is this painting so significant for you, and what was its destiny?

JD   It is an abstract painting, but it is not what Ćelić, Lubarda or Protić wanted. It is an entirely auto-referential painting and as such a rather special one. It is interesting

how that painting got to the Museum of Contemporary Art
in Belgrade at all. When we were preparing the exhibition
of the 'sixth decade',[30] our remit was to find exhibits from
various institutions throughout Yugoslavia. So the curator
Dragoslav Đorđević went to the Modern Gallery in Rijeka,
and there a curator told him that they had a painting by
an artist who must have been a Serb, since his surname was
Jovanović. They told him that they didn't know the origin
of the painting, so they hadn't registered it. Đorđević was
a very meticulous and responsible curator, and he began
trying to contact various people in order to find out who the
painter was. It was then confirmed that Bogoljub Jovanović
was the painter in question, but nobody knew his whereabouts. Thus, the painting came to Belgrade, and it was seen
for the first time at the exhibition *Yugoslav Painting of the
Sixth Decade* in 1980. In addition, the security guards at
the museum told us that one man regularly came to look at
the painting. Afterwards, we thought that it was probably
him. So, it was the first auto-referential painting in Serbian
post-war art, and it is something entirely different compared
to Lubarda, and especially to the December Group. These
are the anomalies of small milieus, namely, that something
so epochal in art remained so marginalised.

BD   Why then is this not the case in Zagreb, which is
an even smaller milieu, and the phenomena you single out
nevertheless assumed an important place there?

JD   Well, talking with my colleagues in Zagreb I have
heard just the opposite. EXAT 51 was a marginalised
phenomenon, doubted from the beginning. They were
attacked fiercely, and at the forefront of this assault was
Grgo Gamulin, who was very influential in those days.
For Gamulin, this type of practice demolished the national-
regional corpus of Croatian art. If you say that one small
milieu has relations such that some phenomena occur
simultaneously, you will be able to find an environment in
which this phenomenon has its contemporaries and its
wider context. The artists knew how to make something the
way they wanted – let's return to Alois Riegl's *Kunstwollen*
('will to art').

BD   Did Riegl, and the Viennese School of art history in general, constitute some kind of basic foundation in your education?

JD   My professor at the Advanced School in Split, Kruno Prijatelj – who certainly had the greatest impact on me – was a student of Ljubo Karaman in Zagreb, and Karaman studied in Vienna with Max Dvořák. The art history department in Zagreb had the rather strict expectation for people to read the works of the Viennese School, and preferably in German, too. Perhaps I wouldn't have graduated up there at all. [Laughs.] There were no such expectations in Belgrade.

[1] Ješa Denegri, 'Jedna nova perspektiva: kompjuteri i vizuelna istraživanja' ('A New Perspective: Computers and Visual Research'), *Bit International,* no. 2, Zagreb 1968, p. 3–8.

[2] Giulio Carlo Argan, 'Projekt i sudbina' ('Project and Destiny') (1964), *Studije o modernoj umetnosti (Studies in Modern Art)*, Nolit, Belgrade 1982. Denegri edited another book of Argan's essays: *Arhitektura i kultura (Architecture and Culture)*, Logos, Split 1989.

[3] Ph.D. thesis at the Faculty of Philosophy in Belgrade, later published as the book *Umjetnost konstruktivnog pristupa – EXAT 51 i Nove tendencije*, Horetzky, Zagreb 2000. Available in English with the title *Art of the Constructive Approach – EXAT 51 and New Tendencies*, Horetzky, Zagreb 2000.

[4] Ješa Denegri, 'Za jednu umjetnost građenja' ('For an Art of Building'), *Anale mladih (Annals of Youth)*, no. 1, Galerija Dom Omladine, Belgrade 1965.

[5] *Cubism and Abstract Art*, exh. cat., Museum of Modern Art, New York, 1936.

[6] Giulio Carlo Argan, 'Projekt i sudbina', p. 32.

[7] Ibid., p. 77.

[8] The latest in the series of Denegri's essays about Lubarda can be found in a publication that deals in detail with the painting exhibited at the São Paulo Biennial in 1953 where Lubarda received an award. See Petar Ćuković, Ješa Denegri, *Lubarda – Besta Fantastica (Lubarda – Fantastic Beasts)*, Klepić kolekcija, Belgrade 2017.

[9] Ješa Denegri, 'Beogradski nadrealizam: Izvan ili unutar druge linije' ('Belgrade Surrealism: Outside or Inside the Other Line'), *Košava*, no. 15, Vršac 1994.

[10] Hanifa Kapidžić Osmanagić, *Srpski nadrealizam (Serbian Surrealism)*, Svjetlost, Sarajevo 1966.

[11] This refers to Marko Ristić and the bequest he made to the Museum of Contemporary Art in Belgrade.

[12] Ješa Denegri, 'Beogradski nadrealizam: Izvan ili unutar druge linije'.

[13] On the art and politics of Belgrade Surrealism, see Dejan Sretenović, *Urnebesni kliker – Umetnost i politika beogradskog nadrealizma (Hilarious Clicker – Art and Politics of Belgrade Surrealism)*, Službeni glasnik, Belgrade 2016.

[14] This refers to the part of the conversation from August 2016 that was not included here, since it relates to Yugoslav art of the 1980s, which is beyond the scope of this book.

[15] See Ješa Denegri, 'Povjesno djelo Aleksandra Srneca' ('Historical Work of Aleksandar Srnec'), *Aleksandar Srnec – Prisutna odsutnost (Aleksandar Srnec – Present Absence)*, Edicija Sudac, Zagreb 2008.

[16] In reference to Krleža's polemical treatise 'Dijalektički antibarbarus' ('Dialectical Antibarbarus') published in *Pečat (Seal)*, vol. 2, no. 8–9, 1939, p. 73–232.

[17] Predrag Brebanović, *Avangarda Krležiana (Krlezian Avant-Garde)*, Jesenski i Turk, Arkzin, Zagreb 2016.

[18] Ješa Denegri, 'Die Gruppe Gorgona: Heute und Damals' ('The Gorgona Group: Now and Then'), in *Gorgona*, exh. cat., Kunstmuseum Liechtenstein, Vaduz 2017, p. 27–39.

[19] See Marijan Susovski, Ješa Denegri, *Vladan Radovanović: Verbo-voko-vizuelna istraživanja 1954–1978 (Vladan Radavonovic: Verbo-Oculo-Visual Research 1954–1978)*, exh. cat., Museum of Contemporary Art, Zagreb 1979.

[20] Ješa Denegri, 'Šesta decenija – period posleratnog modernizma' ('The Sixth Decade – the Post-War Period of Modernism'), *Pedesete: Teme srpske umetnosti (The Fifties: Themes of Serbian Art)*, Svetovi, Novi Sad 1993.

[21] Ješa Denegri, 'Leonid Šejka pre i u periodu Mediale' ('Leonid Sejka Before and During the Mediala Period'), *Pedesete*, ibid., p. 208–218.

[22] See Ivana Bago and Antonia Majača, 'Removed from the Crowd: Dissociative Association – Associations outside the Programmatic Collectivities in the Art of the 1960s and 1970s in the Socialist Republic of Croatia', in Zorana Dojić, Jelena Vesić (eds.), *Political Practices of (Post-)Yugoslav Art: Retrospective 01*, exh. cat., Prelom Kolektiv, Belgrade 2010.

[23] Ješa Denegri, 'Decembarska grupa', *Pedesete*.

[24] Ivana Simeunović Ćelić, Ješa Denegri, *Bogoljub Jovanović*, exh. cat., Muzej Zepter, Belgrade 2016.

[25] Stojan Ćelić, 'Naknadne beleške uz izložbu Bogoljuba Jovanovića u galeriji Grafički kolektiv 1953. Godine' ('Subsequent notes to the Bogoljub Jovanović exhibition at the Grafiki kolektivgallery in 1953'), *Umetnost (Art)*, no. 21, 1970, p. 29–42.

[26] Zoran Mišić, *Bogoljub Jovanović: ulja, crteži, litografije (Bogoljub Jovanović: Oils, Drawings, Lithographs)*, exh. cat., ULUS Gallery, Belgrade 1953.

[27] Vasko Popa, *Bogoljub Jovanović: Crteži i ilustracije (Bogoljub Jovanović: Drawings and Illustrations)*, exh. cat., Grafički kolektiv, Belgrade 1953.

[28] Stanislav Vinaver, 'Boba Jovanović', *Republika (Republic)*, no. 399, Belgrade 1953, p 3.

[29] According to this anecdote from some 10 years ago, during his visit to Belgrade the curator Hans Ulrich Obrist was interested in meeting Neša Paripović to talk with him about an exhibition. But Paripović did not come to the meeting arranged at the Museum of Contemporary Art because he had decided to go for a walk.

[30] *Jugoslovensko slikarstvo šeste decenije (Yugoslav Painting of the Sixth Decade)*, exh. cat., Museum of Contemporary Art, Belgrade, 1980.

A New Perspective: Computers and Visual Research
Ješa Denegri

Published in *Bit International*, no. 2, 'Computers and Visual Research' issue, Galerije grada Zagreba, Zagreb 1968.

All the phenomena conditioning
basic human behaviour in life,
society and production are reflected
directly or indirectly in the spheres
of both culture and art, determining in that way not only the
character of man's existence in
the material world, but also within
the spiritual and mental zones.
The current era is essentially
characterised by the unprecedented
omnipresence and power of technology, with the result that the
relationship between certain knowledge established by science and
the artistic imagination is becoming
increasingly important. Here, at
the very core of the relationship,
there is no potential danger of the
domain of art being subordinated
to the domain of science, but there
is, preceding that, the necessary
opportunity to coordinate man's
many creative and imaginative
capacities with those phenomena
arising out of the current of everyday life in all its complexity in
order to get a view that is as clear,

immediate and sufficient as possible, of the very foundations of our common existential framework under the actual historical conditions. Generally speaking, modern art has taken two diametrically opposed attitudes towards these conditions. On the one hand, it warned of the emergence of symptoms related to witnessing the loss of the human core under the changed social context of rapid industrialisation. It also pointed to the phenomenon of alienation and the reifying of the human personality while considering technological progress as a whole as a reality – admittedly unavoidable – which, nonetheless, is causing concern at the way in which it is endangering man. On the other hand, it expressed an unshakeably positive attitude towards the enlargement of living horizons based on the assistance of positive applications of manifold scientific knowledge, while in this situation art itself has gradually prepared and adapted not only human individuals but society as a whole for this new reality, towards which humanity has been inevitably gravitating since the first industrial revolution.

Art could not do otherwise owing to its capacity for complex effects on our spirit and psyche. This belief was also shared by the pioneers of modern architecture and the proponents of the first artistic avant-garde groups of the 20th century, from the Futurists to De Stijl and from Russian Constructivism to the Bauhaus. Throughout their purely spiritual actions we can see a basic attempt to guide human thinking and many practical habits all directed towards building a highly productive yet happy human society in the industrial epoch. This is true, as we know, since many modern historical facts prove that reality has twice brutally crushed these strivings in successive world catastrophes, interrupting all the newly opened prospects leading in the direction I have described. So, the emergence of the ideal imagined society was and remains utopian, lacking even today in practically all the preconditions for its fulfilment.

The Second World War and the reaction of the suffering individual to this universal threat to security brought about the rise of the art of public confession, the resentful and essentially tragic striptease of the lonely individual unable and unwilling to cling steadfastly to anything but the eternal and lasting power of raw matter itself. The art that dominated in the 1940s and 1950s is,

as regards its best and most powerful examples, the art of
heroic revolt, but it is simultaneously also the art of lonely
scepticism. It is an art characterised by the pain and cries
of an individual on the plane of expression; by the agnostic
and the existentialist underlying the fact of existence on
the philosophical plane, and on the plane of ideas it is
characterised by the acceptance of the present as it stands
and by relinquishing efforts to guide the active forces
towards the paths of the future. In different parts of Europe
an intuitive belief in the idea that a constructive action is
possible has emerged under the pressure of that psychosis
of uncertainty, meanwhile no one any longer believes in
the existing and imposed historical, national, cultural and
ideological 'myths' included herein. This intuitive belief
sprang up spontaneously among many young artists in
various parts of Europe. So, art offered insight into scientific
phenomena again, just as the previous avant-garde movements had once. These phenomena eventually appear as the
only mainstay or shelter in a world of constant political,
social and ethical shifts, and may serve as at least relatively
stable support for those making efforts to build more lasting
and generally more acceptable values. The New Tendencies
movement rose as an attempt to guide the meaning of the
artistic act and art itself in those domains of life where
the only possible and now real picture of modern civilisation
began to form. These particular guidelines began to reflect
not only on the new methodology and technology of design,
but also in the intimation of the ensuing change of the
existing measures concerning artist-work-society relationships. Any merit to be ascribed to the New Tendencies
movement lies in its poignant posing of the question of the
real relations of art and the new reality of life in all its
problematic scope. Also, the movement declared its support
for the stabilisation of the positive spiritual features of
contemporaneity, not for the action of condemning something. Its research methods are those related to its new,
constructive plastic operationality and the new qualities of
work, which came into existence owing to these types of
changed creative acts, which may be subjected to definite
analytic conceptualisation.

    By adopting certain instrumental means immanent
to the premises of scientific thought (namely 'structure',

'programme', 'information' and so on), art has surpassed the status of a specifically emotionally-based human activity and attained some objective value-related hypotheses, meaning hypotheses that are the themes of precise design processes as well as of the realisation and verification of meaning of this new type of work of art. At this juncture, where with the artistic act one overcomes the entirely transcendental component of expression and opens the way towards an exact definition of certain problems, some stage has been reached that enables the utilisation of advantages offered by certain instruments of cybernetics and automation, all with the aim of building up new design structures. Now the prophecy of Norbert Wiener, who was aware of the complex and extremely developed interactive involvement between man and machine in the most diverse manifestations of life and its activities, is beginning to emerge. In the same way, basing his research on empirical data, Abraham Moles has pointed to the fact that the human race today is faced with the dawn of a second technical revolution, namely the automation revolution, which will by virtue of sheer volume radically change almost all spheres of man's creative behaviour, which with its all-out penetration of the very essence of human work will inevitably infuse the sphere of art and bring with it certain repercussions. In these circumstances, the modern artist and the artist of the future in particular will become conscious of the prospects opening up to him. These lie in the computer, the instrument that has already found widespread applicability in the most diverse domains of social and productive practice; and it will, with its specific properties, play an exceptionally important role in defining a new type of artistic creation. Here it is essential to realize the real possibilities and roles in such a process, as well as to define more precisely the operative tasks of the artist himself under such changed working conditions. As Moles said, the person who employs the computer to obtain 'artistic information' will be a type of 'aesthetician-programmer'. He will have to combine artistic inclination with specialised scientific training so that he will not only possess a clearly defined design awareness as regards the forms and structures he investigates, but will also be able to operate the computer in such a way that best enables him to fulfil, as efficiently and desirably as possible, his initial concepts. Namely, the computer here acts as an 'amplifier of complexity' (Moles' term), as the medium that processes the data that is planned and posed by the responsible aesthetician-programmer. The machine, therefore, is not a 'creator' but a 'tool', a tool capable of producing exceptional results to and transmutations of the given problems. In some cases, the results may even, in their ultimate visual expression, surpass the norms and constraints of the given 'programme'. This may be the result of auto-regulatory units in the computer generating a certain quantity of unpredictable relationships, systems and combinations. However, the real point is for the programme at the end of the operation to transform numerical or sign-repertory data supplied by the aesthetician-programmer into autonomous visual or auditive data that is accessible to our senses, with a view to ensuring the preservation of the necessary 'artistic' quality of the final work. This should be independent of what is obtained by the process, which in certain phases of design requires strict scientific conceptualisation.

The above premises only really contain some basic indications of the relations operating between the artist's motives to express man's pure spiritual activity and automatic tools, these technical means that help obtain the most complete, content-rich and otherwise fruitful results. Our immediate forthcoming task to be realised through the practice of research is the continued working out of those formative principles, on which are based those results that could make such operationality the best and most efficient, not only from the standpoint of methodology but also from the viewpoint of 'aesthetics'.

I believe the solution to this problem will also depend on the real value of the character of the whole enterprise. The way to its opening up is through the meeting and coming together of art and cybernetics. If these results prove satisfying at a specific level of aesthetics in the future, then surely a new sequence of gaps will open up in the already tottering forms of the present-day workings of the psychology and sociology of art in the contemporary world. At the moment, we are unable to realise all the detailed implications that will result from these changes.

III. Exhibitions of Yugoslav Art
Ješa Denegri in Conversation with Branislav Dimitrijević and Jelena Vesić

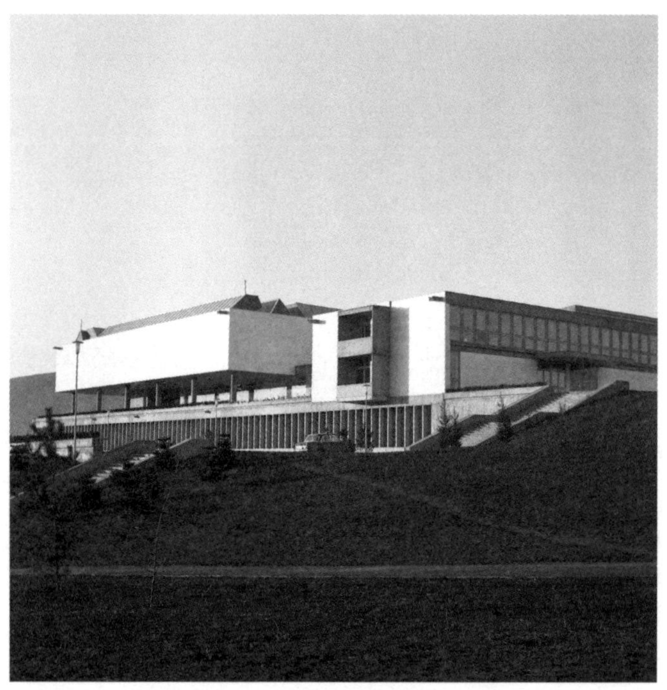

View of the Museum of Contemporary Art inaugurated in 1970, Skopje, 1970

1. <u>Exhibition Politics and Curatorial Practices</u>

JELENA VESIĆ   Let's continue our discussion about art under socialism and the making of the Yugoslav Art Space, now focusing on exhibition practices. Numerous exhibitions representing Yugoslavia abroad were put together as so-called cultural packages, a practice that you, while collaborating with groups of artists and critics gathered around the Belgrade Student Cultural Centre (SKC) Gallery, harshly criticised.[1] The point of your criticism was that most of the artists selected to be part of these cultural packages, who received generous state support and were involved in most international exchanges, were mediocre. In your essay for the catalogue of the 1977 Paris Biennial you criticised the reproduction of 'the human and the sentimental' in official socialist Yugoslav art institutions, and claimed that such practices are 'legitimising mediocrity'.[2]

As a museum curator you yourself worked on large, representative exhibitions that were held abroad; but as an independent critic you were interested in very specific art phenomena that didn't easily fit into the institutional mainstream. Clearly you found a way to link and present all these dualities and contradictions together. We are now talking about the exhibition that was held in Germany, France and Italy during 1978–1980, under the title *Tendencies in Yugoslav Art Today*.[3] It was organised by the Belgrade Museum of Contemporary Art, and curated by you. Interestingly enough, the word tendency is used in the plural – 'tendencies' – and was taken from György Lukács' writings on critical realism in art, and it became imbued with a new, different meaning in the context of the New Tendencies movement in art. Could you tell us something about that exhibition? Does its organisational and presentational model stand apart in some way – if we take into consideration the broader issue of the official exhibition policies connected with Yugoslav art – and if so in what way?

BRANISLAV DIMITRIJEVIĆ   Let me add one more thing. When we speak about modes of cultural policies in socialist Yugoslavia, we're also speaking about the affirmation of Yugoslav art abroad. The topic of art in the context of the cultural diplomacy of the SFRY (Socialist Federal Republic of Yugoslavia) is not at all marginal. These are cultural-political concepts that were developed from the mid-1950s onwards by the Federal Committee for Foreign Cultural Relations and its chairman Marko Ristić, and additionally developed through the founding of the Museum of Contemporary Art in Belgrade and other institutions. If, for example, we look at the catalogue of one of the most representative exhibitions of that kind, *Contemporary Yugoslav Painting and Sculpture*, which was held in London's Tate Gallery in 1961, and subsequently in several museums in the USA, and which was organised by the Federal Committee for Foreign Cultural Relations, we see that what was presented there was exclusively modernist painting.[4] In the introductory text for the catalogue, Zoran Kržišnik explicitly writes that the exhibition is not 'a survey' of Yugoslav art of the time, but that 'its balance was tilted in favour of non-figurative art'.[5] Also, the catalogues of the exhibitions *Contemporary Yugoslav*

Painting and Sculpture and *Tendencies in Yugoslav Art Today*
are very similar, even though the first is from the beginning
of the 1960s and the second one is from the late 1970s.
Both employ the motif of the tricoloured Yugoslav flag,
but without the red star in the middle – as if this crucial
ideological symbol that occupied a prominent place on
the SFRY flag was kept out of sight in view of the Western
political establishment's sensitivity during the time of Cold
War tensions. As if a symbolic concession had been made,
through which the country's culture was also promoted as
modern and free – the culture that didn't 'force' its ideology
onto the autonomy of art. I mention this in connection with
the possible continuity, as well as the discontinuity, with
these policies during the 1970s. During the 1950s, and during
the times of Marko Ristić, the role of art in cultural diplomacy was clear and unambiguous, as it was in the type of
cultural modernisation that came from above, from the
position of state politics. Thus, for instance, at the opening
of the exhibition *Modern Art in the United States* in Belgrade
in 1956, Ristić said that not only are these kinds of exhibitions 'tools for creating mutual understanding between all
peoples in the world', but they also represent 'a step further'.
He added: 'Here, it is not just a matter of understanding,
but of something much deeper and higher, of international
cooperation between the nations and civilisations of the
present day, around the building of culture, which has no
other goal than to become a common culture of all of
mankind. In contemporary art, in its various tendencies
and currents, one can clearly see that it is only in mutual
contacts, in bringing us together, that particular national
arts find their proper space and meaning.'[6]

The exhibition *Tendencies in Yugoslav Art Today* was
assembled 20 years later in another historical context.
By that time such statements had already become a ritually
repeated commonplace, in relation to which the new
generation of artists took a critical stance; for them, such
rhetoric had become mere empty speech because it was
so systematically exploited. In that exhibition, through your
curatorial intervention, this new generation followed the
previous one in the context of the narrative on the Yugoslav
Art Space, but their critique of the established art mainstream was clearly manifested. The exhibition featured

Murtić, Bernik and Mića Popović! It also included Goran Trbuljak, Raša Todosijević, Goran Đorđević and the OHO group. So it spanned from Bernik to Đorđević!

JEŠA DENEGRI   The cultural politics of Yugoslavia's visual arts is a major topic that calls for far more extensive research. At the very beginning of the 1950s we have this crucial exhibition initiated by Krleža, *Medieval Art in Yugoslavia,* an exhibition we have already discussed in detail. We should look favourably on the fact that the cultural politics of the day saw art as the realisation of its social and political project, due in part to the fact that a leftist elite was gathered around such programmes – from Krleža to Oto Bihalji Merin, Marko Ristić and Aleksandar Vučo, who were early exponents of Belgrade Surrealism. A certain continuity with the most progressive currents in pre-war Yugoslav culture was established, which for the most part, particularly back in those days, had communist affiliations. They had very influential positions, and at that point an entire series of grandiose international exhibitions had been staged. We should situate this chronologically. First, the exhibition *Contemporary French Art* was held in Belgrade, Zagreb, Ljubljana and Skopje in 1952. Then the exhibition of the British modernist sculptor Henry Moore opened in Zagreb, Belgrade and Ljubljana in 1955. You just mentioned the exhibition *Modern Art in the United States* from the collections of the Museum of Modern Art, New York, organised by the Federal Committee for Foreign Cultural Relations, and held in the Pavilion at Kalemegdan in Belgrade in 1956. Yugoslavia was the only socialist country to host this exhibition, which was also held in prestigious European museums in London, Paris, Vienna and others.[7] After the end of the 1950s there followed an entire series of international exhibitions in Yugoslavia: the exhibitions of Dutch art, Italian art, then French art again, as well as another exhibition of American art in 1961. This exhibition, together with the work of the protagonists of Abstract Expressionism, including Robert Rauschenberg and Jasper Johns, was held in Belgrade, Zagreb, Skopje, Ljubljana, Rijeka and Maribor.

From the 1940s and up until the mid-1960s a large number of art institutions were established in the country: the Art Gallery of Bosnia and Herzegovina in Sarajevo

in 1946, the Modern Gallery in Ljubljana in 1948, the Gallery
of Contemporary Arts in Zagreb in 1954, the Modern Gallery
in Titograd (today Podgorica) in 1961, the Modern Gallery
in Rijeka in 1962, the Museum of Contemporary Art in Skopje
in 1964, the Museum of Contemporary Art in Belgrade in
1965, the Gallery of Contemporary Visual Art in Novi Sad
in 1966, the Art Gallery in Priština in 1979 and more.
In Belgrade, the Museum of African Art was founded in 1977.
The Gallery for the Art of Non-Aligned Countries named
Josip Broz Tito was founded in Titograd (Podgorica) in 1981.

BD   I'd like to emphasise that the Museum of Contemporary Art in Skopje is particularly interesting as it was built
as part of the project of renewing the city after the disastrous
earthquake in 1963. The construction project was funded
by the Polish Government and many works in the collection
were donated by well-known artists after an international
campaign of solidarity. This institution became an important
contributor to the general modernisation of the city and
helped the development of a contemporary art scene there;
today it is one of the most active institutions of this kind
in the Balkans.

JD   Indeed. This all contributed to the international
reputation of Yugoslavia and was the result of a highly
competent foreign policy and cultural diplomacy. Throughout this period we had important international exhibitions
coming to our region, while at the same time there was a
strong reciprocal arrangement as part of this international
cooperation. At the renewed Venice Biennale after the war,
socialist Yugoslavia was present from 1950 onwards, and
retained the pavilion from the times of the Kingdom of
Yugoslavia that was built in the 1930s at the initiative of the
writer and art historian Milan Kašanin. Yugoslavia did not
participate at the first post-war Biennale in 1948. Želimir
Koščević, in his research on Yugoslav participations at the
Venice Biennale, explained that from 1946 the exhibition
entitled *Yugoslav Peoples' Painting and Sculpture of the 19th and the
20th Century* had been touring the countries of the 'peoples'
democracy'. Perhaps in 1948 it was all about boycotting a
cultural manifestation in the West. What were the governing
structures in Yugoslavia back then, thinking about the

Venice Biennale? Grgo Gamulin, one of the few critics to write about that edition of the Biennale, provided an account in one of his reviews.[8] Despite an utterly negative image of the Biennale, however, the authorities decided that Yugoslavia should be among the participating countries at the next iteration, with Petar Šegedin as the commissioner, and a selection that included Boža Ilić, Ismet Mujezinović, Ivan Kos, Lubarda, Augustinčič, Kršinić, Radauš, Vojin Bakić and Angeli Radovani. The list of names and the accompanying documentation on the works lead us to conclude that the majority of artists and works represented the spirit of Socialist Realism, with some occasional aberrations – first with the painter Ivan Kos, and then with the young sculptors Bakić and Radovani. But such a selection wasn't entirely exceptional at the Biennale. We might have observed something similar at the Italian pavilion, where the neo-realists Guttuso, Pizzinato and Zigaina exhibited, and which is why some critics of the 1950 Biennale called it the 'Biennale of Realism'.[9] And then, in all of these more notable manifestations – the São Paolo Biennial, the Tokyo Biennial, the Alexandria Biennial, and especially the Venice Biennale – Yugoslavia appears with straightforward ambitions. Whether these ambitions were optimally worked out, in terms of expertise, is another question that would require the criteria particular to the profession; but the state was looking to manifest itself through and with contemporary art, and the new cultural politics was committed to articulating itself after the break with Stalinism and the USSR.

Yugoslavia aspired to be an open, democratic country, and its modern art was to be the symbol of that process. At a certain moment, the question of expertise arose: how to do this? In the beginning, the Federal Committee for Foreign Cultural Relations had its board of experts. They appointed notable art historians as commissioners. Very often, Aleksa Čelebonović was selected for the role, and it is important to say that he was one of the few critics who knew the international scene very well: he and his brother, the painter Marko Čelebonović, had lived in Paris and they knew what was going on. So there was a true desire to present what was of real value at these exhibitions. Whether it was really so is now a matter of contention. If we take into account the book we have already mentioned by Želimir

Koščević, you can actually see the unstable nature of the criteria applied.[10] Not only were our commissioners aware of the international contexts and thus tried to fit in with them, but it appears that domestic interests were also playing a part which, very often, was driven by career concerns. International appearances promised to build careers, and here the idyllic story of Yugoslavia and its cultural politics breaks down entirely.

JV   You wrote about this in your essay 'The Language of Art and the System of Art' for the project *Oktobar 75* (*October 75*) where you pointed to the continued tradition of the bourgeois institution of art under Yugoslav socialism and the increasing class differences amongst artists.[11] You wrote: 'As we know, there is no private art market in Yugoslavia, which does not mean that no opportunities to make a considerable profit exist for various groups who pursue a professional artistic practice. Also, the principle of freedom of creation is proclaimed and applied, although the reality of artistic life actually shows that for some artists – most often the proponents of new and progressive orientations – that freedom was no more than freedom of expression deprived of adequate material compensation for the results of their work; whereas for other artists – mostly the relatively broad group of artists involved in the system of academies and other pedagogical or cultural institutions – it also meant freedom that brought a whole lot of privileges and, in the final analysis, influence when it came to regulating the existing system of art. The practice of Yugoslav artistic life points to a paradoxical fact: the social and political elites in this country are most suspicious of the very phenomena that endeavour, through the critical nature of their language, to democratise artistic communication, thus involving themselves in the broader trends of social and ideational change.'[12]

So, in reading this we can conclude that there was a big difference between the nominal and the actual, between the rhetoric and the practice. What was the official position on the selection and evaluation of Yugoslav artists?

JD   The official opinion was that we cannot present ourselves abroad with something that is not verified. This means that the said verification in the domestic milieu needed to be achieved first. So, although there was an international context for this, no bolder attempts were made – for instance, to include EXAT 51 in the selection for biennial exhibitions during the 1950s. Important artists like Bakić, Stupica and Pregelj, although they participated in biennials, in fact didn't get the chance to enjoy a more extensive and timely presentation. The entire artistic context produced during the 1960s by the New Tendencies (and we've talked about this already) was not represented in the context of the Venice Biennale in those years. And when artists from that circle finally found themselves in the Yugoslav pavilion (for instance Richter in 1972 or Knifer in 1976) it was with a significant delay. The OHO group, which was very much present in international exchanges at the beginning of the 1970s, was obviously too radical to be presented in the national pavilion, and would only get the chance later in 1978 with a different group makeup, such as the Šempas Family Art Commune. Marina Abramović did take part on three occasions in thematic international exhibitions in the central Biennale pavilion (in 1976, 1980 and 1984), but never in the selection of her country. And was not the promotion of Neo-Expressionism (1980) and Anachronism (1984) an ideal context for Sedar and Kulmer to appear there? Finally, let's just say this: the role of the commissioner was never offered to competent connoisseurs of international art, like the critics Vera Horvat Pintarić or Matko Meštrović, perhaps because from 1960 onwards this role was entrusted to experts from the museums and galleries.

JV   What did your 'verification of the artists in the domestic milieu' mean in practice? You said it was used as a qualification for the international presentations of Yugoslav art.

JD   It meant that an artist needed to have major exhibitions, they needed to have a social reputation, their works needed to be purchased by institutions, they needed to be a professor at the academy, they needed to hold a master class and so forth.

BD   There was this concept of master classes – some famous artists held their own master classes.

JD   Hegedušić held a master class in Zagreb, Milunović held one in Belgrade and so on. Filo Filipović, in whose summer house we're having these conversations, attended Milunović's class.[13] Antun Augustinčič had a sculpture class in Zagreb. Today, it seems more than clear that these were obstacles, that in fact these great artists were obstructing the presentation of Yugoslav art in its best and most vital aspects, that at issue was some kind of toll that had to be paid to those eminent actors on the scene, and this is the context behind our discussion of an internal corruption of the art system. So the art system was very complex, and people who were making important exhibitions abroad could launch or present real innovations in their curatorial selections only sporadically. One positive example was the appearance of Olga Jevrić at the Venice Biennale as early as 1958. Lubarda received an award at the São Paulo Biennial in 1953, and in 1955 he got the award at the Tokyo Biennial. An analysis of the situation, in which we should move from case to case, would be worthy of a study all its own.

However, when specialised cultural institutions were established, and when they began to work on exhibitions locally as well as internationally and largely autonomously, the Federal Committee for Foreign Cultural Relations was of the opinion that its responsibility to represent contemporary art could be eased, and it assigned the task of international cooperation to these institutions. From the mid-1950s, the Gallery of Contemporary Art in Belgrade (which was to become the Museum of Contemporary Art in 1965) under the management of Miodrag Protić, and the Modern Gallery in Ljubljana under the management of Zoran Kržišnik, were given a mandate to deal with these activities. Our museum produced many exhibitions of this kind, but not to the extent that Protić felt the museum should do – above all with the historicisation of Yugoslav art, which is why our work focused on those seminal decennial exhibitions. Also, as an active artist and art critic he was trying to maintain a certain distance from such appearances, so that neither he nor the museum could be rebuked for taking on a monopolistic role in this process. As a result, we only staged these exhibitions periodically. Most were realised by the Modern Gallery in Ljubljana, which served as the organiser of the International Biennial of Graphic Arts. Since graphic art was an appropriate medium – meaning that it was much cheaper and more easily available for exhibiting than painting and sculpture – the majority of exhibitions in the Second and Third World were of that kind. You can often duplicate that type of art material and send it off to several nearly identical exhibitions almost anywhere in the world.

2.   The Case of the International Biennial of Graphic Arts in Ljubljana

JV   In 1955, the same year that Arnold Bode established documenta in Kassel, Zoran Kržišnik established the International Biennial of Graphic Arts in Ljubljana. The aim of this was the concept of a 'mega-exhibition', an exhibition that would open itself towards the international world of art par excellence. Very important critics, theoreticians, artists and curators came to this, so it became a place of gathering where Yugoslav art was internationalised. And it was done in a most economical way – through graphic media – which was understood as suitable for the dissemination of art in an art world envisioned in a far broader sense – as a venue outside the main centres. The biennial is connected with the founding of the Non-Aligned Movement during the period – the late 1950s and early 1960s – as artists from almost all the continents participated in it, including so-called Third World countries. What did the exhibition mean within the Yugoslav Art Space?

JD   Well, there's no doubt that the Ljubljana International Biennial of Graphic Arts has long been a very distinctive international event and an important expression of graphic arts and beyond. Nowadays, there are several extensive historiographical texts about the entire undertaking, and one can follow the history of the Ljubljana Biennial on the basis of that literature.[14] This topic is highly interesting, and provides answers to a basic question: how did institutions function under that socio-cultural system called 'socialist modernism'? To put it briefly: at the initiative of Zoran Mušič and Božidar Jakac, Zoran Kržišnik, who was then a young curator at the Modern Gallery in Ljubljana, visited the Venice Biennale. Then, following the model of

Venice, which is in the regional neighbourhood of Yugoslavia and Slovenia, they came up with the idea of establishing an institution in Ljubljana – which has enjoyed a graphic arts tradition going back to Expressionism, and which also continued with the Partisan graphic arts of the Second World War – an institution that would specialise in graphic arts. Similar manifestations existed in post-war Europe, in Lugano, in Krakow and so on. Due to Kržišnik's agility, and to the social, cultural and political support the idea gained, the Ljubljana Biennial was established and for some time mapped crucial events in graphic arts around the world. And to top it all off – if we're ready to celebrate such a history today – in 1963 the highest award of the Ljubljana Biennial was given to Robert Rauschenberg, just one year before he was awarded the Grand Prize at the Venice Biennale.

JV   Is that when you started attending the Biennial?

JD   I didn't see that exhibition. I started to follow the Ljubljana Biennial sometime after 1965, when I became the Curator for Graphic Arts at the Museum of Contemporary Art in Belgrade. As a curator, I was expected to visit these exhibitions every two years, as was the entire curatorial team at the museum. I was a member of the selection jury on three occasions, while Miodrag Protić was a member of the jury that granted awards many times.

BD   Curator for Graphic Arts was your first position at the Museum of Contemporary Art?

JD   Yes, it was the collection that somehow 'belonged' to the youngest curator, as one of the less important assignments.

BD   Less important?

JD   The most important for the institution was painting, followed by sculpture. I was the curator for the Graphic Arts Collection until the Collection for New Media was established in the mid-1970s.

JV   Graphic arts have a special meaning and thus place in socialism. What was the concept of the Ljubljana Biennial in this regard?

JD   First of all, graphic arts, as a mass medium based on technical reproduction, well suited the conditions and capacities of Yugoslavia's economy. It was possible to organise an event of this kind within the framework of that medium and draw a large number of participants from all over the world, which permitted including some very prominent names. What is more, the idea of the wider social reach and distribution implied by graphic art as a medium may in an ideological sense have been a good fit for the cultural politics of the time. The International Biennial of Graphic Arts in Ljubljana enjoyed and maintained a markedly rising trajectory for several decades and represented – at least for us here – a window on the world because it was possible to see, here in this country, an impressive body of international production every two years.

BD   Was this the first instance of an artistic event of such a scale that was consistent with Yugoslavia's creation of and participation in the politics of non-alignment, which was ultimately articulated precisely at that moment in time? The Ljubljana Biennial was launched the same year that the Afro-Asian Conference was held in Bandung, and a year before the signing of the Brioni Declaration, which actually inaugurated the politics of non-alignment.[15]

JD   Yes. That can be seen in this history. Yet, when the first exhibitions were held, it seemed as though there were still some doubts amongst the authorities themselves as to what it was all about. The politician Krste Crvenkovski was mentioned in the process, a high official and one who made an official visit to the exhibition in order to dispel any doubts.[16]

BD   He was the State Secretary for Culture and Education at that time. He is considered to be a 'liberal' Party member.

JD   It all fits. I think that the Ljubljana Biennial is a matrix, on the basis of which all of these cultural-political initiatives can be distinguished. So, Crvenkovski comes to the exhibition, allegedly at the explicit request of Tito himself, and offers a favourable evaluation, saying it is all very good, and much needed as far as our society is concerned. And the exhibition gets a green light in the full sense of the word. In any case, it was supported by political officials from Slovenia itself. It is said that Boris Kraigher, and maybe even Kardelj himself, also supported the initiative. And interestingly enough, Božidar Jakac was there. Jakac is one of the artists who made a portrait of Tito in Jajce, during the Anti-Fascist Council for the National Liberation of Yugoslavia (AVNOJ) Session in 1943.[17] So, the Ljubljana Biennial, which was founded on an initiative from the art circles, presents itself as something very convenient, precisely as a manifestation that could develop cultural and political aspirations and endeavours that were a good fit with the cultural and political strategies of socialist Yugoslavia.

BD   How were the selections for the Ljubljana Biennial made?

JD   Some selections came as packages through state channels.

BD   But some turned up through alternative channels, especially those from the Soviet Union, and here Kržišnik's story is interesting.

JD   Yes, the 'unofficial' Soviet artists came through Riga. Why? Because the Baltic countries – Lithuania, Estonia and Latvia – were less rigid compared to Moscow and Leningrad in relation to their systems for the unions of visual artists.

JV   How were artists from the West selected?

JD   Those were different political circumstances. In a book that describes the history of the Biennial there is an interesting text by Riva Castleman, who was the Curator for Graphic Arts at the Museum of Modern Art in New York, where she mentions that the first Curator for Graphic Arts and the founder of the graphic arts, photography and other reproductive media collections in those days, was William Lieberman, who was the first to contact Kržišnik.[18]

The Americans were looking to break into European art, and we can see from their strategies that Rauschenberg was one of their favourites — and then Rauschenberg got his first European award in Ljubljana.

BD   Rauschenberg's award in Venice is usually interpreted as a result of aggressive American private interests, of the American gallery system. Before Venice, he was awarded in Ljubljana by European experts.

JD   Yes. But Lieberman was the one who did the mediating, and he was also on the jury.

BD   European experts whom one might suspect were, shall we say, sceptical of the American art scene?

JD   Yes, but that graphic work really was exceptional. *Accident* (1963) was made from a lithographic stone broken into two pieces. It was an instance of art that was undergoing a change, and the jury realised this. But we can see here that Lieberman had this idea on coming to Ljubljana of introducing Rauschenberg, and in some way was lobbying for his award.

JV   Here in the catalogue, we have the names of the jury for the 5th International Biennial of Graphic Arts in 1963: Umbro Apollonio, Jorge Romero Brest, Alexei Fedorov-Davydov; then Walter Koschatzky, Zoran Kržišnik, Jacques Lassaigne, William Lieberman, Mieczysław Porębski and Lazar Trifunović.[19]

JD   Lazar Trifunović! How about that!

BD   So, Lazar Trifunović was in the jury that awarded Rauschenberg in Ljubljana in 1963! It is interesting, bearing in mind that he, as a critic, was known to have a certain animosity towards American art …

JD   Yes, but this is how it was: after some time, certain circles close to me began to express criticism towards the Ljubljana Biennial. First there were charges that it was a cumbersome, overly-large exhibition, and non-selective;

secondly, that it was assembled according to national selections; and thirdly, that the organisers were not really able to discern what was really happening in graphic arts. Matko Meštrović was the first who, on the occasion of the 5th iteration in 1963, began to push the idea that the International Biennial of Graphic Arts was organised rather arbitrarily – and if I may say so, was of no particular consequence … Because it was already the time of the New Tendencies, and a time of new emerging technologies, and graphic arts were changing.

Also, it appeared that Kržišnik had developed a parallel network for launching businesses and enterprises, using his position as director of the Modern Gallery – from which our museum and Miodrag Protić kept a strict distance – and gathered a group of important artists around himself and his various initiatives. These were the leading figures of what was called the Ljubljana Graphic Arts School – Janez Bernik, Vladimir Makuc, Andrej Jemec and Bogdan Meško – which from my perspective proved to be a conventional and rather retrograde expression of a market-driven type of art. The same thing was happening with the Belgrade Graphic Collective: they supported the idea that the print runs of graphic art productions couldn't be endlessly large, even though that's exactly what the new silk screen techniques enabled and what served to mark the progress of graphic art techniques as reproductive techniques, which tend towards ever greater possibilities of duplication and multiplication. Nevertheless, the Ljubljana and Belgrade graphic schools advocated a form of fetishisation of traditional graphic art techniques.

JV   So, from the initiative behind Jakac, and this idea of the social function of graphic arts, we came to the question of how to constitute the market for graphic arts and how to balance the private interests of particular artists around the Ljubljana Biennial?

JD   Jakac was no longer a paradigm in those days; he was already a veteran. In some way Debenjak was the founder. He was Božidar Jakac's successor at the Graphic Arts Department of the Ljubljana Academy. And this is interesting: there were several ateliers and master classes where graphic arts techniques were taught – etching, aquatint, copperplate engraving, dry point – where Slovenian artists, again due to the network developed through the Biennial, studied these techniques abroad. They went to places like the studios of Johnny Friedlander in Paris and Stanley Hayter in Great Britain. Back then I coined a term for that kind of graphic arts, which I saw as a 'heritage of a noble craft'. As a curator for graphic arts at the Belgrade Museum of Contemporary Art, I was making exhibitions where graphic arts were treated in a very different way. First of all, I was focusing on what was called the Zagreb School of Serigraphy,[20] because within the New Tendencies, and under the aegis of the ideas of Victor Vasarely and Max Bill, this idea about the large number of prints continued. My curatorial work appeared as an aberration of this matrix of graphic arts, which produced five or ten exclusive prints, because the graphic plate for printing becomes worn out after a certain number of imprints are made. The serigraphy in Zagreb had its foundations in the ideas of Ivan Picelj who, at the time, worked with Denise René's gallery, and then in Brane Horvat who was Vera Horvat Pintarić's husband, and who opened a studio for serigraphy where the aforementioned Vasarely and Bill, as well as Fontana and Soto, printed their works. Then the artists from the EXAT 51 days, like Picelj and Srnec, and later the younger ones like Feller, Dobrović and Mladen Galić worked there. In 1967–1968, I presented an exhibition of the Zagreb School of Serigraphy in the Salon of the Museum of Contemporary Art – this was the first exhibition I curated.[21]

BD   So, you wanted to change the very way in which the graphic arts techniques were institutionalised in the Yugoslav context by the Ljubljana Biennial?

JD   Serigraphy challenged the traditional techniques of graphic arts and a kind of split developed: on the one hand everything that was happening at the Ljubljana Biennial became retrograde, and on the other these business arrangements that developed there appeared strange to me. So, even though you're interested in hearing something about the Ljubljana Biennial, I also want to outline my position on all of this.

JV   Of course. Here, the Ljubljana Biennial is an example
of an official international manifestation where cultural
politics was reflected, in relation to which you took a critical
stance.

JD   I have a good understanding of these cultural-
political issues: in the way that the Yugoslav space, internationalisation, pluralism, non-alignment, artists from Riga,
Rauschenberg – all these things are extraordinary, and
should be historically evaluated objectively. However, what
about the critical doubts? The doubts are based on the
fact that the International Biennial of Graphic Arts and its
organisers did not make or intend all these strong gestures
within graphic arts to be critically evaluated, nor was
Kržišnik able to do such a thing, because he was essentially
just a very skilful organiser and manager. Various trends,
tendencies and phenomena were simply piling up within
a huge event, which almost couldn't be properly evaluated
or surveyed. The Modern Gallery in Ljubljana as a space
was not able to host such large exhibitions. The works
were densely displayed one next to another, one on top of
another. And finally, there was the issue around the formation of Group 69.

BD   What was the issue?

JD   The case of Group 69 resulted in one of the most
interesting polemics in the Serbian art space, and involved
the painter Zoran Pavlović and Miodrag Protić when the
Belgrade Museum of Contemporary Art organised an
exhibition of Group 69 in 1978.[22] Protić subsequently joined
Group 69, which emerged in Slovenia and which was linked
to Kržišnik and the Ljubljana Graphic Arts School.[23]
Serbian members of Group 69 also included Stojan Ćelić
and Vladimir Veličković, while Miroslav Šutej came from
Croatia. Kržišnik and the group of artists around him wanted
to build on the achievements of the Ljubljana Biennial and
to capitalise on them. Numerous exhibitions were staged
that the Federal Committee for Foreign Cultural Relations
arranged through institutions such as the Modern Gallery,
and partly also through the Museum of Contemporary Art
in Belgrade. And while we were doing this, thinking that

we were exhibiting our art with the aim of presenting what we considered to be the best of it, or similar, it became clear that the Ljubljana Biennial was establishing a relationship with the art market. In other words, the purpose was to focus on particular achievements of the Biennial in such a way that one circle of artists linked to that institution would break through internationally.

BD   One gets the impression that a process began in Yugoslavia where certain attitudes about socialist art about which we have been talking, started becoming ever more suppressed, and art was becoming linked above all to the market, and the artist was becoming simultaneously both an institutionalised protagonist and some kind of competitive entrepreneur. Here we have the catalogue of the 1978 exhibition, which carries an unsigned introductory essay that can be seen as a kind of would-be manifesto of Group 69. The essay argues for 'constant competition within art', for the need to create better conditions for artists 'engaging in competition in the international arena', and the like. The essay ends quite unusually for a text in a Belgrade Museum of Contemporary Art catalogue – with Group 69 expressing satisfaction at being included in 'the working and festive atmosphere of the eleventh Congress of the Communist League of Yugoslavia'.[24]

JD   The essay was most probably written by Kržišnik himself. As far as I understood it, Kržišnik had organised international exhibitions of the artists who were members of Group 69 with the help of our embassies. He was doing all this with the idea of selling graphic arts in diplomatic circles, and graphic arts were well suited to this, because prices for works weren't excessively high. For us, the Ljubljana Biennial was in fact a stronghold of mediocrity.

JV   Who was this 'us'? Who among your colleagues shared such an attitude?

JD   First off, Matko Meštrović. Also Radoslav Putar, who was perhaps the crucial one here, because he belonged to the first post-war generation who began, rather early on, in what is called Aesopian language, to launch precisely this idea of the renewal of modernism on constructivist principles, and to abandon all conservatisms inherited by pre-war bourgeois art, which unfortunately remained relevant on the scene – and remain so even today.

BD   And what was the essence of the dispute between Zoran Pavlović and Miodrag Protić around Group 69?

JD   The Group 69 exhibition in Belgrade was opened by the high-ranking politician Stane Dolanc.[25] This time Protić, as a member of the group, lost his proverbial sense of self-control and caution in his efforts not to become involved in the exhibitions staged in the Museum of Contemporary Art. Otherwise, Protić and Pavlović had a good relationship. They were both artist-intellectuals and they supported each other. But something happened to Pavlović on this occasion, and he published a venomous piece in the weekly magazine *NIN*, where he accused Protić of misusing the institution in order to present this exhibition. Then he raised a big fuss against the Museum, and against the very phenomenon of Group 69. He called it 'a society for social prestige'.[26] Protić was at his wit's end. He hadn't expected this.

BD   So, Protić with all his caution overplayed his hand for the first time?

JD   He didn't expect it. But, then Protić replied in the next issue of *NIN*.[27] He said something to the effect that this was a group of prominent artists who, both as individuals and as a group, had appeared in many exhibitions at home and abroad. So why wouldn't the Museum present these renowned artists whose works are also in the collection? And finally, he said that this exhibition was to be seen as part of the overall programme of the Museum, into which it most certainly fits, and that such an exhibition is intended to inform the art public in Belgrade about a particular prominent phenomenon. This way he somehow restrained Kržišnik's game. All in all, it was a rather skilful reply. And so the issue was concluded. Afterwards, Pavlović and Protić became close again.

BD   How were these goings-on viewed in Slovenia?

JD   There were tensions. For instance: how did the Belgrade Museum of Contemporary Art acquire half of the entire opus of Mario Pregelj? Because Pregelj was in conflict with Kržišnik. Pregelj was a dedicated leftist, a man who spent the war years in a camp, and who established his artistic and social stature on the basis of that experience. For several years, Pregelj was the chairman of the Yugoslav Association of Visual Artists and often came to Belgrade. And Protić considered him to be one of the four greatest Yugoslav modern painters – in accordance with his insistence that great artistic individuals should oppose both political tendencies and ephemeral artistic trends. The line of argument was: no, never again, after Socialist Realism, no tendencies, no trends, only the great artist-individual.

JV   Who were those four painters?

JD   Besides Pregelj there was Stupica – who is indisputably also a great painter for the three of us – and then of course Petar Lubarda and finally Krsto Hegedušić. Hegedušić, but not Tabaković.

JV   As though the four artists were linked through their tendency to make work in large formats, to achieve some painterly monumentality. Tabaković didn't produce large-format work.

JD   True, one might put it like that.

BD   Great artists, large formats.

3.   *Tendencies in Yugoslav Art Today*: Through the Catalogue

BD   The example of the International Biennial of Graphic Arts in Ljubljana, as well as various examples of presenting Yugoslav art abroad, speak clearly of an enlightened cultural politics, but also about petty or large-scale instances of corruption of that same system through the creation of an artistic elite that was close to the political establishment. You have written many essays that unambiguously testify not only to your feelings on art, but also to your critical position as regards the 'mandarin' system of art in Yugoslavia. And yet you have taken part, directly as a curator at the Belgrade Museum of Contemporary Art, in carrying out institutional politics and thus also in presenting Yugoslav art abroad in an official capacity. You have done this in order to promote the artistic mainstream in Yugoslavia, regardless of your personal view of the Art of the Constructive Approach and, in the 1970s, your openly expressed view of the New Art Practices. So let's return now to the exhibition *Tendencies in Yugoslav Art Today* (1978–1980), where you became the curator of a representative manifestation of this type. How did this come about?

JD   As I have already explained, the institutions took over some of the responsibilities of the Federal Committee for Foreign Cultural Relations, but it was through the Committee that these initiatives, on the basis of various bilateral agreements, were realised. According to such agreements the Belgrade Museum of Contemporary Art had the opportunity to organise several exhibitions with Germany; and as for contacts and initial organisation, the mediator was the renowned writer and translator Ivan Ivanji. In fact, the Museum had the opportunity to prepare exhibitions in three very distinguished institutions, which otherwise would not have organised them on any conventional grounds. Simply put, they had their reputations and professional criteria. These were the Museum am Ostwall in Dortmund, the Kunsthalle in Nuremberg, and the Staatliche Museen zu Berlin – Preussischer Kulturbesitz in Berlin.

JV   Are you saying that these institutions had certain professional principles and didn't operate exclusively in the

context of international diplomacy and state channels,
but were dealing with art in an autonomous capacity?

JD   These galleries thought that if they opened the doors
to Yugoslavia they did so out of genuine interest; they
wanted to see what was going on in the country. The same
thing also happened later in our cooperative actions with the
Italian institutions – first of all, there was emerging interest
in a particular artistic value in Yugoslav art, and certainly
there was curiosity about presenting art from a socialist
country. After the initial agreements were made, the Museum
appointed me to organise the exhibition in Germany, and I
was obliged to write the text for the catalogue.[28] In general,
the procedure was rather simple. The Museum engaged one
of its curators to prepare an exhibition that could fit in well
at several large spaces of European institutions – on the
condition that it should take place under the resounding title
Tendencies in Yugoslav Art Today. It was also expected to be
pluralistic in terms of representing the various Yugoslav
cultures, while at the same time singling out specific themes
and underlining specific currents.

JV   Was this written or implied? Were there particular
defined criteria that the Museum was supposed to meet?

JD   It was implied. There were no written documents
outlining the criteria. Our art scene was already considered
to be rich in various artistic solutions and the Museum was
logically entrusted to present this richness professionally and
responsibly. We didn't identify a single tendency that should
be established and stand resolutely behind that. From today's
perspective, all this could be understood as a mega-culture
of modernism that was both official and considerably open.
But in those days the task of such an ambitious exhibition
in such important venues would have been to provide a single
comprehensive view of the scene, with all its specificities,
particularities and contradictions. Therefore, we couldn't
have just a single phenomenon analysed according to the
individual taste of some critic; instead, the implied task was
to present a range of different phenomena. In contrast to
the Gallery of Contemporary Art in Zagreb which, through
organising the New Tendencies exhibitions, had already

resolved to follow Neo-Constructivism, a more radical type of modernism, the Belgrade Museum of Contemporary Art had to commit itself to a different path. The exhibition *Tendencies in Yugoslav Art Today* had to be constituted out of different languages of art, of different generations of artists and from various milieus. Today, we can say that these exhibitions were subject to quotas from among the republics in the Yugoslav federation, so you had to steer a middle course; namely, there had to be one Slovenian, then one Croat, then one Bosnian, then one Serb, etcetera. This exhibition avoided such a drastic profile, but the complexity of the very notion of Yugoslav art was implicitly presented in it.

JV   We have the exhibition catalogue here in front of us. Your introductory essay is followed by pages showing the artists' works, which are ordered neither chronologically nor alphabetically, but according to your curatorial concept.

JD   I begin with Marino Tartalja, who is one of the interwar artists and goes through an incredible post-war transformation. Gorgona also refers to him. Now, as you see Petar Lubarda is not here as the artist who was exceedingly present and received all kinds of local awards. Instead, I begin here with Tartalja, and with a different notion of the landscape.

BD   So, the idea is that the exhibition speaks about an historical development through a roughly chronological sequence of works from the 1950s onwards. But there are some near-heretical incursions into the usual narrative, bearing in mind that only Stupica, out of Protić's 'four great artists', is included in the show.

JD   Yes, neither Hegedušić nor Pregelj were there.

BD   On the pages following Tartalja and Gliha we have paintings that we might include in the currents of gestural abstraction and Art Informel from the late 1950s and early 1960s.

JD   These works indicate certain relations to Abstract Expressionism and organic abstraction. For example, there is a lot of influence of Wols in the work of Ordan Petlevski. The next one is Bata Mihailović, and then Zlatko Prica and Edo Murtić. But let's recall that the latter two created a lithographic map *The Pit* (1944) on the basis of Ivan Goran Kovačić's poetry about the horrible atrocities of the fascists, which had already been published during the war. Murtić and Prica served in Partisan units; and what I indicate here is the way that as respected combatants in the 1950s they now make modernist abstractions. It was important to exhibit such figures.

BD   But there follows an interesting juxtaposition. On the left side there is Mića Popović, about whom we talked earlier – and you see, you included him in this show! Popović is a protagonist of, let's say, a moderate Serbian-national orientation, and on the right side there is an Albanian artist from Kosovo, Xhevdet Xhafa.

JD   Yes, Xhevdet Xhafa was a well-respected artist in those days. I would not have simply included him in order to fulfil the quota because he was from Kosovo, where the art scene was less developed back then, but because he was a very interesting artist who made collages out of textiles. Next to Xhafa's soft materials there is Mića Popović, who worked with sheet metal.

BD   As we've already discussed, you weren't interested in national-cultural identity, but in material practices. So, this match is about a historical-material encounter, between fabrics and sheet metal. Popović's artwork here is representative of his Informel phase of the early 1960s.

JD   This painting is in the Belgrade Museum of Contemporary Art Collection. A large part of the painting is a metal sheet taken from a barrel that he ripped. In a certain way this was a very courageous painting for the standards of the time and place.

BD   After him follow Bernik and Ivačković, who convert some seemingly free painterly strokes into a form of 'graphism'. Which in turn leads you into the segment that deals with graphic arts. Before anything else, there are those artists we've linked with the Ljubljana Biennial and, in general, with the Ljubljana Graphic Arts School.

JD   Yes, here we find one part of the Ljubljana Graphic Arts School, with Riko Debenjak and Andrej Jemec; and then another section that deals with the representation of objects, with Bogdan Borčič and Adriana Maraž. On the next two pages are artists from Bosnia-Herzegovina, who were also educated in Ljubljana, like Dževad Hozo, who developed various manual graphic techniques and dubbed his works 'multi-originals'. This is an expression or result of that dominant idea about the uniqueness of the graphic arts craft that I have criticised; but on this occasion of such broad representation, I certainly had to include it as one of the tendencies. Hozo was Debenjak's student – like Borislav Aleksić next to him. And then there is a drawing by Virgilije Nevjestić, who lived in Paris and who was also a noteworthy artist from Bosnia-Herzegovina, followed by a work by Mehmed Zaimović, also from Sarajevo.

JV   You clearly take into account two criteria established by Protić in those decennial exhibitions at the Museum of Contemporary Art in Belgrade – the exhibitions of *Yugoslav Art of the 20th Century*. Alongside national and republican representation, there is a clear division in terms of artistic media, the way the Museum's collections were created. After graphic arts there is a section on sculpture. Here you begin with Kosta Angeli Radovani.

JD   This bronze sculpture of his is from the beginning of the 1960s. I wrote about him in my first essay for the journal *Umetnost* (*Art*). He was a student of Marino Marini, the Italian sculptor whose work represented a reaching back to the Etruscan tradition. Radovani created a specific style of reduced figuration with these swollen forms. Then come two powerful figures who made their reputation in the 1950s, Olga Jevrić and Dušan Džamonja. Džamonja's work is made of iron, while next to it is the work of Jagoda Buić, who worked with textiles. Jagoda revolutionised our understanding of tapestry and became internationally renowned, exhibiting in Amsterdam's Stedelijk Museum, where her work was purchased for their collection. She didn't work on cardboard; instead, she and her co-workers wove these fabrics three-dimensionally. Even more famous was the Polish artist Magdalena Abakanowicz; and the two of them were behind those woven sculptures that were known as Fibre Art.

JV   The catalogue employs a classification scheme according to materials and follows with sculptures in wood.

JD   It was rather a diverse range of work, with Šime Vulas and Branko Ružić, followed by metal sculptures by Stevan Luketić, Petar Hadži-Boškov, France Rotar and Oto Logo.

JV   As we see, you followed a specific line – representing a certain phenomenon that emerges in a certain context, which is then transferred to another. Precisely through such a juxtaposition of artists, you demonstrated the material connections inherent in the artistic tendencies of the Yugoslav space.

JD   Let's take Stevan Luketić. He was a Montenegrin who lived in Zagreb and made a lot of monuments in Croatia. Some of these monuments were destroyed during the war of the 1990s, because he was of non-Croatian origin and had a Partisan past. He made sculptures out of waste metal – car radiators, wheels and similar. He was working in the very in vogue style of 'junk sculpture'. These were abstract forms with unusually treated surfaces. He, as well as Petar Hadži-Boškov, made work by pressing hard materials. Luketić found pieces in the junkyard and welded them together. Such techniques represented various micro-tendencies in the circles in which these artists appeared. What follows in the catalogue are some 'mechano-forms' that do not consist of junk, but are cast in bronze, by Oto Logo and France Rotar. Here we have a sculpture by an artist who was connected with the Zagreb School of Animation, Zvonimir Lončarić. He directed a few animated films and appeared in many as a background painter, including the animated film *Ersatz* by Dušan Vukotić, which won an Oscar in 1962. It takes the form of figuration with a bit of humour, as is also the case with Vasko Lipovac, an artist from Montenegro.

BD   All in all, these artists represent this very developed culture of 'high modernism'. In the catalogue we come back to painting, but this time with figural motifs. Here are two emblematic paintings by Gabrijel Stupica and Radomir Reljić, which make for an unusual juxtaposition.

JD   They are artists of different generations, but the treatment of the figure drowned in signs is common to both.

BD   And after that are those artists who would be closest in terms of tendency to Mediala, even though there is no Mediala here, nor is there any Šejka either. Here is a graphic print by Dado Đurić and a painting by Vladimir Veličković. On the next page is Dušan Otašević, whose work provides a remarkable bridge or link to Pop art. And here we have a serigraphy by Zmago Jeraj.

JV   And then there are the photorealists. This would appear to have been a significant trend in the mid-1970s.

JD   Herman Gvardijančić and Boris Jesih. They exhibited at the Venice Biennale in 1976, when Putar served as commissioner.

BD   On the next page, we suddenly turn back, in terms of chronology. Here are two paintings from the 1960s by Tabaković and Ćelić. Are these different instances of geometric abstraction?

JD   Yes, and they are followed by Miodrag Protić, and next to him Tanas Lulovski, a Macedonian painter. These types of abstraction lead us to Dušan Perčinkov and Miroslav Šutej, who was working on a type of 'mobile graphic art'. Back then he was seen as belonging to Op art. After that is the sculpture *Svjetlonosne forme* (*Light-Bearing Forms*) by Vojin Bakić, and a work by Aleksandar Srnec, and here the selection becomes radicalised in a way that was closest to me, as represented by Picelj and Richter. These are those structural 'micro-units' of theirs. Here there is no longer any sense of the ideology of sculptural composition, as in their previous work in sculpture; instead of composition, at issue are structures that consist of identical elements organised according to a particular system in order to construct a form. Everything is based on the principle of the structural order of equivalent building blocks as modules organised according to a precise numerical programme.

BD   And here follows what we could point to as something related to American Minimal art: objects in plexiglass by Vasa Mihić.

JD   These smooth and glazed forms were not common in Yugoslav art. Vasa Mihić had already lived in the USA and had some contact or relationship with Californian Minimal art. These are flawless forms made using new technological means and synthetic materials. This shows how an artist who was no longer living in Yugoslavia developed in relation to Western artistic trends. Next to him is Mladen Galić, who also produced these smooth forms, but this was made in metal. He was an exceptionally important graphic designer. Then, in this context we can go on to look at the graphic art of Juraj Dobrović and Eugen Feller. Feller was an autodidact, and for me an exceptionally important artist. On the following page you see these forms made of plastic, then pressed, which was done by Ljerka Šibenik. She took a surface with plastic on it, and then pressed reliefs into it. Or, for instance, this work called *Aquamobil* (1968, *Aqua Mobile*) by Slavko Tihec, which we can call Kinetic art. He fills the container with water and connects it to an electric power source, and the electricity produces waves that make continuous concentric circles on the water surface.

JV   Which leads us to Lumino-Kinetic and Computer art, and to the last part of the exhibition, which indicates well your particular critical preferences.

JD   These lumino-kinetic objects were made by Koloman Novak. His work here is in the collection of the Belgrade Museum of Contemporary Art. On the next page is Vladimir Bonačić, about whose significance we've already talked – and here we can see his connection with the New Tendencies. Then, Zoran Radović's electronic 'ornamentograph' from 1970, which is in fact an oscilloscope that creates specific forms. On the other side of the spread is

Vilko Žiljak, who was involved with computer generated graphic art. He was an engineer and wasn't active as an artist at all, nor did he study art or actually even exhibit his work.

BD   And then come Damnjan and Knifer, which again may seem an unusual connection at first glance.

JD   Only seemingly. Damnjan was the only Belgrade artist invited to exhibit with the Gorgonists way back in 1962. Back then, Matko Meštrović had written a short essay in which he wrote about how he saw a break in this work in relation to existential depression and the nihilism of Art Informel.[29] We've already talked about the connections between artists from Zagreb and Belgrade, and this was a significant one.

BD   Now follow two other Gorgonists, Sedar and Vaništa.

JD   This is Vaništa's seminal painting, which ended up in the Museum, and boasts that famous formula for the way it was made — a silver line of a certain thickness drawn horizontally in the middle of the painting. Which is how Vaništa arrived at his great reduction, at emptiness.

BD   On the following page we see the work of the graphic designer and typographer Mihajlo Arsovski. This serigraph is a variation on the letter 'a'. This reduction to a single letter may be similar to Vaništa's reduction to a single line. But, also Arsovski may be considered one of the key graphic designers of the 1960s and 1970s. Koščević said about him that he invented entirely unexpected tangles of consonants and vowels, words that only after optical identification become the meaning, the information. Which is why a graphic designer is included in such a representational survey of art.

JD   And then we have Josip Stošić with his spatial-verbal structures from 1972. These are words that he or someone else can combine and arrive at new combinations to form a kind of poetry. So, Stošić is a poet, Arsovski is a designer and Žiljak is an engineer — and here they are all introduced in the context of institutional art.

BD   And finally, another Gorgonist, Ivan Kožarić, who here apparently has the role of marking the transition to Conceptual art, because on the next page there is the project of the OHO group with Walter de Maria.

JD   Yes, Kožarić. I found it interesting that this is actually a sculpture and not a painting, even though it is a canvas hanging on the wall. Not only is this a sculpture, but it is a sculpture that can be hung on a wall as a two-dimensional surface. If we understand it in this way, we see that it is a conceptual approach. But there's an interesting story attached to this piece in the context of this exhibition.

BD   We're listening!

JD   After the exhibition finally returned to the Museum, I got a phone call from one of the technicians who were unpacking the trunks. He told me that all the works had come back except one piece by Kožarić that was on the list but was not in the trunk. Of course that was a very unpleasant situation, because we had borrowed it from the artist and the work was not owned by the Museum. Protić was really angry. But after a couple of days he relaxed a little and asked me to come to his office. He told me to go to Zagreb and visit Kožarić, and arrange with him an acquisition by the Museum of one of his representative works – and that this lost piece we had exhibited in *Tendencies in Yugoslav Art Today* was to be reckoned as his gift. That's how the Museum purchased that famous black sphere by Kožarić. In the meantime, the sheet of paper was found in the packaging in which the exhibition was shipped from Italy. It seems it was used to wrap one of the sculptures. [Laughs.]

BD   This issue of recognising and codifying something as art, and this counter-system ethos of Kožarić's, and generally of Gorgona's – which has enormous importance for your understanding of art in its 'other-lineish' continuity – leads us to the presentation of conceptualism in the exhibition *Tendencies in Yugoslav Art Today*.

JD   First, four well-known photographs present the work of the OHO group with Walter de Maria. Then the works

of Goran Trbuljak and Braco Dimitrijević, who were close
at the time. By the end of the 1960s they had formed one
of the first groups of the New Art Practices in Yugoslavia,
the group Pensioner Tihomir Simčić. After them are the
works of artists who gathered at the Student Cultural Centre
Gallery in Belgrade: *Aksiomi* (1971–1973, *Axioms*) by Zoran
Popović, the series of self-portraits by Neša Paripović
in front of a blank sheet of paper, and photographs of the
performance *Art Must Be Beautiful, Artist Must Be Beautiful*
(1975) by Marina Abramović. Next to her is Bálint Szombathy,
as part of the Subotica conceptual scene that emerged very
early with the Bosch+Bosch group. The work featuring a
xerox of a watch ticking is Gergely Urkom's, followed
immediately by Raša Todosijević. First is his photograph of
a single line that he drew in a small private space – one
small insignificant line. In the second photograph is a work
exhibited at the Paris Biennial in 1971 – *300,000 Lines* – a
large manifestation, and therefore more lines! And finally,
conceptual text works by Vladimir Kopicl and Goran
Đorđević, which now take us into radical analytical conceptualism. It ends with a work by Vladan Radovanović, a
photograph of photographic paper developed on this same
photographic paper. Kožarić and Radovanović, as artists of
the older generation, appear here next to those who belong
to the time of the New Art Practices, which looks like they
provided a certain framework for the most radical tendencies
expressed in the exhibition. All of this passed the verification
process of the Federal Committee for Foreign Cultural
Relations without any objections. And we made a spectacular
selection.

BD   What is your view of this exhibition today?

JD   Bearing in mind the context and the background,
I'd say that I acted as a curator who wanted to map various
phenomena in various milieus, regardless of how fond I
was of each and every one of them. I acted as a curator who
has both a very particular interest and the professional
opportunity to recognise the problems these artists were
dealing with, in their circles and in their positions. I selected
a larger number of artists of different generations, but
I didn't ultimately manage to escape my own position either,

since almost half of the exhibition was inherited from
EXAT 51, Gorgona and the New Art Practices, that is to say:
the Other Line.

JV   I would suggest that unlike the concept of great
artists and master classes characteristic of the 1950s and
1960s, the corpus of Yugoslav art now came to embrace
artworks that were linked with the micro-policies of alternative institutional spaces. These are younger artists, most
often people from the margins; they are no longer 'local
greats' but represent other positions that inherited a critical
view of the cultural mainstream, not only in Yugoslavia, but
also in a far wider context. Behind these positions are
alternative student organisations, such as Gallery Nova and
the Student Centre in Zagreb, the Student Cultural Centre
in Belgrade, the Youth Forum (Tribina mladih) in Novi Sad
and the like.

JD   *Tendencies in Yugoslav Art Today* implied a far broader
spectrum of art and many positions that were quite distant
from the art policies of these Student Centres, but one
could say that the novelty in representing Yugoslav art was
that the language of the Other Line, and thereby also of
the New Art Practices, here became part of a comprehensive
institutional survey of Yugoslav art.

4.   Exhibition Production and Intra-Institutional
        Matters

JV   We are also interested in the material structure of
the exhibition, in the process of making. How did the process
of communication unfold between the Belgrade Museum
of Contemporary Art and the Federal Committee for Foreign
Cultural Relations, between the curator, the artists and the
international institutions?

JD   The majority of the works had already been acquired
by the Museum, and if something needed to be borrowed
from the artists, we had to tell them that the works would be
on loan for more than a year, until the entire international
tour was over. That could have created an unfair situation for

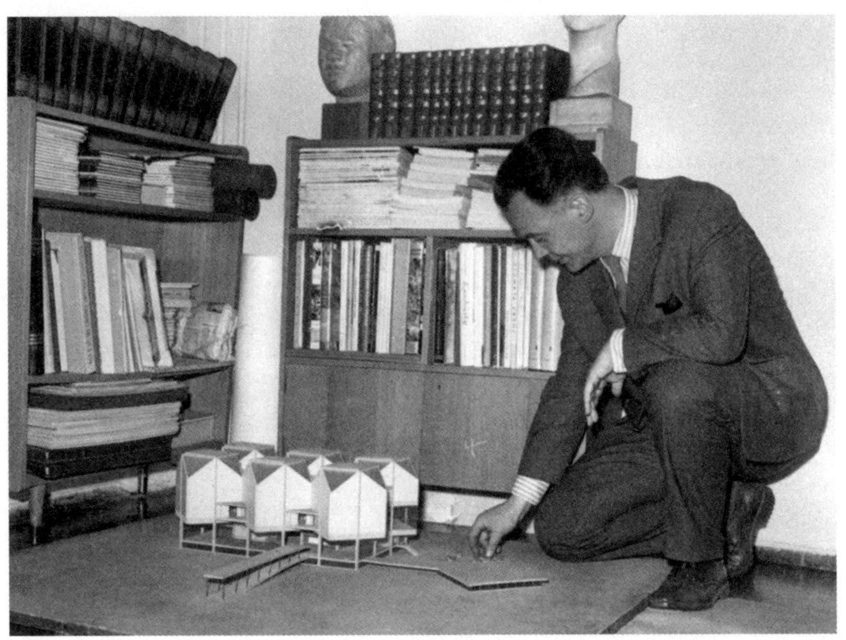

Miodrag Protić with a model for the Muzej savremene umetnosti (Museum of Contemporary Art) designed by Ivan Antić and Ivanka Raspopović and inaugurated in 1965, Belgrade, 1962

those artists who were not in the collection and so would be
lending their works, so there were initiatives launched to
purchase such works. Which was a good plan. However, the
funds available were rather modest, basically not enough
to cover the required costs. On that occasion, the Museum
purchased Braco Dimitrijević's *Looking for: Tiziano Vecellio-
Siro de Polo* from 1975, which is reproduced here in the
catalogue.

BD   That was the first work of its kind that I ever saw,
and it was in the Museum when I was there as a teenager
with my school, in the early 1980s. And you were the curator
who gave us a talk about that particular work. But to return
to the exhibition, you used this high-profile project to
initiate acquisitions of conceptual works. We should point
out, however, that apart from the acquisitions made during
your time there, and most considerably again in the early
2000s, the Museum does not have a significant number of
works from the New Art Practices period, especially compared to the thousands of other works in the collection.

JD   Yes, that's true. For example, this work by Gergely
Urkom from 1971, *Six Minutes of the Hour as Recorded by Xerox,*
was the first work of the New Art Practices purchased by
the Museum. And there emerged a little problem with my
colleague, who was the head of the Graphic Arts Collection
in which this work was to be included. She said: 'that work
will fade and may vanish entirely one day, and I wouldn't
want it to be in my collection, because it could happen that
after a few years the Museum's inspection committee comes
and asks to see the work, and there is no work because it
has vanished irreparably'. So there were various doubts
expressed as to whether this was an artwork at all, and so on.
But the Museum invested in order to purchase what was not
yet part of the collection.

JV   Were there any negotiations regarding what would be
purchased from the exhibition? It would be interesting to
find out what was not purchased.

JD   I wouldn't know the details – whether for instance
this work by Goran Đorđević was purchased, that should be

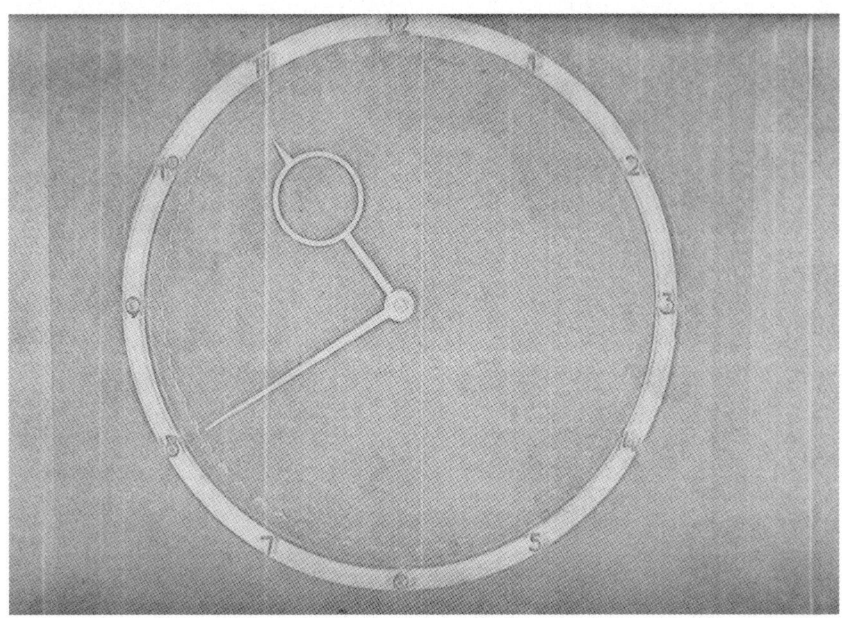

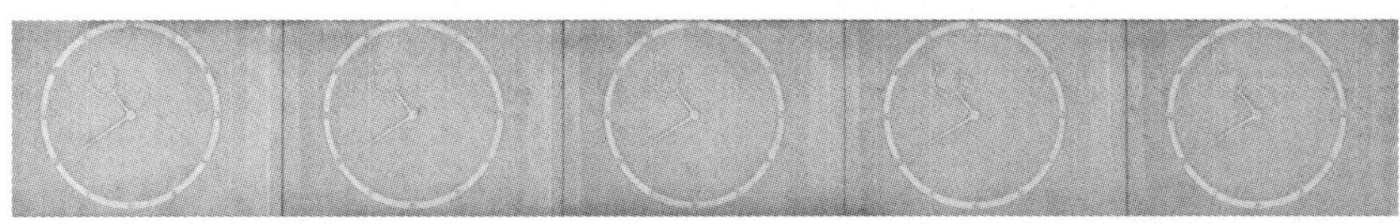

Gergely Urkom
Šest minuta sata snimljeno Xeroxom (Six Minutes of the Hour as Recorded by Xerox), 1971
Xerox paper, 20 pieces, each 21 × 29 cm; bottom: detail

checked from the archive.[30] But what was quite exceptional was the fact that Protić pretty much gave me carte blanche to do this. As was the fact that he, as a director, legitimised this kind of exhibition, regardless of how it may look now – either as a kind of grand compromise or as an audacious institutional gesture. The exhibition was backed up by the Museum and was entrusted to a curator to think it through as a whole. It was not conceived in terms of some bureaucratised institutionalism, in accordance with the specific interests of particular departments. The authorship of the exhibition was entrusted to a single curator.

JV   And how is this single curator, the one entrusted with the authorship of such a representation, delegated? How was your exhibition concept disseminated or communicated through the institution?

JD   It was communicated the same way I just demonstrated by going through the catalogue. Back then there were no computers. I presented each particular work and the exhibition as a whole to the Museum's Curatorial Council. I had to demonstrate my concept to all the curators and the director. And I had to tell them that this would not be ordered alphabetically or chronologically, but according to the concept of the exhibition, which starts with Tartalja and ends with Vladan Radovanović. And the Curatorial Council of the Museum agreed that I would work autonomously with this concept – within the framework of the institution of course. Not a single colleague, including Protić himself, told me: 'you can't do this like that'. The institution stood behind the exhibition. Not only that, but it stood behind the curator who was, to a great extent, the author of the exhibition. The Museum was a complex institution, and other curators were in charge of other projects. And it had operative departments that prepared documentation, set the budget, and sent the project to the Federal Committee for Foreign Cultural Relations and wherever else it was needed.

JV   You explained the concept by means of photographs and an oral presentation of the ideas. Did you have to write a text, what we call today a 'curatorial proposal', an essay that briefly introduces the concept of the exhibition?

JD   The essay for the exhibition was written subsequently for the catalogue.[31] At the meeting of the Museum's Curatorial Council I presented the concept, showed the images, and then a conversation among us followed. Every crucial decision was made at a meeting like this, which had the character of a public hearing. It was not a closed or private agreement with the director or anything like that. A meeting of the Curatorial Council entailed taking minutes of the proceedings during the meeting, and what was recorded had to be verified and updated if necessary by all the members of the Council, and then this procedural protocol would remain in the Museum as a document.

JV   What happens in terms of the curator's regular work? Who is in charge of taking care of the collections in the case of extensive project-based work?

JD   When a curator was tasked with something like that, they did not have to deal with anything else, only with the current assignment at hand. I did not participate in other colleagues' projects, just as they didn't get involved in what I was doing. When I received the mandate to prepare the exhibition *Tendencies in Yugoslav Art Today*, I only worked on that. There was also an aspect of my work that was far less romantic, related to the organisation of packing, transport, insurance and the like.

BD   All of that fell to you?

JD   For Dortmund, only one technician and I ended up travelling there. Protić came for the opening. Ljiljana Simić helped me and travelled to Berlin and Nuremberg, because she was the curator in charge of international relations at the Museum. She knew English very well and I didn't.

BD   She had the very important role of arranging and organising the Museum's international exchange during the 1970s and 1980s. I must add that I knew her personally; my parents were close friends with her and her husband Dušan Simić, who was a well-known journalist, editor and international correspondent. I was 16 years old when she brought me to the Museum on the occasion of the retrospective exhibition of Robert Smithson held there – in 1983 no less! The exhibition was an example of the Museum's international programme, and I must say that this exhibition changed my life.

JD   Ljiljana and I had a very good relationship and worked well together – the Smithson exhibition that you mention is one of the examples of this excellent collaboration. We took *Tendencies in Yugoslav Art Today* further on to Luxembourg and Belgium, and so new catalogues were published. I went to Luxembourg where the exhibition was hung in the foyer of an important theatre, and in Brussels it was held in the Musées Royaux des Beaux-Arts. So this exhibition visited very important centres and finished up in Rome and Genoa.

JV   What did the process of installing the show in all these spaces look like? Did you receive the floor plans in advance, or did you just take the works with you and decide how to hang them on the spot?

JD   I cannot recall, but it was a huge exhibition, and some artworks were enormous – in the catalogue you saw the dimensions of those paintings. The paintings by Damnjan, for example, and Veličković's painting, they were monumental, not to mention Jevrić's sculptures. We hefted a lot of heavy stuff. As for the setting, there was no virtual planning of the installation. I'd have to say that today exhibitions are designed and set up far more professionally, together with many more details and requirements. Back then we managed to do something, but no one knows quite how. The gallery in Dortmund was a very serious and spacious gallery, but it could not stage the exhibition the way it was conceived, bearing in mind the size of the works and the space required between them. It simply could not accommodate such a vast amount of material.

BD   So you basically adjusted the exhibition to the space on the spot and improvised, and the exhibition was adjusted to the programmes that came out of the new cooperation and interstate agreements – in this case exclusively with Western European countries.

JD   When Yugoslavia ratified the convention on cultural
cooperation with Italy, we received an exhibition of Italian
art that came to the Modern Gallery in Rijeka.[32] The issue
of a reciprocal exhibition arose, and we tried to respond
with this exhibition. Comune di Lazio was hosting us, and
they showed me a couple of spaces they were planning for
exhibitions. One palace, Palazzo Braschi, was particularly
striking. It had a classical spatial arrangement, but the space
was not large enough to accommodate our exhibition. And
what was the curator's job in this case? First of all, I had
to go to the Yugoslav Embassy – in those days Borisav Jović
was the ambassador[33] – and there was a cultural attaché
who was helping me, as it were. So our exhibition was much
larger than the spaces that we were offered, and I had to
get in touch with our state representatives and tell them that
we were being offered inadequate spaces, while our Italian
colleagues thought they were offering us extraordinary
spaces. True, Palazzo Braschi enjoyed a very good reputation,
but it was small for this type of setting, with low ceilings.
And suddenly, regardless of all the state agreements,
institutions, regulations, everything came to a halt there.
In the meantime, we tried, through our attaché, to get the
Galleria Comunale d'Arte Moderna as a space, but it was
an autonomous organisation and they did not want to have
the exhibition. Meanwhile, that same year, in 1977, the
exhibition entitled *Beograd '77* (*Belgrade '77*) was held at the
Belgrade Museum of Contemporary Art. It was a multi-
perspective selection of artists from various countries
prepared by curators from a host of international museums,
and had an important political dimension, as it was staged
on the occasion of the OSCE (Organization for Security and
Cooperation Europe) Conference that was taking place in
Belgrade.[34] The curator of the Galleria Nazionale d'Arte
Moderna in Rome, Pia Vivarelli, was present for the opening,
and she brought Michelangelo Pistoletto, Michele Zaza
and Valentino Vago as the Italian representatives. The major
sensation at the exhibition was Willem de Kooning, whose
works were being shown again in European museums after a
break of some time – and here his work served to represent
the USA in Belgrade. Pia Vivarelli was impressed with all
this, and she recommended us to the director of the Galleria
Comunale d'Arte Moderna to accept our exhibition. Which

was a significant step, and finally we installed our exhibition in that space. I used some time during the installation process to visit Argan in order to resolve definitively the catalogue we were just thumbing through. Just to remind you, Argan was the mayor of Rome at the time.

JV   Did Argan come to the opening?

JD   No.

JV   Did the local press, international or domestic, publish anything about the exhibition *Tendencies in Yugoslav Art Today*?

JD   Some articles were written in Germany, because Protić came for the opening, and I remember seeing a photograph of him with the director of the Dortmund Gallery in the paper. There might have been a paper or two, but the practice of reviewing foreign exhibitions abroad was not common in newspapers – regardless of the fact that this exhibition was the most ambitious and most representative exhibition of Yugoslav art internationally.

JV   Do you recall any similar exhibitions?

JD   I remember the exhibition that the Zagreb Gallery of Contemporary Art staged in Vienna a couple of years previously, which was good – inspiring.[35] It was put together by Matko Meštrović. And of course there were graphic arts exhibitions that were circulating in various places, especially in non-European countries. I think that *Tendencies in Yugoslav Art Today* was the biggest project of its kind.

JV   The budgets for events related to international cooperation were always guaranteed – they were provided by the state. As a curator did you have to get involved in additional fundraising, as is the case today?

JD   The Federal Committee for Foreign Cultural Relations, besides bearing the organisational costs, also provided some kind of honorarium for the institution. We had to outline the various necessary expenses, and our colleague Marija Pušić, who became the director of the Museum when

Protić left in 1980, was very skilful in putting together such preliminary calculations. She always took the trouble to secure a 25% reduction of the total sum of the project, and then this bonus could be turned into a so-called thirteenth salary, which was a legitimate profit for the Museum. Why did we have three master craftsmen in the carpenters' workshop, and a fully equipped photographer and the like? In order to make crates and the rest of the exhibition material directly in the Museum, so that the work could be listed as an expense. Although there were situations when we did certain things 'guerrilla style' – for instance we tried to recycle and repair old or damaged crates and the like.

JV Protić also took part in the exhibition *Tendencies in Yugoslav Art Today*. Was that considered a conflict of interest?

JD I included Protić in this exhibition. He nodded his head reluctantly; on the one hand he was pleased, but on the other he was the head of the Museum. And it was always a delicate issue that stood between him and the institution. He kept his distance so it would not become a subject of public discussion in the media or other institutions – I told you about the case of Group 69. But Protić deserved to be at that exhibition; he had a good reputation as an artist. I can confidently say that his type of painting was consistent with the concept of the exhibition.

BD The most interesting thing in relation to Protić is the fact that he agreed to be included in the exhibition, which demonstrated an artistic trajectory that he could no longer control. You included him in the narrative, but the outcome of the narrative was no longer subject to his influence. As the director of the institution, he lent legitimacy to such a narrative. Someone else from his generation, from those circles in Belgrade, would not have allowed such things, would have prevented something like that.

JD Protić stood behind these events in every respect. He believed that the Museum should work well and work honestly, that a curator should be professional, and that they must have free hands, and not to be restrained by any institutional hierarchy. Moreover, he also helped me to secure a scholarship in the late 1960s, and believed that curators had to keep informed and abreast of trends and developments in art, at home as well as abroad.

JV   Protić stepped out of the usual cultural routine of competition, infighting and gossip, and acted with an incredible measure of official decorum and formality for the Belgrade context. We could also call it a Constructive Approach. He really was a true modernist.

BD   And importantly, he didn't yield to the nationalism to which his generation of bourgeois intellectuals largely succumbed. Just as a reminder, he was a member of the Yugoslav Academy of Sciences and Arts in Zagreb (JAZU), and not a member of the Serbian Academy of Sciences and Arts (SANU), which is a rather symptomatic fact.

JD   Yes, he was a member of JAZU and not SANU – all of the local evil-doers considered him a Yugoslav and prevented him entering the SANU. The fact that Protić didn't become a member of the Serbian Academy is the biggest disgrace ever to tarnish Serbian culture. Because not only is he a significant painter, he is also the originator of the Museum, the author of seminal books, and in view of such qualities and accomplishments he should have been a member of such an institution. However, he was rejected three times.

BD   And he neither joined the nationalist dissidents nor was he a member of the Communist Party. He initiated and founded the Belgrade Museum of Contemporary Art without being a Party member.

JV   That's why his attitude was important in the context of art. It enabled him, during the liberalisation of socialism at the end of the 1950s and the early 1960s, to become a respectable figure, to occupy a position in which he could advocate for the autonomy of artists and curators; to work hard, together with other cultural institutions; to cultivate a certain prestige for Yugoslav art at home and abroad. It is obvious that Protić was a figure who, through his work and character, legitimised the values of Yugoslav socialism in its developed phase.

JD   I was invited to write a monograph about Protić,
and it was rather a delicate task for me.[36] Protić was three
distinct things: a painter, a writer and a manager – the
founding director of the Belgrade Museum of Contemporary
Art who served in that capacity until 1980. So I had to find
a way not to deal in parts with such a figure and such an
opus, which developed across three extensive yet distinct
segments, but to find an interaction between all these
functions within the matrix of an enlightened modernism.
Because everything Protić paints is compatible with what
he writes. His painting has in some way this formal treatment
of the text, this pure and clear articulation. The configuration of the Museum building is almost compatible with his
opus.

JV   Museum cubes. It looks like Protić is painting the
Museum or vice versa.

JD   He is a person whose activities, although seemingly
divided into three different sectors, are integrated with the
same ideological-professional code. He's always operating
within the frame of high modernism in all that he does.
And it is international in terms of the extent to which he
understood these matters: just as he was not inclined to the
New Art Practices, he was also not inclined to the New
Tendencies – for him, this was simply too radical. His type
of geometry and his understanding of a painting implied
some notion of a semantic key, meaning that the painting,
even when geometrically reduced, has to be inclined towards
some object. But the painting may also be pure structure,
and there is a limit, where he comes to a halt before the
forms of Gorgona or the New Tendencies. Protić couldn't
comprehend the idea that a painting might be a single line,
the way Vaništa could draw it. However, he very much
supported various tendencies; he could separate his affinities
and inclinations without creating any impediments to his
appreciation or understanding of them, regardless of
whether they were consistent with his thinking.

JV   Can we sum up what people held against Protić
within the circles of experts in Belgrade, in Serbia and in
Yugoslavia? Let me start: his bureaucratic spirit, his cold

and rational style of painting, his Yugoslavism, his authoritarianism … But, above and beyond all, his modernism and progressivism. The latter are well epitomised in Ivo Andrić's comments at the opening of the Museum in 1965.[37]

BD   This anecdote can also be found in his memoirs.[38] At the opening ceremony of the Museum, in the course of looking around this new modern space, Andrić – the most respected writer and already a Nobel prize winner – approaches Protić and, after congratulating him, says that he feels sorry for him. Protić asks him: 'Comrade Andrić, is everything all right? Is there something you don't like – the way the Museum is built, the way everything looks?' And Andrić tells him: 'No, I like it, everything is done very nicely, I have seen exceptional artworks in an extraordinary building.' And Protić asks him: 'But why do you feel sorry for me?' Andrić replies: 'Well, many people will resent this. Because this does not belong to our environment. This has nothing to do with us. All of these modern forms, this progressive concept, this is not us.'

JV   Who is this 'us'?

BD   'Us' is the sum of the people who live here and to whom these ideas were somehow alien. Let's go back to Argan. Andrić states that there exists an unchangeable 'destiny' that will eventually prevail over Protić's 'project'.

[1] The points of this critique were given in an extremely condensed way in the counter-exhibition project *Oktobar 75* (*October 75*), initiated by Dunja Blažević. See Jelena Vesić, '*Oktobar 75*–An Example of Counter-Exhibition (Statements on Artistic Autonomy, Self-management and Self-critique)', available on http://tranzit.org/exhibitionarchive/oktobar-1975 (last accessed May 2024).

[2] Ješa Denegri, 'Some New Artistic Attitudes in Socialist Societies', in *10ᵉ biennale de Paris*, exh. cat., Paris 1977, p. 39–44. See p. 90–98.

[3] The exhibition was held in Germany, France and Italy, and had separate catalogues in all three languages. The first was made for the German exhibition under the title *Tendenzen in der Jugoslawishen Kunst von Heute*, Museum am Ostwall, Dortmund, Staatliche Museen zu Berlin – Preussischer Kulturbesitz, Berlin and Kunstalle Nurnberg, Nuremberg, in 1978–1979.

[4] *Contemporary Yugoslav Painting and Sculpture*, Arts Council and the Tate Gallery, London 1961. Zoran Kržišnik, curator of the Modern Gallery in Ljubljana, curated the exhibition and wrote the catalogue's introductory essay.

[5] Zoran Kržišnik, 'Introduction', ibid.

[6] Marko Ristić, 'Govor na otvaranju izložbe "Savremena umetnost u SAD"', *Međunarodna Politika* (*International Politics*), Belgrade, 10 July, 1956.

[7] On this exhibition, see Branislav Dimitrijević, 'Iron Curtain Raisers – An Exhibition of American Modern Art in Belgrade and its Relation to Socialist Modernism and Socialist Consumerism in the SFR Yugoslavia in the 1950s', in *Different Modernisms, Different Avant-Gardes – Problems in Central and Eastern European Art after World War II*, Eesti Kunstimuuseum, Tallinn 2009, p. 313–342.

[8] Grgo Gamulin, 'Retrospektive s XXIV biennala,' *Umetnost*, no. 1, 1949.

[9] See Ješa Denegri, 'Bijenale u Veneciji i jugoslavenska moderna umjetnost 1895–1988. Galerija suvremene umjetnosti, Zagreb, lipanj-srpanj 1988' ('Biennale in Venice and Yugoslav Modern Art 1895–1988. Gallery of Contemporary Art, Zagreb, June–July 1988'), available on https://www.ipu.hr/content/zivot-umjetnosti/ ZU_45-46-1989_132-135_Denegri.pdf (last accessed May 2024).

[10] Želimir Koščević, *Venecijanski biennale i jugoslavenska moderna umjetnost: 1895–1988* (*Venice Biennale and Yugoslav Modern Art: 1895–1988*), 12 October 1975, hectographed volume with essays by artists, critics and curators gathered around the Student Cultural Centre, Belgrade 1975, SKC Archive.

[11] Ješa Denegri, 'Jezik umetnosti i sistem umetnosti' ('The Language of Art and the System of Art'), *Oktobar 75*, Student Cultural Centre, Belgrade 1975. See p. 196–202.

[12] Ibid.

[13] Most of the conversation with Professor Denegri that was edited for this publication was held at the extra-territory that is Filo Filipović's summer house. Filipović was active as an artist in the Yugoslav Art Space and internationally from the early 1950s until his death in 1997. The editors are grateful to Mrs. Dušanka Filipović, who kindly supported these conversations by making the house available for the editorial team's stay there.

[14] Denegri refers to Breda Škrjanec, *Zgodovina grafičnih bienalov* (*History of the Graphics Biennial*), Mednarodni grafični likovni Centre, Ljubljana 1993; Vesna Teržan (ed.), *Mnemosyne – The Time of Ljubljana's Biennial of Graphic Arts*, International Centre of Graphic Arts (MGLC), Ljubljana 2010.

[15] The Non-Aligned Movement as an organisation was initiated on the Brijuni Islands in Yugoslavia in 1956 and was formalised by signing the Declaration of Brijuni on 19 July 1956. The Declaration was signed by Yugoslavia's President, Josip Broz Tito, India's first prime-minister, Jawaharlal Nehru, and Egypt's second president, Gamal Abdel Nasser. A passage in the Declaration states that 'Peace cannot be achieved with separation, but with the aspiration towards collective security in global terms and the expansion of freedom, as well as terminating the domination of one country over another.'

[16] Krste Crvenkovski (1921–2001) was a Macedonian communist politician who held influential positions in the Yugoslav government and was the president of the League of Communists of Macedonia from 1963 to 1969. Because of his liberal views he was forced to withdraw from public duties in 1974.

[17] The Anti-Fascist Council for the National Liberation of Yugoslavia (AVNOJ) was the political umbrella organisation for the national liberation councils of the Yugoslav resistance against the Axis occupation during the Second World War. At the second AVNOJ conference in the Bosnian town of Jajce, held on 29–30 November 1943, Tito declared AVNOJ to be the superior executive authority.

[18] Riva Castleman, 'The Recollections of the Americans in Ljubljana', in Teržan, p. 97–113.

[19] Škrjanec, p. 120.

[20] Ješa Denegri, 'Zagrebačka škola serigrafije' ('Zagreb School of Serigraphy'), *Arhitektura–Urbanizam* (*Architecture–Urbanism*), no. 59, Belgrade 1969.

[21] *Izložba serigrafija (Exhibition of Serigraphs): Juraj Dobrović, Eugen Feller, Mladen Galić, Ante Kuduz, Ivan Picelj, Aleksandar Srnec, Miroslav Šutej*, Salon of the Museum of Contemporary Art, Belgrade, 16 January–10 February 1968.

[22] *Grupa 69 – Janez Bernik, Jagoda Buić, Jože Ciuha, Stojan Ćelić Dušan Džamonja, Dževad Hozo, Andrej Jemec, Adriana Maraž, France Mihelić, Štefan Planinc, Miodrag B. Protić, Vjenceslav Richter, France Rotar, Gabrijel Stupica, Miroslav Šutej, Slavko Tihec, Drago Tršar, Vladimir Veličković, Mehmed Zaimović*, Modern Gallery, Ljubljana, and Museum of Contemporary Art, Belgrade, July–August 1978.

[23] Group 69 was founded during an exhibition in Bled in 1969 by Janez Bernik, Jože Ciuha, Riko Debenjak, Andrej Jemec, Bogdan Meško, Adriana Maraž, France Rotar, Marko Šuštarčič, Dževad Hozo and others. Until 1975, the group was enlarged with the inclusion of artists from other parts of Yugoslavia in various exhibitions.

[24] *Grupa 69*, n. p.

[25] Stane Dolanc (1925–1999) was one of President Josip Broz Tito's closest collaborators and one of the most influential figures in Yugoslav federal politics during the 1970s and 1980s. He was Secretary of the Executive Bureau of the Presidium of the Central Committee of the League of Communists of Yugoslavia from 1971 to 1978, Federal Secretary of the Interior from 1982 to 1984 and a member of the Presidency of Yugoslavia from 1984 to 1989.

[26] Zoran Pavlović, 'Šezdeset devet nedoumica' ('Sixty-nine Doubts'), *NIN*, no. 1435, Belgrade, 9 July 1978.

[27] Miodrag Protić, 'Šezdeset devet nedoumica i njihov smisao' ('Sixty-nine Doubts and their Meaning'), *NIN*, no. 1436, Belgrade, 16 July 1978.

[28] Ješa Denegri, foreword to the exhibition catalogue *Tendenzen in der Jugoslawishen Kunst von Heute*.

[29] See Ješa Denegri, 'Jedan beogradski gost Gorgone: Radomir Damnjanović Damnjan' ('A Belgrade Guest of Gorgona: Radomir Damnjanović Damnjan'), *Gorgona*, ARTinova, Zagreb 2018, p. 624–627.

[30] No record of the acquisition of this work was found in the Belgrade Museum of Contemporary Art archive.

[31] Ješa Denegri, foreword to the exhibition catalogue *Tendenzen in der Jugoslawishen Kunst von Heute*.

[32] *Talijansko suvremeno kiparstvo* (*Italian Contemporary Sculpture*), Modern Gallery, Rijeka 1976.

[33] A Serbian Communist politician who supported the political rise of Slobodan Milošević in the 1980s.

[34] *Beograd '77 – Međunarodna izložba likovnih umetnosti* (*Belgrade '77 – International Exhibition of Fine Arts*), Museum of Contemporary Art, Belgrade 1977.

[35] *Aspekte Gegenwartige Kunst Aus Jugoslawien* (*Aspects of Contemporary Art from Yugoslavia*), Akademie der Bildenden Kunste, Vienna 1975.

[36] Jesa Denegri, Radmila Matić-Panić, *Miodrag B. Protić*, Clio, Belgrade 2002.

[37] Ivo Andrić (1892–1975) was one of the most prominent Yugoslav novelists. He won the Nobel Prize for literature in 1961.

[38] Miodrag B. Protić, *Nojeva barka I* (*Noah's Ark I*), Srpska književna zadruga, Belgrade 2000, p. 636.

Response to the 'Museums and Galleries of Modern Art in Yugoslavia Questionnaire'
Ješa Denegri

For the purposes of gathering data related to the current state and activities of the museums and galleries of modern art in Yugoslavia, the Zagreb Museum Documentation Centre prepared a questionnaire that was sent in 1983 to the most important institutions of this kind in the country (with a note clarifying that not all the museums and galleries of modern art were included). Assembled by Jadranka Vinterhalter, Museum Documentation Centre, Zagreb.

The respondents were:
—   Ješa Denegri, art historian, senior curator, Museum of Contemporary Art, Belgrade
—   Dr Jure Mikuž, art historian, curator in the research department of the Modern Gallery, Ljubljana
—   Berislav Valušek, art historian, curator, Modern Gallery, Rijeka
—   Azra Begić, art historian, museum advisor, Art Gallery of Bosnia and Herzegovina, Sarajevo
—   Viktorija Vasev-Dimeska, art historian, curator in the exhibitions department, Museum of Contemporary Art, Skopje
—   Božo Bek, art historian, museum advisor, Gallery of the City of Zagreb – Gallery of Contemporary Art, Zagreb
—   Zdenko Rus, art historian, senior curator, Modern Gallery, Zagreb

Questionnaire

1. Tell us something about the history of the museum/gallery that you are working in: when was it founded? How were the collections formed? What is in them? How many objects are there?

2. What is the concept behind the collection(s) that your museum/gallery builds? Bearing in mind the chronic material difficulties in all our cultural institutions – including museums – what is the acquisition policy of your institution? In what way do you supplement your collections? Do you focus on acquiring works from current art production generally, or do you attempt to consolidate the opus of a single artist in your collection? Who ultimately decides on acquisitions and how are they carried out?

3. What is the concept of the permanent display/exhibition

of the museum/gallery? When was the last time it was changed, and when do you plan to change it? Is the permanent display/exhibition in your museum/gallery conceived as a 'changeable part'? Does the display/exhibition follow the development of art in its continuity, showing different phases in the work of an artist, or does it show only the key styles and best periods of a single artist? Do you try to present the most significant names and works of a single style period, or do you try to complete the holdings with less relevant artists and works?

4. The notion of the museum/gallery of contemporary art is linked to actual art, namely the exhibitions. What is the exhibiting activity of your museum/gallery, and what is the concept of the exhibitions themselves? How are the exhibitions organised and realised? Is there any interest in exchanging exhibitions, or in joint projects with other similar museums/galleries?

5. The works of contemporary art in museums/galleries require a very committed following of the art of today, of what is created in studios. They require direct contact with artists, timely decisions about when and what to present to the public through an exhibition, when and what to purchase. What is the role of the curator of the museum/gallery of contemporary art today?

6. The educational role in museums/galleries is considered to be their central, essential activity, especially with respect to the materials of contemporary art. In the museum/gallery that you are working in, do you have elaborated educational programmes, for instance curators and departments dealing specifically with this?

7. Are the changes in contemporary art reflected in the concept of the collections in your museum/gallery, in the setting and in the temporary exhibitions? In other words, the general course of art in the 1970s included a specific kind of material – Conceptual art, photography, drawings and other works on paper, various media, analytical painting, etcetera. The art of the 1980s turns to painting, sculpture, installation,

to works employing heterogeneous materials. Has
your museum/gallery been sensitive to these changes,
and is it equipped to deal with new types of materials?

8. The problem of museum architecture is very important, especially for museums/galleries of contemporary art, because it is expected that architecture itself
will reflect the modernity of time. Unfortunately, in
Yugoslavia there are very few new museum buildings,
or buildings specifically designed as museums and
galleries. Who designed the building in which your
museum/gallery is located, and when? How do the
permanent and revolving exhibitions 'behave' in that
physical architecture – what are its advantages and
shortcomings? Do you plan to resolve the problems
of the interior and exterior space of the building, and
in what way?

9. From the museological point of view, what would you
highlight as characteristic for the museum/gallery
in which you are working?

* * *

Answers by Ješa Denegri, Museum of Contemporary Art,
Belgrade

It is hard for me to answer according to the order in which
the questions are posed – this is something that could
in fact only be done by an ideal (non-existent) good genius
at the museum who would be simultaneously present in
all the objects and manifestations of that museum.

But museums (museums of modern art, the Museum
of Contemporary Art) consist not only of the art objects
they possess and exhibit, but at the same time comprise all
the worker-colleagues we today call 'associate labour'.
The physiognomy (the politics, as it were) of every institution
of this kind depends considerably on ideas, capabilities and
knowledge, but also on the lack of ideas, on the incapacities
and ignorance of those who are the associate labour in
such institutions. And to engage in these kinds of discussions would be not only impossible, but also completely

unnecessary. Therefore, it has always seemed more appropriate to me that on occasions like this I should not talk in the first person plural (we as the Museum, we in the name of the Museum), but only in the first person singular. Not in order to stress my own egotism, but because today it is the only possible way to take responsibility for what I think and say.

So, instead of following the order of the questions raised above, I shall try briefly to share a projection of mine – more concretely, a projection of the art critic employed as a curator at the Museum. I would like to say right away that in principle I separate these two practices, because at issue here are two different vocations, although in certain circumstances, they can be performed concurrently and simultaneously without damaging either of them, or at least without creating internal difficulties. Because someone who is a critic should be critical, but not of art and artists (because that is the easiest way, and the least courageous); a critic should be critical primarily of the functioning of art/cultural institutions and the system itself, within which museums are an important part. It is hard for a critic to be a curator (or for a curator to be a critic); they are expected to try to improve the institution from within, which in principle they should criticise, and if they are not able to do this the only thing left for them is to be engaged in the operation in which their position as a curator becomes a disguised form of some kind of critique in practice.

Therefore, the integration of the critic into a museum institution sometimes conceals serious moral dilemmas that the critic, it seems, cannot resolve other than with the following alibi: they agree to this integration with their own internal justification, that they begin a long march through institutions not to serve them but to fulfil within them (by means of them) their duties that stem from the vocation of critic. One can label this behaviour, if you will, subversive. However, in fact this is neither a compromise nor a form of deceit, but is primarily searching the ever-broader area in which the practice of the critic is necessarily performed today. For we know all too well that a critique is not only an essay published in newspapers or journals, or broadcast on radio or television; a critique is rather the concept and organisation, even the setting of an exhibition; a critique is the acquisition politics, the building of a museum's collections, a selection of works for the museum's permanent display, and so on. The critic, therefore, does not disguise themselves as a curator in order to be integrated within the institution of the museum; they still act as a critic knowing that without the support (and the power) of that institution they would be deprived of many instruments necessary today to their own work, which is why they decide for the 'long march' while at the same time remaining aware – as in many other situations – that they pay in one way and gain in another.

So, if one can speak about the diverse vocations of the critic and the curator, they both (and equally the critic-curator) basically have one common ultimate goal: to promote the value of contemporary art, to shed some light on its problems and to draw closer to and project those problems and values towards an ever wider public. It would be ideal if museums of contemporary art could be primarily, or even exclusively, educational platforms, and therefore separated from the competing circle of artists and critics, from their struggles for prestige and influence, together with everything else that goes with this prestige and influence. But is this at all possible when we know that in contemporary social and cultural practice (of which museums are an integral part) we live in an inevitably and essentially healthy competitive environment consisting of different concepts, perspectives and orientations? This is a state of affairs that we should not try to conceal if we do not want culture-related issues (and within them also museum-related issues) to be outside the real frames of life and thus to deprive us of any demanding requirements related to their critical problematisation. Finally, it may seem that these answers deliberately overlook or avoid the very clear and concrete questions posed. But perhaps not, for I thought it would be more important to cast a shadow of doubt over these clear and concrete questions than to answer them with positive factual indices, behind which one cannot see or foresee that in basically everything people do (as for museums equally) there always exist different human needs and different human interests.

PART 2

The Language of Art
and the System of Art
Ješa Denegri

Published in *Oktobar 75 (October 75)*, Student Cultural Centre, Belgrade 1975.

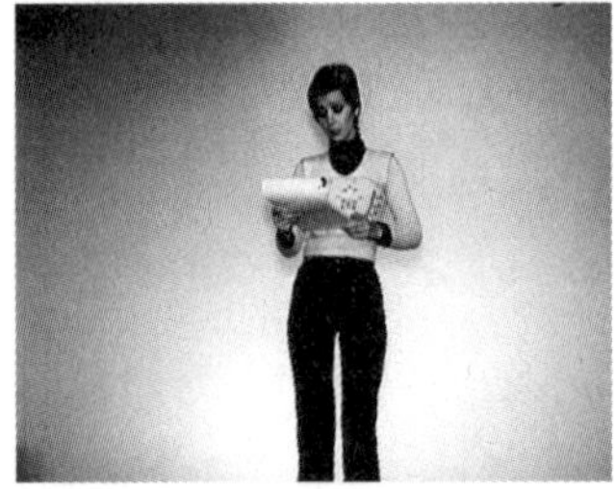
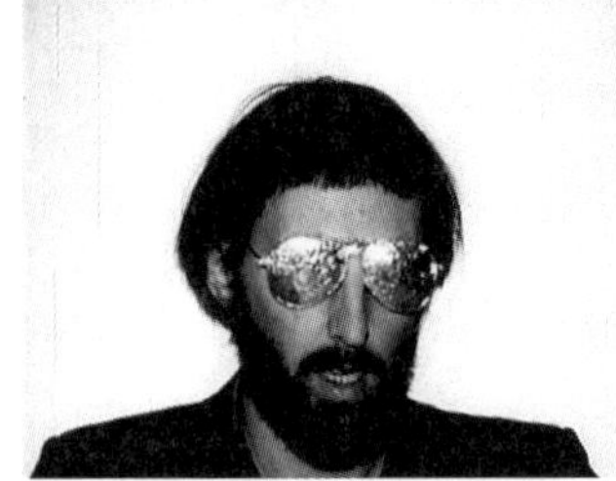
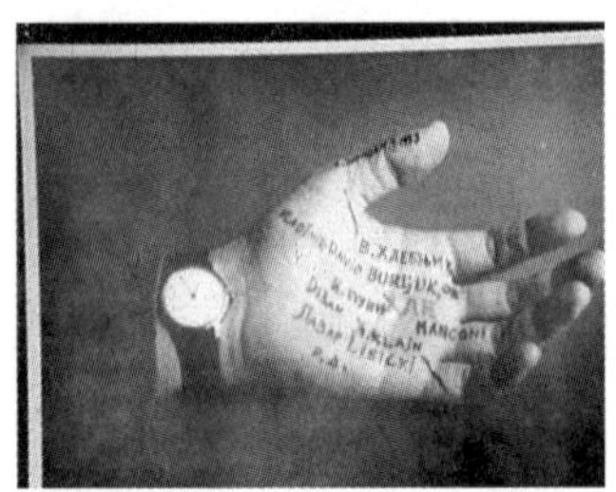
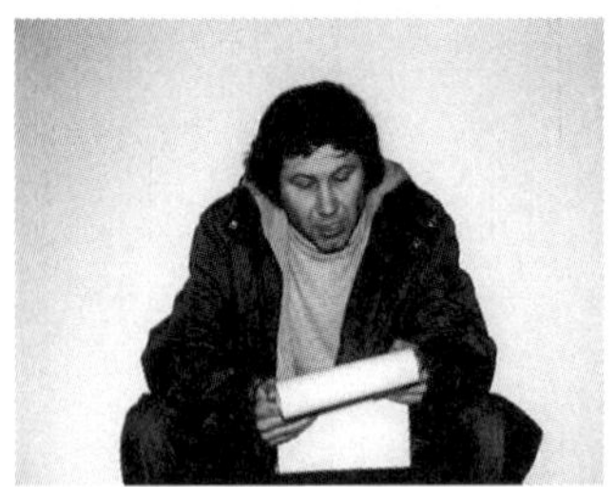

Lutz Becker
Kino Beleske (Cinema Notes), 1975, first screened at the Student Cultural Centre (SKC) Gallery, Belgrade
Video stills, 30'
Clockwise, from top left: Dunja Blažević, Zoran Popović, Ješa Denegri, Radomir Damnjanović Damnjan

Any examination of the function of art in the contemporary world must proceed from the supposition that art as a phenomenon is not an isolated, unchangeable and neutral sphere of the spirit; on the contrary, it is an integral part of the broadest socio-economic reality that not only influences the organisation of artistic life in the existing social context but also conditions the essential character of the language through which artistic views are formed and mani-fested. Such an approach must always bear in mind the existence of two equally complex and mutu-ally permeated areas of examination which, on account of their specific natures, can by no means be reduced to identical parameters: one is the language of art, that comes into being on the basis of various immanent historical laws, and on the basis of irreplaceable existential experiences of particular artists; while the other is the system of art, which emerges on the basis of those general determinants that condition not only consciousness and imagination but also the position and status of artists within a particular social context. It is understood that between these two factors – the language of art on the one hand, and the system of art on the other – there exists a sensitive structure of dialectical mutual conditioning. If we accept these propositions in principle, the next step brings us to the first specific question: what are the socio-economic bases upon which the complex of contemporary art is built in today's reality?

The characteristic mechanisms of global systems – neo-capitalism on the one hand, and socialism on the other – essentially determine the form and position of art within the general processes of the functioning of these systems. Pursuing this thesis further, we can establish that the form and the position of art within these systems are actually profiled through the possibility of a reaction to the dominant factors of social power, irrespective of whether this power at various moments manifests as the economic, the ideological or the political structure of power. Thus, the face of contemporary art at this historical moment is nothing more than a form of resistance formulated in a specific language, or a form of integration in relation to the notion and the instruments of power, and the specific modes of its manifestation may be subsumed under the three basic forms of the social behaviour of artists as direct producers of art. One is a form of acceptance and passive reflection of reality; another is a form of partial attempt at reforming reality; while the third is a form of radical criticism or even total denial of that reality, where the notion of reality should be understood not in the sense of diverse very general surroundings but, on the contrary, in the sense of the most particular socio-economic and cultural institution. It is an illusion to believe that an artist can act in a space between these three modes of manifestation. After Antonio Gramsci had once and for all destroyed the myth of the alleged neutrality of intellectuals, and thereby also the myth of the neutrality of artists, it is inevitable that the examination of the status and function of art in the contemporary world should eliminate the phraseology about an imaginary freedom of expression, and that the element of freedom should from now on be viewed only within that fundamental

Marxist diagnosis of freedom as the possibility or impossibility of specific action under the real social and historical circumstances.

Proceeding from these two basic theses of Gramsci's, according to which intellectuals, and therefore also artists, are not an isolated and entirely autonomous social stratum, but are actually always more or less closely connected with either the ruling or the revolutionary powers, let us now try briefly to specify the modes of their behaviour within the global socio-economic context of the contemporary world. The context in which art develops today, that is, that cultural sphere that we call the West, is still, despite all the factors of resistance, a context of the domination of neo-capitalism, where the market mechanism has an exceptionally pronounced role. The consequences of the functioning of the market mechanism are twofold. On the one hand, the artist as the direct producer of art is deprived of the possibility of exerting any decisive influence on the further destiny of his own work. Not only is he unable to prevent the process of financial manipulation of the results of his work, which specifically means that one who is not the actual producer of the work of art in question reaps the profit; he is also unable to choose his own collocutors or to control the trajectories of his own discourse – which is of no less importance to the artist as a person participating in the struggle of ideas. As the final consequence of the above, even the most progressive artistic attitudes, when they are caught in the net of this system, cannot avoid the humiliation of being treated as a commodity, and this is how any pronounced spiritual or ideational projection can be exposed to the danger of being compromised. Closely connected with this is another characteristic moment of the assimilating strategy of the system of art of neo-capitalism: for, precisely because of the easy acceptance within and the equally easy entry into the web of dominant market circulation, all new artistic proposals, initially created as more or less radical acts of social opposition, gradually end up in the marginal zone of consumer culture. This culture, whatever its creators might think of it, is nothing but an instrument in the hands of the dominant socio-economic structures in the existing makeup of contemporary civilisation.

Therefore, in order to be able to understand various forms and processes of contemporary art in their very essence, we must bear in mind the fact that an immanent resistance to the alienated function of the market has crept into the core of the ideational motivation and operative techniques by which progressive artists are guided and which they make use of today, not only through its anti-aesthetic manifestations but also through a radical spiritual and political orientation. Which is why we by no means accept the general extremely negative assessment of art arising in the context of contemporary neo-capitalism as provided by the representatives of vulgar, materialistic aesthetics, but examine the character of this problematic by referring to the analyses and conclusions of the authentic Marxist approach employed by Karel Teige who, in his texts written as far back as the 1930s, polemicising from the point of view of a Plekhanov-type mechanism, established that revolutionary elements in art created within the system of bourgeois society are revealed to be elements of conflict and indicate a crisis in the relationship between art and the society within which it is created.

If it is possible to say of artistic practice within the context of neo-capitalism that it is exposed to the danger of alienation on account of the pernicious influence of the market, it is also true that art is exposed to other kinds of deformations, no less severe, in systems that are referred to as socialist. From the time of the liquidation of the Soviet avant-garde right up until the present day, ideology has exerted permanent pressure in its efforts to determine and limit the function of art in advance, treating it solely as an instrument of its own strategy of controlling all the material and spiritual resources of society. If art can exist, even in an alienated state, as per Theodor W. Adorno's negative perspective, in the 'bad infinity' of bourgeois society, it does indeed wane in the Stalinist solution. Such a solution demands an unconditionally apologetic presentation of the existing reality, all the more so because history unequivocally confirms that this reality has been full of all kinds of aberrations that the artist, as an ethical being, could not fail either to see or to hide. This has resulted in a situation that, in an environment otherwise characterised by a great tradition of revolutionary art, has constituted a total regression of

goals and ideals imposed up on its authentic social function.
Under such circumstances, the space of artistic action
becomes the space of a more or less illegal underground,
which leads to its enforced isolation from the necessary
mass of potential or actual collocutors that it addresses.

A specific form of alienation also threatens the artist
who works in the context of social trends in the under-
developed countries of the Third World for, even if we leave
aside the total anachronism of linguistic experiences that
artists in these surroundings use, contemporary demands
for an enlightenment-oriented approach may entail a loss
of any critical distance from the inner developmental trends
in these environments.

What is necessary here is briefly to review the current
Yugoslav situation. As we know, there is no private art
market in Yugoslavia, which does not mean that no opportunities to make a considerable profit exist for various groups
who pursue a professional artistic practice. Also, the
principle of freedom of creation is proclaimed and applied,
although the reality of artistic life actually shows that
for some artists – most often the proponents of new and
progressive orientations – that freedom was no more
than freedom of expression deprived of adequate material
compensation for the results of their work; whereas for
other artists – mostly the relatively broad group of artists
involved in the system of academies and other pedagogical
or cultural institutions – it also meant freedom that brought
a whole lot of privileges and, in the final analysis, influence
when it came to regulating the existing system of art.

The practice of Yugoslav artistic life points to a
paradoxical fact: the social and political elites in this country
are most suspicious of the very phenomena that endeavour,
through the critical nature of their language, to democratise
artistic communication, thus involving themselves in the
broader trends of social and ideational change. On the other
hand, what is supported, directly or indirectly, are those
views that are based on the neutral aestheticism, intimism
and sentimentalism of the local models of bourgeois artistic
tradition, or those whose arbitrary literary-narrative
symbolism could easily adapt to the frequent demands for
apologetic and solely affirmative interpretations of the
current political and cultural situation.

What, then, remains to art and artists today, in the concrete historical circumstances in which one cannot even remotely see the potential and real forms of de-alienation towards which they must strive owing to the nature of their engagement?

The global political situation in the world today is such that we increasingly believe that Marcuse was right when he claimed that contemporary art would never free itself from the state of alienation in which it had actually always been throughout history. If that is its real and only possible perspective, then the only thing we can do, despite all the idealistic prejudices on which the human spirit feeds steadfastly, is to characterise this phase in its historical existence as part of a process of the probable and inexorable death of art, based on those forms and those functions that we encounter in the existing historical experience.

I. The New Art Practices: Attitudes, Procedures and Institutional Perspectives

Ješa Denegri in Conversation with Branislav Dimitrijević and Jelena Vesić

I. <u>Shearing for Art</u>

JELENA VESIĆ   We have already talked about your participation in the selection committee for the 1977 Paris Biennial, and your essay in the catalogue on the art of socialist states that is published in this book. However, today we go back six years earlier to speak about the 1971 Paris Biennial. You were the curator of the Yugoslav selection?

JEŠA DENEGRI   That's right. In 1971 I was the national selector for the Biennale Internationale des Jeunes Artistes de Paris (Paris Biennial), and then in 1977 I was a member of the curatorial team of the same biennial that had been restructured in-between. Look at the catalogue to see how that was done at the time — there are also photographs. That's me here and here … and here (showing with his finger). Here's what I looked like, with that long hair! [Laughs.]

BRANISLAV DIMITRIJEVIĆ   Nice haircut!

JD   Come on, it was much longer than that in 1971!
Once they stopped me on the border for that long hair
I had, because in my passport it was much shorter. On that
occasion, we were going as a group of curators from the
Belgrade Museum of Contemporary Art to Milan to see an
exhibition about Futurism. There was a fund for educating
curators, for internal training purposes within the institution.
And you won't believe it, but of all the artists and curators
going, they only stopped me at the border.

JV   Because of your hair?

JD   Yes. Because in my passport I had short hair and the
Italian passport control didn't want to let me pass despite
all my assurances. I got a very stubborn guy. We said that we
were going to an exhibition, that we worked in the arts,
that I was a curator from the Museum of Contemporary Art.
Nothing worked. Luckily, we had Kosta Bogdanović with us,
a master of all difficult situations, who gave me a haircut
in the toilet at the border control. If I had been alone or
with someone else, I would have been sheared like a sheep,
but Kosta knew how to give me a little style, so I passed.

JV   So that was 'shearing for art'!

BD   When we look at the artists you selected for the Paris
Biennial in 1971, long hair was very much in vogue. This
was the first time you participated professionally in a large
international exhibition?

JD   Well, I had had only limited experience with the
Venice Biennale. I wrote the foreword for Stojan Ćelić who
was part of the Yugoslav pavilion in 1964 and I was included
in the team for that occasion. The exhibition featured the
works of Branko Ružić, a sculptor from Croatia, the graphic
work of Riko Debenjak from Slovenia and the paintings
of Ćelić.

BD   It is clear that for that and for similar events artists were selected according to two criteria: according to a proportional presentation of artistic techniques and media, and according to nationality. Stojan Ćelić was a Serbian artist and painter, and a representative of high modernism oriented towards geometric abstraction. Six to seven years later, your selection had nothing to do with the type of art in which Ćelić figures as one of the most prominent and influential individuals, and also nothing to do with the nationality of the artists, and particularly not with traditional techniques of painting, sculpture or etching.

So let us note, for the record, the list of artists in your selection for the 1971 Paris Biennial. It comprised not only so-called *likovni umetnici* (fine artists), but also people who worked in film, photography, installations, theatre – so here you proposed an expanded notion of fine art that was entirely novel in the Yugoslav Art Space of the time. The following artists from Yugoslavia participated in this exhibition: Karpo Aćimović Godina, Slavko Bogdanović, Vladimir Bonačić, Boris Bućan, Slobodan Dimitrijević (Braco Dimitrijević), Čedomir Drča, Sanja Iveković, Jovan Jovanović (a.k.a. Joca Jovanović), Vladimir Kopicl, Tomaž Kralj, Miroslav Mandić, Dalibor Martinis, Milenko Matanović, David Nez, Vladimir Petek, Marko Pogačnik, Mirko Radojičić, Zoran Radović, Ana Raković, Andraž Šalamun, Slobodan Tišma, Goran Trbuljak, Peđa Vranešević, Miša Živanović and Gorki Žuvela.[1] The list was very long – like their hair! So, what therefore happened to you, what happened on the scene in those six years between 1964 and 1971? Of course, we know the historical background, the political movements, the politicisation of art practices and finally also the institutional affirmation of Conceptual art. But let's look at the question of what happened from a micro-perspective, which you personally witnessed.

The degree of changing attitudes
amongst the youngest generation
compared to previous generations
indicates a shift of consciousness
unprecedented since Josip Račić
(1885–1908). The belated romantic
rebellion of the young Račić
expressed in *Manet hat nicht so gemalt*
(*Manet Did Not Paint Like This*)
had outgrown its revolutionary
dimensions according to the
thinking of our cultural ideologues
and critics led by Krleža. Today,
in the world of the recently
adjusted attitudes of the youngest
generation, this Račićian-Krležian
revolution has been reduced to
the right size: that of the modest
wish to approach one's own time,
without counting the approxi-
mately half-century delay of the
one-and-the-same friction of the
canvas against the easel.

It seems that the revolution
was brought by the 'long-hairs'
some 70 years after Račić – the
very ones who have recently been
chased by our honest citizens
and sheared like sheep. Both the
cutting and growing of hair are
attitudes. And ways of behaving.
The former need not be explained,
but the word on the second has
still not been determined as to
whether it was actually a revolution.
After so many centuries, we see a
revolution in human behaviour.
But hence also a shift in consciousness, and perhaps also one of the
preconditions for the great shift
that will be manifested in the
revolution of thinking that will
come soon – or not that soon.[2]

—Mangelos

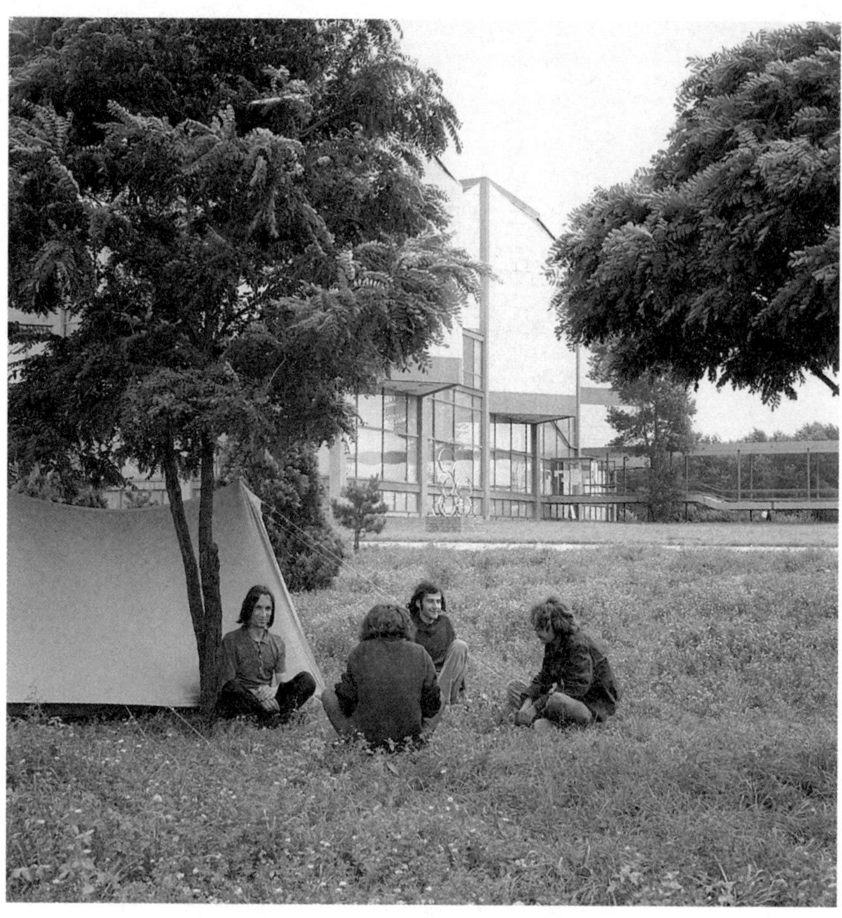

The OHO group in front of the Muzej savremene umetnosti (Museum of Contemporary Art),
Belgrade, during the 4th Yugoslav Triennial of Visual Arts, Belgrade, 1970

2. <u>Micro-Perspective: the Museum of Contemporary Art
    and Conceptual Art</u>

JD   When we talk about the international presentations
of Yugoslav art, it is important to emphasize the points of
view of the Federal Committee for Foreign Cultural Relations
that were imposed on cultural institutions – in our case on
the Belgrade Museum of Contemporary Art and its curators.
The 1971 Paris Biennial got in touch with the Committee
to organise the Yugoslav participation, but since they no
longer organised exhibitions, as they had done in the 1950s
and 1960s, the invitation arrived at the door of the Belgrade
Museum of Contemporary Art. That correspondence also
included something that helped facilitate such a radical
selection: it literally said that the Paris Biennial that year
would present Conceptual art, artistic interventions, art films
and so on. It was clear that a different type of exhibition
was coming, an exhibition that included a new thinking of
art in terms of spatial or environmental installations, new
technologies, ephemeral artforms, etcetera. Back then I was
the only curator at the Museum who expressed an interest
in the various manifestations of the New Art Practices as we
used to call them. I socialised with artists and critics who
worked in the field and frequently collaborated on their
exhibitions. I was appointed commissioner for the Yugoslav
participation in this biennial at a meeting of the Museum's
Curatorial Council. We had the Museum behind us, its
authority and its logistical support. This meant in the
formal/institutional sense that the state allocates the
resources: the Federal Committee for Foreign Cultural
Relations transfers them to the Museum, and the Museum's
curators conscientiously and professionally organise
the project.

JV   What is actually very interesting, if I may add, for our
international readers, is that in explaining the procedures
practised by an art institution in a socialist state your thesis
is that the institution, in its foreign dealings, seeks to fit
itself into a thematic frame and to choose the most competent professionals in that field in order to respond to the
particular theme and concept. On the one hand, it could be
said that this is the simple logic of fitting in with global

trends. On the other, it confirms a relative degree of autonomy for art established in the Yugoslav Art Space, which resulted in opening up a very different space for art, one which was autonomous from both the state dictates and the art market. And the Paris Biennial exhibition would effectively test the horizons and limits of this double-bound autonomy. It would become a place for the subjectivisation and differentiation of the Yugoslav group of conceptualists.

BD   In addition to these cultural-political issues summed up by Jelena, it is very important that we map the situation on the microlevel of the local cultural mainstream and the museum itself. The director of the museum, Miodrag Protić, was one of the main protagonists of high modernism in Yugoslavia. In relation to the type of selection that you proposed, he represented a very different position. But he obviously understood that art was changing. That is one of the reasons such a selection of artists for the Paris Biennial in 1971 was possible.

In other words, to simplify, you didn't feel any type of political pressure whatsoever? In Yugoslavia, the early 1970s mark a backlash against the liberal tendencies in politics, but particularly against the so-called anarcho-liberal tendencies in culture. Like Protić, you were also not a member of the Communist Party, nor were any of the artists you took to the Paris Biennial.

JD   You should bear in mind the ways that the various institutions worked. The Federal Committee for Foreign Cultural Relations was active from the beginning of the 1950s onwards and charged with overseeing the representation of Yugoslavia abroad. Formally speaking, it was an institution of the bureaucratic-ideological type. The institutions of contemporary art that took over these responsibilities in the 1960s were established to be both representative – and therefore partially ideological in character – as well as professional bodies. We were never briefed or in any way under the influence of the Party in our professional decisions relating to programmes and projects. Of course we could not engage in any major provocations, but no institution of that kind would do that anywhere. The selection for the 1971 exhibition was provocative, but for the mainstream cultural milieu, not for the Party as such – we already talked about my acceptance of Richter's notion of socialism as a civilisational level. From the first exhibition of the New Tendencies in 1961, it became clear to me that I was neither embracing nor rejecting the existing political system, but trying, within the field in which I operated, to contribute to a type and direction of socialism represented by new and constructive forms in contemporary art produced in a socialist society.

3. Operational Procedures and the Dynamics of Life

JV   The New Art Practices did not play a formative part in your development. You were already an established critic when they appeared at the end of the 1960s. Your experience of observing the New Tendencies exhibitions was crucial for your understanding of the international contemporary art context. And what is interesting to point out in this conversation is that you learned about contemporary art precisely by viewing exhibitions. Your encounter with the New Tendencies was the product of life's contingencies. But it was also decisive for the future of Yugoslav art histories, particularly today, now that the art phenomena you joined as a critic and curator have become crucial.

JD   The story of the New Tendencies is an enormous subject, which today has been revalidated internationally, most of all through the research conducted at ZKM Karlsruhe.[3] But at the beginning of the 1960s it was a new and experimental phenomenon that I encountered and became connected with by chance, as follows. When I was studying in Belgrade I often went to Split to visit my parents. Since I was interested in keeping up with events, I would usually first go to Zagreb to see the exhibitions, and then I would take a train to Split. I came across the first exhibition of the New Tendencies in 1961 by pure chance. I saw the exhibition not knowing anything about the art they were showing, but it was fascinating to me that the works were typologically completely different from everything we were used to seeing in our exhibitions. I recall Piero Manzoni's famous *Achrome* (1958) – an enormous white surface … nothing … only white. This painting was canvas dipped in paint, so it wasn't even painted in a painterly way. I found myself confronted with other forms of knowledge and criteria by which to make art. I was not easily able to understand it, but I found the situation intriguing – to try and grasp something new and seemingly impenetrable, to understand the materiality of the new artistic method. I also saw many other new phenomena there: for example, how Otto Piene, a member of the group ZERO, drew a circle with a candle on the canvas – or more accurately, with soot. Not a single type of this work existed within the horizons of the students and the adherents of artistic life in Belgrade at this moment. Nor did I know what was going on there, but I did notice, at least in some small corner of my mind, that I had distinguished two typologically very different art practices: something that was in the New Tendencies and something that we then saw at the first Yugoslav Triennial,[4] or at the October Salon,[5] or at other large-scale exhibitions in Belgrade, Zagreb, Ljubljana and so on. When I visited the New Tendencies exhibition in 1964, I had a similar experience – from a typological point of view the art had changed from the previous exhibition. The exhibition presented luminescent environments and spatial installations in a meeting of art and technology. Since these encounters with the New Tendencies, I have lived in two parallel worlds. On the one hand, I followed that which was our artistic reality, and on the other, I knew that there was something completely different, that there was an Other Line of artistic thought and action. When Biljana Tomić and I went to the Venice Biennale in 1964, I was writing the catalogue foreword for Ćelić at the Yugoslav pavilion, and at the exhibition I came across the new American art – Pop art, Rauschenberg, Claes Oldenburg, Frank Stella, etcetera. Thanks precisely to the experience of seeing the New Tendencies, I already knew how to approach these phenomena and also to understand how they might be thought yet further. It wasn't easy to write about that in relation to the references we were raised on in our local art history.

JV   How, from today's distance, do you see these moments of rupture in your work and your way of thinking? And we could also say the ruptures in the history of art. What stands behind your enquiring mind, your urge to research?

JD   I could answer that in several ways. One of those ways might not be strictly professional, strictly art historical, but could also come out of the whole spectrum of life – from companionship, friends, urban culture, sport. I'm not an expert on general culture and everything that might be understood by it. My interests and enquiries were driven more by a way of life. When I began my studies, Belgrade opened itself up to me as a large city with many art events, many different worlds, sports events, beautiful girls and so on. Also, when I was studying, I socialised with people from the Kino Klub[6] and also acted in the films of Ivan Martinac,[7] with whom I then shared a flat. Many things actually came about from going out and friendships. Again, that produced two relationships in me: one with the academic history of art that I was being taught at the university, which we respected, and the other with Belgrade, which offered a particular dynamic of the life of that time, which is emblematically captured in the film *Ljubav i moda* (1960, *Love and Fashion*) by Ljubomir Radičević.[8]

BD   So, as opposed to the institutional-scientific method of creating a national historical narrative of art, what was actually essential for you was the relation between two extremities: one being everyday life, the active pursuit of the everyday, and the other being the reading of theoretical literature and learning about the new intellectual positions that were dismantling the existing historical narratives and the local traditions. In this coexistence of active life and theoretical curiosity, you felt that you were able to discern, recognise and interpret changes in the historical-artistic paradigms.

JD   You see, I tried to follow what art history said about our recent artistic heritage as far as possible. After all, that's what we were studying. I was aware of one thing – my obligations with regard to my life in Belgrade, and also to my parents, so I had to finish my studies. I didn't come here not knowing what to look for, but rather to finish my education, above all else. Accordingly, I studied dutifully, as I was obliged to.

JV   But you were reading much more than was required of you. What for you was exceeding the norms, what wasn't required?

JD   Look at it this way – there was, in one way, the history
of art and art criticism as an elevated and metaphysical
discipline about understanding artistic phenomena. But there
was also another type of art criticism, or explanation of
artistic phenomena, and that is where I was able to place
myself, which explains a concrete work of art in terms
of its *operative procedures*. What was decisive for me? While
I was still in Split, when I was volunteering at the Meštrović
Gallery, I came across an essay written by Vera Horvat
Pintarić about Dušan Džamonja.[9] In that essay she begins
roughly with the following: Džamonja takes nails of various
sizes, then welds them in such and such a way – and that's
how a sculpture is produced! You couldn't find that way
of writing, where art is interpreted in such a materially
grounded way, in many art discourses of the time. Great
humanistic narratives were circulating then … But my
position was the following: not having a highly developed
literary or philosophical education, I couldn't recognise
myself in all those grand narratives, but I could in the
operative procedures of art: how one paints, with which
materials the artist works, how materials are processed,
how the form is structured and so on. Therefore, the debate
came down to something that was visible, verifiable. That
way I developed an affinity for the artist whose work I appreciated most in Serbian art, and that was Olga Jevrić. I had
seen how she worked and when we met, she also explained it
to me very simply: 'I take cement and I put rods in it and so
on …' Of course, there is a symbolic projection in her art,
but that is a level in art that was inaccessible to me, whereas
what is accessible can be verified as an *operational procedure*.

JV   So you weren't interested in any grand humanist or
theoretical narratives that, as you said, often served the
mystification of art and its symbolic projections. Instead
you observed art as a material practice and, I would add,
as a practice that is demystified by the procedure of its own
production.

JD   Yes. I constantly asked myself: what do I think about
this work? And more particularly, what can I say or write
about this work? There are works where my affinities,
my culture, and my knowledge fail me, and I cannot grasp

them. But there are others that I managed to grasp. And then
I make intuitive choices and question my own affinities.
Ultimately, what you're asking about my reading and methods
– if I may make a small comparison – is similar to what
Protić did with the 'reconstruction of the artistic persona'
that he borrowed from Lionello Venturi.[10] That's why his
reach is so wide; it takes into consideration personalities as
diverse as Lubarda and Tabaković. I, however, came across
Umbro Apollonio and Giulio Carlo Argan, and the way they
talked about the reconstruction of the formative process.
For me, there is a fundamental difference between the
reconstruction of the artistic persona and the *reconstruction of the
formative process*. At that time, for example, I wasn't able to
think about Lubarda as a great artist who was moving hills
and valleys, who talked about something between heaven
and earth, and where everything existed in a mystical space
… With some artists in our cultural context the meaning
of art, as they understood it, was completely beyond my
comprehension. My individual psychological constitution
couldn't grasp such a world and align itself with it.

JV   And Manzoni, whose works you had chance to see
at the New Tendencies exhibition in Zagreb, was precisely
parodying that figure of the great modern artist and the
mythical nature of high art – everything that you actively
did not identify with.

JD   Exactly. So, by keeping up with events on the international contemporary art scene, visiting exhibitions and
lectures, reading magazines, I encountered new forms of art,
new artistic statements and interpretations and a particular
way of writing about these phenomena. Reading the essays
of Argan was pivotal. It helped me understand how to write
about contemporary art in an operative, formal, semantic,
but also culturological way. Secondly, after a thorough inquiry
into the legacy of Futurism in Italy and their ideologically
problematic avant-gardism in the context of fascism,
I realised that art history should think in two directions:
about art in its social context, and about the operational
procedures of art. In the works of Lucio Fontana, Alberto
Burri or Emilio Vedova, we see a certain building on the
legacy of Futurism, not as an ideological affiliation but

rather as an operational procedure. The reconstruction of the formative process generates a new relation to culture, heritage and ideology, and to the various continuities and interruptions in the development of art. If art has no base from which to depart, as was provided by the historical avant-gardes, then we ask: what does it take as its point of departure? And, in the case of Yugoslav post-war art, we see that its base, its point of departure, is pre-war bourgeois modernism. That, in my opinion, was its impasse. And that is the reason I thought it would be valuable to make a breach, so as to think about Zenit, Yugo-Dada and other similar phenomena.

I encountered these phenomena when I began systematically to follow and later to associate with EXAT 51, and with Picelj, who said that he knew of Zenit, of *Dada Tank*, of Šumanović's cubist period. And I saw that there are artists who consciously start from different historical premises and who have the capacity to invoke their own historical role models and references. I found my own art historical way of thinking in all of these transformations and moments of artistic self-construction and self-invention within the larger field of historical options. I found out that the knowledge one gains from the practice, and not only from books, is very important, sometimes decisively so.

4. 1971

BD   The Paris Biennial ran from 24 September to 1st November, 1971.

JV   And the exhibition *Examples of Conceptual Art in Yugoslavia* ran from 3 to 22 March the same year, in the Salon of the Belgrade Museum of Contemporary Art. You worked with Biljana Tomić on that exhibition.

JD   Biljana and I had just had our daughter, so Biljana was not able to take part in setting up the exhibition in March. Biljana wrote a short text in this leaflet – a text of some three sentences – which was enough for her to announce her curatorial intentions. Her text describes the way the scene was spoken about at that time, and how art was communicated.

idea = artwork = communication
idea = art = value
idea = utopia = reality[11]

–Biljana Tomić, 1971

JV   I will read it [see previous page]. Biljana's concept or curatorial statement for me condenses three arguments that primarily comment on the new paradigm of process in Conceptual art and, as we would say from today's perspective, the new political economy of art.[12]

JD   The exhibition wasn't adequately documented by today's standards, nor according to the standards of the Museum at the time. We made a leaflet in the spirit of a curatorial statement because there wasn't enough time to make a catalogue. But the form of a leaflet suited the exhibition well since the exhibits were mainly documents of artistic actions.

JV   Your art historical approach was very important in the context of such a pioneering exhibition. In your essay for the leaflet you give a broad historical overview of artistic developments, within which you situate these new practices.[13] I have pointed out several times the educational aspect of your museum exhibitions in relation to the experimental exhibition forms characteristic of the Student Cultural Centres (SKC).[14] Briefly, the protagonists of the SKC worked with notions of the exhibition as a medium (what I call conceptual exhibitions), while you were the only individual in the Museum at the time interested in this type of art, and you worked on the educational aspect of the New Art Practices by simultaneously promoting and historicising them.

JD   Indeed, we spoke about this for another occasion, and it is interesting to me that now someone reads my work through the language and practice of the exhibition.

JV   What is often important for us are the details that show how some things have been historicised – the process of historicisation itself – and not the singular artwork. For example, the title of your essay published in the leaflet – 'For The Possibility of A New Type of Artistic Communication' – is very symbolic of the act of establishing an approach to art that is outside the field of aesthetics. And here for the first time we can say that the paradigm of communication is emphasised as the key paradigm to the whole lineage of contemporaneity that one can draw from the art of the 1960s and 1970s to today's artistic and media-based events. You are also addressing the historical references: from the avant-garde movements of the 1920s and 1930s to the radical modernist practices and the New Art Practices of the 1960s and 1970s. You connect the theory of the dematerialisation of art by Lucy Lippard with the Primary Structures of Donald Judd and the theory of Anti Form of Robert Morris. You are tracing a possible way for a different type of history.

What interests me here is this: it is precisely the New Art Practices that prompt you to question the necessity for another historical approach to these artistic phenomena. And it is precisely from that point of contemporaneity and moving backwards to the beginning of the 20th century that the Other Line emerges.

JD   Exactly. The New Art Practices, and before them the New Tendencies, were triggers for me to begin thinking about a different genealogy of art.

BD   And now, when we talk about the artists with whom the New Art Practices in the Yugoslav Art Space began, these are the artists you exhibited in the Salon of the Belgrade Museum of Contemporary Art, and several months later you brought them to the Paris Biennial. And these two exhibitions were already functioning in an institutional register, and you were a curator of a public institution, of a museum on a state budget. And the Belgrade Museum of Contemporary Art in 1971 supports a type of art that ideologically and aesthetically is oriented towards something for which the entire socialist-modernist mainstream had no affinity whatsoever. What did that imply in an organisational and institutional sense?

JD   We are talking about March 1971 and the exhibition *Examples of Conceptual Art in Yugoslavia,* and then the Paris Biennial in autumn of the same year. The choice of artists and artworks wasn't questioned and was facilitated by the propositions for artworks set by the Biennial. Had that not been the case, maybe the Federal Committee for Foreign Cultural Relations, maybe the Museum itself, would have adopted the position that the selection should come out of an entirely different, let's say academic, point of view, and should not pay attention to world trends in contemporary art and Western propositions. However, the exhibition embodied a particular thematic and genre-specific precision, and there is probably documentation of this in the Museum. All foreign engagements had to be discussed at the Curatorial Council and were probably recorded in the minutes from that meeting. Protić was very thorough, and also a legalist. There was no room for mistakes. Our museum functioned perfectly, like a Swiss watch, in the operational and procedural senses.

BD   There are records in the Museum archive from March and April 1971, which note that your plan for the selection of the Paris Biennial was accepted, but they do not provide any details. It seems you were only given a few months to realise your curatorial plan.

JD   From a curatorial point of view the work with the artists differed from the previous studio visits and selection of existing works. The concepts were to be realised on site or in relation to the ongoing situation. Things happened quickly and frequently, and sometimes they brought tectonic shifts in understanding the material existence and the social role of art. These two exhibitions took place when the OHO group disbanded and one of its wings joined the Šempas Family Art Commune. The second instance of disintegration unfolded in Novi Sad, with the fusion of the groups KÔD and (Э, which no longer constituted two independent groups but which in a single moment merged in a process fraught with friction. In Zagreb there was also a clear division between the early protagonists of the New Art Practices, whose work was seen as a part of Conceptual art, and the second generation of artists whose work was more closely associated with the legacy of the New Tendencies. These distinctions are apparent in the essays of Nena Baljković and Davor Matičević who analyse the New Art scene in Croatia in the catalogue *Nova umjetnička praksa 1966–1978* (*New Art Practices 1966–1978*).[15]
      Curatorially, these two exhibitions were not easy amidst such micro-social events and the dynamics within

different artist groups. When I set off from Paris back to
Belgrade, I felt: 'It is good I'm leaving!' The whole exhibition,
to which I had taken so many artists, had left me exhausted
and caused me so many problems. One particular problem
arose – and this relates directly to the New Tendencies
and the ensuing manifestations of technologically-inspired
art in the works of the artist-scientists Bonačić and Radović.
When I finally found the Parc Floral de Paris, which was
one of the exhibition spaces, it didn't have any electrical
sockets nor any technical support to help get their equipment
working. I went to the Yugoslav Embassy to ask them for
a nominal amount of money with which we could make
a wall and purchase cables to draw electricity from a nearby
source, so that the two pieces of equipment belonging to
Bonačić and Radović could function. There were an unprecedented number of setbacks with this show, such that
I was asking myself why the hell I was taking on such an
unmanageable selection, putting myself in a position that
made it seem like I might be unable to complete the task.

JV   Was there a central Biennial organisation team
coordinating the installation of the works and the production of the exhibition, or was everything delegated to
individual curators?

JD   The official instructions were as follows: you can use
this and that part of the wall to put your works on. You have
to take into account that this was a biennial of young artists
and that the organisation depended on a lot of improvisation, on a lot of ad hoc circumstances. Also, the artists were
not grouped by nationality but rather were dispersed across
different spaces and events. This is the time of Conceptual
art, installation art, interventions, Happenings, improvisation, communication and things that developed organically.
Nonetheless, as I said, the organisation and the whole
curatorial responsibility was stressful.

BD   What did Bonačić's work look like?

JD   His work was a big computer that was programmed
so that the lights on the screen flickered endlessly, yet that
same image on the screen would only repeat itself once

every hundred years. The final consequence of the New Tendencies was Computer art. Abraham Moles introduced us to computer and visual research during the fourth exhibition of the New Tendencies (1969). Computers were incorporated into visual research and were called 'amplifiers of complexity'. If their mathematical capacity is exceeded by a number of combinations that become unimaginable, then a different system of computing takes over. By introducing the first computers, which were still very rudimentary then, a historic trajectory from the white surfaces of Manzoni to large digital displays was processed during the course of the New Tendencies.

JV   How did you present Bonačić and Radović's works? Were the parts of their installations made on site or beforehand?

JD   They had already been produced. The boxes were made at the Ruđer Bošković Institute. At the time Vladimir Bonačić was an engineer at this scientific institution and ran the laboratory for cybernetics and cybernetic art. He was a genius who had arrived at the conclusion that it was more interesting for him to work with this type of art than to pursue some potentially great scientific career. And this is how his life was turned upside down and he went to Israel, where he founded the Jerusalem Programme in Art and Science at the Bezalel Academy of Arts and Design. After that he moved to Germany, where he passed away in 1999. In Germany, he undertook projects in visual communications for television. So you see just how unusual and brilliant these characters were. Bonačić wasn't just a science nerd who made a type of computer art, but rather an important protagonist, an authentic person and artist.

JV   Let's return to the Paris exhibition. How was it structured? In the catalogue it is divided into 'expanded' artistic media: Conceptual art (*art conceptuel*), Mail Art (*envois postaux*), Hyperrealism, Interventions, collective works (*œuvres collectives*), musical compositions, performances (*spectacles*), filmmakers' films, artists' films, architecture and so on. The national selections as such are listed only in the long colophon.

JD   Before the 7th Paris Biennial in 1971, the exhibition
had been organised in terms of national selections, like the
Venice Biennale. But what was the goal of the Paris Biennial?
It was initiated when André Malraux was the French minister
of culture, when there were important cultural-political
debates about whether Paris would become a world centre for
modern art again, as it had been before the war and as
New York became, and took over this leadership in the late
1950s and early 1960s. The Paris Biennial was created at the
end of the 1950s, more precisely in 1959, as a place of encounter that would bring the new generation of European artists
to Paris and provide them with stipends, accommodation at
the Cité internationale des arts, studios and contacts. The
rejuvenation of the Parisian art scene through its internationalisation meant that it would once again attract artists from
various milieus, and that these artists would stay there, like
Picasso and Miró had done in their time. From the local
artists, I know that Vladimir Veličković was one of those who
got a stipend and stayed in Paris.[16] He received an award that
gave him the opportunity as a young artist to find out what
interested him in this renewed artistic-galleries-market environment and to stay in the city. This is how many other artists
who found themselves in the city also came to stay in Paris.

     The most important magazine for the new movements
in art in Paris was *Art Press*. The magazine was edited by
Catherine Millet, with whom I worked at the Paris Biennial
in 1971 and later in 1977, and who came to Belgrade after our
first collaboration.[17] At that time, I was working with the
magazines *Opus International* and *Artist*, but I hadn't written
anything for *Art Press*. In order to understand the atmosphere
around the Paris Biennial, you had to know what was happening in Paris, again in that wide cultural-political sense;
a battle was being fought on the one hand to maintain the
continuity of the Paris School, and on the other to maintain
Paris as an art centre by opening it up to the experiences
of the American and other art circles. Millet was one of the
proponents of the new cultural politics that looked to open
Paris up to the new art scene, which was also the project
of the 7th Biennial. Millet was the most important critic for
this new wave in art, and she was the editor of *Art Press,*
which at the time was one of the most influential art
magazines in the world. There was a debate within the Paris

milieu, the details of which weren't clear to us at the time, about how Paris should be positioned with regard to itself and the notion of French culture. Millet and the organisational team of the Biennial made the decision not to organise this iteration of the Paris Biennial around national selections but rather according to media. If we were to locate this shift in the wider international sense, a certain accumulation of similar exhibition projects was developing. As a result, we had already seen Harald Szeemann's *Live In Your Head: When Attitudes Become Form* (Kunsthalle Bern, 1969), as well as Kynaston McShine's exhibition *Information* (Museum of Modern Art, New York, 1970) and many others.

JV   Did you have any contact with these events in real time? Did you visit any of these exhibitions?

JD   No, but the new exhibition practices were not outside our immediate purview. I told you about my experience of seeing the New Tendencies, which also presented a contemporary exhibition form in a sense. I had the opportunity to attend some significant Arte Povera exhibitions because I went on study trip to Italy at the end of the 1960s and, in the meantime, I met Germano Celant and many other protagonists of this movement.

BD   It seems that Celant and Millet made the strongest impression on your own approach when dealing with the arrival of this paradigmatic change in art. Millet visited Belgrade in 1971. What was she doing there?

JD   She gave a lecture at the Student Cultural Centre's Gallery about Conceptual art, and her experience of the Paris Biennial.[18] She had become very important in the Yugoslav Art Space because of the translation of her essay 'Conceptual Art as the Semiotics of Art', which had been published in the journal *Polja* (*Fields*) in Novi Sad. New direct contacts, translations of essays and the distribution of new forms of knowledge and methods were really of great value in the local experience of art. *Polja* magazine and the Novi Sad Conceptual art scene really played a crucial role in this.

BD   We will get back to Novi Sad later.

JD   In Paris, Nathalie Aubergé and Alfred Pacquement
were the other curators; and much later Pacquement became
the director of the Musée National d'Art Moderne at the
Centre Pompidou. It was important for us to keep up with
and understand the many changes that were coming our
way. Paris was interesting precisely by virtue of its schisms:
Paris or New York as the centre, Picasso or Duchamp as
the principle? You can imagine that in one deeply stratified
scene (in terms of classes and concepts) there are circles
that wish to preserve the orthodoxy of Paris as a great centre
with all its traditions and values. The whole story is split
over this, over Yves Klein and Nouveau Réalisme. That
is certainly one dissonant line in Parisian art. In Yugoslav
art the model is Picasso; I'm speaking above all about
Yugoslavia's interwar traditions, about the first half of the
20th Century, as this was an experience that remained
deeply inscribed in the post-war art of this space.

The Duchampian model of the artist that emerges
onto the scene later in the 1960s begins to dismantle this
stereotype of the great artist of the modern age. When Paris
Nouveau Réalisme begins to engage with the Duchampian
legacy by abolishing the art object, by engaging with the
production of actions, with the process-based works of Klein,
the scene collapsed internally. Also, giving a small group of
young people the opportunity to conceive the Paris Biennial
according to their own preferences marked a precedent
in Paris, because no platform was constructed on which to
develop a narrative about Conceptual art in the strict sense
of that word, unless it was Bernar Venet or Daniel Buren
in their own ways … The question of what exactly was and
is Conceptual art is (still) relevant, and it was, in a way, an
invention of the American art scene. So, the question 'what
name should this new art take?' had many strings attached.

But we are talking here about Paris of that time, and
how the cultural establishment of Paris wanted to preserve
the personality and type of art that was inherited from
the Paris School. The type of exhibition platforms that made
the expansion of the traditional Paris School possible was
the Salons: the Salon d'Avril, the Salon de Mai, the Salon
d'Octobre, the Salon Grands et Jeunes d'Aujourd'hui, and
so on. Both the older and younger generations participated
together in these exhibitions that enjoyed long traditions

and great reputations, including some of our artists who had already been in Paris, like Bata Mihailović, Petar Omčikus and others. There was a fascination in the Yugoslav art scene with Paris, from the prewar to the post-war period. The Paris Salons, if seen from the conceptual standpoint of exhibition making, were conglomerates of vastly different productions. The salons maintained that image of Paris in which the art market and the rebellious life of the artist met. In fact, many of the artists who received awards at the Paris Biennial are seen as 'innovators' on the international art stage – primarily the Europeans, who revitalised the Paris scene and resisted the competition from New York.

Catherine Millet, with Galerie Templon, produced a key moment in the reception of American art in France – the first French exhibitions of Frank Stella, Andy Warhol, and later Joseph Kosuth and others. Certain circles situated the new approaches in Paris by dealing with the Duchampian and post-Duchampian legacy, although that had already been done somewhat earlier by the artistic circle around Pierre Restany. When I consider your question in this context – how my 'radical' selection of artists for the Paris Biennial was possible vis-à-vis the institutional, professional and political apparatuses of Yugoslavia at the time? – I would say that the change in the concept of the Biennial made this 'radical' selection possible, which was clearly articulated in the propositions they sent us. The institution was first confronted with these propositions, and then with my exhibition. If that hadn't happened, Yugoslavia would probably have exhibited the works of individuals who were seen as gifted artists in the local context.

5.　　Youth Culture and the Art System: Career or Revolt

BD　　How did the artists you selected position themselves with regard to all these cultural-political constellations? What relation did they have to the exhibition in Paris and the artistic trends they saw there? How did they react? I wouldn't ask if we weren't talking about very young people who, for the first time, now had the opportunity to participate in an international event of that institutional importance.

JD   Various changes were taking place in then. If we start from the OHO group, we see their participation in the *Information* exhibition (MoMA, New York, 1970) which represents a great international breakthrough for the group, but also resulted in its disbanding. The OHO group members David Nez, Milenko Matanović and the poet Tomaž Šalamun went to New York. Šalamun ran Atelier 69 in the Modern Gallery in Ljubljana, where the OHO group had exhibited for the first time in 1968 in an exhibition organised by Tomaž Brejc. OHO was splitting up at the same moment that I was making the selection for the Paris Biennial. Pogačnik was a representative of the ideas of the New Age, of hippy culture and a non-conformist way of life, and not (strictly speaking) of the professionalisation of art and the legitimisation of one's work within such major international scenes as New York or Paris. From this belief system he and his family, with Matanović and Nez, formed the Šempas Family Art Commune.[19] The Paris Biennial took place within this framework. The second split and reorientation happened in the Novi Sad groups. (Ǝ group is theoretically-linguistically oriented, while the KÔD group has a demonstrational practice. Mirko Radojičić is a member of the KÔD group, but also the link between these two groups, in a narrower sense, derives from his theoretical occupations with Conceptual art. Various steps were taken to withdraw from the art world and to find a different way of life in certain types of micro-communities.

JV   And exhibiting at the Paris Biennial triggered the ruptures within these art collectives?

JD   While I was working on organising the 1971 Paris Biennial, I got the opportunity to see a particular polarisation developing between the artists and the art groups with whom I worked. Some of them were very radical in their attitudes and actions, like Miroslav Mandić, who was the most radical of all. He wasn't looking, like Pogačnik, for an opportunity to present work at an international exhibition and to be on a stage of this kind. For some of the protagonists from Novi Sad the situation was not about building an artistic career, rather they had a purely intellectual interest in the problematic of Conceptual art.

Such was the case with Mirko Radojičić, who was interested from a theoretical perspective, and was the editor of the famous 156th issue of *Polja* magazine and the translator of the majority of essays that have proved important for our understanding of Conceptual art.[20] On the other hand, not all the artists who came along had dilemmas like this. You can see in the Biennial catalogue, here on page 56, a reproduction of the work *Casual Passer-by* (1971) by Braco Dimitrijević, for which we obtained permission to install it in the public space on Boulevard Saint-Michel. The publication of that work in the catalogue made his participation in the exhibition even more visible. Braco was a very lively artistic personality and knew that an appearance in one important artistic event could help him build an international reputation. The photograph from the Paris Biennial became the image that 'branded' Braco Dimitrijević as an early conceptualist, and it is very important, because it has been reproduced countless times in various international contexts ever since.

All in all, in the Paris exhibition and the Yugoslav selection I see various forms of behaviour determined by the context and the positioning of the artists in relation to that context. There are artists who do not strive so hard to be noticed on the international scene; rather the fact that they are protagonists of a particular social and cultural trend serves as the impetus for their participation. But there are also those who, through exhibiting, wish to build their artistic career, and who managed to do so later. And finally, there is this most radical position, which is realised in the medium of life itself, in a philosophy of life that distances itself from the art system.

An ongoing wish for the total
autonomy of art is nothing other
than art's effort to attain a self-
conscious and efficient functioning
within the framework of its own
language.
　　Only when it is functioning
as a critique and an analysis of its
own language is art capable of
raising the issue of the analysis
and critique of social practice and
demanding its change.
ART THAT CELEBRATES
VICTORY STOPS FIGHTING.

—Raša Todosijević, *October 75*, 1975

6. <u>Before the Work of Joseph Kosuth</u>

JV   You once told us a very illustrative anecdote about a visit paid by the group of Yugoslav conceptual artists we have just been talking about to an exhibition by Joseph Kosuth held during the Paris Biennial. Would you tell it to us again? Because that story produces a very strong image of the different subjective attitudes of the Yugoslav group of conceptualists in relation to the rapid process of the institutional co-opting of dematerialised art.

JD   I was very busy with the organisational duties connected with the exhibition, and I wanted to take a short stroll through Paris. Which is how we found out that Joseph Kosuth was exhibiting at Galerie Templon. And one afternoon, as we had completed all our tasks, Trbuljak and I and a group of the Novi Sad artists who knew Kosuth's work well headed over to the gallery. Then I saw Kosuth's enlarged texts on black canvas, and that was phenomenal. However, there followed a very lively discussion among the artists: why are they large format? Why this aestheticisation and commodification? Why does Kosuth's work look different from the way they had understood it from his essays, namely that it is typed on a sheet of paper and the like? Thus, a true sense of incomprehension arose in our small group of visitors to Galerie Templon: does even he, our greatest role model, a pure conceptualist, this linguistic conceptualist, have to do something that restores the spectacle of objecthood? Is he actually doing that for the sake of the market; and why couldn't he be like us, a real alternative? This raised many questions.

BD   In other words, the Novi Sad group of artists recognises a moment in which it appears that that dematerialised, conceptual practice is becoming commodified.

JV   Through enlargement and post-production, which in the 1990s become a global phenomenon.

JD   In the early 1970s Kosuth was definitely not in the same situation as the Novi Sad conceptualists, who had very radical political and artistic attitudes. He was on the list of the Leo Castelli Gallery artists and was active in the developed art system of the West. If you read Kosuth and the artists and critics of that time, you will see that Greenberg is their target, and that in essence they conduct a critique of his doctrine and hegemony in the American art context. Kosuth and other protagonists from that circle are sharply critical of the great authorities, and as a result we see them as some kind of avant-garde. Which is the reason for our moment of perplexity at Galerie Templon. Mirko Radojičić was highly disappointed, as were the others in their own ways. I wasn't, because as an art historian I was interested in seeing the work of Joseph Kosuth. The following dilemma resulted from this: are the protagonists of the artist groups that associated with the Novi Sad Youth Forum (Tribina mladih) more a youth subculture, albeit a highly educated one, or are they professional artists?

BD   But judging from your story, I would say that they understood the context in which they exhibited very well, and actually resisted the idea of becoming institutionalised.

JD   They knew the context and acted from a very specific standpoint, which wouldn't be repeated in the Belgrade circle of protagonists of the New Art Practices.

BD   The Belgrade circle of conceptual artists came onto the scene somewhat later, and they were artists who came out of the Belgrade Fine Arts Academy, unlike the artists of the Novi Sad scene who had no relation whatsoever to the standard art education system.

JD   Yes, although these phenomena did to some extent coincide with each other. But the Belgrade artists would never consider a position like that represented by the Novi Sad groups.

JV   The Belgrade scene will be a separate topic of our conversation. But we can maintain the following difference between them and the Novi Sad groups – that for the artists and critics who gathered around the Belgrade Student Cultural Centre, the New Art Practices was not so much a question of the philosophy of life or of immediate social and political activism, but rather of a critical consideration of art, a break within art itself.

JD   That is, they thought from inside art, and that is why they found themselves in a different position, maybe a very difficult position, because they realised – and this is a discussion now about Marina Abramović, Neša Paripović, maybe least of all Era Milivojević, but certainly Zoran Popović, Gergely Urkom and Raša Todosijević – that they had been educated during those years at the Belgrade Fine Arts Academy in a way that left them unprepared to make art that expressed the contemporary historical moment.

BD   Let's return to the 1971 Paris Biennial and its Yugoslav selection, as well as to the exhibition you curated with Biljana in the Salon of the Belgrade Museum of Contemporary Art the same year. Those exhibitions didn't feature anyone from the group of Belgrade artists we just mentioned. Were both exhibitions prepared at a moment when you, as a curator and critic, had still not registered what they were actually doing?

JD   No. I had registered what they were doing.

JV   Yet the Belgrade scene was activated by the founding of the Student Cultural Centre and with certain landmark exhibitions, both in 1971: *Drangularijum* (*Trinketarium*) in June, *Objekti i projekti* (*Objects and Projects*) in September and finally the exhibition *Oktobar 71* (*October 71*) the following month.

JD   But from today's perspective they all melt into one another and the chronological difference of a few months does not seem terribly important to me. In reality it wasn't so important, because this was a simultaneous process that became visible at different moments and in different situations.

BD   And you also made it visible as a museum curator who showed an instant interest and thereby provided institutional verification at the moment that this practice emerged on the Belgrade art scene. Shall we say that, in some way, you institutionalised it: you put it in the Salon

of the Museum and exhibited it as a national selection at
an international biennial. You were an important participant
in this very complex dynamic between the artists and the
institution, which in any case represented the main agenda
of the protagonists we have been talking about.

JD   Did I bring the New Art Practices into the institutions
and did I lay the ground for their disintegration? You will
have to decide for yourselves.

BD   You definitely didn't split them up; but did any of
them decline your invitation to the Paris Biennial?

JD   No one declined. I had one conversation with Miroslav
Mandić, who told me that an invitation to carry coal to
people's cellars would have impressed him much more than
going to the Paris Biennial. That's how it once was, people
needed fuel for winter, and the young often helped out.
Marko Pogačnik also expressed some type of anti-art senti-
ment by forming the Šempas Family Art Commune, but
no one declined the opportunity to exhibit in Paris. I have
to emphasise that regardless of the fact that as a curator
I represented the Museum on this occasion, I knew all the
participants in other ways; they didn't see me as a bureaucratic representative of a state institution, but rather as
a curator who worked with them. I had a good relationship
with all the artists I invited to the exhibition and didn't
encounter any insurmountable problems during our time
working together.

JV   Nevertheless, there existed very different positions
and attitudes among the artists you took to the Paris
Biennial.

BD   Yes, for example, you mentioned that Braco
Dimitrijević stood out from the others as someone intend-
ing to engage in art as a profession. That means that he
already had a very different agenda than the others. It looks
to me like he was the only one of the participants in the
Yugoslav selection who actually had such an agenda. A few
years later he would be selected for documenta 6 in Kassel,
which would serve as a trampoline for his artistic career.

JD   So you see, I think his agenda is apt. We have since seen that Conceptual art is no more than one kind of artistic phenomenon.

BD   And not some kind of revolution in art?

JD   Maybe also a revolution.

BD   Maybe a revolution in the *language of art,* but not in the *system of art*?

JD   There was no revolution in the art system. If we look at the genesis of this art in the larger centres it was immediately clear that art cannot disturb the functioning of the system, at least not in any enduring way. In America, the artist knows that art cannot change the world, because it is clear that art is a part of all of the mechanisms available to it. In our case, the logic of the 'sixty-eighters' still existed (although I'm not claiming that the artists themselves thought and said so): here we have 'socialism with a human face', and we must not fall under capitalism and the art market. That gives rise to an utopia in which stepping out of line produces an extreme attitude, and then one is penalised, as was the case with Slavko Bogdanović and Miroslav Mandić, who were sentenced to several months in prison for their 'Open Letter to the Yugoslav Public'.[21]

Political and administrative decision-making created an atmosphere of fear and endangered progressive thinking and freedom of creation, and made working in the field of art sickening and hazardous. Self-management practices in a reign-of-terror atmosphere are impossible, because the trust of the government is always given to politically 'correct' individuals.

—Excerpt from the 'Open Letter to the Yugoslav Public', 1971, signed by the February Group

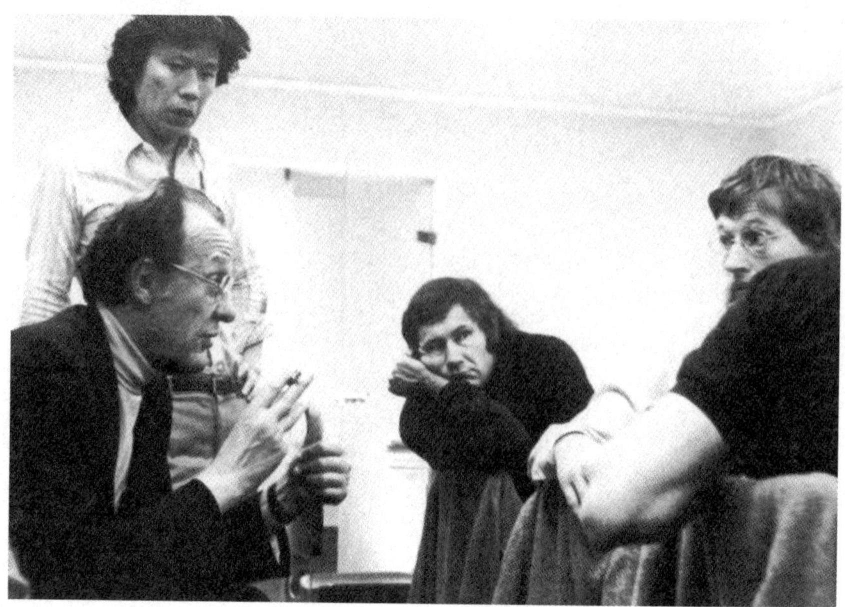

Georges Boudaille, Toshiaki Minemura, Ješa Denegri and Armin Zweite during a meeting of the Selection Committee of the Biennale Internationale des Jeunes Artistes de Paris (Paris Biennial of Young Artists), Paris, 1977

7.   <u>My Dear Friends, You Have No Idea</u>

BD   Now you are talking about the situation in Novi Sad, where there was a backlash against the artists of the 'false avant-garde', which is how the regime's press of the time labeled them. This effectively brought about the demise of the Novi Sad neo-avant-garde and the Conceptual art scene that revolved around the Youth Forum (Tribina mladih) and the *Index*, *Új Symposion*, and *Polja* magazines, and it brought prison time for Mandić and Bogdanović. 'Open Letter to the Yugoslav Public' and other political provocations of the members of the KÔD group, later the February Group, brought the process full circle in 1971 with the activities of the January and February Groups which became monthly meetings and a temporary way of working for these artists.[22] One gets the impression that, in contrast with the situation in other bigger cities in Yugoslavia, the authorities came down hard on the Novi Sad scene and that this was orchestrated by people from cultural circles close to the Communist Party and the security services.

JD   Well, on the one hand we have the iron hand of the regime that puts artists in prison, and on the other we also have the same artists, marginalised and condemned, exhibiting in state-run institutions and taking part in state representation at the Paris Biennial. While this sounds rather paradoxical, it also speaks of the heterogenous nature of the socialist system in Yugoslavia.

BD   In 1977 you returned to Paris, again for the Paris Biennial, but this time as one of the curators of the entire programme.

JD   This time I was invited by the organisers because the Biennial's concept had changed in the intervening years. It changed from nationally made selections to an international curatorial team within which there was an artistic director who presides. That time it was Georges Boudaille. Here you see in this photograph the international team of curators: Georges Boudaille, Michael Compton, me, the American curator Nina Felshen and Catherine Millet. This is Tommaso Trini, a very important critic and curator at the time – he

was easiest to communicate with him because of our
common language – and Armin Zweite, the curator and later
the director of the Städtischen Galerie im Lenbachhaus
in Munich. Then there is Ad Petersen, also a very important
curator at the time who later became the director of the
Stedelijk Museum in Amsterdam. And finally, this is the
Japanese critic and curator Toshiaki Minemura, who had
also been very involved in several of the preceding Biennials.

BD   How did you come to be invited to join the curatorial
team? You were the only one from a socialist country.
Were you actually referred to as the curator in charge of
Eastern Europe?

JD   During preparations for the 1977 Paris Biennial the
decision was taken that, instead of national selectors, an
international team of curators would conceive the exhibition
based on artists' portfolios. We gathered in Paris and meetings were held over the concept of the exhibition, and
then we examined the hundreds of submitted portfolios.
The working day began about 10 or 11am and ran until late,
as long as our patience and attention held out.

JV   How were the portfolios gathered? Was there a
competition, an open call, or was it by invitation?

JD   The artists' portfolios were gathered in various ways.
Some artists personally delivered them, while others sent
them by post from abroad. The portfolios were delivered in
large numbers. The artists were informed and invited in
a variety of ways. The commission sat for days and made its
selection – those who were more familiar with the work of
certain artists spoke about them; we exchanged opinions
and there were many discussions. On the whole, everything
went smoothly, but there was one incident that caused
quite a lot of consternation. Our jury turned down two
members of the group Supports/Surfaces, Marc Devade
and Louis Cane, who were very important artists in France
at the time. As the key representatives of the group of
painters of Marxist provenance they were important because
they had given the problem of painting a radical leftist
ideology, which is a context that should be acknowledged.

It so happened that in the process of making the selection, Compton and Minemura did not like their work. I was familiar with the problematic they dealt with, and I was all for them, but they were rejected in the final vote.

BD   So although the decisions were made by consensus, this time it was decided by a small margin of votes?

JD   Exactly. We would review a portfolio and together we would say 'yes' or 'no'. A number of artists had international reputations. Sometimes differences of opinion arose. Also, several Yugoslav artists were selected: Mladen Stilinović, Raša Todosijević, Group 143 and Šalamun, on this occasion with his paintings. A very cooperative and congenial atmosphere prevailed. The artists made their submissions on the basis of a set of propositions that they had to meet. Which meant they had to submit a biography, a self-authored text, or an essay by a critic about their work, together with photographic documentation. This had to be available in the selection process. It was a demanding job, but it was also a pleasure to see, hear and learn about the work of so many artists.

BD   Did you notice in the selection that a change of artistic paradigms that became evident at the end of the 1970s was approaching in relation to what had been characteristic of the 1971 Biennial?

JD   This was 1977, almost ten years after the events of 1968. The selection includes critics from diverse backgrounds, and there are no longer, strictly speaking, any more dominant ideas and trends. My proposals were still in the vein of Conceptual art. If we look at this historically, here you will find the first indications of Transavanguardia, the return of painting, a softening of the position that the New Art Practices represented a *break*. The realignments in art that happened in Yugoslavia in the 1980s were already under way in the West by the end of the 1970s. Art was understood as the great aggregate of all possible languages. This is the pluralistic approach of postmodernism. The Paris Biennial itself is perceived as an art institution that should cultivate all these languages in anticipation of artistic

globalism. And then, precisely in 1977, they invited curators
of all kinds from all the global centres. I was given the job
of writing an essay on art in the socialist countries. Jelena
already commented on this in our previous conversations.
One year later, in 1978, I was a jury member at the Lisbon
Biennial of Drawing, at which Georg Jappe, Achille Bonito
Oliva and Julião Sarmento were presiding. During the review
of the works, I realised that I was still looking through the
lens of the 1970s, though I did register the changes in
the scene. Bonito Oliva, however, proposed an award for a
young German artist whose work was akin to that of the
Neue Wilde, to Neo-Expressionism, but it wasn't accepted.
At that moment I learned about Transavanguardia from
Achille. After the judging session, we sat in a restaurant and
Bonito made the following comment: 'My dear friends,
you have no idea – that art that will appear within a year on
the world art stage will be just like the art I proposed that
you wouldn't accept.' This was directed particularly at Georg
Jappe. And then, the new exhibitions begin to appear:
Transavanguardia Italiana, *Transavanguardia Internazionale*,
etcetera. This was about one whole manoeuvre, about a new
trend which, as we see, was critically and organisationally
set up through galleries and the accompanying writing. I see
the Lisbon Biennial of Drawing and our role in the jury as
a story that opened up a professional dilemma for me over
the question of how to position myself in the transition
announced by the arrival of the art of the new decade, the
art of the 1980s.

8.	Stipends for the Advancement of Curators:
	Italy, Czechoslovakia, Poland (Vignette)

JV	The research trips you went on thanks to the stipends
which you received via the Museum were important for the
work you did for both biennials in Paris. First your trip
to Italy in the late 1960s, and then to Czechoslovakia and
Poland in the 1970s.

JD	I first received a stipend in 1968–1969 for a six-month
trip to Italy. The stipend was intended for one person, but
Biljana also joined me. One day Protić asked me: 'Why don't

you go somewhere on a stipend?' He was interested in
facilitating education for curators. I was thrilled, of course.

JV   You were also the only curator in the Museum at
that time who showed an affinity for the New Art Practices,
as well as for academic-museological research.

JD   I didn't even think of that as being an academic
pursuit. Our duty in the Museum was to research art history,
to learn about the works of artists and critics from the
20th century, and the decennial exhibitions (*Yugoslav Art of
20th Century*) were a particular focal point. For example,
for the exhibition *Treća decenija* (*The Third Decade*) in 1967
I was allocated the task of writing an essay about art criticism
of the 1920s, and then I studied Rastko Petrović and Antun
Branko Šimić and realised that there had also been a major
discussion about the reorientation of the art scene in those
years.[23] It helped me to connect my interests in art production with the historical research. I didn't lose out in any
way from the research and historicisation activities of the
Museum – that was a challenge in its own way – but I was
also inclined towards a more informal type of education.

JV   At the time, the paradigm of education had become
central, particularly in the context of socialism, which
insisted on making it available to everyone. Protić himself
probably held similar ideas: education and research. Some
kind of internal staff development was evidently a part
of his programme and policies for the museum staff. The
second trip we singled out here was an exchange project
with Czechoslovakia and Poland. You travelled to Prague
and Łódź.

JD   Education was important, but I was also simply
curious. I went as a museum curator to Czechoslovakia and
Poland through an inter-institutional exchange of curators,
and I was introduced to the art scenes which had just then,
if not later, become internationally recognised. Immediately
upon arrival I recognised the very artistically advanced
nature of these centres, and of their traditions and languages
– both in the historical avant-garde and in the New Art
Practices. That knowledge and opportunity to research

developments in the field helped me when I was invited
to write this essay about the Eastern European art scene
for the 1977 Paris Biennial.

And this is how that came about: Protić, in the
capacity of a member of the jury of the International Biennial
of Graphic Arts in Ljubljana, frequently visited Zoran
Kržišnik, and since the Ljubljana Biennial is a matrix of
the non-aligned strategy of cultural politics, Kržišnik asked
very important figures to be jury members. This is how a
collaboration was established with Jiří Kotalík, the director
of the National Gallery in Prague, and Ryszard Stanisławski,
the director of the Muzeum Sztuki Łódź. The museum in
Łódź is part of the Polish cultural heritage of Constructivism.

JV   The Museum in Łódź has a highly developed permanent exhibit, which was valuable for me, to be able to see
the avant-garde part of their history.

JD   You cannot imagine the feeling of admiration I had
when standing before the greatest phenomena in avant-
garde art, for instance Władysław Strzemiński. Kotalík,
Stanisławski, and Protić came up with the idea of a curatorial
exchange, and it seems that this was important above all for
curators from the Eastern Bloc who couldn't travel so easily.
First the curator Mahulena Nešlehová of the National Gallery
in Prague visited us as part of this exchange. She later
worked with the Czechoslovak Informel. When our curators
were asked if they would like to go to Czechoslovakia and
Poland, no one was interested. I put myself forwards. Some
of my colleagues sighed: 'What's there for us?' Many people
from here still lived in the conviction that we belonged
to the free world, and that people didn't live freely in the
Eastern Bloc. But I was curious. I visited Poland again later
when I went with their curators to a Solidarność meeting
in Gdansk. I owe all this knowledge to the Museum.

9. Influences from Italy: Arte Povera and
    Acritical Criticism

BD We are talking about your involvement in the events
associated with the New Art Practices, and also about the
theoretical premises you used to interpret and read that
paradigmatic change that emerged in the late 1960s. Your
engagement with the art of the 1960s and 1970s was, as we
have seen, very close in theoretical terms to Argan. And then
Germano Celant was a major influence for you when we get
to the New Art Practices. As you say in your book which
addresses the issues in the Serbian art of the 1970s,[24] you
adopt the four categories laid out by Celant: Conceptual art,
Land art, Arte Povera and Body art. You take those four
concepts as the four concepts of the New Art Practices.

JD My acquaintanceship with Celant started an interesting exchange of information about the current events. We
met in 1965 at the third exhibition of the New Tendencies in
Zagreb and at the international conference in Brezovica,
close to Zagreb, at which experts from the different fields of
Kinetic art and Computer art gave talks. Umbro Apollonio
was also a guest, a very important critic, and at the time the
director of the Archive of the Venice Biennale and the editor
of the magazine *La Biennale*. Celant was his assistant at that
time, and it was then the custom that an older critic takes
along a younger critic, to introduce him around. Celant was
already a serious expert about the artistic events of the time,
and we became friends and afterwards kept up correspondence. In one letter he wrote: 'What we saw in Zagreb [the
New Tendencies], that's a fait accompli, now completely new
ideas are emerging in art.'
    After some time, I found essays by Celant in the
magazine *La Biennale* which he later collated into a book,
and which represented a kind of chronological retrospective
of the events important to the development of the New
Art Practices. In 1966, Lucy Lippard curated the exhibition
Eccentric Abstraction at the Fischbach Gallery in New York,
which evoked a surrealist notion of the subliminal and set
the scene for what would later be seen as Postminimalism.
Also, Robert Morris published his famous essay 'Anti Form'.
Celant followed current developments thoroughly and

in detail. The new phenomena were the artists of Genoa, Turin, Milan, Rome, and their use of 'poor' materials, on the basis of which Celant came up with the term *arte povera*. In 1967 I went with Biljana to Rome where the AICA Congress was being held, and then to the 6th Biennial in San Marino, where in 1963 Argan had organised *Oltre L'Informale,* an exhibition that brought Art Informel to an end and asked what came next.

JV   How would you translate the title of this exhibition?

JD   *Beyond Informel.* Therefore in Italian, not *dopo* (after) but *oltre* (beyond). I wholeheartedly endorsed that definition, because Art Informel had by this point lasted ten years, and it had already become academicised. What comes after: the New Tendencies in the constructivist vein, the Nouveau Réalisme promoted by Pierre Restany, the new figuration as heterogeneous phenomena; and all these fall under the new directions of *dopo l'informale.* That was 1963.

    When Biljana and I arrived at the San Marino Biennale in 1967,[25] there were still exhibits of lumino-kinetic works in the central exhibition spaces as there had been at the New Tendencies exhibitions. Everything spun around, everything was in a dark space and illuminated in some way so that lights flashed when you entered. But Biljana looks around and sees something in one corner that looks like a discarded chain, and in the other corner something that looks like someone had taken a newspaper and put it on the floor. Biljana says: 'That's the best, here! That and that …' – and she points out these two works. And I say: 'Are you crazy? How can that be the best after all the things we have seen?' – because Lumino-Kinetic art had evolved from objects to whole environments and there was a lot of fascinating stuff here. But Biljana had such a sense for things, an intuition, something existential and inclined towards very modest things that were discrete in their pre-sentation, impoverished in the sense of a spectacle. She had in essence a very deep and vital relationship to what had brought about the New Art Practices and that whole turning point in the second half of the 1960s and the beginning of the 1970s. She leaned more towards immaterial forms and in those two installations, which were so ephemeral that one

might have easily overlooked them, she found something
that seemed to be of the greatest importance to what
was going on in art in that moment. One of those works,
the newspaper on the floor, was indeed one of the most
important works of Arte Povera, made by Luciano Fabro.
It was called *Floor/Tautology* (1967).

Finally, we get to 1968, and without it and all its
further implications many things in art simply could not be
understood. As the critic Maurizio Calvesi said: 'prima e
dopo sessanta otto' – art divides before and after 1968. This
periodisation speaks about something that happened on
an existential level. There can no longer be such a fascination
with new technologies and Computer art, but rather there
is a turn towards impoverished and discarded materials,
towards the work of young artists, towards experimentation.
And my selection for Paris reflects that dilemma; there are
Bonačić and Radović as the artists who brought the story
of Neo-Constructivism to an end precisely through their
use of computers, and there is this younger generation of
conceptual artists. Even though I followed Celant's writing,
it seems I learned the most about the New Art Practices
from Biljana.

The San Marino Biennale was a ground-breaking
exhibition for the coming artistic developments in Italy and
around the world. We met many artists, critics and gallerists.
That break would have further consequences on both
existential and cultural levels. At the Venice Biennale of
1964, the Golden Lion was awarded to Robert Rauschenberg,
and at the next Biennale in 1966 the same award was given
to Julio Le Parc for his Kinetic art, and at the 1968 Biennale
Pino Pascali received the award as a representative of Arte
Povera.

By pure chance Biljana and I happened to be at the
source of some of these events. We travelled from city
to city and looked at the old architecture and art. Arezzo,
Siena, Verona, Milan, Turin, Genoa, Pisa, Bologna, Perugia,
Florence, Naples … Celant is from Genoa, Northern Italy,
which began to develop rapidly at the end of the 1950s.
It was said that Arte Povera is in essence the art of industrial
society, and it isn't about a return to rural culture like some
aspects of the hippy culture/movement. It is more a continuation of urban high culture but without the exaltation of

modern progress and is rather a particular critical position and confrontation with the dynamics of the times. The new generation of the time no longer believed the story of a priori modernist progress. The story's validity was questioned in intellectual circles, in education, among students, and that is the essence of Arte Povera. I felt we were in the presence of a change in paradigm. In Rome, where we were stationed in 1969, we met Jannis Kounellis and his wife Effi. We learnt a great deal about Kounellis's work, even though he usually said nothing about it. We attended his exhibition at Galleria L'Attico where he exhibited 12 horses. I remember that we arrived very early for the opening, so that we had the opportunity to see how the horses were led in and out of the gallery. The horses were powerful and dignified. A magnificent exhibition: live animals in the gallery were marking a moment of great change.

BD   What was Galleria L'Attico's exhibition policy?

JD   Galleria L'Attico was run by Fabio Sargentini, the son of the owner of the Galleria L'Attico Senior. 'Senior' was a collector of the top art of the modern period, and he had some paintings by Gabrijel Stupica. However, the son as the heir had his own idea for a gallery. L'Attico Junior wasn't a classic white cube gallery space but rather a garage in the street, at Via Cesare Beccaria, a large space in which Kounellis could put his horses. The next exhibition was Mario Merz with igloos and neon scripts, then Gino di Dominicis, a phenomenal, controversial artist who inspired many of today's artists – Maurizio Cattelan among others. Fabio Sargentini was also interested in performance, video, new dance and minimalist music, which were all brought into the gallery space – artists like Trisha Brown, La Monte Young and others. Biljana was interested in performances that were based on dance and symbolic movement, so later on she invited Simone Forti to Belgrade as a guest at the April Meetings at the Student Cultural Centre.

JV   Arte Povera had two centres: Rome and Turin. And here we come to the problematic that you are speaking about – the question of the interpretation of Arte Povera as an urban, anti-industrial art in the time of the industrial boom in Northern Italy. The pride of Italian industrialisation and modernisation is found in Turin, the Fiat factory in the district of Mirafiori, where during the 1960s the workers' strikes took place and resulted at the end of the decade in the autonomist movement and the famous 'refusal to work'. What was your impression of Turin then, and what in general were the connections between Arte Povera and these social movements?

JD   Turin is a complex city with many social phenomena and events, and it is the city in which the most artists appeared within this particular artistic tendency – Mario Merz, Michelangelo Pistoletto, Giulio Paolini, Giuseppe Penone, Gilberto Zorio and Giovanni Anselmo among others. There were also numerous contradictions in Turin – the social context in which 'poor art' is formed, the famous gallery of Gian Enzo Sperone which was important for the international promotion of Arte Povera. Sperone developed strategies that helped this art to spread vigorously and to be acknowledged relatively swiftly by the art system. He joined forces with the American gallery Westwater, which had launched Anti Form art. This is how a strong bridge between Arte Povera and Anti Form, between Europe and America, was established, the way world trends come to be created. However, in that moment we were more interested in the meaning of Arte Povera and we used our acquaintance with Sperone in the hope that he would show us his enormous attic, which served as a storage space for all the works he had acquired. This is how we got to see a great number of Pop art paintings and the early Arte Povera works.

BD   Who else did you meet that time in Italy?

JD   Our correspondence with artists and gallery spaces was very open and hospitable. The acquaintance with Pistoletto was especially interesting. Pistoletto organised an impressive performance using his heartbeat there in his studio, which he even made available to us to spend the night. One sat in the dark and listened to these loud beating sounds; it was very compelling. On another occasion Pistoletto and Maria Pioppi made a performance using huge trumpets into which they blew and then said: 'I am poor, you're rich – that's wrong; I am rich and you're poor – that's wrong; I am rich and you are rich – that's ok; I am poor and you are poor – that's ok.' Pistoletto was very rich indeed. But that was the time of the culture of the commune and communitarianism, and that's how all of us ended up together in a flux of contacts and communication.

Also, as we have already noted, the new conceptual principles developed by Celant were important for the development of this art and some of its interpretations. He launched the critical theory known as acritical criticism.[26] This was also close to Susan Sontag's concept of 'against interpretation' set out in the text of the same name.[27] Both concepts served as an attack on the old institution of the critic, as represented by Clement Greenberg. Celant says that the critic can no longer criticise the artist, because we don't know from which position to criticise them if we assume that the artist is aware of what they are doing and why they do it precisely the way they do. According to this new approach the role of the critic is indeed to provide a platform for the artist. And that marks the beginning of the relationship between curating and criticism. Celant refers to Sontag when he says that the role of the critic is to provide platforms for art practices, from which comes the concept used in Italy and further afield, and which we here translate as criticism at work. Therefore, *critica in atto*, criticism in the act, *kritika na delu*.

BD   Criticism in the making, criticism as an active approach, and not criticism that relates to the finished work.

JD   Indeed.

JV   The term 'applied criticism' (*primenjena kritika*) was in circulation within the Belgrade Student Cultural Centre, which may have derived from Celant's theory but may also be an autonomous term. Our research into the Belgrade Student Cultural Centre touched upon this term, primarily through Dunja Blažević, and we understood it as a kind of euphemism for curatorial practice.[28]

JD   You could put it that way. You need to return to the Yugoslav space of the 1960s and 1970s, when cultural events, film, theatre, literature, art, media and so on, were thriving on all levels. Communication between the Yugoslav and European centres was very intense. Every centre had a certain linguistically structured profile by which it was recognisable. In Belgrade in 1967 a group of artists, architects and art historians initiated Galerija 212 in the theatre Atelje 212. They were Damnjan, Reljić, Kalajić, Šejka, Slobodan and Saveta Mašić, Irina Subotić, Biljana and me. Biljana organised the international art programme for the BITEF theatre festival from 1968 to 1973. The Student Cultural Centre opened in 1971 and a busy programme of great events began with the April Meetings: the Festival of Expanded Media and the October exhibitions of 1971–1975, bringing about the international meetings of critics and architecture, design and art symposia. The new mood calls forth a generational divide vis-à-vis the decade of the 1960s and the expanded media and performative ways of behaving in the multidisciplinary context of the 1970s that had just come onto the scene. Everything became possible!

10.   <u>Lotta Poetica</u>

BD   Does the appearance of artist performances at the BITEF theatre festival in 1968 and 1969 mark a turning point for the emergence of the New Art Practices in Belgrade?

JD   At that time *Teatro povero* was current. At its first iteration in 1967 the BITEF theatre festival hosted Jerzy Grotowski, who created that concept. We quickly began to discern the logic behind all of this: in place of technological exaltation, there is *poor art*. In Celant's manifesto of Arte Povera it is introduced as 'the new guerrilla art',[29] and this is all impregnated by the ideas of 1968. Tommaso Trini was also an important protagonist on the scene. He edited the magazine *Data Arte*, which was important for all these topics at the time. Biljana published an essay there about Marina Abramović, when she had her two key performances in Italy, *Ritam 4 (Rhythm 4)* in Galleria Diagramma in Milan in 1974, and *Ritam 0 (Rhythm 0)*, which would become particularly famous, in Galleria Studio Morra in Naples the following year.[30] Later, I wrote a long essay for them about the New Art Practices in Yugoslavia.[31] On an earlier visit to Italy, to the Festival of Visual and Concrete Poetry at Viterbo, Biljana met the various protagonists of this movement, like Adriano Spatola, with whom Bogdanka Poznanović later worked. She also met Milenko Matanović and the members of the OHO group who had come out of visual poetry, which they called 'Reism'. There were slogans like *Lotta poetica* ('poetic struggle') or *Lotta continua* ('the struggle goes on'). It is not easy to understand the transition from these actions if you don't bear in mind how they involved building, dissolving or splitting a word or an idea into letters. And then from the idea and the word you came to something concrete that has no additional meaning and is a pure construction. If the word is a poem and you break it up, then the letter 'e' remains, and nothing else. This art developed entirely out of the tautology of a letter.

JV   Poetry had already ceased to be a metaphysical idea with the historical avant-gardes, but here we're speaking about a new deconstructive turn.

JD   The poem becomes a *poem*, and the early theoreticians of this movement or these experiments emphasise the materiality of the thing itself, of the word and the letter. Taras Kermauner says: 'The poem is made from letters.' We can think about Marko Pogačnik's plaster casts of bottles in a similar way. They are the type of objects that could be an integral part of a classical artistic composition, but here they are reduced to their pure materiality. Pogačnik takes a bottle, makes a plaster mould, smashes the glass, and does it all over again. He has made hundreds of such moulds. In 1969 we found ourselves in Zagreb at the OHO group exhibition entitled *Pradjedovi* (*Great-Grandfathers*). The exhibition featured the work of David Nez, who took roof tiles and laid them out flat on the floor. Tomaž Šalamun built a haystack. Biljana was already in contact with them, so they exhibited at the BITEF theatre festival in 1968 and again in 1969. The first Happening of the OHO group in Belgrade was called *Pasija* (*The Passion*) – *Crossing the Red Sea*. OHO liked titles like that. They took rolls of paper and pierced them and put their heads through the holes. The appearances of the OHO members were absolutely in the spirit of the youth culture of the day – hippies with long hair and a specific way of dressing. They also acted that way, like slackers, sometimes smoking grass and so on.

BD   Seen from the perspective of Yugoslav art history, it is the first time marijuana appears on the art scene. Were the previous generations of artists taking some kind of narcotics?

JD   No. They were more inclined to alcohol. But this thing with OHO, this isn't part of a 'drug culture' in any serious way, they were just smoking pot. This is more about a cultural coding, not about heavy drinking or drug addiction.

JV   We're not talking about that. We just want to make a distinction, purely from the perspective of popular culture and art, because alcohol is associated with the bohemian figure of the artist and the notion of artistic individuality. And now we are talking about a different, more communitarian spirit, and the urban youth culture, which became the substrate of many art collectives and forms of collective action at the end of the 1960s and into the 1970s.

JD   This is another type of culture and another type of art. Which is why we constantly thought about the 'new'. These phenomena, and all those forms of refusal about which we spoke with regard to the Paris Biennial and the Novi Sad art scene, are more closely tied to hippy culture – particularly OHO. And for me there is that constant dilemma, as well as the question as to whether we should make a distinction between this counterculture and the art in the fullest sense of the word. For OHO and one part of the Novi Sad artists this is definitely art, because people were able to conceptualise and think of what they do as art, but their lifestyle is more a question of counterculture.

JV   But that very lifestyle was the basis of such a way of thinking.

JD   Exactly. I remember I had to take the OHO artists around Belgrade and entertain them for a while. For them the city was a place in which to have a good time. While we were strolling around, we found out that Spaghetti Westerns were being shown in the Dom Sindikata (Union Hall) cinema, so we headed there. I learnt from them that this was something really phenomenal, and to this day there isn't anything more enjoyable for me than watching a Sergio Leone film. This was a revelation for me, and when we arrived at the cinema, they said that they didn't want to watch only one, but three films in a row. So, they spent the whole day in the cinema. It was still a working day for me at the Museum, and I still had work to do, things to attend to. But the OHO group were very authentic in their lifestyle, in their way of seeing and their art. For example, at BITEF they performed *The Passion*, as well as their Street Theatre. The procession started at Dom omladine (Youth House), and whoever wanted could join in.

BD   How did the people there respond?

JD   Some watched, not knowing what it was about; some were curious, paused to look and then went on their way. For them this was some youngsters' mischief. But when you say Street Theatre – that was already an important artistic concept – La MaMa, the Living Theatre, they all took part in the early manifestations of BITEF. I listened to Grotowski's lectures; I remember he was speaking in Polish, which was a problem, and the organisers almost didn't find an interpreter.

We were witnessing all that flux that Celant had told us about a few years before. But the story we had learned about since we had met him back in 1965 was already changing two years later, because something quite different was happening. This became clear when the revolt of 1968 unfolded. If that hadn't happened, there wouldn't have been the New Art Practices and all their socio-political implications. Many exhibitions were realised spontaneously with impoverished materials, so they didn't have to mean some great step forwards but rather a preoccupation with contemporaneity. We understood such phenomena on the one hand as a breaking point, a provocation, a precedent and, on the other, as something that could be seen as a continuation of other ruptures in art, hence this story about continuity and ruptures. Not only Kounellis and his horses

come to mind. They followed Lucio Fontana and Alberto
Burri, and Biljana and I also thought of comparisons
with the paintings of Cy Twombly. Kounellis used a garage
instead of a canvas.

JV   You want to say that these developments in art were
not an issue of discontinuity, or a break with the previous,
even though there was an evident change in the political
climate and way of living, but rather that they came out of
the entire corpus of art history. Therefore, it wasn't about a
generation of artists that made an absolute break with all
previous practices, but rather about establishing a new kind
of continuity.

JD   It was also a break to some degree because artists
certainly identified with the way of living and the political
options the 1960s and 1970s brought with them. In Italy,
the intellectual circles and the youth were especially politicised. Then the armed actions of the Red Brigades and
other radical groups emerged. One Yugoslav artist, Ilija
Šoškić, took part in some of these radical political actions
in Italy. This was a scene in which everything was mixed up
with politics – everyone was politicised to the maximum.
But on the other hand you had to be aware that if you
wanted to construct a type of art that would become a world
phenomenon, and if Sperone was working with the Westwater gallery, if you wanted to work with Robert Morris or
the group of artists from the Galleria Sperone, you had
to be on the same plane, you had to construct a language
based on continuity. In the same way Greenberg created
a continuity between Pollock and Noland. A continuity had
to exist in order for something to be considered art.

II.   Once Again on the Other Line

BD   In other words, the consequence of all this was
that it would be very difficult to develop a 'new art practice'
in those centres that didn't already have at least some
tradition of radical artistic activity, namely a tradition of
the avant-garde, if we may call it that. And that's exactly
why you developed the thesis of the Other Line.

JD   The proposal for the Other Line in the Yugoslav Art Space is founded on the principle that there is a continuity between the historical avant-gardes of the 1920s and the post-war avant-gardes.[32] Confirmation of this continuity was provided by the first revalorisations of the groups within the historical avant-garde, such as Zenit and Yugo-Dada, in Miodrag Protić's study for the exhibition catalogue *Treća decenija – konstruktivno slikarstvo* (*The Third Decade – Constructivist Painting*) for the Belgrade Museum of Contemporary Art in 1967.[33] This is how we gained insights into the graphic art of Mihailo Petrov that was published in the magazines *Zenit*, *Dada Tank* and *Út*. Certain members of EXAT 51 displayed a knowledge of the Zenit period of Josip Seissel, otherwise known as Jo Klek, and later Vera Horvat Pintarić curated his retrospective in the Galerija Nova in Zagreb in 1978.[34] His invention was pure abstract painting, which he named after the materials he used: ARBOS for ARtija-BOja-Slika (paper-colour-painting, or in German PAFAMA (PApier-FArben-MAlerei). Members of the OHO group likened the historical legacy of Kosovel and Černigoj and members of the Bosch+Bosch group to Lajos Kassák and Hungarian activism. The actual existence of this continuity is supported by the fact that individual members of the neo-avant-garde of the 1950s and 1960s and the New Art Practices of the 1970s built on the legacies of their predecessors from the 1920s.

BD   I will pose the question another way because it concerns art history and methodology. We are talking about tradition and the interruptions made in it by the avant-garde. And here you are talking about the necessity of seeing things in a historical way, through art history. The point of the Russian avant-garde is a revolutionary break, the aim of Futurism is to sink Venice; therefore, to break with art tradition. But by using the concept of the Other Line you are establishing a 'new tradition' that begins with the avant-garde, even though it actually lies in politico-artistic breaks and ruptures. The avant-garde was not about continuity, but about a cultural and political rupture.

JD   Yes, the Soviet avant-garde cannot be thought without the October Revolution.

BD   But speaking of traditions there is also a major reference made to the legacy of Russian icon painting, as well as to Russian folk art, to *lubki* woodblock prints, within the Russian avant-garde. Even in the case of Malevich himself.

JD   Futurism came out of symbolism, and it cannot be conceived in any other way. Look at the early Umberto Boccioni. Not one of those avant-garde artists proposed the idea of a beet without a root … I had the chance to go to Zurich and visit Cabaret Voltaire. The works of Hugo Ball clearly indicate how everyone has to start somewhere. I think that the great artists, the great artistic events, re-codify their predecessors in a profound way, and do not ignore or discard them completely.

JV   Let's return to the beginning of the discussion and the interpretation of the Other Line. When we organised the exhibition *Political Practices of (Post-)Yugoslav Art: Retrospective 01* in 2009, at one point we looked back at the sense of that term which, in how I read it, actually emphasises the dialectic of continuity and rupture.[35] I would see the Soviet avant-garde as well as Dada and Futurism as moments of breaks with the dominant traditions, but there is still the question of how to look at this now, taking into account a certain type of literacy in the language of art, in the formal thinking that was crucial for the case of the historical avant-gardes. It seems to me that your concept of the Other Line tries to think this dialectic of continuity and rupture. The Other Line assumes a connection, historical and conceptual, between the various points of rupture with the dominant art traditions. The Other Line binds these points of rupture together.[36]

BD   Is it then a *tradition of ruptures with tradition*?

JV   Yes, but I am not very keen on the word tradition. I would say a *continuity of ruptures* within artistic traditions. That continuity is stubbornness, persistence, the necessity of an historical break, a break with the institution of art if we speak in Peter Bürger's terms.

JD   The thesis of the Other Line is indeed polemical, but it isn't destructive or exclusive because – which is after all a completely reasonable and indisputable supposition – it acknowledges and accepts all preceding traditions and their values. The Other Line is indeed an addition, and is no way a rejection of the central and prevailing 'main line' or the 'mainstream' if you will, of the local artistic heritage and existing historiography of modern art. But the interesting paradox is that it is precisely those phenomena that fall under the term the Other Line, unlike locally-oriented modernism, which has recently become the main point of reference for the international art scene. Evidence of this are the exhibitions of EXAT 51 at Krefeld, Gorgona at Vaduz, the New Tendencies at Ingolstadt and Karlsruhe, as well as numerous Yugoslav presentations of the New Art Practices of the 1970s, of the OHO group members, Marina Abramović, Braco Dimitrijević, Todosijević, Paripović, Popović, Urkom, Damnjan, Stilinović, Goran Đorđević, Goran Trbuljak, Sanja Iveković, Gotovac and so on. Research and new knowledge of the historical avant-garde – Zenit, Dada, Slovenian Constructivism, Belgrade Surrealism – owe much to the noteworthy studies and appearances of a small number of art historians who address these subjects at various gatherings of professionals. All this has significantly contributed to changes in the criteria of the valorisation and reception of the art of the 20th century from the Yugoslav cultural space in the relevant European and international contexts.

12.   Meetings with Grgo Gamulin: On Unitarism, Nationalism and Generational Differences (Vignette)

BD   The works of some artists of the New Art Practices were exhibited in the Yugoslav pavilion at the Venice Biennale in 1976 when Putar was commissioner. This seems to be an advanced decision. Braco Dimitrijević and Damnjan were included in the exhibition with two Gorgona members, Knifer and Kožarić, as well as two hyperrealist painters, Jesih and Gvardijančić, who were something of a trend. Once you told us an anecdote about the renowned Croatian art critic Grgo Gamulin, who objected particularly to this exhibition.

JD   I frequently went from Belgrade to Zagreb to see exhibitions and meet with artists and colleagues. The train arrived early in the morning and I went for a cup of coffee, to wait for the museums and bookshops to open. There was one specialist bookshop on Cvjetni trg (Flower Square) and I headed over to it to spend a bit of time and buy something. And I saw that Grgo Gamulin was approaching me from the side. I thought he was not close enough to notice me, so I turned my head away and swiftly entered the bookshop. However, as I was leafing through some magazines in the morning quiet, he approached me from behind and said: 'Were you trying to avoid me?' I replied: 'Oh, Professor Gamulin (even though he had not been my professor), what a surprise! It is a pleasure to see you, how are you?' He was the type of man that made your blood run cold – severe and uncompromising on everything. He said: 'How am I?? Don't give me that! There's something I need to discuss with you.'

JV   An informal chat? [Laughs.]

JD   He said the following: 'You young critics' – and that refers to Igor Zidić, Želimir Koščević, me and others – 'instead of taking responsibility and finally openly saying to those two Croatian artists, Kožarić and above all Knifer, that they are just endlessly repeating the same sterile ideas and concepts, you urge them on by writing about them and their delusions'. He said that this was an example of the irresponsible nature of the young critics, who are conformist and pander and do not take a critical view of the development of art. 'You know what', I said timidly, 'I wouldn't say that each one of Knifer's meanders is the same.' Then he got still angrier and moved onto Kožarić, who was exhibiting his works in the form of a type of dump or heap at the Venice Biennale in 1976: 'Kožarić is showing his attitude at the Biennale by throwing his works around and depriving them of their sculptural status.' He was probably thinking that Kožarić devalued the sculptures in some way by placing them in heaps, because until recently he had always placed them on plinths. And I said, again sheepishly: 'Maybe he didn't just throw them around as you are saying – this can be interpreted as a kind of collage/installation in space, which

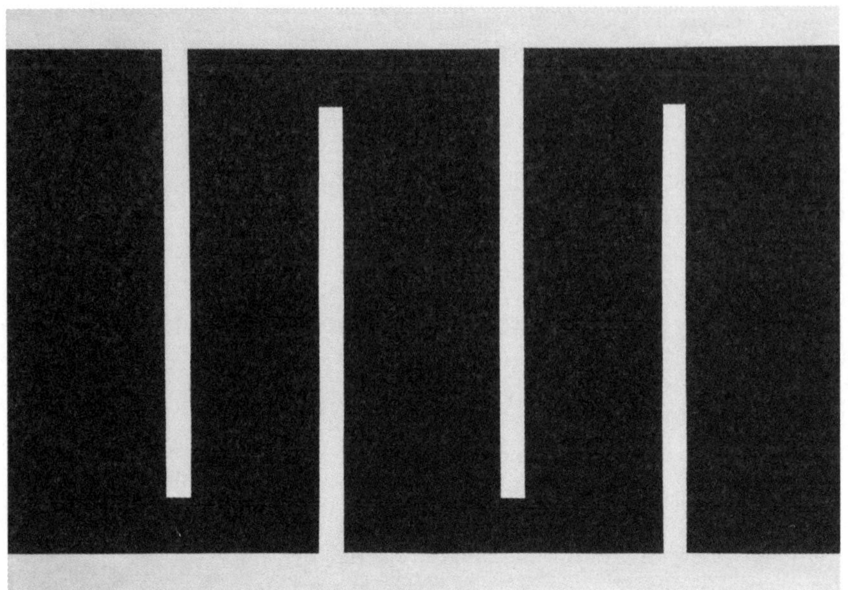

Julije Knifer
Composition I, 1960–1962
Oil on canvas, 88 × 130 cm

the artist made from his own sculptures.' Then he got even more upset because he didn't want to admit that he didn't think of that: 'No, it can't be like that, that's not collage!' I was now feeling quite nervous, so I said: 'He does this to his own work, and if he does so it is to his own detriment, and that is an artistic attitude.' But then he said to me solemnly: 'But the *Patria* may not lose a single one of its artists!'

JV   What does he say? *Partija* may not lose a single artist?[37]

BD   Not *Partija,* but *Patria*! What year was that?

JD   As I said, it was after the Biennial of 1976. In the 1970s such nationalist discourse was already very common in Yugoslavia.

BD   The homeland may not lose a single artist …

JD   Which means that the artist doesn't have the right to devalue their own work because they don't own it, but rather the homeland does.

BD   Gamulin was indeed associated with the 'Croatian Spring'[38] and for us he is the embodiment of an exceptionally influential art critic who in the climate of socialism never abandoned the idea of national culture – nor is he the sole example in Croatia or Serbia. There is a second part to your anecdote that concerns an exhibition organized by the Belgrade Museum of Contemporary Art in Zagreb.

JD   Yes. The next time I met him was in 1986 when Kosta Bogdanović was the director of the Museum in the mid-1980s and we had produced the large exhibition *Yugoslav Graphic Arts 1950–1980*.[39] The Museum had agreed with the Zagreb Art Pavilion to take the exhibition there. I was the head curator and wrote the introductory essay, and Kosta accompanied me for the installation of the exhibition in Zagreb. On the day of the opening, everything had already been installed and Gamulin came to look around. I greeted him and explained a bit about the show – but immediately his first objection was why hasn't the exhibition been laid out according to the nationality of the artists? According to him, the exhibition should be divided into Croatian artists, Slovenian, Serbian and so forth. But here we employed Protić's way instead: the list of artists in the catalogue was organised according to nationality, but the exhibition in the gallery space was presented in stylistic sequences. That's how Protić described it – *stylistic sequences*. So I explained this to Gamulin, but he shook his head. In the end I said to him politely: 'Mr Professor, it would be a great honour for us if you were to come to the opening.' He replied: 'Certainly I'll come, when is it?' I answered: 'Seven o'clock'. Alas, however, the opening was scheduled for six o'clock, they were running on winter hours.

JV Ouch. Now you're in big trouble.

JD And he arrived precisely at seven, but the visitors had already left. I rushed up to him to apologise, but he said sternly: 'You deliberately misled me.' This was unpleasant for me and I asked: 'How?' He said: 'You deliberately misled me so that I would not hear your unitarist speech at the opening.' And that was the scene in which we moved.[40] There were those who viewed the Yugoslav Art Space as a unitarist idea. Even though Kosta only said a few lines about the cooperation with the Zagreb Art Pavilion and the representatives of the Pavilion talked about technical things. There had not been any such 'unitarist story' at the opening.

[1]   See *Septième Biennale de Paris*, Biennale Internationale des Jeunes Artistes de Paris, Parc Floral, Paris, 1971.

[2]   Ivana Bašićević Antić (ed.), *Dimitrije Bašićević Mangelos (Essays)*, Museum of Contemporary Art, Belgrade 2017.

[3]   Margit Rosen (ed.) with Peter Weibel, Darko Fritz and Marija Gattin, *A Little-Known Story about a Movement, a Magazine, and the Computer's Arrival in Art: New Tendencies and Bit International*, 1961–1973, MIT Press, Cambridge, Massachussetts 2011.

[4]   The first Yugoslav Triennial of Visual Arts was held in Belgrade in 1961, and then every three years at the Belgrade Fair until 1979. The Triennial was founded by a decision of the National Committee of the City of Belgrade as an independent institution with the task of 'organising the public exhibition and presentation of the best visual artworks of Yugoslav and foreign artists', and to 'keep up with the development of visual art in the country and to collaborate with similar institutions here and abroad'. The Triennials were large and administratively demanding exhibitions, granting awards for the widest spectrum of artistic orientations. A total of seven Triennials were held.

[5]   The October Salon was founded by a decision of the City Assembly of Belgrade in 1960, modelled largely after the Paris Salon exhibitions as a display of the best works from the field of visual arts in Yugoslavia, and from 1967 from the applied arts as well. The Salon changed its concept and organisational form over the years and in 2004 became an international event.

[6]   The Kino Klub Belgrade was an amateur working film cooperative founded in 1951. During the 1950s and 1960s some of the most important filmmakers were attached to the Kino Klub and made their first films through it: Dušan Makavejev, Živojin Pavlović, Marko Babac, Ivan Martinac, Kokan Rakonjac, Srđan Karanović and others. Kino Klub ended with the dissolution of the Organisation of National Technology (Organizacije narodne tehnike) in the late 1960s.

[7]   This concerns the experimental documentary film *Rondo* (1962) that Ivan Martinac made during his time studying architecture in Belgrade and when he was a member of the Kino Klub Belgrade. He later returned to Split to become not only the leading filmmaker of the Split Kino Klub, but also one of the most important experimental documentary filmmakers in Yugoslavia.

[8]   *Ljubav i moda* (*Love and Fashion*, 1960) by Ljubomir Radičević is a popular musical that aestheticizes the urban life of Belgrade youth during the 1950s and 1960s. The film gained enormous popularity and is seen as announcing the liberal reforms, market economy, emerging consumerism and the general orientation towards the Western style of living of that time. For more about this film and the rise of consumer culture in socialist Yugoslavia, see Branislav Dimitrijević, *Potrošeni socijalizam: Kultura, konzumerizam i društvena imaginacija u Jugoslaviji (1950–1974)* (*Spent Socialism: Culture, Consumerism and Social Imagination in Yugoslavia*), Fabrika knjiga, Belgrade 2017; and 'Consumerist Imaginary in SFR Yugoslavia (Case 3: Beba Lončar on a Lambretta scooter)', in Branka Ćurčić (ed.), *Ideology of Design*, Autonomedia, New York 2009.

[9]   Vera Horvat Pintarić, *Džamonja*, Naprijed, Zagreb 1960.

[10]   Lionello Venturi, *Od Giotta do Chagalla* (*From Giotto to Chagall*), Mladost, Zagreb 1952.

[11]   Biljana Tomić, 'Examples of Conceptual Art in Yugoslavia', curatorial essay, Museum of Contemporary Art, Belgrade 1971.

[12]   See Jelena Vesić, 'The Three Exhibitions – Simultaneity of Promotion and Historisation of the New Art Practices (From Alternative Spaces to the Museum and Back)', *Parallel Chronologies*, an exhibition archive by tranzit.hu, Budapest, 2014, see http://tranzit.org/exhibitionarchive/the-three-exhibitions-simultaneity-of-promotion-and-historization-of-new-art-practices-from-an-alternative-spaces-to-the-museum-and-back/ (last accessed May 2024).

[13]   Ješa Denegri, 'Examples of Conceptual Art in Yugoslavia', curatorial essay, Museum of Contemporary Art, Belgrade 1971.

[14]   For more on this, see Jelena Vesić, 'Od Alternativnih prostora do muzeja i natrag. O simultanosti promocije i istorizacije Novih umetničkih praksi u Jugoslaviji: Beogradski kulturni prostor' ('From Alternative Spaces to the Museum and Back. On the Simultaneous Promotion and Historicisation of New Art Practices in Yugoslavia: Belgrade Cultural Space'), *Prilozi za istorizaciju Muzeja savremene umetnosti* (*Contributions to the Historicisation of the Museum of Contemporary Art*), Museum of Contemporary Art, Belgrade 2016.

[15]   Marjan Susovski (ed.), *Nova umjetnička praksa 1966–1978* (*New Art Practices 1966–1978*), exh. cat., Gallery of Contemporary Art, Zagreb 1978.

[16]   Vladimir Veličković received the award at the Paris Biennial in 1965.

[17]   The Belgrade Student Cultural Centre Gallery invited Catherine Millet in 1971. See Ješa Denegri, 'Konceptualna umetnost u izboru Catherine Millet' ('Conceptual Art in the Selection of Catherine Millet'), *Jedna moguća istorija umetnosti: Beograd kao internacionalna umetnička scena 1965–1998* (*One Possible History of Art: Belgrade as the Centre of an International Art Scene 1965–1998*), The Serbian Society of Art Historians, Belgrade 1998, p. 468–471.

[18]   See ibid., p. 468–471.

[19]   It is interesting that only a few years later Pogačnik represented Yugoslavia at the 1976 Venice Biennale with the Šempas Family Art Commune.

[20]   *Polja*, vol. XVIII, no. 156, Novi Sad, February 1972. In this issue, titled 'Konceptualna umetnost' ('Conceptual Art') are published the essays of Catherine Millet, Joseph Kosuth, Victor Burgin, Robert Barry, Douglas Huebler, Mario Merz, Sol LeWitt, Ian Burn and Mel Ramsden, Mirko Radojičić, Vladimir Kopicl and others.

[21]   'Open Letter to the Yugoslav Public' was an action by the February Group on 12 February 1971, and was signed by Slavko Bogdanović (who drafted the letter) and other group members. The letter asserted that a strong-arm policy, absolute bureaucratisation, the monopoly of a few in positions of authority from which they drew material and political power, the disqualification of new phenomena in culture, all prevail in culture and that this hinders the democratisation of culture and maintains a climate of fear. As stated, the letter was sent to the most prominent State and Party functionaries, institutions and the media. The letter was seen as the key reason behind the instigation of a police investigation, followed by the trials of individual artists from the Novi Sad avant-garde and conceptual scene. Miroslav Mandić was the first to be given a prison sentence, followed by Slavko Bogdanović who was sentenced to eight months in prison in May 1972 for 'inciting resentment amongst the citizens' in another of his texts, 'Letters from the Underground', published in the Belgrade magazine *Student* in December 1971. See *Slavko Bogdanović – Inventar discernacije* (*Slavko Bogdanović – Inventory of Discernment*), exh. cat., Orion, MSUV, Novi Sad 2018, p. 227, 286–287.

[22]   The January and February Groups were short-lived iterations of the KÔD group aimed at the bureaucratisation of culture. January Group made two appearances during January 1971: one during the Belgrade film festival FEST, and one at the Youth Forum (Tribina mladih) in Novi Sad. February Group had an action in Dom omladine (Youth

House, Belgrade) in February 1971 and issued the 'Open Letter to the Yugoslav Public', after which a full-blown political backlash against the group and the Novi Sad alternative scene in general was orchestrated.

[23] Ješa Denegri, 'Jerko Denegri, ka u Srbiji i Hrvatskoj' ('Jerko Denegri, as in Bosnia and Croatia'), *Treća decenija – konstruktivno slikarstvo'* (*The Third Decade – Constructive Painting*), exh. cat., Museum of Contemporary Art, Belgrade 1967, p. 41–51.

[24] Ješa Denegri, 'Sedamdesete: Radikalni umetnički stavovi, redukcije materijalnog objekta, novi mediji, mentalni i analitički postupci, ponašanja umetnikove ličnosti' ('The 1970s: Radical Artistic Attitudes, Reductions of the Material Object, New Media, Mental and Analytical Procedures, Behaviour of the Artist's Personality'), *Sedamdesete: Teme srpske umetnosti* (*The 1970s: Themes of Serbian Art*), exh. cat., Svetovi, Novi Sad 1996, p. 5–31.

[25] This iteration of the San Marino Biennale was titled *Nuove Tecniche d'Immagine* (*New Image Techniques*) and took place from July to September 1967. The Biennale Committee included Carla Nicolini, Giorgio Veronesi, Maurizio Calvesi, Jürgen Klaus, Maurizio Fagiolo, Otto Hahn, Robert Delevoy, Harold Rosenberg and others. Giulio Carlo Argan wrote the introductory essay for the catalogue. The best known European and American galleries were involved.

[26] Germano Celant, 'Per una critica acritica. Inchiesta sulla critica d'arte in Italia' ('For an Acritical Criticism: Investigation of Art Criticism in Italy'), *Nac*, 1970–1971.

[27] Susan Sontag, *Against Interpretation*, Farrar, Straus and Giroux, New York 1966.

[28] See 'SKC and New Cultural Practices: Prelom kolektiv in Conversation with Dunja Blažević', in Jelena Vesić, Dušan Grlja (eds.), *The Case of SKC in the 1970s – Exhibition Notebook*, Ljubljana–Zagreb–Belgrade, 2008, p. 84; available on http://www.prelomkolektiv.org/eng/PPYUart. htm (last accessed May 2024).

[29] Germano Celant, 'Arte Povera: Notes for a Guerrilla War', *Flash Art International*, no. 5, 1967.

[30] Biljana Tomić, 'Marina Abramović', *Data Arte*, no. 18, 1975, p. 74–75.

[31] Ješa Denegri, 'La Situazione Iugoslava' ('The Yugoslav Situation'), *Data Arte*, no. 27, 1977, p. 40–43.

[32] See Ješa Denegri, *Razlozi za Drugu liniju: Za novu umetnost sedamdesetih* (*Reasons for the Other Line: for a New Art in the 1970s*), Sudac and Museum of Contemporary Art Vojvodine, Zagreb/Novi Sad 2007; and Ješa Denegri, *Prilozi za Drugu liniju (1–3)* (*Attachments for the Other Line*), Horezky, Zagreb 2003; Macura, Vienna and Belgrade 2005; Edition Sudac, Zagreb 2015.

[33] Miodrag Protić, 'Treća decenija – konstruktivno slikarstvo, Jugoslovenska umetnost XX veka' ('The Third Decade – Constructive Painting, Yugoslav Art of the Twentieth Century'), *Treća decenija: Konstruktivno slikarstvo (1920–1930)*, exh. cat., Museum of Contemporary Art, Belgrade 1967, p. 7–39.

[34] Vera Horvat Pintarič, *Jo Klek Seissel*, exh. cat., Galerija Nova, Zagreb 1978.

[35] See Jelena Vesić and Zorana Dojić (eds.), *Political Practices of (Post-)Yugoslav Art: Retrospective 01*, Prelom kolektiv, Belgrade 2010.

[36] Jelena Vesić, 'Two Times of One Wall: The Case of the Student Cultural Centre in the 1970s', ibid., p. 128.

[37] *Partija* means 'Party', i.e. referring to the Communist Party.

[38] The Croatian Spring (*Hrvatsko proljeće*) or MASPOK (*masovni pokret*/mass movement) was a nationalist political movement that emerged from the League of Communists of Croatia in the late 1960s. It opposed the unitarisation of SFR Yugoslavia and demanded greater autonomy and more self-governing rights for Croatia within Yugoslavia. In 1971, the Yugoslav authorities suppressed the movement.

[39] *Jugoslovenska grafika* (*Yugoslav Graphic Arts*) *1950–1980*, exh. cat., Museum of Contemporary Art, Belgrade 1986.

[40] Although *federalism* was a governing doctrine in socialist Yugoslavia, there were also proponents of political *unitarism*, which was connected with the pre-war notion of 'integral Yugoslavism', meaning with the idea of the actual existence of the Yugoslav *nation*. A segment of the cultural elite, most notably Miroslav Krleža as the highest authority, argued for a Yugoslav cultural identity based on the shared language and similarities in historical legacy. By the end of the 1960s, Yugoslav unitarism was heavily criticised, especially in Croatia, because of the centralist political tendencies that threatened the autonomy of the republics within the federation. Although the Croatian Spring was suppressed at the beginning of the 1970s, the Yugoslav constitution of 1974 gave greater power to the individual republics and political centralism was significantly weakened.

The Other Line

This term refers to the avant-garde, the neo-avant-garde and the radical modernist models of artistic language and forms of behaviour articulated in the Yugoslav Art Space from the early 1920s to the early 1980s. Precisely because of its temporal range, the Other Line is not an idea that encompasses linguistically-related artistic phenomena interconnected by a strong stylistic coherence, nor is it a term that depends on a strict theoretical foundation. It is rather an operational, critical and polemical procedure that seeks to emphasise differentiation, deviation, parallel existence, separation and even the opposition to artistic phenomena that are recognised, valued and accepted as mainstream and major tendencies, and which as a rule are concentrated within the mindset of a moderate form of modernism with its varying linguistic species and sub-species. —Ješa Denegri, 2024

The Reason for the Other Line
Ješa Denegri

Published in *Jugoslovenska dokumenta '89* (*Yugoslav Documents '89*), exh. cat., Skenderija Olympic Centre, Sarajevo 1989, p. 13–20.

The concept of the Other Line, which is conditional and theoretically unestablished, anticipates and suggests the contemplation of a single set of events in modern Yugoslav art. These events are contrasted or consciously separated from certain dominant streams in art, and form a specific area that basically aspires to the radicalisation of the notion of art and, therefore, towards the radicalisation of artistic behaviour. The Other Line is not an artistic expression that can be recognised or applied in advance, but rather a mentality and a reaction of certain artists and artist groups to cultural and social circumstances. It is, in fact, a way of shrinking back from being integrated within those very circumstances and, thus, a way of searching for an independent artistic attitude. The Other Line is not an ideological opposition to the alleged 'official' status of certain ineradicable streams in modern Yugoslav art, nor is it a local version of the epochal conflict between the avant-garde and tradition – a conflict which is, in the present circumstances, groundless. The Other Line could, it is true, be conceived as an alternative to various different artistic expressions and behaviours, but it would be more accurate, more moderate and certainly more realistic to see it as a set of phenomena that are connected by a particular language and psychological similarities and spiritual affinities into a possible art historical whole.

The beginnings of the Other Line in Yugoslav culture may be found in occasional – but for the circumstances of that environment highly valuable – inclusions in those streams of international art known as the historical avant-garde. In the early 1920s, various artists and groups associated with art magazines followed the trend – Ljubomir Micić's magazine *Zenit* and Dragan Aleksić's *Dada Tank* and *Dada Jazz*. Another member of this group was August Černigoj, who attended the Bauhaus in Weimar in the summer of 1924 and, having been introduced to the ideas of Russian Constructivism, assembled a group of sympathisers in Trieste who worked in accordance with the ideology of this movement. It was not, of course, an entirely uniform group – there were uncompromising fundamental and personal conflicts between certain members (such as a Zenit/Dada conflict between Micić and Aleksić) – but, on the whole, these should not now prevent us from seeing them all as part of the same movement, one characterised by the aim of radicalising the idea of art and artistic behaviour.

That radicalisation was set out in manifestos, proclamations and theoretical texts written entirely in the spirit of the ideology of the historical avant-garde. It could also be observed in artworks – collage, photomontage, graphics, spatial constructions, drawings and occasionally the paintings of Bijelić, Klek, Petrov, Černigoj, Stepančić and others. Although few in number and short-lived, these artistic phenomena, directly connected to similar international processes, represented a heroic chapter in modern Yugoslav art. Its language denotations, its behaviour, its understanding of the artist's vocation and the object of art served as the inheritance, foundation and example to all later events referred to herein as the Other Line.

In post-war social and cultural circumstances, the notion
of the avant-garde as it had been established in the first
decades of the century could no longer survive, although
there were certain trends that claimed a discontinuance,
or at least a fundamental change, from the existing and
inherited spiritual climate of their environment. In the
early 1950s, the art group EXAT 51 appeared and demanded
respect for the experience and the introduction of abstract
art, which was, at the time, ideologically dubious. Through
the synthesis of the artistic and architectural design of
space, they strove to reconstruct their surroundings. They
saw the role of the artist not as a producer of aesthetic
objects, but as an active participant in the modification of
the everyday milieu. Although these aims could not be
achieved during EXAT 51's time, the mere expression of
such needs was enough to place this group and its members
among the initiators of new problems in various areas of art,
including abstract painting, architecture and urbanism,
graphic and industrial design, scenography, cartoon and
visual art pedagogy. The members of EXAT 51 were well
aware of the theoretical and practical principles of their
activity, as well as those of the cultural inheritance of which
they were a part (in their own milieu). The words of one
member, Ivan Picelj, testify to an awareness of this kind:
'Just creating a piece of art wasn't enough. It had to be
defended. It was a confrontation … Amongst all the plausible
and implausible arguments against our painting, the most
repeated one was that we didn't belong here. The fact
that Aleksić (Dada), Micić (Zenit), Šumanović (post-Cubism)
and Seissel (Bauhaus) worked in this city [Zagreb] was
overlooked.'

 The supposition on which EXAT 51 acted was based
on the ideology of the structure, project and Constructive
Approach to the problems of form as was, both constructively and projectively, the behaviour of its members.
A decade later, in the early 1960s, similar attitudes were
once again expressed through the affiliation of most of the
former members of EXAT 51 with the international movement – the New Tendencies who, owing to their work, made
Zagreb their centre. The New Tendencies had all the traits
of the typical post-war neo-avant-garde; its sole and final
aim was not the linguistic dimension of artistic work itself,

but rather the analysis and criticism of the conditions that affected artistic work. The movement aspired to the pre-qualification of certain fundamental suppositions of artistic practice and, therefore, to the pre-qualification of social determinants and the social status of art in general. Apart from the artists, critics and organisers also took part in these events and became integral components of them. One of the leading theoreticians at the time, Matko Meštrović, best expressed the essence of the New Tendencies: 'the New Tendencies appeared spontaneously in the climate that old Europe was first to feel. A positive attitude towards scientific achievements is an integral part of the tradition of the pioneers of modern architecture, Neoplasticism and those members of the Bauhaus that were still alive. Also alive was a confidence in the potentially transformative power of technology and industrialisation. Deep-rooted Marxist thought made their approach to social change and problems constructive. These factors made the first criticism in Europe possible, and with it came the first opposition to corruption and alienation. A resolute demand was raised for the demystification of art and artistic creation, and for the unmasking of the dominant influence of the art market, which speculated in art and treated it in a contradictory, hypocritical way – as both a myth and a commodity. The tendency towards the suppression of individualism and the promotion of the spirit of collective work also became possible. A progressive political orientation was clearly expressed, and art was focused on the problem of plastic and visual research, endeavouring to establish the objective psycho-physical principles of the plastic phenomenon and visual perception.'

But the social and psychological tensions of the time did not allow the radicalisation of artistic expression and behaviour to be introduced solely through a projective and constructive approach. Furthermore, there was a tendency towards the idea of artistic negativity or negative artistry, which, instead of creating forms and works, was inclined towards the destruction or, at least, the reduction of material and plastic factors.

When an artist fails to see the possibilities and reasons for his social integration, when he loses faith in collective efforts and the commonly accepted direction of the development of civilisation, then he unavoidably turns to his own inner world and problems. But, in so doing, he also turns to various general questions about the survival of art itself. This creates a climate that results in an exceptional and conscious defence of the uncommunicative nature of modern painting. The painting is a gesture of the artist's will, and there are authentic reasons for its creation. But it is no longer the author's link with the world. The painting is an amputated, independent organism, living off its proud self-sufficiency. Such were the positions of a non-iconic and anti-artistic, extremely radical art stream in the Informel of the late 1950s and early 1960s – the Informel of Gattin, Feller, Kristl, Seder and Jeršovar. This stream was separated linguistically, spiritually and psychologically from other streams in the same climate and artistic environment. It had nothing in common with those subgroups that turned from the subversive attitude typical of the mentality of this other art *(un art autre,* as Michel Tapié called it) to the production of paintings as aesthetic objects. Some members of the radical Informel were at the same time members or close associates of Gorgona, a loose gathering of artists and intellectuals who were active in the early 1960s and contemporaries of the New Tendencies. Gorgona aspired to dislodge the established notion of art and founding *behaviour* as a means of artistic and, in general, spiritual existence. It was said of Gorgona that it existed rather than worked, since the group was not publicly active, even though its members were all well-known public personalities, mostly artists and critics. But, because of its dual position – one of which was public, the other underground and cryptic – this artistic behaviour stressed, for the first time in Yugoslav culture, the acceptance of existential unease and alienation as a driving force of the artistic impulse. Thus, it laid bare the perception that creating art was not a matter of professional education or social status but, on the contrary, it was a matter of not having any other choice. In other words, being an artist meant being condemned to the only means of expressing oneself in the apparently shielded but completely limited and otherwise inaccessible field of art.

It was no accident that the re-examination of Gorgona and the radical Informel occurred more than a decade after their formation. It happened in a spiritual climate that could be seen as the result of another break in the trajectory of post-war art amidst the social and ideological turmoil of the late 1960s and early 1970s. Today, Renato Barilli's prediction may seem exaggerated. He claimed that in the future historiography of modern art, 1968 would be marked as a turning point, but he distanced himself from the idea that this break could be directly connected with the political circumstances of the time, linking it rather with cultural processes and psychological moods. Art produced at that time throughout the world, including Yugoslavia, was not limited to the production of completed aesthetic objects (such as paintings and sculptures) but was transferred to the artist's actual behaviour, his personality, his body and his 'speech in the first person'. It was only natural that such historical circumstances would lead to an explosion of emotional outbursts that created the mood of a 'new sensitivity'. This spread throughout the media and alternative culture, fields that should not be equated with those forms of artistic expressions formed between 1966 and 1969 (Arte Povera, Conceptual art, Land art, Body art and others). A succession of artistic groups (OHO, Bosch+Bosch, KÔD, (Ǝ, etcetera) and individuals (Damnjan, Šoškić, Gotovac, Dimitrijević, Trbuljak, Abramović, Paripović, Popović, Todosijević, Iveković, Martinis, Stilinović and so on) were part of this new trend. The shifting of this trend from the dominant stream into those milieus gave cause for the recognition of the phenomenon of the Other Line in modern Yugoslav art. This phenomenon was characterised by breaks in conceptual links and a discontinuity from many central streams within that art but, at the same time, leading to a different continuity, one with a heritage of the historical avant-garde (Zenit, Aleksić and Černigoj and his circle) as well as post-war neo-avant-garde trends (EXAT 51, the New Tendencies, the radical Informel and Gorgona). Despite considerable differences between these artistic expressions, it is possible to establish certain traits they all had in common. They aspired towards extreme means of artistic expression, and endeavoured to think art and do art without being obliged to realise it in a completed work of art. Even when classic methods and techniques were used, it was evident that the means could be subjected to aesthetic and artistic evaluation in terms of a final result. On the other hand, artistic expressions were either completely depersonalised or completely personalised, and a different mental language and metalinguistic processes were employed. The orientation was a radical asceticism of visual form and a conscious turn to the field of silence.

Susan Sontag convincingly demonstrated that this stratagem of artistic behaviour was not a question of denouncing the work of art, but an extremely responsible approach to reflecting upon the sense of creating art according to the usual practices. It was those many characteristics of the art that could, according to every standard and conventional artistic criterion, be regarded as unartistic or as outside art, although they were most significant from the artistic point of view. They were artistic in the seriousness of the dilemma to which they gave rise, and were referred to in the well-known and only seemingly paradoxical statement made by Argan, that 'everyone can do art, but only a true artist can do non-art'.

The proposition of the Other Line in the spiritual climate of the last decade, which has been strongly marked by the ideas of postmodernism, may seem burdened with an exclusivity that is characteristic of the culture of the historical avant-garde, the neo-avant-garde and modernism. There is little doubt that, in view of the character of art during the last decade, many of the earlier categorisations no longer exist. Artists and art groups no longer suffer under the former ideological polarisations, and the idea of pluralism, though exhausted by incorrect usage, remains one of the basic traits of the art orientations of the current historical moment. Therefore, it is not difficult to agree with Gilles Lipovetsky's statement: 'In general, the sudden breaks are becoming less frequent, and the impression of déjà vu is stronger than that of novelty […] We no longer feel that we live in a revolutionary period. The constant decline of the level of the creative power of the avant-garde coincides with the difficulty of behaving in an avant-garde way […] The weariness of the avant-garde does not mean that art is dead, that artists no longer have imagination, but that the most interesting works have gone in another direction and no longer strive for expression without traits. They are, to an even greater degree, subjective and often obsessional. The search for purity has replaced the search for novelty.'

But the basic truth of this statement should not obstruct the need for selectivity, for differences in type and value, and an open display of artistic expressions that qualify art as an ethical vocation, rather than art as a mere profession, a source of material commodities or as a lever for gaining social status. There is a great need today for a safe orientation in critical attitudes, positions, choices and decisions, which does not, of course, entail dominance and indoctrination by this orientation. As Tomaž Brejc rightly said: 'Perhaps it is a consequence of the desire to find some regulating mechanism, a model of awareness in the chaos of modern art production.' In the art of the last decade, such a mechanism could not be found at the level of formal expression and technique, but it could be detected, at least generally, at the level of emotions, and through the similarity of mentality and individual psychology. In other words, this mechanism could be noticed at the level of that particular instinct with which the authenticity and originality of an artistic statement can be recognised, quite apart from all theoretical criteria. The art of the last decade, created in an atmosphere of fiery arguments about the nature of postmodernism, has different features from those of the previous period, and different, too, from the traits of the Other Line. Nonetheless, it is possible to feel, claim and even demonstrate that, in some individual cases in modern Yugoslav art, a mentality akin to that of the Other Line has been inherited and continued, and a psychological and spiritual unity has been established. It is true that this art, as was the case with the historical avant-garde and post-war neo-avant-garde, no longer cultivates utopian projections, no longer seeks deeper changes in the evaluation of tradition and no longer radicalises the means and forms of artistic creation. But, nonetheless, it shares with former experiences the consciousness of the critical and independent behaviour of the artist and believes in the defence of his moral integrity. An artist is an independent intellectual who stands apart from ruling ideologies with which he is forever confronted. Thus, not merely by expression, technique,

tendencies and style, individual artists participate on equal
terms in establishing ways of thinking, behaviour and
attitude similar to those manifested in the phenomenon
of the Other Line.

II. New Art Practices in Yugoslavia: Youth Culture and the Ruptures with Art and within Art itself
Ješa Denegri in Conversation with Branislav Dimitrijević and Jelena Vesić

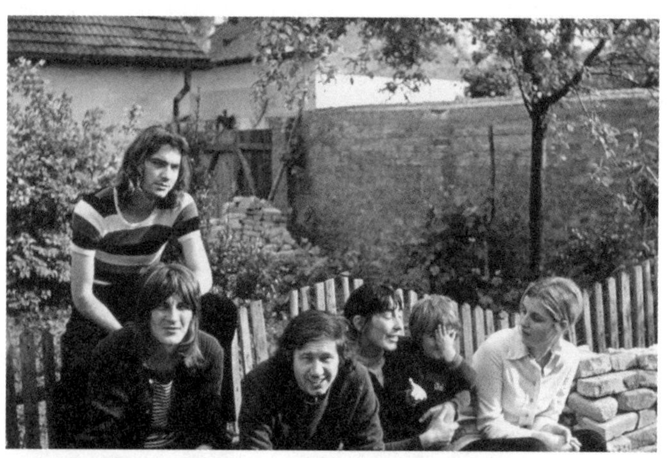

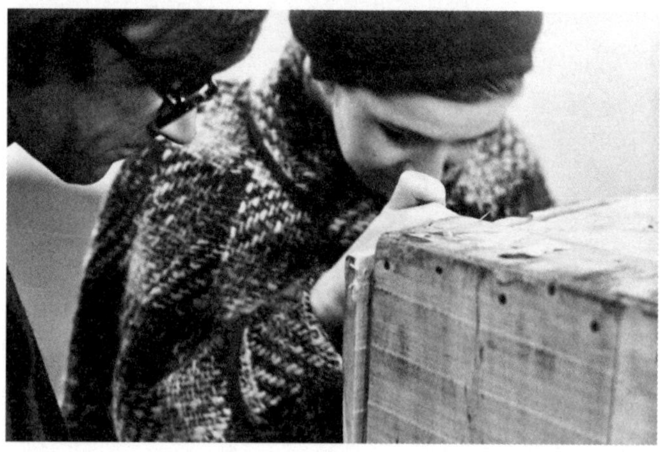

Ješa Denegri and Biljana Tomić with the members of the Bosch+Bosch group, Subotica, 1972
From left to right: Bálint Szombathy, Slavko Matković, Ješa Denegri, Biljana Tomić holding Zaviša Matković, Valeria Matković

View of the exhibition *Postal Packages* curated by Želimir Koščević, Student Centre Gallery, Zagreb, 1972, showing Želimir Koščević and a visitor peeping through the package

I. <u>Transversals of Conceptual Art in Yugoslavia</u>

BRANISLAV DIMITRIJEVIĆ Let's begin this part of the discussion with the film recently made about the Novi Sad scene of the early 1970s, whose title is taken precisely from your term: *Druga linija* meaning the Other Line. We watched it together at the Beldocs International Documentary Film Festival in Belgrade.[1] So let's start with some of your impressions and memories from that time that were prompted by your watching the film, in which you also participate as a commentator of the time. The film seems to follow faithfully what you made visible in your exhibition *Examples of Conceptual Art in Yugoslavia* in 1971, which we have already discussed. The film is about a transversal that was established by the protagonists of the New Art Practices between Ljubljana, Zagreb and Novi Sad, as well as Subotica and finally Belgrade.

With regard to Belgrade, the film also mentions your thesis
that the scene that began in 1971 at the Student Cultural
Centre was primarily focused on resistance to the Belgrade
Fine Arts Academy – about which Raša Todosijević talks
explicitly in the film – whereas the Novi Sad scene was more
focused on the linguistic aspects of Conceptual art. Furthermore, with regard to the part about Belgrade, the film also
emphasises the importance of the magazine *Rok* (*Time Limit*),
and especially Branko Vučićević and Bora Ćosić, who were
thus introduced to the concept of the Other Line, which is
one intervention into your narrative, and I would welcome
your taking it into consideration. The film *Druga linija*
certainly leaves no doubt about the vital importance of the
connection between the Novi Sad scene and the OHO
group, who in Novi Sad in 1969 carried out a series of street
actions. Also, the significance of the connection with
Goran Trbuljak from Zagreb, who participated with the
KÔD group in the *Public Art Class*, which was one of the key
events of the New Art Practices in Novi Sad. Therefore,
this film articulates your own position again and talks about
the actual exhibition of 1971.

JD   The exhibition *Examples of Conceptual Art in Yugoslavia*
in 1971 in the Salon of the Belgrade Museum of Contemporary Art and the exhibition of Yugoslav artists at the Paris
Biennial of the same year are mentioned in the film.
The latter exhibition, which also included members of the
Novi Sad groups KÔD and (Ǝ that had briefly united as the
short-lived group (Ǝ-KÔD, was the only exhibition ever
of this group. The film brings me back to times long ago.
I have spoken about my contact with the conceptual artists
through their works on paper to the actions of the OHO
group in natural and urban environments. I have also spoken
about the collective conception of the Gallery 212 at Atelje
212 from 1967 and the BITEF art programme up to 1973.[2]
The Novi Sad artists participated in the exhibition *At Another
Moment* organised in 1971 by Braco Dimitrijević and Nena
Baljković at the Student Cultural Centre in Belgrade. Thus,
this is the general context in which the exhibitions *Examples
of Conceptual Art in Yugoslavia* and the Yugoslav selection at
the Paris Biennial were organised.

The leitmotif of this film is that this type of art caused major disagreements, and it seems particularly in Novi Sad. There wasn't the custom in our milieu, nor the educational context, to facilitate the reception of free forms of individual activity as art. Such experiments were only possible in small circles – those who were acquainted with the early work of the OHO group knew that unlike the Italian situation, for which extreme exhibitions such as Kounellis's horses were fairly normal, this wasn't possible here.

BD   The Novi Sad scene was primarily driven by personalities such as Bogdanka and Dejan Poznanović who, through their educational, practical, publishing and translation work, furthermore opened up a mental and actual space in which young people gathered – or let's say young intellectuals, whose goal or vocation wasn't artistic but for whom the New Art Practices were a space for thinking, the place where theory and life met. They gathered around the Youth Forum (Tribina mladih) and the magazines *Index*, *Uj Simpozion* and *Polja*. At the beginning of the 1970s the KÔD group was formed by Mirko Radojičić, Miroslav Mandić and Slavko Bogdanović, among others. It focused on public actions and socio-political activities while the (Ǝ group focused on radical linguistic conceptualism, such as in the work of Vladimir Kopicl. This scene wasn't connected to the art academy but rather to the literary field, and some of its protagonists fall outside this actual period, among them the most important Yugoslav neo-avant-garde poets and novelists: Vujica Rešin Tucić, Judita Šalgo, Slobodan Tišma. In Subotica the Bosch+Bosch group had already formed in 1969 by Slavko Matković, Bálint Szombathy and others. Szombathy then moved to Novi Sad where he continued his own work. What were your relations with the Novi Sad scene?

JD   They were a very self-aware crew. There was plenty of youthful rebelliousness and institutional resistance. They were not interested in the continuity of artistic practices nor in any artistic professionalism. They were interested in linguistic theories, and in technical sciences, but primarily in the relation between art and their own lives, life as actually *lived* life, and therefore in actually practising art as life.

The groups KÔD and (Э were short-lived, both due to
political circumstances, and to the very radical attitudes
of their protagonists. Some of their members continued
afterwards with their individual work, which aimed at a form
of self-annihilation or at exploring the radical invisibility
of the artistic act. They aimed at voicing and practising a
clear distance from what was understood as 'institutional
culture'. They didn't want to have anything in common with
institutional culture, and they were highly outspoken in
their position, whose ethical basis lay in avoiding complicity
with any institutional legitimisation. Which is why their
participation at the Paris Biennial was so troubling for them.
They were not interested in operating as artists within the
art system. But more than that, they conducted social and
political provocations in their public appearances and written
statements, which were met with harsh response.

When speaking about KÔD, it is clear that they
wanted to challenge the alleged tolerance of the system that
declaratively supported 'youth culture' but was alienated
from it because of the growing cultural bureaucratisation
that required a maintaining of the cultural status quo. These
groups wanted to expand the limits of artistic freedom fully,
all the while being well aware how existentially risky their
position was.

BD   The notion of 'artistic freedom' is a modernist trope
par excellence. However, the conceptual groups we are
talking about here aimed their critical stance at the institutional culture of modernism. As Art & Language put it,
Conceptual art was the nervous breakdown of modernism!
It took the notion of freedom from modernism but rushed
towards its radical linguistic and political consequences.

JD   They were part of the culture of refusal instigated
by the 1968 upheaval. But there is a connection that could
also be established with some of the more radical aspects
of local modernism, primarily within the Informel painting
in Vojvodina. The pioneer of Informel in Vojvodina,
the painter József Ács, wrote about and supported the
Bosch+Bosch group. One of the most significant protagonists of the New Art Practices in Novi Sad was Bogdanka
Poznanović, herself initially an Informel painter. In 1970

she performed her first actions in public space, including the legendary action *Heart-Object*. She and her husband Dejan, as well as Judita Šalgo, provided a link between the 'institution' of the Youth Forum (Tribina mladih) and the rather anarchistically inclined members of KÔD and others.

JV   If you were to compare these various institutional situations – first the gallery as the site of production and gathering, and then the interpretation in the sense of the reinvention of the role of criticism – what would you say is the basic difference between the Novi Sad situation and the Tribina mladih, the Zagreb Student Centre that had already been active since 1966, the work of OHO in Slovenia and these other more developed situations from the Italian context, above all in Rome in L'Attico with the young Fabio Sargentini, and in Genoa with Germano Celant?

JD   They can't be compared. In any way. The very phenomenology of these expressive acts and languages was essentially different. Which is why I am still undecided. I wonder – although any question of such a categorical nature seems superfluous today – if these phenomena *constituted a youth subculture or if they were absolutely committed to art?* It is very apparent that the OHO group and the individuals and groups from Vojvodina who gathered around Tribina mladih and the *Polja* magazine were a group of artists who were aware of Conceptual art and a linguistic approach to art practice. They were familiar with conceptualism in the strict sense of the word – the translations of Joseph Kosuth and Sol LeWitt in *Polja* magazine were available and visible enough at the time, which means that there was a very clear theoretical background to the thinking behind the New Art Practices. But these two scenes were quite different, and when we speak about the American conceptualists and Arte Povera, these are entirely other lines of thinking. Phenomenologically, the products of Arte Povera are large environmental and artistic installations that changed the constellation of the way that art is exhibited and presented, like Merz's igloos, Pistoletto's installations or Kounellis' horses. There were no surprises in the various Italian traditions that ran from Futurism to the post-war phenomena – that is in the work of Fontana, Burri and

Manzoni – or at least none in the sense of new phenomena fundamentally disrupting the way art was understood or that could cause people to ask whether that really is art or just pure provocation. Secondly, this all takes place inside the gallery system, even when that system has been invented for that new art.

JV   As is the case, for example, in the United States with the activities of Seth Siegelaub. He profoundly changed the normative way of exhibiting, but by doing so he also invented a new institution – the institution of the curator as producer, gallerist and art dealer.[3]

JD   Or young Fabio Sargentini in Italy, whose radical steps in making and exhibiting art had a radical effect on the scene itself. But historically speaking such radicalism has been connected with the lines of tradition that go back to Futurism. In our milieu there isn't such a historical back-drop. Again, we are tackling the question of continuity and rupture. The continuity of the Other Line in Yugoslav art that came to mind was my way of creating the missing historical backdrop for the New Art Practices phenomena. If they can't be explained as an art practice, then they will be treated like some type of ad hoc youthful infraction limited to the internal culture of places like Dom omladine (the Youth House) in Belgrade, Tribina mladih (Youth Forum) in Novi Sad and later on the Student (Cultural) Centres. All these alternative institutions, if observed as hypothetically divorced from art history and art practice, will remain places of youth culture.

BD   You have now introduced the question of youth culture, which is particularly important when we talk about the Novi Sad scene. Its protagonists were very young, some of them still in secondary school when this all began.

JD   They were mostly students of philosophy and litera-ture, but also of the law faculty.

BD   Who was in charge of the gallery programme at Tribina mladih when that scene was forming?

JD   Biljana ran the gallery programme from 1969 to 1970. KÒD group had their first exhibition there in April 1970 with an action which had the character of a neo-dadaist, Fluxus-like event. But I remember there was also a Zenit exhibition there in 1972, curated by Zoran Markuš, shortly after Ljubomir Micić died.[4] Biljana had already exhibited the works of Mangelos in Belgrade in 1968, and then he took part in the organisation of the Mangelos exhibition in Tribina mladih in 1972.[5] So there were clear inclinations manifested in organising exhibitions of Zenit, of Mangelos, of visual and concrete poetry, and all of this was connected to what was happening with the emerging generation in Novi Sad. Unfortunately, these were times of particular political tension, which by 1973 heavily affected their situation, and the progressive role of this cultural centre was terminated. I did not witness first-hand all these events in Tribina mladih, and the first interpretations of this scene came from the protagonists themselves, primarily from Mirko Radojičić,[6] and also from Bálint Szombathy, who was a member of Bosch+Bosch.

JV   You have said that you had a connection with the members of Bosch+Bosch?

JD   I once went with Biljana to meet them in Subotica in 1972. We visited Slavko Matković at Stipe Grgića number 8 – I remember it like it was yesterday – and we stayed there for a while. In discussion with Bálint Szombathy he said that the historical avant-garde served as their background, which would later become an important part of my argument for the idea of the Other Line. Szombathy said that their 'forefather' was Lajos Kassák, and that they were the 'descendants' of this historical practice. Then we tried to find an answer to this crucial question: is the Novi Sad scene gathered around Tribina mladih a kind of phenomenon connected with youth subculture or a deeply embedded artistic process that requires its own historical stage? Because if the artists can't be put onto such a stage, they are vulnerable to the fleeting whims of youth.

BD   Here we come back once again to what is essential in the concept of the Other Line: the affirmation of a particular genealogy.

JD   Indeed, that is the essence. I wrote an essay in 1978 for the journal *Umetnost* called 'Three Historical Stages – The Related Aspects of Artistic Behaviour' in which I set out this thesis for the first time.[7] The term the Other Line still didn't exist at this time, although I introduced the idea of how these artistic interventions build on one another in an art historical way. The three stages are: the historical avant-garde (Černigoj, Micić, Seissel, Aleksić); Gorgona and radical Informel; and finally the New Art Practices. As an art historian I realised that there is a reason for returning to the historical avant-garde as a form of dialogue inside the system and the synchronised activity of art and history. It happens that the New Art Practices are, as a phenomenon, very unusual in terms of the experience of art of the time, and in order to be able to discern it as such in any way it is necessary to create some connections to it and to show how this form of art has its roots in earlier artistic phenomena. That is, at a time when art history itself is undergoing change owing to the rediscovery of Duchamp.

BD   The rediscovery of Duchamp was an institutional move in the United States. His exhibition at the Pasadena Museum of Art in 1963 marked a renewed interest in his work.

JD   That's how great disruptions and ruptures take place. But strictly speaking the professional circles do not react in a timely manner. They register the fact that something new is approaching, but do not consider that it will automatically change the entrenched local situation, where everything is already known, where the rules by which things are evaluated are known. But when a new phenomenon emerges, as in the case of the New Art Practices, values are changing, as is the phenomenology of art. This cannot be understood through the existing instruments, so some type of legitimacy in the historical context has to be invented.

BD   We mentioned the decennial exhibitions of Yugoslav art at the Museum of Contemporary Art in Belgrade (*Yugoslav Art of 20th Century*). The historical avant-gardes entered the narrative of art history created by the institutions of modern art of that time and from which the Yugoslav Art Space was constructed. Which means that in that moment – and we

are now referring to the exhibition of 1967 that dealt with
the Constructivism of the 1920s – the historical avant-
gardes were visible to the new generation of artists. And if
we now return to the exhibition of 1971, *Examples of Conceptual
Art in Yugoslavia,* we can see how the Museum acknowledges,
in a timely way for that period, these new radical practices.
How was that possible? Are we able to look at things from
this perspective since, as we have already concluded,
institutions promoted a type of mainstream modernism,
and here we are making a step away from that?

JD   We talked a lot about this when Jelena was working
on a critical historicisation of the exhibition *Examples of
Conceptual Art in Yugoslavia* and other pioneering exhibitions
in the context of the New Art Practices in Belgrade.[8]
It was necessary to go into the employment structure of the
Museum of Contemporary Art. The Museum functioned
as a working community according to the principle of self-
management, and represented what was then called a
plurality of interests. I think, and this turns out to be very
important with regard to these questions and differentiations, that I was able to combine my own work and interests
with the institutional format of the Museum. The exhibitions
were thus me 'speaking in the first person', but also within
the discourse of the institution. Our team of curators and
colleagues respected the existence of different interests
and tried to be as collegial, democratic and professional
as possible as regards decisions about procedures for and
the elaboration of new projects and so on. I would propose,
explain and discuss the new phenomena in the scene
that were of interest to me, and the Museum was interested
in the right things at the right moment and frequently
responded positively to my proposals.

BD   What do you think marks the earliest manifestation of
all these phenomena? In the film *Druga linija* this question,
because it addresses the way these channels were developed,
makes it seem like the OHO group was in some way key to
everything.

JD   That is the OHO exhibition in Novi Sad in November
1969, just before the OHO exhibition in Dom omladine

(Youth House, Belgrade) in December 1969. I wrote the preface in the catalogue for both exhibitions, which consisted of five environmental works.[9] The first time the OHO group was invited to Belgrade was in September 1968, as part of the BITEF art programme with the exhibition and performance/Happening of Milenko Matanović and David Nez, with Tomaž Šalamun and Tomaž Brejc. They came back at BITEF in 1969 and 1970. Before Belgrade, they first exhibited in 1968 in Ljubljana, invited by Šalamun and Brejc, and then in Zagreb, invited by Želimir Koščević. Biljana and I returned from Italy in 1969 and we visited the OHO exhibition *Pradjedovi* (*Great-Grandfathers*) in the Gallery of Contemporary Art in Zagreb. The title of their exhibition afterwards in Novi Sad was *Great Great-Grandfathers*. The exhibition in Belgrade at the Dom omladine Gallery was split into sequences, into five solo exhibitions, each of which ran for a week, by Andraž Šalamun, Tomaž Šalamun, Marko Pogačnik, David Nez and Milenko Matanović.

JV   Conceptual art and the New Art Practices, at least in Novi Sad and Belgrade before the Student Cultural Centre, came about through theatre, philosophy and literature. Of course, that was counter-current to the system of education at the Belgrade Fine Arts Academy. This would be a crucial point of departure for the Belgrade group assembling around the Student Cultural Centre.

JD   The aim of all these institutions like the Student Cultural Centre was to educate the younger generations in line with the new worldviews. Did student centres in Yugoslavia become dissociated from their original functions? This is the core question. Initially, student centres were established to serve students' broader cultural needs and to serve as rather populist institutions, like houses of culture (*domovi kulture*). If they had really done this, the developmental scenario we have today wouldn't have happened, but it did happen, thanks precisely to the young professionals who began to work in these institutions. In Zagreb Želimir Koščević ran the Gallery of the Student Centre,[10] and Dunja Blažević and Biljana Tomić headed the Belgrade Student Cultural Centre.

BD   Koščević may well have been the first contemporary art curator (producer in today's terms) active on the Yugoslav scene.

JD   Koščević was very well aware of what was happening on the contemporary international scene, and he was truly an engaging figure in exhibition practice. I remember he travelled to Stockholm and worked with Pontus Hultén at the Moderna Museet for his specialisation in curating. Koščević produced an important exhibition, *The Exhibition of Men and Women,* which our colleagues WHW from Zagreb recently re-created in a contemporary context, and which was originally presented in the Gallery of the Student Centre in Zagreb in 1969.

JV   It was one of the first exhibitions that entailed thinking its own context of production, its own medium, in line with the new paradigm of Conceptual art.

JD   And it was a very early exhibition in this sense. In 1958 in Paris, Yves Klein made his ground-breaking work named *The Void* at Galerie Iris Clert as an artistic action, which was precisely an example of this Duchampian line in art that we discussed in the context of the 1971 Paris Biennial. And I agree, what Koščević did in our art space was a great experiment in exhibition-making. We should remember that at the end of the 1960s, Fluxus and some branches of Conceptual art were indeed organised around notions of immateriality, performativity and the democratisation of art practices. The latest was also among the key operative terms of art in the 1960s and the 1970s in Yugoslavia. Koščević often organised exhibitions and art events outside the gallery and was the first curator to publish newspapers instead of issuing regular catalogues. Like me, he was also interested in the kind of radical modernist thinking promoted by the New Tendencies, and we collaborated on a few exhibitions. We shared an interest in popular culture, and I remember Koščević was among the first, organizing the 'fairs' of science fiction that he conceived in his usual experimental style.[11]

JV   Koščević's conceptual interventions in exhibition-making are quite important when you are thinking about curatorial practices in Yugoslav and post-Yugoslav art.[12] But if I understood you properly, and in reference to our main line of discussion, it was largely the experimental approach and the knowledge of contemporary art that played an active role in this displacement of student centres from their original institutional functions and frameworks – from the populist-socialist approach to youth culture – towards a determined cultural-political attitude. We spoke about Želimir Koščević, and I would suggest that Dunja Blažević and Biljana Tomić shared similar attitudes and brought these attitudes to the Student Cultural Centre in Belgrade. This shaped it as an alternative institution. Biljana already had experience in experimental curatorial practice and the New Art Practices through her work at BITEF and Tribina mladih, while Dunja, with her knowledge of art history, managed to shape a clear profile for the artistic politics of the gallery. The principles of democratisation of production and reception, the experiments in exhibiting and viewing art, were an important part of both the Student Cultural Centre in Belgrade and the Student Centre in Zagreb.

One of the first exhibitions of Conceptual art at the Student Cultural Centre, upon the arrival of Blažević and Tomić, was staged in 1971, the year we discussed in terms of the production and promotion of the New Art Practices in the Yugoslav and international art spaces. This is the exhibition *At Another Moment* conceived by Nena Baljković and Braco Dimitrijević together. Heralded as 'the first international exhibition of Conceptual art', it was one of the pioneering experimental curatorial projects in the Yugoslav Art Space. The exhibition was originally staged in a hallway at Frankopanska 2A in Zagreb where the artist pair lived. Under the title *At the Moment* it presented the work of artists like (and I am reading from this experimental catalogue produced by the Student Cultural Centre) Giovanni Anselmo, Robert Barry, stanley brouwn, Daniel Buren, Victor Burgin, Jan Dibbets, Braco Dimitrijević, Barry Flanagan, Douglas Huebler, Alain Kirili, Jannis Kounellis, John Latham, KÔD, Sol LeWitt, OHO, Goran Trbuljak, Lawrence Weiner and Ian Wilson among others.

JD   The Student Cultural Centre in Belgrade was formed as one of a series of multi-programme institutions, of which the Student Centre in Zagreb was the first, having opened in 1959. The Belgrade Student Cultural Centre opened in 1971, and the Ljubljana Student Cultural Centre opened in 1972; after that, similar spaces for students were established in Sarajevo, Skopje and Podgorica. The individuals running these places, like Koščević, Dunja Blažević, Biljana Tomić, Taja Brejc and Marina Gržinić, were of crucial importance, as were the artists and critics affiliated with them. The Tribina mladih in Novi Sad had been active since the early 1960s, when the film director Želimir Žilnik was the main programme manager there, who was to become a key figure in the New Art Practices in Serbia at the end of the 1960s, just as he would become key to the New Yugoslav Film.

There was tension and conflict around the student centres because, as I said, these institutions had been 'dispossessed' of their original functions, functions that had been established by the socialist order and in accordance with the dominant view of the younger generations. Socialism was in principle inclined towards young people and was prepared to establish new institutions for them. But, in order for cultural institutions like the student centres to play such a ground-breaking role, young professionals had to be installed in leading positions at these institutions. Judita Šalgo was the programme manager of the Tribina mladih in Novi Sad, while Biljana organised numerous exhibitions in 1969–1970 in their gallery and collaborated with Bogdanka Poznanović and members of the KÔD group and others.

BD   It is interesting that the programme managers of these youth and student institutions were precisely those who sought to carry out such a displacement and move away from the institutional mainstream. Ultimately, that is exactly what you were doing as a curator at the Belgrade Museum of Contemporary Art, introducing Conceptual art in a very timely manner into the museum programme and more generally into local art history.

JV   We can even write a short note on the history of historicisation. After the exhibition of 1971 in the Salon of the Museum of Contemporary Art in Belgrade, things begin to take shape. In your exhibition of 1973 entitled *Dokumenti o post-objektnim pojavama u jugoslovenskoj umetnosti 1968–1973* (*Documents of Post-Object Phenomena in Yugoslav Art 1968–1973*), again at the Salon, you replaced the notion of Conceptual art with the notion of post-object phenomena.[13] The first comprehensive institutional historicisation of the New Art Practices in Yugoslavia followed several years later with the exhibition *The New Art Practices* organised by Marijan Susovski at the Gallery of Contemporary Art in Zagreb in 1978. That's when the New Art Practices became firmly established in Yugoslav art history, even though its practitioners never rose to the level of the 'local greats', which remained reserved for those practising traditional forms of expression, like painting and sculpture.

JD   That is the first case of a historicisation effort to unite all these artistic phenomena. I worked on that exhibition and wrote the introductory essay called 'Some Problems of the Art Practices of the Past Decade' (1978).[14] The making of this comprehensive publication was a difficult task; it wasn't easy to find an art historian who was sufficiently familiar with the subject, so some of the essays had to be written by the protagonists themselves. Mirko Radojičić wrote about the Novi Sad scene, Bálint Szombathy about the Subotica scene. Of the art historians, Jasna Tijardović wrote about the Belgrade circle, and Nena Baljković wrote about Dimitrijević and Trbuljak. Both historians were very close to the protagonists and became familiar with this type of art as the result of real-life contacts, and not because of their education and background in art history. Vladan Radovanović wrote about himself. In addition to the introductory essay, I also wrote short essays on Goran Đorđević, Damnjan and Tomislav Gotovac because they were not part of the circle of the Student Cultural Centre informal group of six artists, whose work was covered by Jasna Tijardović. Miško Šuvaković wrote about Group 143, of which he was a member. The entire development of the New Art Practices in Yugoslavia was addressed through the collected critical texts. The exhibition from 1971 was given the title *Examples of Conceptual Art in Yugoslavia*, but the one in Zagreb in 1978 was called *The New Art Practices*. These different titles reflect the dynamics of promotion and historicisation that Jelena wrote

about in her dealings with the New Art Practices exhibitions.
I began from Conceptual art, and from a text written by Sol
LeWitt. Once we had historicised the Belgrade phenomena
it became clear that I couldn't call these phenomena
Conceptual art, as the term largely refers to a very specific
practice in art related to linguistic, analytic and iconoclastic
tendencies. We used the term New Art Practices because
it was more comprehensive and exemplary of all those
different trends and ways of working; and we owe the
decision to emphasise the term in the title for the exhibition
in 1978 to Marijan Susovski, the curator of the Zagreb
Gallery of Contemporary Art.

JV   This was the first integral exhibition of the Yugoslav
New Art Practices, the first attempt at a single, all-
encompassing historicisation through which this whole
scene comes to be documented.

JD   It was a major exhibition for this type of art. And the
essays read well even today.

2.   <u>The Student Cultural Centre as an Art Scene:</u>
        <u>Individuals, Platforms and Collective Acts</u>

BD   We discussed the exhibition *Examples of Conceptual
Art in Yugoslavia* and the selection for the 1971 Paris Biennial.
The same year a completely new institution for culture
opened that would become canonised in art history as the
place where the New Art Practices in Belgrade emerged:
the Student Cultural Centre (SKC).

JV   We are curious about your own memories from the
time of the SKC founding, because we are now holding our
conversation from the plasticity of individual experience.

JD   The SKC was founded as a result of the events in 1968,
and it opened in 1971. Dom omladine (the Youth House)
in Belgrade already existed as an institution dedicated to the
culture of the younger generations, and the SKC appeared
as structurally connected to the University of Belgrade.

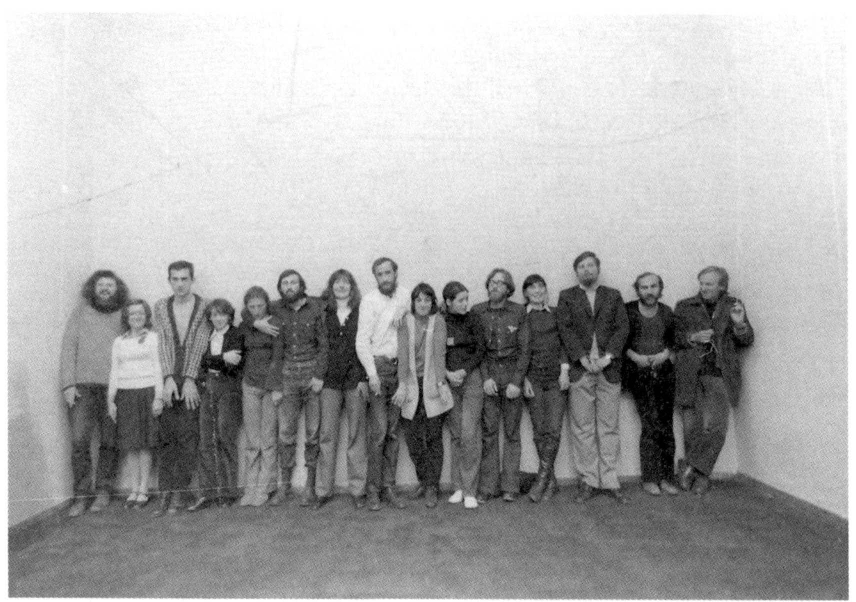

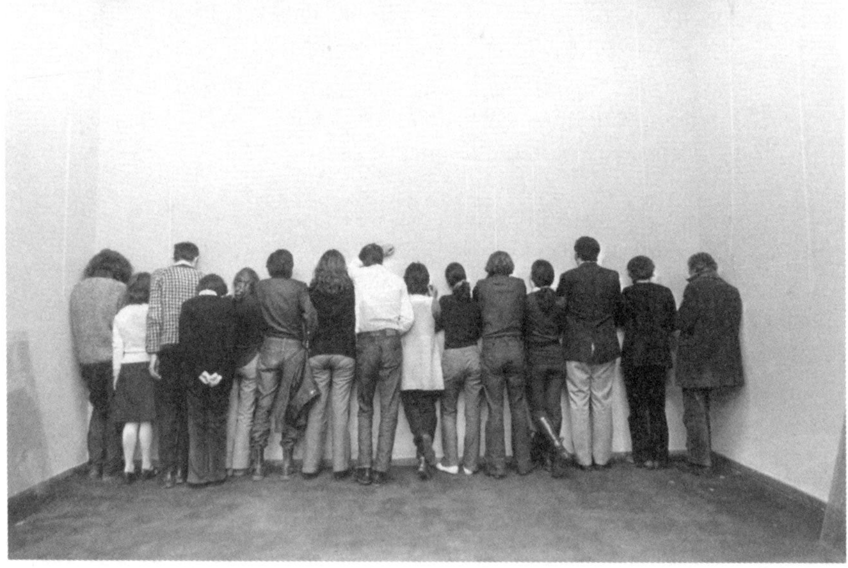

Six artists and nine art historians, Student Cultural Centre (SKC) Gallery, Belgrade, 1972
From left to right: Slavko Timotijević, Dragica Vukadinović, Milan Jozić, Ljubica Stanivuk, Jasna Tijardović, Zoran Popović,
Marina Abramović, Raša Todosijević, Goranka Matić, Dunja Blažević, Gergely Urkom, Biljana Tomić, Nikola Vizner,
Era Milivokević, Neša Paripović
Photographs by Milan Jozić

BD   The SKC first director was Petar Ignjatović, from 1970 onwards, who was an art historian by education. From 1976 to 1979 it was led by Dunja Blažević.

JV   You and Biljana worked with Dunja. Moreover, Biljana very quickly got involved with the SKC Gallery.

JD   Everyone worked together. Dunja had a clear view of it all, which could be summed up in the motto 'new art for a new society'. Could the New Art Practices create a new society, or was the new society in that period of socialism after 1968 already in a state of crisis? These are considerations that already called for attention. In any case Dunja, as the programme manager of the Gallery, and later as the SKC director, contributed to the profile of the cultural events held at the SKC in the 1970s.

JV   And to the institutional profile itself?

JD   Yes, also to the Gallery's entire institutional profile, as you have shown in your research on SKC. Dunja's initial profile of the space aims at creating an open sequence of events which grow out of a dialogue, out of the reality from which the New Art Practices scene developed. Resistance to the academies and institutional critique grew out of the events associated with BITEF, the Student Centre in Zagreb and more. Then there is also the new collectivist way of life, and heated debates about art in group discussions. All these things are definitively the approach observed by all those connected with the SKC Gallery.

JV   Unlike the Belgrade Museum of Contemporary Art, the artistic policy of the SKC wasn't based on a defined programme that should then have been put into practice, but rather favoured process and immediacy – immediate actions and ideas. In the interpretation of the SKC, which I prepared together with Prelom kolektiv in the exhibition notebook *The Case of SKC* (2008), the profiling process that ran both top down and bottom up through the institutional framework and in the form of self-organisation, this very specific internal dynamic, was an important feature of the SKC's new institutionalism.[15] Unlike the museum as an official cultural institution organised hierarchically and professionally, a certain type of informality played a big role at the SKC: the social networks, personal ties, affinities, affections and the way Dunja opened up the gallery at the SKC to participative and collective action. For me, the institutional essence of the SKC lies in the fact that it is neither the museum nor the Šempas Family Art Commune, that it accommodates neither the logic of the white cube nor the politics of exodus. And I would argue that there isn't any singularity of authorship of the institutional profile that could be divided between Dunja and Biljana, but rather their authorship is to be found precisely in the gesture of the abdication of the curator, of opening the space up to a type of communitarian participation in institutional profiling and programming. That is where Dunja and Biljana's invention lies, precisely in that type of refusal of authorship and authority, in the decision to share it with others. Out of this grow the exhibition and the programmatic singularity and specificity of the SKC, for which many deserve credit. And that is why the photograph taken by Milan Jozić, in which the various protagonists lean against the main gallery wall, is in fact an ideal institutional representation of the SKC. However, speaking of the very earliest beginnings, it is obvious that someone had to open the door to such a possibility. That was Dunja and Biljana. And this for me is a clear example of what we called *critica in atto* (*criticism in action*).

JD   I would say that professional experience was important for the institutional profiling of the SKC. It was crucial for the beginnings of the SKC. Biljana brought a well-developed line-up of programmes that encompassed concrete poetry, performance and Arte Povera, and Dunja developed the concept of a politically involved new art.

BD   It is also important to emphasise all this because of the speculation and gossip characteristic of the Belgrade art scene, like the rumour that Dunja Blažević became the programme manager because of her Party connections …

JV   Because from such speculation her role is reduced to that of a purely bureaucratic function, to an apparatchik.

JD   That kind of nonsense I will not comment on.
The gallery programme and its overall orientation were
conceptually conceived by Dunja Blažević and a very wide
circle of collaborators: Biljana Tomić, Bojana Pejić, Jasna
Tijardović, Jadranka Vinterhalter, Milica Kraus, Goranka
Matić, Dragica Vukadinović, Seka Stanivuk, Mića Vizner,
Slavko Timotijević, Milan Jozić, Žarana Papić, Ivan Vejvoda,
Filip Filipović and others. There were the artists Marina
Abramović, Neša Paripović, Raša Todosijević, Zoran Popović,
Slobodan Milivojević Era, Gergely Urkom and more. All
these people were members of an informal type of editorial
board that took part in discussions about the programme
and in the programme itself as collaborators. It was crucial
that the status of an institution intended for youth culture,
and primarily for the student population, was raised to that
of a highly professional institution. I think the essence
of the SKC is that the protagonists of the programme, from
the curators and artists to the general public, had a clear
concept of the institution and knew what they were doing,
they understood what they were taking part in and what they
represented. Young critics and numerous collaborators,
Dunja and Biljana at the vanguard, pulled off a major about-
face, in which they made the SKC Gallery, initially opened
to students and the youth population alike, the best platform
for the curators, critics and artists of the New Art Practices.

BD   What were the exhibition procedures in other
galleries that supported young artists?

JD   Artists began showing in galleries in Belgrade whose
exhibition programmes were run by selection teams, like
at the Dom omladine (Youth House) Gallery or the Gallery
of the Kolarac National University and other exhibition
programmes that were largely conventional. The Student
Cultural Centre Gallery, however, created a platform on
which a continuous dialogue between artists, the public
and critics could develop, and it was quite logical in such
a vibrant atmosphere for new concepts, attitudes and
approaches to creative practice to come out of these
discussions and the exchange of ideas.

BD   The exhibition *Drangularijum* (*Trinketarium*) is considered to be the first exhibition of the New Art Practices at the SKC. I have certain reservations as to whether that was really the case, given the wide range of artists shown at the exhibition who were not associated with the conceptual paradigm.

JD   *Drangularijum* took place very soon after the SKC was founded in June 1971. We agreed to give the exhibition this particular title and to allow free expression to all the participants when we were setting it up.[16] Because of this departure from the classic conventions of exhibition-making, *Drangularijum* is seen as a unique project at a crossroads.[17]

JV   *Drangularijum* is indeed a turning point in the exhibition discourse for me, regardless of any inconsistencies. It is a turning point precisely as the result of all its departures from the classical white cube imaginarium – the forms of sacralisation and religious narratives on eternal life – that Brian O'Doherty described so well when speaking about the behaviour at the gallery space, drawing parallels between the gallery and the church. Museum-type exhibitions of the time and all other representative exhibitions operated within this paradigm. *Drangularijum* abandoned the canonical modernist practice of exhibition-making, of showing artists and artworks according to the curatorial/professional authority selection, and instead appeared as a ready-made type of exhibition that I also called a 'People's Cabinet of Curiosities'.[18] The exhibition concept resulted from the discussions of the gallery's informal editorial board and from the Wednesday meetings: no one claims ownership over the exhibition, it doesn't have an artist (no single curator); it doesn't show art objects, but instead shows artistic life from a number of different angles. The idea was to show a particular relation towards an object.

JD   From its very inception *Drangularijum* became an important departure point from which things could branch out. A similar example of an exhibition that Biljana and I knew about was *Amore Mio* (*My Love*), organised by Achille Bonito Olivo in Montepulciano in the summer of 1970.

Art should be changed! As long as
we leave art alone and keep on
transferring works of art from studios to depots and basements by
means of social regulations and
mechanisms, storing them, like
stillborn children, for the benefit of
our cultural offspring, or while we
keep on creating, through the private market, our own variant of the
nouveau riche or Kleinbürger, art
will remain a social appendage,
something serving no useful purpose, and yet something that neither ethically nor culturally we
should be without.
   The self-managing system of
free exchange and association of
labour through self-managing communities of interest represents a
new non-ownership relationship
that examines and revises the
existing models of artistic work
and behaviour.

—Dunja Blažević, *Oktobar 75*,
Student Cultural Centre, Belgrade,
1975

For this exhibition, Bonito Oliva suggested the artists should not exhibit their work, but rather what they love.

JV   In the invitation to exhibit in *Drangularijum* it was proposed that people should exhibit 'things that are important/dear to them'.[19]

BD   But that means that it has to be a thing, some type of object. In the title of the exhibition itself – in the word *drangulija* – there is an insistence that this 'beloved thing' needs to be an object. I think that the title leads one into a trap in which the New Art Practices are experienced simply as a kind of freedom not to exhibit paintings and sculptures, and that this is its main feature. That was how the majority of artists took it, apart from Raša Todosijević, who exhibited his girlfriend Marinela as part of the little *tableaux* he made for the occasion.

JD   Yes, but Damnjan exhibited a sheet of paper on which he had written 'spiritual freedom'. Certainly, there were many artists at the show who were not protagonists of the New Art Practices either before or afterwards: Radomir Reljić, Milija Nešić, Stevan Knežević …

JV   When did the informal group of six artists who were most closely identified with the work of the SKC Gallery in the first half of the 1970s begin to split off from the other participants at *Drangularijum*? I am referring to Abramović, Urkom, Todosijević, Paripović, Popović and Milivojević?

JD   I think that happened immediately after *Drangulari-jum*. Biljana invited these six artists to participate in the exhibition *Objekti i projekti* (*Objects and Projects*) in September 1971, which was part of the BITEF art programme. She asked Dunja for permission to organise the exhibition in the SKC Gallery, which Dunja granted, and then also proposed that Biljana should run the gallery programme until Dunja's return from the United States.

BD   *Drangularijum* took place in June 1971, *Objekti i projekti* happened in September, and then finally there was *Oktobar 71*, of which you wrote: 'Only with this exhibition

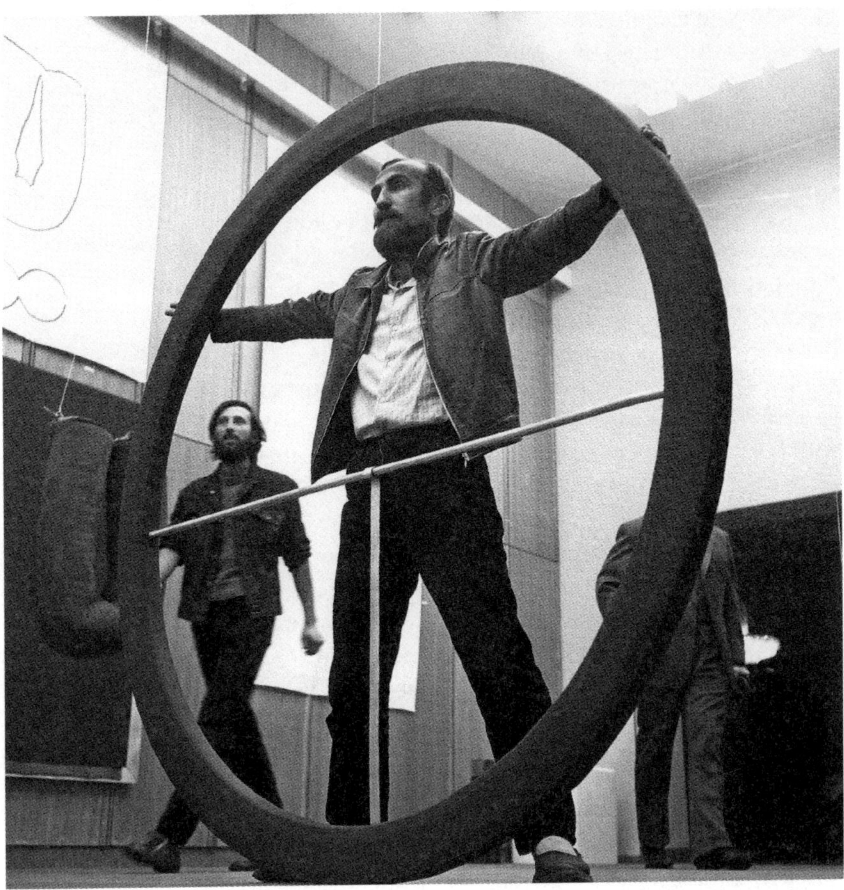

Zoran Popović (left) and Era Milivojević in the exhibition *Objekti i Projekti* (*Objects and Projects*), Student Cultural Centre (SKC) Gallery, Belgrade, 1971

can it be said that we have decisively entered the space of the New Art. This is the point at which its bold and hard kernel of six artists begins to form, plus Damnjan. For all the other participants *Drangularijium* will be but a passing episode as they return to their previous practices.'[20]

JV   You have written a great deal about the SKC, the artists who exhibited there and the New Art Practices in the Yugoslav Art Space. However, the title of your book *Studentski kulturni centur kao umetnička scena* (*The Student Cultural Centre as an Art Scene*) appears best to describe the singularity of the SKC with one stroke.[21] It was not an institutional space in the strict sense of the word – a building populated with bureaucracy and hierarchy – meaning everything that served as an object of the institutional critique by Robert Smithson, Daniel Buren, Hans Haacke and many others. Rather, the SKC was an institution of semi-permeable walls, the institution-movement, the layering of different individual and collective positions within a discursive process, in a flux of people and ideas. This is the type of dynamic for which your term 'scene' is well suited and which title of yours I borrowed for one of my essays on the SKC.[22] The difference lies in the fact that you see the artists as the main protagonists of the scene; your essays, criticism and books focus on the artists and the artworks, while in your later observations the protagonists are not only artists, but also curators, critics, institutions and the analogous networks of collaborators in the Yugoslav space and beyond. I don't think that one artist can be the sole bearer of this idea and the guarantor of the character of such an institutional programme. It rather encompasses all the agents of the scene. Which is why that question of the collectivity, community and exchange seem important to me; I think that without this, this type of development of singular artists wouldn't be possible. The artists gathered around the SKC through the New Art Practices became 'more than artists', which is the tendency broadly negotiated by Art & Language in Europe, the United States and Australia, who insisted on questions of artistic education, artistic theory, self-reflection and so on.

JD   I wrote primarily about the SKC from the position of a critic who approaches artistic phenomena and works of art from a social and cultural perspective. For me, the position of the artist and their work is key. With the New Art Practices, artists become interested in interpretation, context and semiotics. These are mutual processes. The scope of artistic action expands. It is no longer tied solely to the work, but rather to a broader context, which is why I write about the phenomenon of the 'Artist in the First Person'.[23] That relates in the strict sense to performance and the dematerialisation of the art object, but also to the new role of the artist, which is based on a knowledge of and attitude towards social issues. It was of key importance for the SKC that these platforms and facts should acquire a profile, that the curators of the gallery and the programme editors should consciously and intentionally produce an alternative, that they should open the space to far greater spontaneity and participation. It was key that something happened every day between the groups of these artists. Ideas caught fire, multiplied and, what is more important, all of this could be manifested, expressed and shared. When you wanted something to happen, it could always happen at the SKC Gallery.

3.   'I Will Take These Medications'

JV   I also consider these processes to be mutual. I would by no means place the curator in a central role. Nor the critic. Nor, I have to admit, the artist. All of this could be a part of a theory about authorship, about which much was written in the 1960s and 1970s. But, as we are speaking about the actual terrain and the materiality of artistic practice it seems that this way of interpreting the SKC in relation to a wider analysis of the scene also produces certain problems, because with all credit to you, Dunja and Biljana created a sense of irritation among the artists. Today, most of the artists, namely those who gathered around the SKC Gallery, claim to be the progenitors of these ideas – that their reflections on art retroactively created, so to speak, the SKC phenomenon. That is, in their witnessing the artwork there remained some kind of central lever that moved everything

The concept was proposed and introduced in critical terminology at the exhibition of the same name in the Salon of the Belgrade Museum of Contemporary Art in October 1975. The exhibition presented documentation of artistic actions and other forms of behaviour which, in their linguistic origins, range from Happenings, Fluxus, Nouveau Réalisme, Body art, Performance art and other means of personal artistic intervention that have been voided of any mediation via the material object. The thesis behind this concept came to light in the circumstances of the heightened atmosphere around and within the New Art Practices.

The sense and the goal of the idea of the 'Artist in the First Person' are here not exhausted by the assertion that the artist, with their presence and physicality, appears as the actor and protagonist of some artistic form of behaviour. This term also rather explicitly advocates and insists on the need for the artist to manifest an exceptionally individualistic and subjective presence according to radical decisions in life; and anarchistic political options that are irreconcilably opposed to the art system, in which the demands of the market prevail, and against the entire social system, in which the demands of the dominant ideologies prevail.

—Ješa Denegri, 2024

else around it. That is interesting in another way, because the New Art Practices started out as a critique of the concept of the great artistic individual. Finally, the artwork itself in the New Art Practices is a social fact because it didn't come out of an artist's studio but out of the gallery.

JD   That is the essence of the work of the New Art Practices: not a studio, but rather a gallery. That is where the work comes about.

BD   Let's return to the place where Jelena started. Even though conversations with artists are very important for the historicisation of the SKC and understanding the phenomena of the New Art Practices – for example Zoran Popović can offer plenty of insights and very articulate interpretations of this, as was the case in your interview with him for *Moment* magazine[24] – as art historians we know that the institutions followed the developments around the New Art Practices from their very formation: the exhibition at the Salon of the Museum of Contemporary Art in 1971, and then the first exhibitions at the SKC Gallery of the same year.

JD   The SKC is not an institution that was allocated a particular profile, but rather its profile emerged as the result of the people who ran it, and all the events that took place there in its early years – the Wednesday meetings and other discussions. This institution acquired a profile in a way that was different from the way that other cultural institutions got theirs.

JV   We have talked about the Museum of Contemporary Art in a similar way. It didn't exist as an institution before it was profiled, that is before the idea of Yugoslav art of the 20th century was formed and the practice of decennial exhibitions began. Only then did the institution of the museum become the central institution for representing and generating the Yugoslav Art Space, which was a huge idea.

BD   But also, if it weren't for the system of socialist self-management, which enabled institutions to organise themselves independently as institutions – something that worked better with some than with others – none of this

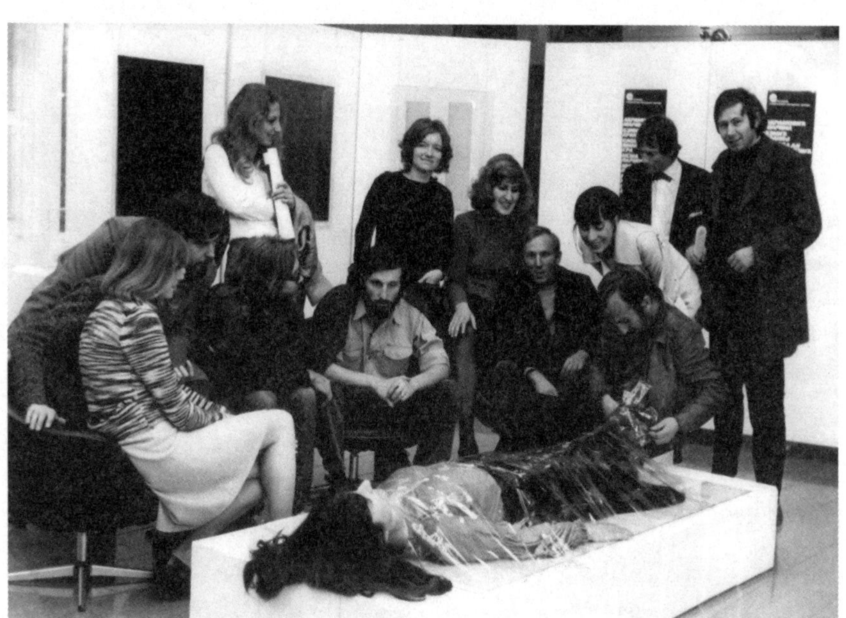

Era Milivojević taping Marina Abramović during the event *Oktobar 71*, Student Cultural Centre Gallery, Belgrade, 1971
From left to right: Marinela Koželj, Nikola Vizner, Gergely Urkom, Jasna Tijardović (standing), Zoran Popović, Ljubica Stanivuk (standing), Bojana Pejić, Neša Paripović, Biljana Tomić, Era Milivojevic, un-identified (standing) and Ješa Denegri (standing)

In order to explain more precisely
where the four of us – Raša,
Gera, Neša and I, and later after
1967–1968, also Era and Marina –
stood in our debates on art … I will
return, via a flashback, to the 1950s.
It was in those years, through
discussions that were a sort of
continuation of the pre-war con-
frontations that were part of the
so-called Clashes within the Left,
that two apparently opposite
opinions crystallised, at least in the
visual arts: on the one hand, there
was the demand that art should be
socially useful to revolutionary
society by performing the tasks
required by a society in the process
of constructing socialism … On the
other hand, there was the position
that the only true task of art was
to explore purely artistic issues.
This political radicalism, known
as the art of Socialist Realism,
soon waned; what remained on
the scene was the middle line,
endorsed by Krleža, as a special
variant of social engagement.

Thus we, as a generation that had only just appeared on the scene, found ourselves squeezed between two apparently opposite opinions, which were both firmly socially anchored, with all their secondary consequences – benefits or repressions – stemming from the economic, the political and the social.

—Zoran Popović, 'Strictly Controlled Representations',
Moment, n°14, 1989

would have happened. Thus, you as workers in art associated your labour through discussions and the exchange of opinions, and you opened up a space for new artistic forms and propositions. But, even in such a context there were very important singular artworks, works that today still draw a lot of attention. Which artworks from the Belgrade scene of the New Art Practices do you classify as ground-breaking, as representing the first works in which you can see a change in language taking place?

JD   One such piece is *Šest minuta rada časovnika snimljenog Xeroxom* (*Six Minutes of the Working of a Watch Recorded by a Xerox Machine*) by Gergely Urkom from 1970 (illustrated on p. 177). I urged the Museum to acquire it. He took a pocket watch, placed it face-down on a photocopying machine and set it to run for six minutes. Here he initiated an interaction between two machines – the movement of the watch as recorded by the Xerox machine, and the action of the Xerox machine recorded for six minutes by the watch. The work was exhibited in the form of a frieze that shows the passing of the six minutes.

BD   We could say that this is a classic example of a conceptual work. But it is also unusual for the New Art Practices in Belgrade. We could say that the works characteristic for Belgrade were performative, and consequently *bodily* in character.

JD   I think that to a large extent they are, and that's the path that was taken further by Marina Abramović, who became a great star of performance art. But also Raša Todosijević, Era Milivojević and, to a degree, Zoran Popović. The first version of his work *Axioms* had already been performed at Atelje 212 as part of the BITEF art programme, and not at the SKC Gallery. Urkom may have had a different sensibility from the other artists of the Belgrade informal group of six artists. Neša Paripović kept his distance from performing in the gallery, and instead presented photographs or films and videos of his performances. If you ask me, one of the key works in performance and Body art in Belgrade appeared with Era Milivojević pasting transparent adhesive tape over a mirror in the foyer of the SKC.

BD   Of those performative works from the early years of the SKC, Raša Todosijević's performance with a carp, known as *Drinking Water* and presented during the April Meetings at the SKC in 1974, for me is seminal. Needless to say I wasn't present at the event, and I only know this performance from photographs and sparse descriptions. But I think this performance is very articulate – since we are talking about that fundamental change in discourse – about the radical abandonment of the humanist discourse by which modern art was institutionalised. Todosijević placed an aquarium on a table in which there was a live carp. During the performance Todosijević pulls the fish out of the aquarium, puts it on the table and while it slowly dies tried to drink all the water in the aquarium. He drinks the water, cannot drink anymore, then vomits it out, and then drinks more water, vomits again and so on – until there is no more water in the aquarium and the carp on the table finally dies. And we could say that that's totally senseless and meaningless, an unnatural and pointless act. The artist drinks the same water that was essential for the fish to survive. And he does it in order to do himself harm, to make himself sick. Which means that pursuing art is an unnatural, or better still, a counter-natural act. This work denounces the humanist fantasy about the artistic gesture with which late modernism is institutionalised – its politics are to be found precisely in the demystification of the humanist rhetoric about art, of the false harmony between nature and art.[25] That is the crucial rupture shown in this work.

JV   Abramović has certainly become the most famous of these artists because of her radical performances from her Belgrade period in the first half of the 1970s. These followed her sound installations. Recently [in 2019], the Belgrade Museum of Contemporary Art organised a Marina Abramović retrospective for which you wrote the catalogue essay.[26] How do you now see her work in relation to the early years of her career? She stands out as the most important personality in a group that was indeed informal, but in which there was much exchange and many joint activities.

JD   The first appearance of Marina Abramović I can remember is her solo show in the Dom omladine (Youth

House) Gallery in November 1970. After that she became involved in the events in the Student Cultural Centre Gallery, with her peers from the same generation. She was making sound installations at the time, installations and photographic works. She participated in the exhibition *Mladi kritičari, mladi umetnici* (*Young Critics, Young Artists*) at the Museum of Contemporary Art in 1972. But how I now experience and understand Marina's work is that her real start in art – which she went on to develop up to the present day – is indeed the performance *Ritam 10* (*Rhythm 10*) in August 1973 at the Edinburgh Festival, and which she then repeated in an expanded version at the invitation of Achille Bonito Oliva for the *Contemporanea* exhibition in Rome in February 1974. Everything that comes after this is part of the epic story of her international adventure, from the subsequent iterations of the *Rhythms* in the Belgrade period through her collaborations with Ulay in art and life and up to the present day. Before she embarked on the joint project with Ulay, a retrospective of her *Rhythms (10, 5, 2, 4, 0)* was organised in the Salon of the Museum of Contemporary Art in April 1975.

BD   You wrote the essay for this exhibition catalogue too.[27] We can therefore say that Abramović's work had had a timely presentation within an institutional framework in Belgrade before she decided to move away. Of course, her artistic ambitions far exceeded the Belgrade context.

JD   I think it all began for Marina at the Edinburgh Festival in 1973. The Edinburgh Festival programmer, Richard Demarco, favoured the art of Eastern Europe. He organised an exhibition of Polish art and he came to Yugoslavia and produced a large exhibition with a catalogue, for which I wrote the essay, and whose cover featured a picture of a red Yugoslav passport.[28] Raša, Marina, Zoran, Gergely, as well as Biljana, Jasna, Irina Subotić and others went to Edinburgh, where Joseph Beuys was also present, and there was an atmosphere in which people could feel completely free, and Marina chose to perform the project *Rhythm 10*. From then on, performance became her primary medium. Of course, she was hugely inspired by Viennese Actionism.

BD   At the time you were already well known in Yugoslavia as an art critic and already an experienced curator at the Museum who was following her work and writing about it. There's that remarkable anecdote about how you were once called to the office of Marina Abramović's mother, who was the director of the Museum of Revolution. Can you share this anecdote with us?

JD   One day, while I was working at the Museum, I received a telephone call from Danica Abramović, Marina's mother, to meet her at the Museum of Revolution where she was the director. The next day, after a warm greeting, she continued in a much sharper tone, accusing me of being a negative influence on her daughter. Surprised, I replied that Marina was such an independent and creative personality that no one, me included, could really have any influence on her. I said that Marina had made very important international performances, that she was supported and valued in serious art circles. However, Mrs Abramović felt that in addition to performance, Marina should continue to paint, especially as she was doing post-graduate studies in Krsto Hegedušić's class in Zagreb. She also made an interesting remark: 'Ivan Tabaković is an experimental artist [like Marina], but above all he is a painter!' I tried to convince comrade Abramović that Marina knew exactly what she was doing, and tried to reassure her with the news that Marina was actually preparing her final performance from the *Rhythm* series – which would soon take place also under the title of *Rhythm 0* in Naples in February 1975. We parted ways amicably.

JV   So, Danica Abramović wanted Marina to do something like Tabaković. Dunja Blažević too had an 'informative discussion' with Marina's mother.

JD   I would love to hear Dunja's story.

JV   The message was that Dunja should take care of Marina's extreme behaviour, that she should tell her to stop performing in such a frightening way in which she hurts herself. Dunja came at this from a position not unlike yours – by affirming Marina's work and the autonomy of her art with reassurance for the concerns of a mother.

JD   In the Gallery of Contemporary Art in Zagreb she performed *Rhythm 2*, in which she took medication to treat acute schizophrenia. Davor Matičević initiated the exhibition. I wasn't the only witness of this performance, which was remarkable and tested many boundaries, and when the performance had come to an end, a brief discussion ensued in order to explain what had just happened. Božo Bek was the director of the Gallery. I remember that he then accused Davor of allowing himself to get pulled into such an event for which he hadn't engaged any medical personnel who could monitor the situation if something went wrong. Božo responded: 'Now, you have gone too far!' Although Božo was very liberal and openminded, he was nonetheless tied to the New Tendencies, and the New Art Practices seemed like a return to Surrealism and the subconscious for him.

JV   Again, we arrive at the conclusion that unlike the constructivist-oriented Zagreb scene, there was this ongoing relation to Surrealism in Belgrade. Both Abramović and Mediala are products of this relation in their own ways.

JD   So, what did Marina do? She swallowed a lot of pills, and then quickly began to convulse violently and shake – and that was really unpleasant for the people watching. After some time, she stopped convulsing and took another medication that helped her return to a more normal state. The performance was documented in photographs and on film.

JV   But there wasn't any pharmacological list. That would have lent the performance another dimension.

JD   You can't present this experience through photography. I remember that my colleagues and the members of the public who were present asked me to interpret the work. I said something like the following: in art we have two forces – the artist makes a rational decision – how they will begin, how they will act out certain creative impulses – but there is also contingency, on the basis of which the work acquires its eventual form. The work on the one hand coincides with the original idea, but on the other it cannot be controlled. What did Marina do? She said, rationally:

'I will take these medications', and that is the original
decision. And what will happen when the medication starts
to take effect? What will happen when she takes the medication that helps her return to a normal state? This is the
contingency factor in art that is immanent to every work
that has not been made such that the first and last instances
of that work correspond with each other. And then one
can say that there is really no difference between the point
at which Marina enters the gallery and begins to work on
her body and the point at which Pollock stands in front
of a large canvas with buckets of paint and begins to pour
and spray, which is also the work of the body.

BD   You spoke to the audience in this way, and then Božo
Bek asked you whether this related somehow to Surrealism?
Even though Pollock's main supporter, Clement Greenberg,
wasn't inclined towards Surrealism, Pollock derived his
approach in part from Surrealism – from the notion of automatic drawing. For Breton, automatic drawing is an immediate expression of the unconscious. And that's how, in the
case of the Belgrade scene, that connection to Surrealism
surfaced. This is apparent with Abramović, and Božo Bek
was correct in his observation.

JV   I see automatism rather in the case of *Freeing the
Memory,* which she performed in Tübingen in 1975. This work
with the pills is rather a critique of modernist rationality,
a critique of that rationalised medical regulation and control
of the body. It is a very typical post-1968, biopolitical,
countercultural and counter-institutional work, a critique
of institutional control over the body. This led to the anti-
psychiatric movement in those years, which was discussed,
among others, at the SKC Forum run by Milo Petrović.[29]
However, in the further development of her work, Marina
discards these references and replaces them with mystical,
shamanistic techniques designed to control and free one
from one's own corporeality.

JD   Her first *Rhythms,* as well as her last *Rhythm o* in Naples
at Studio Morra, are of the same matrix. Marina exhibited
two tables in the gallery, on one of which were various
potentially dangerous objects, and on the other she lay and

declared: 'I am an object, you can do what you want to my body. I take full responsibility.' This for me is of the same matrix as the preceding instance. She says: 'I will do this'; then there are unforeseeable circumstances, and these circumstances are described in an essay written by Thomas McEvilley, who witnessed the performance.[30] Whether Marina is aware of it or not, she posits the fundamental problem of art in her series of five *Rhythms*: the relation between the first act, the first gesture, and that which takes place over the course of the work.

JV   You are talking about the dialectics of decision and process, plan and contingency. We can think this in connection with that long discussion about 'project and destiny' from the beginning of our conversation, or in connection with insisting on the idea of process in the New Art Practices.

JD   I wrote the first essay about Marina for *Polja* magazine in 1974.[31] I organised her exhibition at the Salon in 1975. This is the exhibition in which she brings the series of the five *Rhythms* to a close, before she decided to team up with Ulay and leave independence behind. That was 1975. No one at the Museum opposed this first solo exhibition of hers in a museum context. They considered Marina Abramović to be an artist who deserved such a promotion from (such) an institution.

BD   After this show she left Yugoslavia and began living and working with Ulay. That's the moment, we might say, that this heroic phase of the New Art Practices came to an end. The SKC Gallery continued to be associated with Conceptual art all the way through to the late 1970s. In the mid-1970s a second generation emerged, and they were more strictly tied to analytic conceptualism. In the early 1980s the Gallery turned again to the next generation again, which was forming around the ideas of the return to painting and expressionist art, as well as to some rather generalised postmodernist discourse, from which the alleged sterility and repetitiveness of the conceptual paradigm was criticised. Nevertheless, during that second half of the 1970s some of the key works by the protagonists of the Belgrade New Art

Practices were produced: several versions of Todosijević's video-performance *Was ist Kunst?* (1976–1978, *What is Art?*) or Paripović's film *N.P. 77* (1977), better known as *Preskakanje* (*Leaping Over*). From my experience of meeting foreign colleagues it appears that these are the two best known works of the Belgrade scene from the 1970s after the works of Abramović. What else is characteristic of the second half of the 1970s in the Belgrade SKC?

JD   Let's start with Jovan Čekić, who in fact shot this film for Paripović. Those two were then members of Group 143. This group of artists mainly dealt, according to its members' various capacities, with the analytic approach to Conceptual art, and thus they began to map out an essential deviation from the socially-engaged and political standpoints of the preceding generation. Towards the end of the 1970s Paripović produced some of his key works, such as the film *N.P. 77* which you mentioned, and then *Primeri analitičke skulpture* (*Examples of Analytic Sculpture*) in 1978, *Poruke* (*Messages*) in 1979, *Odnos glava-ruka* (*The Head-Hand Relation*) in 1979 and more. Aside from Paripović and Čekić, Group 143 included Miško Šuvaković, Maja Savić, Paja Stanković, Vladimir Nikolić and others. Occasional guests included Marko Pogačnik and Mirko Radojičić, and sometimes Boris Demur worked with them during his military service in Belgrade. But the next big change in the cultural and artistic paradigm was, in the early 1980s, already on the horizon. The pioneers of the New Art Practices of the 1970s, Abramović and Urkom, had left Belgrade, and those who stayed continue to produce very important works, but in changed circumstances and in a significantly different context. Raša Todosijević performed *Umetnost i memorija* (*Art and Memory*) in 1975, and in 1976 began the performance series *Was ist Kunst?* (*What is Art?*), in its many different versions. In 1976, Zoran Popović created *Filmski autoportret/Privatna moda* (*Film Self-portraits/ Private Fashion*), Gergely Urkom made the series of paintings *Beli međusloj* (*White Interlayer*) in 1977, and Era Milivojević began *Slike-promene* (*Paintings-Changes*). This entire corpus would be shown for the first time in the exhibition *Posle petnaest godina* (*After Fifteen Years*) curated by Dragica Vukadinović at the Happy New Gallery in Belgrade in December 1988.[32]

BD   In the Yugoslav context, 1980 really was a turning point, as Josip Broz Tito died and the socialist federation entered its final decade, leading to the breakup of Yugoslavia and the wars of the 1990s. In the global context, this was the year Ronald Reagan became President of the United States and a new epoch of global capitalism that today we call neoliberalism became demonstrably articulated. In Yugoslav art, this was the year marking the symbolic endgame of the New Art Practices, and I would say that happened with the exhibition *Protiv umetnosti* (*Against Art*) by Goran Đorđević in January 1980 at the SKC Gallery. After that, Đorđević and various other artists, including Todosijević and Milivojević, became more present in another gallery that had opened earlier in the SKC, the Happy New Gallery, run by Slavko Timotijević. This is where the first exhibition of Laibach Kunst in Belgrade was organised, and where Autopsia had their first events, and where Đorđević exhibited the works from the final phase of his artistic practice before his disappearance from the scene in the mid-1980s. All in all this was definitely a moment when one paradigm ended and the term 'the postmodern condition' became increasingly used.[33] That opened a deep rift – once you mentioned a conversation you had with your Slovene colleague Jure Mikuž, who was very sceptical of this paradigmatic change, while you by contrast endorsed it.

JD   At the Venice Biennale of 1980, Achille Bonito Oliva organised the exhibition *Aperto 80* as a programmatic declaration and introduction of the major changes in art at the beginning of the 1980s. This was an exhibition that presented, among others, the Italian Transavanguardia, the German Neue Wilde and American artists like Julian Schnabel and Susan Rothenberg. Georg Baselitz and Anselm Kiefer were shown in the German pavilion. After Venice I went to Portorož with Tomaž Brejc. Jure Mikuž was also present. Naturally, the conversation turned to the Venice Biennale, particularly *Aperto 80*, and our totally contrasting impressions and drastically differing evaluations of the entire current art situation came to the surface, particularly our thoughts on the 'new painting' in Slovenia, of which Mikuž had an extremely negative opinion. Brejc was significantly more moderate because – even though he had,

from the beginning, been very favourably inclined towards
the OHO group and the New Art Practices in general – he
knew that Andraž Šalamun, as a former member of OHO
and as someone whom he trusted completely, had in the
meantime turned to painting. Even though all of this
pointed to a major 'reversal' in art, the new situation seemed
like something that could be seen as an inevitable turn
within contemporary art, and one could only try to do one's
best to deal with the new events and discourses. A young
generation came forth, in whom, in principle, you had to
accord the same trust you had demonstrated in the previous
generation. One of the outcomes of having such trust was
the exhibition *Umetnost osamdesetih* (*Art of the 1980s*) organised
at the Museum of Contemporary Art in 1983, on which
I worked with Jadranka Vinterhalter and Jovan Despotović,
that would soon be followed by the events that resulted in
the exhibition *Umetnost–kritika usred osamdesetih* (*Art–Criticism
of the Mid-1980s*) and the first and second *Documents* in
Sarajevo. Generally speaking we now consider that a significantly different artistic situation appeared from the beginning of the 1980s, which understood the entire cultural
climate in terms of postmodernism and the postmodern.
Numerous protagonists of the New Art Practices of the 1970s
got involved in this trend and also found a prominent place
within its linguistic and media-based pluralism. I think that
their position was justified simply because art, like life itself,
moves on, unceasingly, and both change according to the
new circumstances in which every protagonist in the world
of contemporary art always has to express themselves anew.

[1]   The film *Druga linija* (2016) by Nenad Milošević looks at the groundbreaking moments of the Novi Sad neo-avant-garde and Conceptual art scene at the end of the 1960s and the beginning of the 1970s. In addition to the recollections of the protagonists themselves, the film contains footage from a significant number of films and documentaries of various artistic actions.

[2]   Among the Yugoslav artists were the OHO group with an exhibition and theatre and street performances; Tomaž Brejc and Tomaž Šalamun, Andraž Šalamun, Milenko Matanovič, David Nez and Marko Pogačnik's reistic objects made of plaster; from Zagreb there were Goran Trbuljak and Ida Biard, Braco Dimitijević and Nena Baljković, Sanja Iveković and Dalibor Martinis, Jagoda Kaloper and Željko Koščević. There were also the Belgrade artists Marina Abramović, Slobodan Milivojević Era, Neša Paripović, Zoran Popović, Raša Todosijević and Gergely Urkom.

[3]   See Alexander Alberro, *Conceptual Art and the Politics of Publicity*, MIT Press, Massachussetts 2004.

[4]   *Zenitizam. Predlog za jednu izložbu* (*Zenitism. Proposal for an Exhibition*), Tribina mladih, Novi Sad, 1972.

[5]   *Mangelos – Fenomen Pikaso* (*Mangelos – the Picasso Phenomenon*), Tribina mladih, Novi Sad, 1972.

[6] Mirko Radojičić, 'Aktivnost grupe KÔD, grupe (Ǝ, Umetnički rad van grupa u Novom Sadu', in *Nova umjetnička praksa 1966–1978* (*New Art Practices 1966–1978*), exh. cat., Contemporary Art Gallery, Zagreb 1978, p. 36–47.

[7] Ješa Denegri, 'Tri istorijske etape – srodni vidovi umetničkog ponašanja', *Umetnost*, no. 65, Belgrade 1978.

[8] Jelena Vesić, 'The Three Exhibitions – Simultaneity of Promotion and Historisation of the New Art Practices (From Alternative Spaces to The Museum and Back)', *Parallel Chronologies*, an exhibition archive by tranzit.hu, Budapest, 2014, available on http://tranzit.org/exhibitionarchive/the-three-exhibitions-simultaneity-of-promotion-and-historization-of-new-art-practices-from-an-alternative-spaces-to-the-museum-and-back/ (last accessed May 2024).

[9] Ješa Denegri, *Grupa OHO*, exh. cat., Dom omladine, Belgrade 1969/1970.

[10] See Sanja Horvatinčić, *Inovacije u kustoskim praksama Želimira Koščevića u počecima rada Galerije Studentskog Centra u Zagrebu 1966–1970* (*Innovations in the Curatorial Practices of Želimir Koščević at the Beginning of the Student Centre in Zagreb*, Master Thesis, University of Zagreb, 2020).

[11] See Želimir Koščević, Davor Matičević and Ranko Munitić (eds.), *Prvi sajam naučne fantastike* (*The First Fair of Science Fiction*), design and poster: Ivan Picelj, photographs: Petar Dabac, Enes Midžić.

[12] Ivana Bago, 'Dematerijalizacija i politizacija izložbe: Primjeri kustoske prakse kao antikapitalističke institucionalne kritike u Jugoslaviji tijekom 60-ih i 70-ih godina 20. Stoljeća' ('Dematerialisation and Politicisation of the Exhibition: Examples of Curatorial Practice as Anti-Capitalist Institutional Criticism in Yugoslavia during the 1960s and 1970s'), *Radovi Instituta za povijest umjetnosti* (*Works of the Institute for the History of Art*), no. 36, 2012, p. 235–248.

[13] See Jelena Vesić, 'The Three Exhibitions'. A summary of Denegri's critical text can be found here: http://tranzit.org/exhibitionarchive/wp-content/uploads/2014/09/1_Jesa-text_1973-summary.pdf (last accessed May 2024).

[14] Ješa Denegri, 'Problemi umjetničke prakse poslednjeg decenija'('Some Problems of the Art Practices of the Past Decade'), *Nova umjetnička praksa* (*New Art Practices*), Contemporary Art Gallery, Zagreb 1978, p. 5–13. See here p. 322–351.

[15] See Jelena Vesić, 'SKC as the Site of performative (self-) production: *Oktobar 75*–Institution, Self-Organisation, First Person Speech, Collectivisation', *Život Umjetnosti* (*Life of Art*), no. 91, Zagreb 2012.

[16] *Drangulija* means a knick-knack, a trinket, so the title of the show may translated as *The Knick-Knackarium* or *Trinketarium*.

[17] See Ješa Denegri, 'Drangularijum', *Sedamdesete: Teme srpske umetnosti* (*The Seventies: Serbian Art Themes*), exh. cat., Svetovi, Novi Sad 1996, p. 89–93.

[18] Jelena Vesić, 'Drangularijum – Ready-Made Exhibition or Peoples' Curio Cabinet', *Parallel Chronologies*, an exhibition archive by tranzit.hu, Budapest 2014.

[19] See *Drangularijum*, exh. cat., Student Cultural Centre Gallery, Belgrade, June 1971.

[20] Denegri, 'Drangularijum', p 92.

[21] Ješa Denegri, *Studentski kulturni centar kao umetnička scena* (*The Student Cultural Centre as an Art Scene*), Student Cultural Centre, Belgrade 2003. The book comprises critical essays that Denegri published during the 1970s and his later writings about the art of the 1970s.

[22] See Jelena Vesić, 'Student Cultural Centre (SKC) as an Art Scene', *Parallel Chronologies*, an exhibition archive by tranzit.hu, Budapest, 2014.

[23] Ješa Denegri developed a theory about the first-person artist with regard to the new artistic phenomena, which broke with the 'fixed norms defining the notion and borders of a praxis we call art'. Instead of the white cube as a modernist salon, we now have a space of 'independent artistic expression'. Denegri related his concept of the 'Artist in the First Person' with Duchamp's legacy and the 'unconditional egocentrism of the artist aimed at overcoming and tricking all the attributes that the morality of bourgeois society attached to the phenomenon of art, treating it as both an object of trivial commercialisation and as a phenomenon of often idealised cultural superstructure'. However, Denegri did not see a solution for these problems or any new glorification there, rather the symptom of a certain pessimism linked to the Marcusean end of utopia: 'As the material opulence and the general increase in social standards [of living] did not result in an actual alienation of the living conditions of modern man, the process of imagination in the procedures of new artists could not establish a crucially altered and truly alienated social status of art.' From Jelena Vesić, 'SKC as the Site of Performative (Self-)Productions'.

[24] Zoran Popović, 'Strogo kontrolisane predstave' ('Strictly Controlled Performances'), *Moment*, no. 14, Belgrade 1989, p 20.

[25] See Branislav Dimitrijević, 'Čuvajte se umetnika, oni se poznaju sa svim klasama'('Beware of Artists, they Familiarise with all Classes'), *Reč*, vol. 87, no. 33, Belgrade 2017, p. 193–205.

[26] Ješa Denegri, 'Umetnost Marina Abramović: kontekst, karakteristike i vrednosti beogradskog perioda' ('The Art of Marina Abramovic: Context, Characteristics and Values of the Belgrade Period'), *Čistač/Cleaner, Marina Abramović*, exh. cat., Museum of Contemporary Art, Belgrade 2019, p 242–249.

[27] *Marina Abramović: Ritam 10, 5, 2, 4, 0*, exh. cat., Salon of the Museum of Contemporary Art, Belgrade, 1975.

[28] *Aspects 75: Contemporary Yugoslav Art*, Richard Demarco Gallery, Edinburgh, 1975.

[29] Between the mid-1970s and the mid-1980s, the Tribune programme of the SKC presented several conferences and events: The Week of Spain in 1976, coinciding with the end of Franco's dictatorship; The Week of Latin America in 1977, dealing with the anti-colonial struggles of different militant guerrilla movements in various parts of Latin America; the first women's issues were opened in 1978 through the conference Comrade Women, after which followed the event dedicated to militant revolutionary Chilean cinema, The Second Week of Latin America in the early 1980s. New movements in psychiatry (or more precisely, the positions and attitudes of *anti-psychiatry*) were discussed in 1983, while events in 1984 were dedicated to the critique of the then contemporary Yugoslav society.

[30] Thomas McEvilley, 'Marina Abramović/Ulay – Ulay/Marina Abramović', *Polja* (*Fields*), no. 377–378, Novi Sad 1990, p. 52–55. Originally published in *Artforum*, vol. XII, no. 1, New York 1983, p. 52–55.

[31] Ješa Denegri, 'Marina Abramović', *Polja*, no. 189, Novi Sad 1974, p. 22–23.

[32] Dragica Vukadinović, *Posle petnaest godina* (*After Fifteen Years*) (Marina Abramović, Slobodan Era Milivojević, Neša Paripović, Zoran Popović, Raša Todosijević, Gergely Urkom), Happy New Gallery, Belgrade, 30 December 1988–27 January 1989.

[33] See Branislav Dimitrijević, 'That's The Look That's The Look The Look of Death: Briefly About the Art Scene In and Around Belgrade in the 1980s', *The Eighties Through the Prism of Events, Exhibitions and Discourses*, exh. cat., Moderna galerija, Ljubljana 2018.

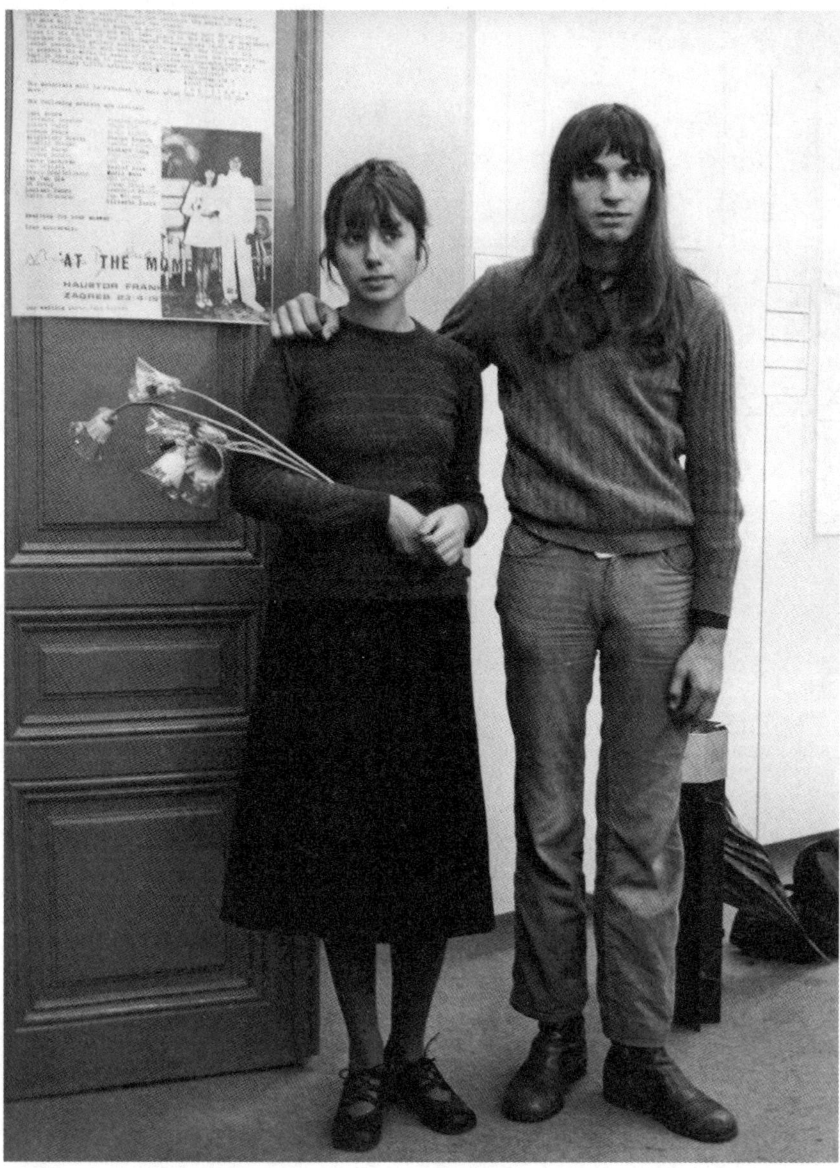

Nena Baljković and Braco Dimitrijević during their exhibition *At Another Moment*, Student Cultural Centre Gallery, Belgrade, 1971

<u>The New Art Practices</u>

The term New Art Practices was chosen because there were no adequate theoretical grounds for the use of the narrow and specific term Conceptual art. The term was chosen because it encompassed the following meanings: the term 'new' tells us that it is about innovative neo-avant-garde phenomena radically different from the other previous currents in the Yugoslav art scene (discrete modernism, Informel, new figuration, Neo-Constructivism, etcetera); the term 'art' or 'artistic' is there to abolish all doubts that it is a legitimate form of art (not an anti-art activity or a work outside the field of art, as many critics who disagreed with this new art often emphasised); and the term 'practices' boldly underlines the fact that it is about processes, operations, durations, events, Happenings and so on, and not about finished and final aesthetic objects (paintings, sculptures and so forth). The term 'practices' also alludes to the philosophical notion of praxis, which could point to the meanings of activism, social critique and political engagement in relation to the radicalism and militancy of artistic phenomena included under this term.

—Ješa Denegri, 2024

Some Problems of the Art Practices of the Past Decade: General Characteristics of the New Art Practices
Ješa Denegri

Published in Marijan Susovski (ed.), *Nova umjetnička praksa 1966–1978* (*New Art Practices 1966–1978*), Contemporary Art Gallery, Zagreb 1978.

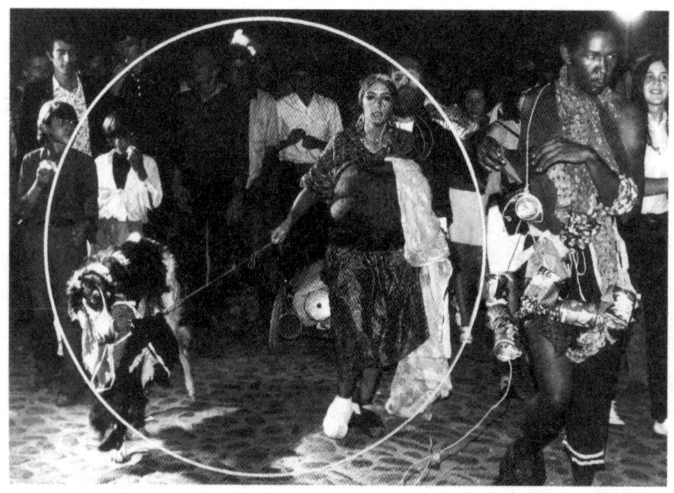

The Lo Zoo Group performing *Dresirani čovek u Skadarliji* (*The Trained Man in Skodarlija*) in the streets of Belgrade, 1970

Although it is widely accepted that art follows a continuous, unbroken line in its development, without sudden interruptions marked by specific dates, various symptoms support the claim that some ten years ago a new situation arose, which, it seems to us, can be justifiably set apart as a specific period in the history of post-war art. It goes without saying that the new development contains many direct or indirect influences and elements discernible in the period preceding it, but it also shows a sufficient number of characteristic constitutive elements that lend it a separate identity. In his *Precronistoria (Prehistory)*, Germano Celant takes 1966 as the beginning of this period and sees the first signs of change in relation to the preceding trends in the exhibitions *Arte abitabile (Habitable Art)* at the Sperone Gallery in Turin and *Eccentric Abstraction* at the Fischbach Gallery in New York. The works displayed at these exhibitions were characterised by a conscious departure from the premises of Minimal art and the art of primary geometrical forms realised in industrial technology and the new media. Instead, the artists were now offering works of non-consistent temporary material structure, bringing into question more prominently than ever before the status of the fixed and permanent art object. This change of the status of the art object seems to be the key issue that sparked the critical debate about the specific characteristics of the new situation in art. Some of the first analyses of the new trends pointed out the reduction of the material character of form applied as a principle; this is also the basic sentiment/statement of the now classic critical texts – *Arte Povera* by Germano Celant (1969) and *The Dematerialization of Art* by Lucy Lippard and John Chandler (1967) – and the programmatic essays of two particularly representative artists of the movement – *Anti Form* by Robert Morris (1968) and *Le ultime parole famose* (*Famous Last Words*) by Michelangelo Pistoletto (1967). The issue of the changed material status of the art object was also treated in some later papers, for instance those on post-object art by Donald Karshan; furthermore, emphasis was laid in the first presentations of the new trend on the artists' attitudes, behaviour and actions in concrete processual operations (the exhibitions *Op Losse Schroeven* [*Situations and Cryptostructures*] at the Stedelijk in Amsterdam and *Live in Your Head: When Attitudes Become Form* at the Kunsthalle Bern, both in 1969); finally, the symptoms of this radical separation of the current artistic practice from previous attitudes led some critics to speak of the whole phenomenon as the 'new art', as was the case in the theme of the exhibition of English artists entitled *The New Art* at the Hayward Gallery in London in August 1972.

However, it has now become evident that this whole development contains a far more structured inner configuration composed of a series of phenomena for which it is increasingly difficult to find a common denominator. The symptom of the art object remains one of their characteristics, though it has to be pointed out that we are dealing here with a change in the visualisation or concretisation of ideas rather than with a definite disappearance of the physical properties of the art object. The work of art is no longer formulated as an autonomous plastic shape but is

constructed in a medium or material as a 'background'
(or a 'container' as Ursula Meyer describes it), within which
there is a thought process at work.

Furthermore, apart from the interest in the use of
physical, organic and natural materials, there arose the
question of how to treat modern media, such as videotape,
film and photography; and within the whole movement
that emphasised the mental components of artistic work,
problems associated with new approaches to the classical
disciplines of painting, sculpture and drawing once again
became of central interest. If we add that these developments
had very definite sociological implications, that individuals
and whole groups of artists took part in ideological discussions and social and political life, we must inevitably
conclude that the new art trend did not merely consist in
an internal stylistic change within an adopted basic concept
of art, but was in many ways an essentially new global
situation, in which there arose and featured equally prominently questions of changed forms and ways of artistic
practice and its projection onto the basic structure of the
cultural and social conditions in some milieus of modern
society.

Writing on the new artistic practice, art critics and the
artists themselves identified a number of separate orientations that today are parts or components of a single whole.
In the initial manifestations, in which a reaction to the
strictly technological orientation of the movements of
Primary Structures and Neo-Constructivism was directly
observable, the accent was on works with non-selected
organic and ephemeral materials, while the meaning was
transferred from the form of the art object to the behaviour
of the artist's subject. The work of art had to be an ideological postulation of the dichotomy culture-nature – a
characteristic feature of the early Anti Form and Earth Works
operations of American and English artists (Robert Morris,
Robert Smithson, Richard Serra, Richard Long, Barry
Flanagan and others), and a similar idea can be observed in
the Italian artists espousing Arte Povera (*poor art*, a term
coined by Celant), such as Michelangelo Pistoletto, Mario
Merz, Jannis Kounellis, Gilberto Zorio, Emilio Prini,
Giovanni Anselmo, Giulio Paolini and others, and equally in

the German representative and precursor of the movement, Joseph Beuys. One thing all these artists had in common was a continuous change of behaviour and action aimed at creating as much room for free manoeuvre as possible. As Celant observes, this was a consciously articulated principle of 'creative nomadism'. In this, the work procedure is intuitive and concrete, and is not pre-determined by philosophical and theoretical motivations, though it is almost always based on the principle of tautology, which indicates the factual character of the elements used in the process of the materialisation and visualisation of an idea. With their tendency to stress natural and physical – meaning organic – media, removed from any confinement within the frame of a fixed object, these operations are directly continued by Land art and Body art. In Land art, natural open areas are used for works on a macro-dimensional scale and the work either perishes quickly or survives for a long time, like a kind of archaeological data (works by Robert Smithson, Walter De Maria, Michael Heizer, Richard Long and others). In Body art, the artist's body becomes the place and medium of work and is often used with all the physical brutality of vital and organic functions. The representatives of this method (Gina Pane, Vito Acconci, Chris Burden, the artists of the Vienna body circle and others) react to the subconscious layers of individual fates, including the components of personal and collective psychological complexes in their actions, endowing the perception of the work with a markedly sensuous character, expressed for the most part in brief and ephemeral performances.

Alongside these artistic trends that developed simultaneously but in different directions and independently from one another in various parts of Europe and America, the field of Conceptual art became more clearly defined; the term had hitherto often been inappropriately used to denote all art developments of the past decade. However, today it is obvious that in its narrower sense it can refer only to the works of a group of American and English artists whose work is based on the principles of analytical philosophy and the philosophy of language, under the influence of Ludwig Wittgenstein and Alfred Jules Ayer. The term itself derives from Sol LeWitt's texts, which suggest the possibility that the physical object may disappear and envisage the

substitution of that object with a notional (mental) level of
its functioning, which he frames as follows: 'Ideas alone
can be works of art; they are in a chain of development that
may eventually find some form. All ideas need not be made
physical' (1969). This is the basis on which the working
principles of the art of the early conceptualists who gathered
around Seth Siegelaub (Douglas Huebler, Robert Barry,
Lawrence Weiner, Joseph Kosuth) evolved, with work
characterised by the approximated choice of solutions for
the conceptualisation and realisation of the object (with
the exception of Kosuth). This is proposed by Weiner in his
well-known formulation: 'The artist may construct the
piece. The piece may be fabricated. The piece need not be
built' (1966). However, it was in this approximation that
Catherine Millet quite rightly discerned a relapse into the
'expressive residue'; it required the strict theory of Joseph
Kosuth to give the term and notion of Conceptual art as
'art as idea' its essentially analytical meaning. 'Artistic
postulates', says Kosuth, 'are not of a factual but a linguistic
nature: they do not describe the behaviour of physical
things or mental processes; they are the expression of art
definitions or are formal consequences of such definitions'.
Art & Language and a few other artists (Victor Burgin,
Bernar Venet) pursued the course of these rigorous analytical
procedures further, insisting on the extreme objectivity
of artistic language or language as an art, with the aim of
eliminating from it any possibility of ambivalence that might
result from the function of the image, form or symbol. All
these artists use language as a medium of artistic practice
(and not as a medium of art criticism or art theory), which is
the ultimate point that the process of conceptualisation
of artistic thought can attain and still be considered a kind
of pattern of perception. One further (and extreme) step
in that direction would be the concept envisaged by Jack
Burnham in his statement that 'the ideal degree of Conceptual art is telepathy', but such a thesis extends beyond the
scope of the known examples of art and therefore has no
meaning for the historical consideration of the phenomenon.

   The further development of this purely linguistic wing
of Conceptual art took an unexpected turn at the beginning
of 1975, when its members did not follow the direction
foreseen by Burnham but, on the contrary, began severely

to criticise the cultural superstructure in the context of the historical and cultural development of contemporary neo-capitalism. In Kosuth's words, the position of the contribution of Conceptual art, already completely assimilated at that time, demanded a new impulse, which necessarily led to a break with the Wittgenstein-inspired first stage. The analytical operations that had resulted from that inspiration were replaced by anthropological and, consequently, ideological and political problems that were pursued to the extent and in the forms that could be achieved in small groups of intellectuals in New York. Working in that direction, Kosuth and the members of Art & Language (Ian Burn, Andrew Menard, Mel Ramsden and others) launched the magazine *The Fox* in 1975, in which a number of texts by these and other authors explain the reasons and motives behind the changes in their ideological standpoint, as well as the strategy of practical behaviour that results from them. Apart from substituting the idealistic position of analytical philosophy with a kind of specific interpretation of Marxism, the concrete consequences of the new attitudes manifested themselves in the criticism of the very principles of the cultural and artistic system to which these artists had themselves belonged. Contributors to *The Fox* were aware of the fact that the politicisation of art cannot proceed effectively on the level of elaborations of contents linked with the developments in the world around us, but only on the level of a dialectic analysis of the situation within the art system itself, which in fact forms an integral part of a much broader spectrum of the dominant social system. Exposing the dependence of art on the broader context of relations in that system, a dependence that obviously exists even when artists act autonomously in their choice of language, the earliest conceptualists made a significant contribution towards a clearer insight into the socially determined position of culture and art in the concrete circumstances of a given reality. However, they have not been able to avoid the dilemmas which, since the time of the historical avant-gardes, have always accompanied the activity of artists with a radical orientation, torn between the need for a continuous development of their ideological stand and its simultaneous neutralisation by the integrative instruments of the existent social organism.

This short and necessarily simplified outline of the various alternatives within the range of new artistic experiences justifies the conclusion that, in spite of the widely differing approaches, they may be classified into two general attitudes. One approach involves turning to the limitless sphere of the real, in which the artist looks for sources and inspiration for their work, using various media ranging from highly developed technologies to primary organic media, and placing almost explicitly the subjectivity of the artist's individuality in the foreground. The other attitude sees research focus on the analysis of the constitutive terms of the art language itself, and the artist thus avoids any contamination with the real and the objective; here the expressive potential of the medium gives way to the verification of its elementary structural factors, which is the very reason for strictly objective and impersonal operative procedures. In an attempt to describe the characteristics and intentions of these two approaches, Renato Barilli distinguishes between 'mystical' (vitalistic or worldly) and 'tautological' conceptualism, the former referring to artists whose work emphasises 'referentiality and subjection to the material context of life', and the latter to those who 'reject any referential link with the world or the environment, either natural or social, bodily or spiritual', and reduce the problem of the work to a rigorous process of self-analysis conducted within the immanent terms of art. The American critic Robert Pincus-Witten makes a similar distinction when he speaks about two types of conceptual artists: 'ontological conceptualists' (whose prototype is Acconci) and 'epistemological conceptualists' (whose prototype is Kosuth). Both critics agree on the existence of a synthetic and an analytic component in the complex of new art experiences, thus bearing out the fact that the new art scene has brought to light numerous integral working approaches, the characteristics of which extend beyond the solutions contained in one and the same style, direction or movement, and form the elements of a much more complex organism characterised by new ways of looking at the nature of art itself.

In the past few years however the internal situation has changed: developments that could be denoted by such terms as Arte Povera, Conceptual art and so on, are now losing those very characteristics that make such definitions possible, and they are growing into a very extensive artistic practice, within which distinctions are possible only on the basis of selecting the media of expression. Artists are becoming aware of the possibilities of a large number of operative instruments that may equally justifiably be natural or technological. This has led to the autonomous use of such techniques as photography, film and video. Initially most often used as a means of registering and documenting processual events, these media have now become vehicles for expressing very individualised themes. Narrative and metaphorical messages have made their reappearance (Narrative art, in a symbiosis of photography and text) and the language of video has been given a more elaborate structure, which sets it apart from the condensed and reduced material of the earliest works in this medium, such as the tapes by Gerry Schum. The stage of testing the technique and language of the media is now over, and they are becoming the basis for transmitting a variety of themes – a series of new works is based on the subjective and private expression of the thoughts and obsessions of the individual. The behaviour of the artist is marked by an emphasis on 'speaking in the first person'; as a consequence, the language of the earlier stage has been abandoned and replaced – as was first explicitly stated on the occasion of the documenta 5 exhibition in Kassel in 1972 – by the acknowledgement of the existence of 'individual mythologies'.

Furthermore, a number of other forms of expression (such as various types of performance and uses of 'mixed' and 'crossed' media) and a simultaneous opening up towards psychological and sociological complexes of individuals often from marginal social groups, have led to increased fragmentation and specification of the causes and means of artistic expression, thus robbing the current situation of the earlier conditional possibility of differentiation according to linguistic orientations. Critics have therefore termed the present state in art 'the time after art movements', meaning a time of very individualistic approaches to art and art problems.

In this post-conceptual stage of contemporary art, we are witnessing a development that seems to contradict

the extreme diversification of media and procedures:
the focus of the artist's attention on studying the basic
constitutive terms of painting. The representatives of this
orientation are Robert Ryman, Brice Marden, Robert
Mangold and others in the United States; Giorgio Griffa,
Claudio Verna, Carlo Battaglia, Marco Gastini and others in
Italy; Raymond Girke, Winfred Gaul, Ulrich Erben in
Germany, Jaap Berghuis in the Netherlands; Louis Cane,
Marc Devade, Claude Viallat and others from the Supports/
Surfaces group in France. A number of exhibitions and
critical texts have given the development such names as
analytical painting, fundamental painting, primary or elementary painting and the like. Filiberto Menna has identified
the territory that Conceptual art and the new painting share:
'Conceptual art and the new painting follow the same basic
course, though each of them uses its own procedures. Their
common denominator lies in the emphasis they place on
problems of language and in the common interpretation of
artistic activity as an autonomous practice. The artist adopts
an analytical and auto-reflexive attitude; he transfers the
procedure from the directly expressive or representative
plane to the metalinguistic level, engaging in discussions
on art and its specific linguistic instruments at the very
moment in which he creates art.' And further on: 'In the
practice of the new painting this procedure is particularly
conspicuous in its disciplinary specificity: a return of the
problems of painting back to painting requires an essential
specification of the visual reality from the artist, an analysis
of the painting process that cannot be accomplished without
the process of creating the painting.' The fact that these
analytical principles of Conceptual art may be applied to
painting (or to sculpture, drawings or graphic arts) gives
weight to the following statement: the new art phenomena
of the past decade do not consist only of procedures
involving media that had hitherto rarely been used, that is
to say, a mere broadening of the existing basis of art: they
are a process of restructuring and redefining the very notion
of art, a consequence that saw the process manifesting
itself not only in the new media, but in penetrating the very
foundations of the traditional and ongoing media of artistic
production. Analytical painting is a characteristic example
of that symptom and testifies, therefore, no less than many

seemingly more radical developments, to the changed character of art in the past decade with regard to the earlier and still present 'standard' model of artistic thought.

The complexity of these processes which, as we have seen, have resulted in basic changes in the very notion of art, calls for an attempt to understand their sociological and ideological causes. Which should start from the fact that they emerged in a situation of conflict and crises in the modern world, a situation characterised on the one hand by the continuous consolidation of hyper-organised social structures with the aim of strengthening their economic and material potential, and on the other hand by a permanent dissatisfaction with the progressive intellectual forces over this one-dimensional development of the dominant course of civilisation, which they tried to oppose by the free and uncodified behaviour of the critically-minded subject. Art and culture were the obvious fields in which such uncodified behaviour would manifest itself, which fact can be found at the roots of any radical art development in history. It is no accident that new attitudes in art coincided with the broader social and spiritual events in and immediately after 1968. Barilli maintains, even in the face of many characteristic facts, that we can justifiably speak about a period before 1968 and a period after 1968 in the historiography of post-war art. There is plenty of evidence that the process of contestation that was sweeping, in different ways, over most countries at the time found its expression in art and culture. One of the symptoms of this was the resistance of new art to the dominant role of the market in the bourgeois art system of the West, which first manifested itself in the temporary, inconsistent and therefore non-commercial status of artistic work. Germano Celant and Pierre Restany, for example, speak about Arte Povera as a kind of guerrilla phenomenon within the existing cultural mechanism. ('Is poor art meant for poor people?' asks Restany; to which Celant answers: 'No, poor art is guerrilla art against the rich world.') The strategies of the resistance were conducted on two levels that were directly included in the internal structure of the language of art: one was the gestures and actions emphasising the subjectivity of the artist through his opposition to the paternalist and institutionalised organisation of cultural

life, and the other was the focus on the utmost objectivity in
analytical procedures, which stress the strict autonomy of
art and its total isolation from the ideological manipulations
of the predominant culture. Since culture is an integral
component of the system, the conflicts within culture are
in fact conflicts within the standards of the system itself.
In this way new art assumes the role of spiritual opposition
to the functionalist demands of the dominant structures,
and the artists involved become one of the minority groups
that hover at the margins of the basic social mechanism.
The alternative offered by this practice of art is the liberation
and expression of individual preoccupations which grow
into acts of social and cultural relevance through the very
process of artistic valuation. Individual preoccupations are
continuously freed through their expansion over the channels
of the media in which they are communicated; in this way
art transgresses the bounds of standard specialised techniques and its practice becomes accessible to forces outside
of professional structures; as a result, the content of artistic
messages becomes so personified as to lead in many cases
to that frequently emphasised element of interpenetration,
and even identification, of the sphere of life and the sphere
of art. This 'aestheticisation of everyday life' is one of the
instruments of the alternative art that stands opposed to the
pragmatic demand for the total organisation of reality based
on the principle of an efficient functioning of predetermined
value parameters. The moving force of such a process is the
demand for continuous changes of behaviour, action and the
evaluation of action, as opposed to the repressive demands
for a continuation of the *status quo*.

Lest the processes described above seem abstract
or even too idealistic, we must consider some contradictory
factors within the socio-cultural situation. First of all, it
is beyond any doubt that there was no direct organisational
link between the various movements of political contestation
and the proponents of the new art practices. This can be
seen, among other things, from the behaviour of a number
of artists during the demonstrations at the 1968 Venice
Biennale, who demanded the right to independent work
free from any direct association with political strategies.
The world of art was reacting with its immanent ability of
resistance to all ideological and operative barriers within

its own nature, and refused to be used as an instrument of political confrontation. On the other hand, the dominant art system (the system of the functioning and evaluation of artistic production) proved sufficiently strong and flexible in almost all environments, and thus, either because of genuine acceptance or in order to neutralise or integrate other developments, sooner or later assimilated a number of new ideas and suggestions. In due course these formed the bulk of the new artistic production presented at the leading galleries and museums and in art journals. It thus transpired that the new artistic experience in both Western Europe and the United States has assumed, over the past years, a leading role in discovering and dealing with new fields of problems, while at the same time it is the most financially stimulated art of our age. This has led to an inevitable cleft in the movement's ethical and ideological foundations, proving yet again the well-known fact that the greatest threat to any radically new art practice lies not in opposition from the dominant structures, but in acceptance and recognition by them. The relatively quick acceptance of all new proposals is one of the basic reasons we can no longer speak, theoretically or practically, about the existence of an avant-garde in the same sense and meaning in which this term was used in the cases of Dada, Futurism, Constructivism and the other developments of the first half of this century. What is more, the working mentality and consequently the social behaviour of the protagonists of the new phenomena in art have varied considerably, owing to specific local social and cultural conditions, cultural traditions, market pressures, public opinion and the like; among the many possible distinctions of this kind are the differences between similar phenomena in Europe and America. Achille Bonito Oliva has identified a number of symptoms in which these differences are directly observable. According to him, the work of American artists is characterised, regardless of individual and formal solutions, by their focus on problems associated with the constitution and functioning of the art language, which corresponds to the empirical and analytical basis of their knowledge of philosophy. As a result, the artist always uses all the available resources at hand to the full, and thus rarely gets into conflict with the social and cultural environment.

It was only with the emergence of a new orientation in the attitudes of conceptual artists contributing to the journal *The Fox* (the members of the first and second generation of Art & Language) that artists began to adopt or cultivate a political dimension. On the other hand, for many European artists the inevitable integration into the art system involved an element of conflict with their own conscience. This led to a further polarisation of ideological attitudes and the introduction of an art of critical and subversive elements into the language, and in some cases also led to political activism (not always entirely homogenous), as in the work of Joseph Beuys, Daniel Buren and some members of the Supports/Surfaces group. What is more, European left-wing artists and critics came to question the very nature of the new trends, their ideological shifts and practical compromises, and these circles began to suggest that the notion of the avant-garde should be dismissed because it is typical of bourgeois culture. They also proposed a different form of socialisation that would go beyond the still dominant models which, as has now become obvious, were not terribly disturbed by the new art practice but continued, with occasional reforms and corrections, to function as before.

Characteristics of the New Art Practices in Yugoslavia

Our purpose in starting this paper with a survey of the general art situation of the past decade was broadly to outline the trends that form the natural time and issue context for related examples in Yugoslavia. We should like to emphasise that the appearance of the New Art Practices in Yugoslavia is not an accidental and isolated phenomenon, nor is it the result of the random and unconnected work of many individuals and groups, a development still awaiting artistic and sociological identification, but it is part of the body of work described in the introduction. There is ample evidence for such a statement: for example, the participation and involvement of Yugoslav artists in events abroad, as well as the presence of foreign artists in the events organised in Yugoslavia. All of this was conditioned and accompanied by an awareness of the many problems that all the artists involved in these trends shared in various environments. Of course, this link is not the basic reason that makes the work in Yugoslavia relevant: it is above all a good indicator of the cultural, social and existential position of that section of the young generation who at a particular moment chose the language of the New Art Practices as a possible avenue of artistic expression. So, apart from the influences and correspondence (which are not negative factors but indicators of the nature and level of certain spiritual affinities), there existed a clear *organic* motivation for the emergence of the movement. It produced a very specific body of manifestations, whose particular features give it an artistic and cultural identity of its own. The problems we should examine or at least indicate here include the following: identifying the procedures of the work and the expression of individuals and groups of artists – a task that calls for an analysis of the application of art language; we should also enquire into the circumstances of their spiritual formation, the ways they behaved in life, the forms of their involvement in the social and artistic environment, their attitudes to the past and present cultural situation, the ideological roots of their attitudes and procedures; and we should gain an insight into some aspects of feedback, namely the reactions of people outside the circle of artists to their art, because they are indicative of the way that social and cultural media worked in Yugoslav conditions.

The emergence of new artistic attitudes in Yugoslavia is not the result of the homogenous action of a new generation (that same generation has also produced many entirely different attitudes, while at the same time several artists of the preceding generation have adopted the new artistic orientation), but it is certainly the fruit of the mentality characteristic of a broad circle of young people – not only their views on art, but their attitudes to life in general. One particularly revealing feature is the development of their affinities related to contemporary spiritual coordinates: as regards the recent past, they have emotionally associated themselves with the movements of historical avant-gardes; from the contemporary scene they have absorbed popular culture, ranging from literature, film and music to cartoons and visual art. The Pop culture we are talking about is not that which belongs to the sphere of mass consumption, but to the so-called underground – small groups of young people who oppose the dominant cultural superstructure of mass society. In Yugoslav conditions this was perhaps the first generation that was brought up without any nostalgia for patriarchal and local considerations and was open to the ways of contemporary city life. Braco Rotar said of the OHO group that 'their production springs completely from an urban environment', and this still applies, albeit with certain qualifications, to the work of all new artists in other centres. This sociological and spiritual dimension should be borne in mind when discussing the mentality of the new phenomena in Yugoslav art.

These spiritual foundations were the source of the orientation and behaviour of the new artists. As they did not find any models of avant-garde art in the cultural scene at home (where examples of this type of art are extremely scarce) and because their upbringing and attitudes to life were such that they could not find much affinity with the work of their immediate predecessors (except, to a degree, for the phenomena in Zagreb, where the work of the New Tendencies and Gorgona was seen as a positive factor), the new art scene in Yugoslavia developed in a direction markedly different not only from the bulk of the art produced by the rest of the country, but also from the very interpretation of the notion and function of art at home. This difference, which was more pronounced than in all previous changes in artistic orientation, produced the impression of a drastic rift between the new and the established art; it would, however, be more correct to say that the rift was not the result of a conscious provocation, but of a natural basic difference in the mentalities of the representatives of these two attitudes to the language of art. The new movement had to look for footholds in international art production, to which the intolerant localist criticism immediately reacted with remarks about 'imports', a criticism that reappears whenever deeply rooted local attitudes are questioned and re-examined. The only truth in this criticism lay in the fact that turning to the international scene resulted in the adoption of some recent formulations (which has always been an unavoidable factor in the creation of a new art language and can be observed in all artistic developments that have emerged in Yugoslav cultural centres over the past decades).

As the New Art Practices were not based on a continuity of existing art concepts and were the consequence of a broader view of the possibilities of artistic expression that did not depend on specific professional knowledge, it is not surprising that a considerable number of its representatives did not come from among the regular students of art but from other fields of study, mainly from those of literature, languages, art history and, perhaps unexpectedly, from various fields of engineering. This was the case with some members of the OHO group, all the members of the KÔD and (Ǝ groups of Novi Sad, the Bosch+Bosch group from Subotica, the Belgrade Group 143 and a number of artists from some other centres. It is interesting to note the initial catalytic role of visual poetry, which was particularly widespread among Slovene artists in the late 1960s. This can be explained by the fact that visual poetry dismisses any metaphysical character of the verbal expression that operates with symbols, images and metaphors, and the poet's attention focuses on reflections on the nature of the language and its constitutive elements which, when adopted as a principle of approach to other media and procedures, made it possible to create works that can easily take on the status of a specific object in the sense of the qualities of new artistic experiences. On the other hand, graduates of art academies (mainly individuals and groups in Zagreb and Belgrade) had to reach the starting point of the New Art Practices by consciously rejecting almost everything they had learned about operative techniques and the very nature of art. It was not a normal process of outgrowing knowledge acquired at school before entering the contemporary art scene, but the first open conflict with one of the instruments of the established art system. It is impossible to gain any insight into the institution of art academies in Yugoslavia from the aspect of their pedagogical function alone, which is quite inadequate by contemporary standards. It must also be pointed out that the institution assembles an all too excessive number of teachers recruited from among artists holding conventional and often outmoded beliefs; their teaching is merely the expression of the financial and, consequently, ideological backing of such artistic conceptions, and in concrete Yugoslav conditions this creates a status of social privilege associated not so much with individuals but rather with the attitudes on which the work and behaviour of such individuals is based. The moment the New Art Practices appeared, this situation manifested itself in an especially acute form; if penetration into the field of contemporary art languages was possible only by by-passing or opposing all the established experiences and training methods, there arose a question: the possibility of the further co-existence of these two largely mutually exclusive trends within an interdependent relationship. The dilemma that was thus opened was as follows: are the New Art Practices really an illicit and consequentially socially questionable form of public manifestation, or have the established training institutions become so inadequate for modern requirements that their social role should be seriously re-examined? It is clear that the few examples of deviation from the standard forms of acquisition and application of artistic training could not lead to any deeper processes of critical re-assessment of the activity of such institutions, whose adequacy is not easily questioned by the social mechanism, but it was the orientation of the new artists that finally revealed some of the latent symptoms, thus revealing the real character of one of the basic instruments of the dominant art system in contemporary Yugoslavia.

The work produced by the New Art Practices in Yugoslavia over the past ten years is so prolific that it would be difficult to register and catalogue it as a whole; furthermore, it demonstrates a variety of approaches and branches out into many solutions, due not only to individual differences but also to the different cultural situation in each centre. As with other art phenomena in Yugoslavia, it is also impossible to speak about 'pure' language examples in visual art (in the sense of adherence to Arte Povera or Conceptual art, etcetera). What we find instead is a mixture of these and other working principles and individual interpretations, which results in syncretic solutions that should be regarded as the artist's search for expression.

    We have already mentioned the mediatory role of visual poetry in paving the way for new experiences. The same transitional functions, especially in artists with a training in visual arts, can be found in the initial leanings on the matrices of Pop art and Minimal art and in the application of lessons learnt from spatial design. From there, they proceeded to create objects of a non-consistent material structure and then on to an even further decomposition of the object. Various processual procedures were applied in condensed time intervals; the action was taken out of the gallery and outside into the natural or urban environment; and the first performances in which the artist participates in person in the action appeared. The further development of these experiences was marked by the following characteristics: the initial, often expressive, tensions were suppressed, the formulations began to show increasingly greater pre-conceived mental preparation and a greater awareness of the conditions in the social and cultural environment, and some artists therefore turned to the re-examination of the criteria of art valuation and the functioning of a broader artistic context, introducing into the internal structure of their works elements that directly confront the spectator with these problems. The repertoire of the mediums of expression was also broadened, and the first formulations of the new technological possibilities of video appeared, while film and photography no longer functioned as mere documents and began to be used as an autonomous language system. Alongside the use of these mediatory instruments, the art scene was enriched by a few radical instances of the direct use of the artist's body in the spirit of the terms of Body art. At the end of the period under review, the mental analytical postulates had been transferred to painting, drawing and graphics, which is yet more evidence that the movement's aim encompasses much more than the use of new media; it is, above all, a new use of all of the means of communication available, both artistic and entirely non-artistic, for the expression of content that results from ideas, thoughts and, ultimately, from existence itself.

All these different procedures have certain characteristics in common. Each art work and each action reveal the actual working process; reality is never described by means of a symbolic or formal apparatus; the artist takes part in reality through the interaction of mental and operative interventions into the very medium chosen as the field of expression. The ubiquitous 'metaphysics' of traditional art, whose alleged purpose is to justify the subconscious roots of artistic activity, has been abandoned; the artist can now verify his procedures – they plan the course of their work, and once the work is performed they recapitulate the stages they have just gone through. For this reason, these activities always emphasise the element of process: the finality of the work is not an end in itself; it is only a stage, which is achieved through the gradual development of the idea. The final physical form is never an 'aesthetic object' that is to be contemplated or experienced only through the senses; instead, it has the characteristics of a materialised and visualised mental operation that tries to induce the spectator to analyse it in the way that it was conceived and realised. Since chance elements have been eliminated from the structure of the work (or chance is consciously included into the working process), the artist becomes the person who controls his own practice; he does not want to expose its courses and results to chance influences, not only in the forming of meaning but also in its reading and use. In this way he manifests his social and political consciousness, which inevitably brings him into conflict with all the factors that strive to separate art from the individual needs of its creator under the pretext of achieving a 'higher' ideological and representative purpose. By stressing the concrete character of his work and aiming at the direct reading of its meaning, the artist wants to eliminate any mediatory illusionism of the presentation of the actual or imaginary reality, because many historical examples offer ample evidence that such illusionistic language served as an effective vehicle for the ideological misuse of art, which was the reason that such an art language has always been accepted by the dominant social structures. The new artistic practice, on the other hand, calls for the perception of art as such, stressing the independence of its own language as a paradigmatic sign of the independent behaviour of the personality that expresses itself through the work. It is this characteristic in the structure of the meaning that expresses the awareness of the freedom to use one's own 'anarchy of imagination', which today is tolerated only in art.

One of the characteristics of the work and manifestations of the new artists is their association with or into more or less homogeneous groups. Mention should be made here of the following groups: the OHO group (some of whose members later joined the Šempas Family Art Commune (Obitelj u Šempasu)), Crveni peristil (Red Peristyle), KÔD (Code), (Ǝ, Bosch+Bosch, the Pensioner Tihomir Simčić, Tok (Course), Ekipa A3 (Team A3), Verbumprogram and Grupa 143 (Group 143). Some of the associations never declared themselves under a name, though they existed in various recognisable forms (phenomena that have been conditionally named October 72 in Belgrade, and Interventions and Exhibitions-Actions in Zagreb). As is well-known, groups in modern art usually appear in situations of cultural and social tension, when many individual orientations look for support in tendencies similar or related to their own in order to express themselves. In Yugoslavia, these associations were not only the result of their members' artistic affinities, but also of the artists' day-to-day contacts based on similar outlooks, and partly on their isolation from other social or professional groups. It should be noted that the groups were never established on the basis of a fixed programme, nor did they share the principles of team work that were characteristic of the earlier New Tendencies movement. On the contrary, group members often vary from one manifestation to another, and each individual retains his full identity in the name and the work of the manifestation, all of which demonstrates that the group functions as a spiritual rather than a professional framework of action. This is particularly obvious in the case of OHO, which at the beginning often changed members; then its members consolidated and finally dispersed, a part of them joining the Šempas Family Art Commune, a group that has functioned as a commune and whose primary aim is not artistic but existential. In some other cases the groups have been either very short-lived or extremely heterogeneous (a case in point is a group of artists in Belgrade who have been meeting since their days at the Academy) and even when the associations take on a more permanent form (as in Group 143), it has been for the purpose of working together, and not because of the usual forms of public manifestations.

Though the language of the New Art Practices in Yugoslavia is essentially international and the followers of the new orientations are linked by close working and human contacts, their art shows certain elements that indicate their association with the cultural and artistic environment in which they have been working. By the same token, the starting points and consequences of their activity have often been conditioned by specific (local) circumstances, which is evidenced in a reading of the meanings contained in the internal structure of the language they use. When, for example, Braco Rotar states that 'the OHO group occupies an exceptional place in the Slovene visual arts because its production is the only one in Slovenia that is not based on a semantic (illusionistic or mystificatory) but an explicitly semiotic transparency', he is referring to their opposition to the art standards enclosed within the co-ordinates of the narrow local environment. However, the ideas and concepts of the OHO group are linked to the so-called 'reistic doctrine', which is characteristic only of the Slovene cultural environment and whose reflections have influenced the literature – poetry in particular – of the young generation there. 'The starting premise of OHO's activity', says Tomaž Brejc, 'was that mystical artistic production should be substituted with the production of articles, and the art product with suitably simple "handicraft" products. Further in the process of development there was a need to change the established model of perception, not only in the creative process but also in the way the spectator views the finished product, and to use the article as a means of directing and transforming the spectator's field of perception, thus enabling him to discover new visual impulses.' In an environment whose visual culture is based on quite different principles, such an attitude naturally produced the impression of a rift, which did indeed exist, because the dominant culture – as Brejc goes on to say – was characterised by 'a long tradition of "quality" promoted by the Ljubljana school, particularly in graphics, with a conservative perception based on collectors' ideals and a fair degree of intellectualism, which was always built into traditional chiliastic structures of meaning'.

Whereas the break of the OHO group with the visual culture of the local Slovene environment was particularly radical – as the quotes above have shown – the situation in Zagreb has a more differentiated and, basically, ambivalent character. Writing on a very different occasion, Matko

Meštrović noted that 'unlike Ljubljana, which has preserved a rather closed environment, Zagreb is a cosmopolitan town, where phenomena of very different origins can persist and develop independently, creating a cultural scene of a very broad spectrum'. In such an environment, very authoritarian and extremely liberal conceptions about the nature of artistic behaviour exist side by side. Which is why the emergence of the new art was accompanied with strong disapproval on the one side and open support on the other. What is more, in Zagreb, unlike in other Yugoslav centres, there existed basic elements in the art of earlier generations that could serve as the initial source of inspiration for the new artists. These can be identified in two different conceptions of work: one originated from EXAT 51's ideas and was developed within the international New Tendencies movement. Its working principles included a broader use of the media, coupled with a belief in artists modifying everyday life and the environment, an idea put into practice by the young artists who worked in the direction of interventions in the urban space. The other is represented by the reductionist and defunctionalist mentality of the Gorgona group, and was realised in those works and actions that were intentionally non-aesthetic, critical, ephemeral, provocative and sometimes openly negative. Both components, then, form part of a specific tradition of the new at home, which brings them into the following ambivalent position: the existence of the preceding climate makes manifestations easier and soothes the open or hidden resistance of reactionary circles; on the other hand it eliminates empty zones in the starting points of new generations, which are sometimes indispensable, and thus robs the latter of the possibility of a break with the inherited cultural scene that similar phenomena have the ability to effect to varying degrees in other environments.

The situation in Belgrade is different again. Deep-rooted attitudes, which originated in the aesthetic experience of the Paris School in the period between the two World Wars, and the ever-present tendency towards deeply emotional and intimate confessions in the visual arts, explain the fact that in Belgrade there were practically no cultural groups that could make it possible for the new art phenomena to come to expression. True, some deviation

from that dominant course came earlier, in a section of the
Mediala group, but the ideology of the group as a whole
was basically alien to the new artists (because of its attempt
at constructing an atemporal integral picture) and they
could not adopt it as a spiritual or operative starting point.
The only element that indicated an alternative existed in the
abstraction of the painted field by Radomir Damnjanović
Damnjan, and this kindred mentality was later confirmed by
the fact that he adopted the New Art Practices in the course
of his further development. Because of these circumstances
the new forms of expression appeared in Belgrade later
than in Novi Sad and Subotica, but after the initial breakthrough they developed rapidly owing to, among other
factors, the favourable work conditions at the Student
Cultural Centre Gallery and to many international contacts
as the result of events like the BITEF Festival and the April
Meetings. The break with the old conventions has resulted
not only in the introduction of new procedures (film,
photography, photocopying as art media, performances and
body expression, primary painting and, recently, analytical
drawing within the framework of 'mental constructivism'),
but above all in the new definitions of the sources and
interpretation of the nature of art language. Like the OHO
group in Slovenia, the new Belgrade artists proposed, instead
of the dominant aesthetic (illusionistic or visual) interpretation of the artistic formulation, the mental (concrete
or analytical) status of the work. It should also be pointed
out that, in contrast to the conformist behaviour that
prevails among the young Belgrade artists, their work and
texts show an awareness of the social and political factors
that determine the nature of art production and of the
conditions of its socialisation and valuation.

It would be logical to assume that the extreme forms
of contemporary art could only have appeared in a few large
towns, in which there already existed at least some cultural
and historical preconditions favouring such a development,
as well as the alternative channels of expression through
which the new artists could manifest their work. However,
the new forms of artistic expressions appeared, although
only sporadically, in Split and, in a much more intense form,
in Novi Sad and Subotica. Since the new artists in these
towns came from fields outside the traditional art scene,

they could not achieve a deeper re-orientation in the local
art events, but they have succeeded in establishing, to
a much greater degree than the other artistic circles, links
with related phenomena in Yugoslavia and even abroad.
The most successful in this respect are the initiatives in
Novi Sad, where, apart from exhibitions and other actions,
two successful publishing ventures were launched in 1972
and made a significant contribution to the understanding
of the theoretical and historical presuppositions of the
new movement: a special issue (no. 156) of the journal
Polja (*Fields*) devoted to Conceptual art, and the publication
The Artist's Body as the Subject and Object of Art which was as
its title indicates devoted to the phenomenon of Body art.

Owing to their specific character and the marginal status
they enjoyed at the beginning in the broader context of the
art system in Yugoslavia, the new art phenomena were at
first presented in galleries that formed part of student and
youth institutions and were therefore only partly treated as
regular exhibition spaces. Though the situation was different
in some places (the exhibition of the OHO group at the
Modern Gallery in Ljubljana in 1968 and that of Serbian
young artists at the Belgrade Museum of Contemporary Art
in 1972, as well as several exhibitions at the Salon of the
same museum and at the Youth House Gallery in Belgrade),
the tone of all these events was set by the manifestations
at the Student Centre Gallery in Zagreb, the Youth Tribune
in Novi Sad, the Student Cultural Centre in Belgrade and,
more recently, Gallery Nova in Zagreb. The Gallery of
Contemporary Art in Zagreb also belongs on this list,
because its orientation towards and open acceptance of the
new art trends has provided a ground for the verification of
their value and problematic relevance. Apart from these
institutional channels, important activities were taking place
outside the galleries, such as the art programmes during
the BITEF Festival in Belgrade and various 'underground'
manifestations, such as the shows in the entrance hall at 2A,
Frankopanska Street in Zagreb and at the Tenants' Gallery,
which, though established in Paris, organised a number
of actions in Zagreb as well. The editorial boards for visual
art at the Student Centre in Zagreb and the Student Cultural
Centre in Belgrade not only provided exhibition spaces,

but have also stimulated the work of young artists from the very beginning, and thus play the role of an alternative educator, in marked contrast to the training offered by the art academies. The association with the new artists, on the other hand, has contributed to the further programmatic development of the galleries: their activity now extends far beyond their work as student institutions and is on the level of professional centres that specialise in following and furthering the most contemporary forms of art production.

A situation similar to that in the galleries can equally be seen in the press. Articles about the appearance of the New Art Practices were first published in student and young people's publications (*Tribuna*, *Index*, *Studentski list*, *Omladinski tjednik*, *Student*, *Polet*, *Književna reč*), then in cultural, literary and sociological journals (*Problemi*, *Polja*, *Pitanja*) and occasionally in art journals (*Umetnost*, *Život umjetnosti*, *Sinteza*, *Čovjek i prostor*). At the same time the daily newspapers (*Vjesnik*, *Delo*, *Borba*, *Politika*) and the weekly journals dealing with social and cultural issues (*NIN*, *Oko)* – which was by no means an accident – gave them very poor ratings in the few articles on the new art that they ran, not only in terms of critical evaluation but also in relation to political relevance, which positions were often extremely tendentious. Attempts to create independent information channels (*Novine*, published by the Student Centre Gallery in Zagreb and *Moment*, published by the Student Cultural Centre Gallery in Belgrade) faltered due to lack of funds and, ultimately, motivation. Nevertheless, these publications constitute a considerable body of valuable documentation.

The programmes of these galleries primarily include the works of Yugoslav artists, and in this way helped form a platform for the new art in Yugoslav art centres. However, they have also maintained contact with artists from a number of foreign countries, which shows that the character of the new Yugoslav art is international, that there exists a strong awareness of this fact, and that collaborations with foreign artists have not been left to mere chance but are part of a strategy of participation in the contemporary cultural scene. Only the most important events are mentioned here. The list is given in order to show the range and variety of artists, critics and organisers who participated in the development of the most interesting and active trends of the past decade.

In 1970, Walter De Maria visited the OHO group in Šempas, during which occasion they produced several of their joint works. In 1971, two exhibitions were organised at the initiative of Braco and Nena Dimitrijević: *At the Moment* (in the entrance hall at 2A Frankopanska Street in Zagreb) and *At the Other Moment* (at the Student Cultural Centre Gallery in Belgrade), when works by Giovanni Anselmo, Robert Barry, Stanley Brouwn, Daniel Buren, Victor Burgin, Jan Dibbets, Barry Flanagan, Douglas Huebler, Alain Kirili, Jannis Kounellis, John Latham, Sol LeWitt, Lawrence Weiner and Ian Wilson were shown. The Gallery of Contemporary Art in Zagreb has organised exhibitions of works by Yves Klein, Bill Vazan, Daniel Buren, Christian Boltanski and Annette Messager, as well as presentations of Conceptual art and the new painting within the framework of *New Tendencies 5* (1973) and a number of international video meetings. However, such events and meetings are more frequent in Belgrade: at the BITEF Festival, the April Meetings and on numerous other occasions the following artists have participated in talks and actions: Michelangelo Pistoletto (with the group Lo Zoo), Franco Vaccari, Claudio Parmiggiani, Mario Ceroli, Jannis Kounellis, Mimmo Germanà, Daniel Buren, Giuseppe Chiari, Gina Pane, Joseph Beuys, Antonio Dias, John Stezaker, Art & Language members Andrew Menard and Michael Corris; Katherina Sieverding, Ulrike Rosenbach, Wolfgang Weber, Tom Marioni, Diego Cortes, Al Souza, Tim Jones, Luigi Ontani, Iole de Freitas, Ugo La Pietra, Francesco Clemente, Lamberto Calzolari, Gianni Emilio Simonetti, G. A. Cavellini, Nicole Gravier, Hervé Fischer, Endre Tót, Natalia LL, Janusz Haka, Szdislav Sosnovski and other artists; Germano Celant, Achille Bonito Oliva, Filiberto Menna, Tommaso Trini, Henri Martin, Catherine Millet, Jean-Marc Poinsot, Klaus Honnef, Barbara Reise, Rosetta Brooks, Marlis Grüterich, Giancarlo Politi, Gislind Nabakowski, Willoughby Sharp, John McEven and other art critics and editors of various art journals. Other events that should be mentioned here include the exhibition of Conceptual art selected by Millet (with works by Victor Burgin, James Collins, Roger Cutforth, Dan Graham, Bernar Venet, Art & Language

and others), the exhibition *Mail Items* from the 7th Paris
Biennial in 1971, selected by Poinsot (with works by Jean
Le Gac, Christian Boltanski, Gerz, Friedman, Higgins
and others), Bonito Oliva's exhibition *Persona* (with works
by Merz, Kounellis, Boetti, Prini, Penone, Vettor Pisani,
Paolini, De Dominicis and others), John Baldessari's one-
man show, video projections by Studio 970 of Varese (with
tapes by Dennis Oppenheim, Nagasawa, Luciano Fabro,
Chiari, Trotta and others) and Art/Tapes/22 from Florence
(with tapes by Vito Acconci, Joseph Beuys, Daniel Buren,
Pier Paolo Calzolari, Joan Jonas, Frank Gillette, Allan
Kaprow, Jannis Kounellis, Giulio Paolini, Urs Lüthi and
others). We should also mention the fact that an exhibition
in 1968 of the Italian Arte Povera with the personal participation of several key representatives was called off at the
last moment due to the sudden death of Pino Pascali in
September of that year, just a few days before he was due to
arrive in Belgrade.

Simultaneously with the events organised at home,
Yugoslav artists took part in international art events that
defined the basic artistic orientation of the period. The first
in the series of such contacts was established by the members of the OHO group, who participated in *Information*,
an exhibition organised by Kynaston McShine at the Museum
of Modern Art in New York in July 1970. This was followed
by presentations of the OHO group and Braco Dimitrijević
at Aktionsraum 1 in Munich in 1971; Marina Abramović and
Braco Dimitrijević at the exhibition *Contemporanea* in Rome
in 1973–1974; Goran Trbuljak (1973), Goran Đorđević and
Marina Abramović (1975) and Raša Todosijević, Zoran
Popović, Mladen Stilinović, Andraž Šalamun and Group 143
(1977) at the last three Paris Biennials; Braco Dimitrijević
at the exhibitions *Projekt* in Cologne in 1974 and documenta 5
and documenta 6 in Kassel in 1972 and 1977 respectively;
Marina Abramović in *Attualita internazionali 1972–1976* at the
1976 Venice Biennale and at documenta 6 in Kassel in 1977;
as well as a series of individual exhibitions, presentations and
events of lesser importance. Exhibitions of new Yugoslav art
were held at the 1973 Edinburgh Festival, the Wspolczesnej
Gallery in Warsaw in 1976 and at the Galleria civica d'arte
moderna in Modena in 1977. It is important to note that
such activity came about as the result of direct invitations

to the artists and not through the mediation of official
Yugoslav cultural agencies and institutions, a fact that speaks
of the presence of Yugoslav artists in events that are at the
centre of the most topical discussions in the world of art
today. The works of some of the new Yugoslav artists have
been registered in books by art critics like Lucy Lippard,
Gillo Dorfles, Achille Bonito Oliva, Germano Celant, Lea
Vergine, Frank Popper, Klaus Groh, Adrian Henri; numerous
essays, photographic documentation and other pieces of
information, as well as articles by Yugoslav critics have been
published in the journals *Flash Art*, *Data Arte*, *Nac*, *Le Arti*,
Alfabeta Inplu, *Art Dimension*, *Europa – arte informazione*,
Bolattiarte, *G 7 studio*, *Opus*, *Art Press*, *Art Present*, *Artitudes*,
Studio International, *The Fox*, *Art in America*, *Avalanche*, *Vision*,
± o and *Heute Kunst*.

With this introduction we have tried to outline both the
general and the specific framework within which a new
approach to art has developed on the Yugoslav cultural scene
over the past decade. The phenomena that have appeared in
that process show the characteristics of their organic growth
in two separate contexts: one is that of related phenomena
in the international context, and the other is activity in
the local environment. Such twofold growth can be found
only in phenomena that are determined by sociological
and ideological factors: the information, the symptoms and
the conclusions presented show that the processes under
review embody the constitutive elements of a clearly defined
cultural organism. The components of this organism are,
on the one hand, the expressive idiom of the new artists
and groups and, on the other, the network of superstructural
factors (exhibition policies, information, criticism and the
like) that have helped to present the new art and have
followed and interpreted its development. Which brings us
to the conclusion that the new art phenomena in Yugoslavia
have operated as multiform, but in their ideas is the relatively homogeneous sum of a multitude of individual
engagements in mutually complementary fields of creation,
organisation and theory. Which activity has been guided
above all by the following basic motive: by the need of the
subject for self-expression and self-affirmation in an active
and contradictory spiritual reality that is always full of

tension. It was the feeling of existential determination and
not a purposely provocative or even socially deviant attitude
that has led to the occasional conflict between individuals
or within the phenomenon as a whole and certain structures
and institutions in the socio-cultural realm. The critical
element in the activity and behaviour of the new artists is
not the result of an a priori opposition to society as a whole;
but it does reflect an opposition to certain institutions
that represent socially privileged or retrograde ideas. The
advocates of the new artistic conceptions have revealed
– not in any planned action but by the nature of the mentality of the open and critical young generation – the appalling
internal configuration of the art system in Yugoslavia,
bringing to light as never before symptoms that, among
other things, show the outmoded method of artistic training,
the inert functioning of most galleries and other institutions
that organise exhibitions, the uninformed criticism, and
the existence of a hidden market mechanism that differs
from that in the West but is powerful and dangerous in its
own way. Since they have directly experienced the effect
of these symptoms, it is to be hoped that the new artists will
not allow their language eventually to develop into a style
that might find its place on one of the steps of that same
system. Our wish for them is that they may persist in their
striving to activate the cultural and artistic scene in a way
that is true to their nature, that they should never follow
predetermined and pragmatic aims, and that they may always
work in such a way as to create fields of free expression for
future generations.

EPILOGUE

The *Yugoslav Documents* Exhibitions in Sarajevo

Ješa Denegri in Conversation with Branislav Dimitrijević and Jelena Vesić

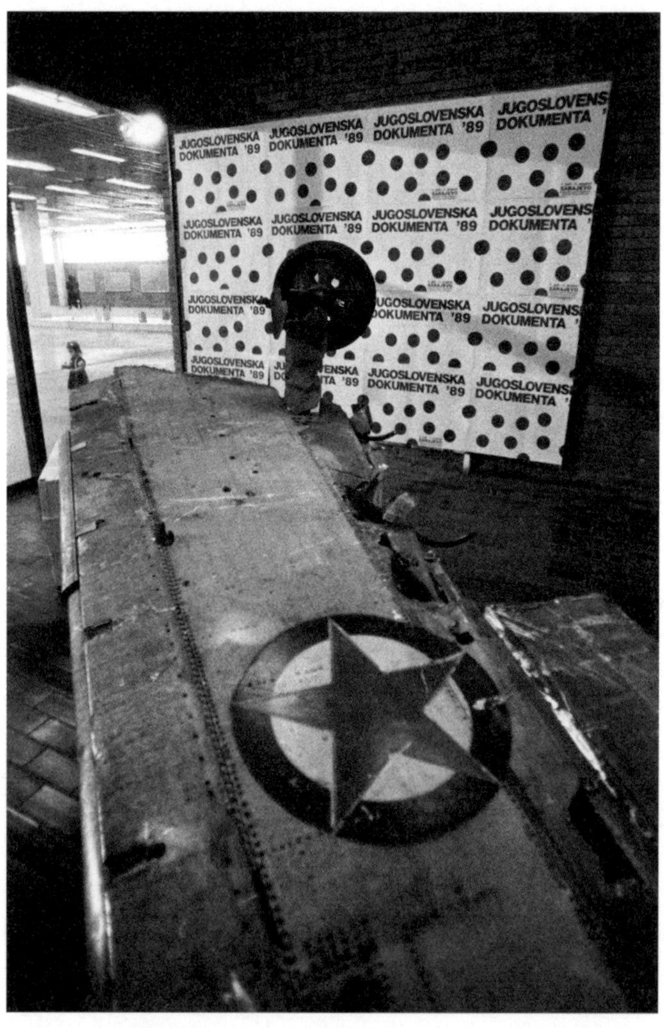

Jane Štravs, view of the second *Jugoslovenska dokumenta* (*Yugoslav Documents*), Sarajevo, 1989

BRANISLAV DIMITRIJEVIĆ   Up until now, our conversation has largely revolved around the artistic phenomena of the 1960s and 1970s in Zagreb, Ljubljana, Belgrade and Novi Sad. To conclude this book, we will plunge briefly into the 1980s and talk about the exhibitions which, so to speak, marked the end of the Yugoslav Art Space, and which took place in Sarajevo. We have mentioned the art scene in Sarajevo, as well as the scene in Skopje, only in passing.

JEŠA DENEGRI   Sarajevo as a scene in the 1960s and earlier does not play a significant role in the dynamics of the Yugoslav Art Space. If anyone is interested in what was happening in Sarajevo in the 1960s, they can turn to the book *Yugoslav Painting of the Sixth Decade*, in which Azra Begić's essay explains the situation.[1] Then in the mid-1970s, a local group Prostor-Oblik (Space-Form) emerged and became important for the Sarajevo scene.

I worked with them, largely owing to Kosta Bogdanović, who participated in this group's exhibitions. I also wrote about them.[2] The Prostor-Oblik group is a late-modernist phenomenon – as its name declares. The group is in a way the conceptual opposite of the Sarajevan artists favoured at the time, like Mersad Berber or Safet Zec.

BD   Were those two considered to be well-established artists?

JD   Yes. One can also say the same of Vojo Dimitrijević, the father of Braco Dimitrijević. Or Ismet Mujezinović, who lived in Tuzla and was an important protagonist of Socialist Realism. But what drew me to Sarajevo was a well-respected magazine called *Izraz* (*Expression*), for which I had written some essays in the 1960s.

BD   Who gathered around that magazine?

JD   Mainly literary critics: Kasim Prokić and Husein Tahmiščić among others. There was also Ivan Foht, a philosopher, and highly esteemed as an aesthetician.

BD   What about art criticism?

JD   There was practically no one writing art criticism. Azra Begić is important as an art historian who, apart from writing about the Bosnian and Herzegovina scene, organised the exhibition of the OHO group in Sarajevo in 1973. That exhibition is referred to as the seed from which things grew later.

BD   Again, we reaffirm how important OHO was for the art events in Novi Sad and Belgrade, and now also in Sarajevo.

JELENA VESIĆ   Did the *Yugoslav Documents* exhibitions of 1987 and 1989 come from the same seed?

JD   I think those exhibitions came about as the result of the conjunction of two different sets of circumstances. First of all, there are the young artists who studied somewhere outside Sarajevo. There is Jusuf Hadžifejzović who studied in Belgrade and brought his experience of the Belgrade Student Cultural Centre to the scene in Bosnia. Then there is also Radoslav Tadić who studied in Ljubljana with Bernik. The second set of circumstances was the Winter Olympics, which transformed the entire city as well as the art scene.

BD   The Winter Olympics were held in 1984.

JD   They really shook that whole centre in a serious way, and many young people were educated for organisational and technical jobs, among them Enver 'Enjo' Hadžiomerspahić. And additionally, an important institution that promoted the New Art Practices was founded – the Collegium Artisticum, which would come to play a significant role in the local milieu. They began to organise small exhibitions in the Collegium called *Dokumenti* (*Documents*), simple exhibitions on walls and panels, mostly made of paper-based materials. Which is why they called it *Documents*. They had practically no budget but still made various exhibitions and brought artists to Sarajevo who on the whole belonged to the New Art Practices.

BD   Like Raša Todosijević, for example.

JD   Or Mladen Stilinović and Vlada Martek from Zagreb. These exhibitions set in motion the process of creating a network of artists. Then another exhibition should be mentioned in this narrative, the exhibition *Umetnost–kritika usred osamdesetih* (*Art–Criticism of the Mid-1980s*).[3] This took place in the Collegium Artisticum, with the Yugoslav section of AICA (International Association of Art Critics) as its patron. This exhibition was actually organised as a reaction to another exhibition, entitled *A View on the 1980s*, which had been held under the auspices of AICA in Sarajevo a year before, in 1985.[4] Zoran Markuš, an art critic from Belgrade, was the curator. But some of us thought the exhibition was badly organised, and at one AICA meeting we questioned an exhibition like this being staged under the patronage of a reputable organisation of art critics. The reply from the AICA was clear: 'If that doesn't work, here you are, we will give you a time slot in which to organise another exhibition dealing with the actual mid-1980s scene', and I was invited to curate the project. But although I accepted the invitation, it was already clear to me that I would not do it alone. Since the AICA was behind this project, it seemed logical to me to use this opportunity to gather together a group of young critics who were more organically connected to the scene. My suggestions led to the formation of the following team: Bojana Pejić and Lidija Merenik from Belgrade; Davor Matičević and Branka Stipančić from Zagreb; Marina Gržinić and Tomaž Brejc from Ljubljana; Nermina Zildžo from Sarajevo; Zoran Petrovski from Skopje. They authored the essays and selected the artists included in the exhibition. Davor and I installed the exhibition, since Davor had a lot of experience as a curator working on large exhibitions in the Zagreb Gallery of Contemporary Art. This exhibition reflected the initial impact of the new image and the changes in the art system that had already been felt across the entire world.

JV   How was the exhibition received in the Yugoslav context outside Sarajevo?

JD   You should know that this type of exhibition was certainly not of any interest to the mainstream, because it was still a kind of radical art for them – only it was not exclusive in the way the manifestations and experiments of the 1970s scene were. But it was positively received in our circles. The exhibition was broad in scope, with a large number of selectors and highly diverse works and artists, but it was nevertheless rigorous with regard to the artistic mainstream. Our approach was pluralistic, but did not include mainstream academic art. We showed artists from different generations, and from different cities in Yugoslavia, and some of them were very young.

BD   *Art–Criticism of the Mid-1980s* took place in 1986, and already the following year the first *Yugoslav Documents* was organised. So it seemed that all of a sudden Sarajevo was hosting major exhibitions of contemporary Yugoslav art year after year. Again you and Davor Matičević wrote the introductory essays in the catalogue.[5] On the whole, the works exhibited relate to the idea of the 'new image', but many of the other-liners we mentioned earlier are also to be found amongst the exhibitors: Mangelos, Jevšovar, Knifer, Kožarić, Stilinović, Todosijević, Urkom, Damnjan and so on. However, after all was said and done, this was about a new scene that showed the great number of phenomena that comprised the Yugoslav art of the 1980s. The term postmodern was already widely used, as was the demand for an age of artistic pluralism after the monolithic modernist project. Is the notion of pluralism in fact some type of relativisation of art discourse? It tends to prevent one from forming clearer evaluations and to form more radical attitudes. Is this notion of artistic plurality employed when it is unclear what we should critically conclude about the art of today?

JD   The exhibition *Art–Criticism of the Mid-1980s* took place in an atmosphere in which it had already become highly evident to us here that the international scene had changed since the beginning of the decade – certainly since the *Aperto 80* exhibition of Harald Szeemann and Achille Bonito Oliva at the Venice Biennale in 1980. In an effort to shed some light on the new situation, a thematic issue of *Polja* magazine was published under the title 'The Postmodern Era – The Art of the 1980s', for which Bojana Pejić wrote the introductory text.[6] The basic aim of the issue, as well as the aforementioned exhibition in Sarajevo, was not to understand the art from the early 1980s as a kind of negation, opposition or denial of the art of the preceding period – as it was being viewed and promoted by part of the local art scene. On the contrary, it was a possible continuation, extension and progression, expressed in other languages and with other means. It became obvious that it is no longer possible, nor even justified, to speak about conflicts between generations, tendencies or determinations, and ultimately, between artistic and non-artistic ideologies.

BD   The second iteration of the Sarajevo *Documents* in 1989 seems to be a more comprehensive and even more important exhibition than the first. Here we have a far greater number of exhibitors and a large number of important artworks. That exhibition can be read today above all in the light of the breakup of the country and the war, which particularly affected Sarajevo. Therefore, it can be seen as one of the last exhibitions to gather together artists from all over Yugoslavia.[7] The Sarajevo *Documents* exhibition in 1989 is also interesting for us because of your essay 'Razlog za Drugu liniju' ('The Reason for the Other Line'), which is published in the accompanying catalogue, in which you fully explain this crucial art historical term of yours.[8] However, the exhibition itself did not include many works or projects that could be classified under this term. Or am I wrong? What happened to the idea of the Other Line after the New Art Practices of the 1970s? And why did this particular essay of yours appear in this catalogue, since it didn't deal with the exhibition itself?

JD   The overall concept of the first and second *Documents* was conceived by Jusuf Hadžifejzović and Radoslav Tadić. They also invited us as expert consultants, which is why Tomaž Brejc, Davor Matičević and I are all listed in the publication. We then together invited curators, or selectors as they were called; there were a full 16 selectors for the second *Yugoslav Documents* exhibition. Brejc, Matičević and I also wrote the introductory essays. We agreed that Brejc should write a text on the theory of art,[9] Matičević should write about the art scene at the time,[10] while I was entrusted with producing a review of the preceding artistic situation. I tried to use this opportunity to write an essay that communicated some of the earlier positions related to contemporary artistic production and subsumed them under the notion of the Other Line. It was important to me to get a text like this published in the catalogue of such a widely promoted exhibition, even though I had to conclude the essay with the admission that the art of the 1980s no longer harboured any utopian vision, nor did it radicalise the means or the form of the artwork. In spite of this, my intention was to insert the idea of the Other Line into the foundations of the vital artistic phenomena of the time, instead of isolating it and treating it as a separate entity, which would have left the art of the 1980s looking like some sort of rebuff and a return to the classical disciplines of painting and sculpture.

JV   The second *Sarajevo Documents* was larger, with a far higher budget than the first, and displayed the clear

intention to adopt the character of a biennial. A third
iteration was also planned.

JD   Yes, a third exhibition was planned. We met in Neum,
that is in Drvenik near Neum, at Enjo's flat, where he usually
spent the summer. Davor Matičević, Jusuf and I were there.
Enrico Comi, the Italian art critic and publisher of the
magazine *Spazio Umano*, was also there. We thought that
the third *Documents* should be an international show. But
here is what was interesting to me: at one point Enrico
Comi asked me: 'Why are artists here organising such major
exhibitions, like Jusuf and Edin Numankadić, and the
others?' And I said to him: 'Because these are a type of artist
who is trained in such a way so as to think not only about
their art, but also about the art of other artists – and as art
historians, we have not extended ourselves enough to play
such social roles.' He then replied to me: 'If that happened
in Italy, those artists would be seen as sacrificing their own
work. Because people would say: "If the artist isn't working
exclusively on their own art, then they have some problems
with their career, which is why they have to organise exhibitions"'. He thanked me for explaining and said: 'Now it is
clear to me why Jusuf is so active and engaged in absolutely
everything in this project.' The third *Documents* never took
place, as the war in Bosnia and Herzegovina soon broke out.

BD   But what are your memories of the atmosphere
surrounding the second *Documents* in the summer of 1989?
The general atmosphere in the country was already very
tense. How did the artists get on with each other? You
were at the opening. Did you sense any nationalist-related
tensions? Could you feel something in the air?

JD   No, nothing particularly nationalist. But one day,
Jusuf complained to me that they had not had any reply from
Stilinović, Martek and Jerman. He didn't know whether
they had agreed to participate in the exhibition and asked
me to intervene. Then I called and spoke to Stilinović on the
telephone. I asked: 'Well Mladen, do you want to take part?'
And he said: 'No, we won't be participating because of Tadić.'

JV   Why?

JD   Tadić was one of the main organisers. I relayed this
to Jusuf and said: 'Look, I spoke to them, they don't want
to take part because of Tadić.' But then Jusuf said: 'Just don't
touch Tadić!' I suspect they didn't really know who Tadić
was, but provisionally he represented someone who was
unacceptable to them. He was a professor at the Sarajevo
Academy. Tadić provided a very important cultural link
between Jusuf, the Collegium and the SIZ.[11]

BD   Which means that he was intimate with the political
structures?

JD   He was intimate with these structures, and obviously
capable of finding the resources for a project like this.
Then there was a second conversation and, as can be seen
from the exhibition catalogue, Mladen Stilinović, Martek
and Jerman all decided to take part in the end.

BD   But you don't know why they initially refused to take
part?

JD   There were artistic reasons, or reasons of art politics.
But I would completely deny the claim that they had any
basis in nationalism.

BD   Tadić was Serbian, I presume?

JD   He was, but that had nothing to do with the antagonism between them.

BD   Which means that there was nothing odd or charged
in the atmosphere?

JD   You are asking me now: how was it possible that an
exhibition was organised in the centre of Sarajevo in 1989
and there wasn't any suggestion of what would happen just
a year or two later – neither in the artworks nor in the
introductory essays? I don't know, but that's how it was.
I cannot give you any more explicit answer to this question.

BD   The exhibition took place in summer, running from
1st July to 1st August 1989. What I am saying is that the

opening of the show came only two days after Milošević's speech at Gazimestan, on St. Vitus' day, 28 June. And it is interesting …

JD   Interesting, indeed.

BD   Yes, two or three days later. That speech was attended by hundreds of thousands of people commemorating the anniversary of the battle of Kosovo. And in that speech Milošević said: 'Today, we are looking ahead to new battles – these battles are not fought with arms, although they [arms] are not excluded as an option.'[12] If the process of Yugoslav disintegration was not already clear before that, then it was perfectly clear after his speech.

JD   I cannot give you an answer. There is no answer. Did we know, or not know, did we ignore it, or were we unaware – and not just me, but also many others, all of us together? The people in Sarajevo – I don't know whether they foresaw it or not …

BD   Well, if all this still wasn't clear in 1989, then it certainly was in 1991. You have said that you were preparing the third *Documents* and that it didn't go ahead because of the outbreak of the war in Slovenia and then in Croatia. A year later, in April 1992, the siege of Sarajevo began.

JD   Which is why I brought you this publication from the Belgrade Circle.[13] This is now 1993. The Belgrade Circle was gathering intellectuals engaged in the anti-war movements. I think I was invited by Aljoša Mimica because I was lecturing at the Faculty of Philosophy at the time, in the Art History department, and he was in the Sociology department. I participated in the sessions of the Belgrade Circle. I would ask you to read this essay. It is called 'On the Ashes of the Sarajevo *Documents*'.[14] I am proud that I attended these sessions, but when Mimica asked me to contribute something I was only able to do so with the story of the *Yugoslav Documents* exhibitions. I was a part of that circle to a certain extent, but I didn't feel sufficiently important or sufficiently informed, or sufficiently eloquent to be able to say something more about that terrible situation.

JV   Perhaps it is best to finish our book with this essay.

JD   During the bombardment of Sarajevo, Enjo telephoned me excitedly and said: 'We got the Maršalka!' The Maršalka are the barracks named after Marshall Tito, which by that time had already been vacated and in which we intended to organise the next *Documents*. Stunned by his call I first asked: 'But, Enjo, how are you? How are you coping?' 'Whatever', he said, 'forget about me, all that's important is that we got the Maršalka!'

[1]   Azra Begić, 'Slikarstvo šeste decenije u Bosni i Hercegovini' ('Painting of the Sixth Decade in Bosnia and Herzegovina'), *Jugoslovenska umetnost XX veka: Jugoslovensko slikarstvo šeste decenije* (*Yugoslav Art of the Twentieth Century: Yugoslav Painting of the Sixth Decade*), exh. cat., Museum of Contemporary Art, Belgrade 1980, p. 69–75.

[2]   See Ješa Denegri, 'Jedinstveno mišljenje – različite tehnike. Nova ostvarenja grupe Prostor-Oblik' ('Unique Opinion – Different Techniques. New Creations of the Prostor-Oblik Group'), *Odjek* (*Echo*), vol. XXXV, no. 10, Sarajevo 1982, p. 19–20.

[3]   *Umjetnost–kritika usred osamdesetih* (*Art–Criticism in the Mid-Eighties*), AICA i Umjetnički paviljon, Collegium Artisticum, Sarajevo 1986.

[4]   *Pogled na osamdesete* (*A View on the Eighties*), AICA i Umjetnički paviljon, Collegium Artisticum, Sarajevo, 1985.

[5]   *Jugoslovenska dokumenta '87* (*Yugoslav Documents '87*), exh. cat., Radna organizacija Zimske olimpijske igre '84, Centar Skenderija, Svetlost, Sarajevo 1987.

[6]   Bojana Pejić, 'Vreme ikonodula' ('Time of Iconodules'), *Polja*, vol. XXIX, no. 289, Novi Sad 1983, p. 103–104.

[7]   See Branislava Anđelković, Branislav Dimitrijević, 'Poslednja decenija: umetnost, društvo, trauma i normalnost' ('The Last Decade: Art, Society, Trauma and Normality'), in *O normalnosti. Umetnost u Srbiji 1989–2001* (*About Normality: Art in Serbia 1989–2001*), exh. cat., Museum of Contemporary Art, Belgrade 2005, p. 9–10.

[8]   Ješa Denegri, 'Razlog za Drugu liniju' ('The Reason for the Other Line'), *Jugoslovenska dokumenta '89* (*Yugoslav Documents '89*), exh. cat., Olympic Centre 'Skenderija', Sarajevo 1989, p. 13–20. See here on p. 266–275.

[9]   Tomaž Brejc, 'Umetnost i teorija na kraju osamdesetih godina: nekoliko otvorenih pitanja' ('Art and Theory in the Last Year of the Eighties'), ibid., p. 28–30.

[10] Davor Matičević, 'Viđenje desetljeća: Osamdesete i kakvim ih upamtiti' ('Seeing the Decade: The Eighties and what Memorialises Them'), ibid., p. 21–27.

[11] SIZ or Samoupravne interesne zajednice (Self-managing communities of interest) were formed by the Constitution of Yugoslavia from 1974 for the organisation and free exchange of duties between workers in organisations from the fields of social activity (education, culture, etcetera) and the workers who practised these activities.

[12] For the full recording of the speech see https://www.youtube.com/watch?v=vdU6ngDhrAA.

[13] Ivan Čolović, Aljoša Mimica (eds.), *Intelektualci i Rat* (*Intellectuals and War*), Beogradski krug, Centar za antiratnu akciju, Belgrade 1993.

[14] Ješa Denegri, 'Na pepelu sarajevskih *Dokumenta*' ('On the Ashes of the Sarajevo *Documents*'), ibid., p. 85–87. See below p. 366–370.

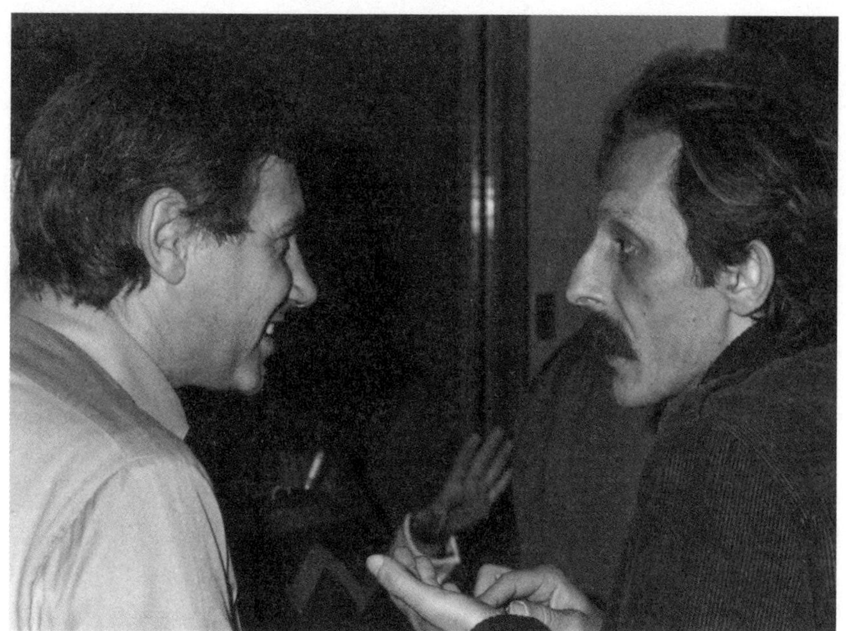

Ješa Denegri and Mladen Stilinović during the exhibition *Towards a Museum of Contemporary Art – 30 Years of the Gallery of Contemporary Arts*, Galerija suvremene umjetnosti (Gallery of Contemporary Arts), Zagreb, 1986

On the Ashes of the
Sarajevo *Documents*
Ješa Denegri

Published in Ivan Čolović, Aljoša Mimica (eds.), *Intelektualci i Rat (Intellectuals and War)*, Beogradski krug, Centar za antiratnu akciju, Belgrade 1993, p. 85–87.

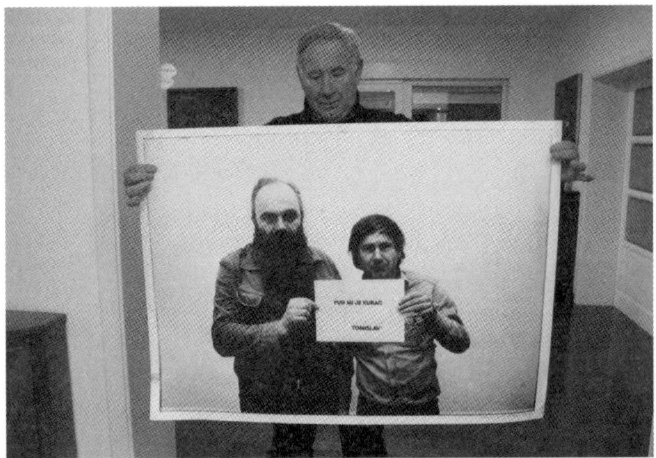

Ješa Denegri holding a photograph showing Tomislav Gotovac and Denegri holding Gotovac's artist's book after his performance in 1978 at the *New Art Practices in Yugoslavia* exhibition, Galerija suvremene umjetnosti (Gallery of Contemporary Arts), Zagreb, 2012

It is with the greatest difficulty that
I engage in writing these few pages
on the topic 'Intellectuals and War',
because I am confronted on a daily
basis with the fact that no words
whatsoever written or spoken
by the people who work in culture
can actually do anything to help
bring this horrible thing to an end.
Sometimes it seems to me that
it would be much easier to deal
with all this suffering in oneself
and with oneself; or, if one is
supposed to talk about it, then
it is only possible to say something
entirely personal, something
that relates only to a personal
experience.

This war has brought tremendous
suffering to individuals, to families
and also to entire communities;
today it is entirely clear that the
result is a catastrophe for everyone,
there are losses on all sides. But
this also has brought something
which, before the breakout of war,
wasn't even possible to imagine:

the death or, perhaps it is better to say, the slow dying of a big city with all its urban institutions; it has brought the destruction of everything built in this town related to art and culture. Many people from the art world have (did have) a Sarajevo of their own – a Sarajevo of their friends, a Sarajevo where perhaps they themselves were able to do something. For me, it is a Sarajevo of the journals *Izraz* (*Expression*) and *Odjek* (*Echo*), of the art groups Prostor-Oblik (Space-Form) and Zvono (Bell), of the Art Gallery of Bosnia and Herzegovina and the Collegium Artisticum, of the Roman Petrović Youth Centre and Gallery, of the Obala Theatre/The Bank and the Academy of Fine Arts. And for me, I repeat, as something unforgettable: it is the Sarajevo of the *Yugoslav Documents*, and particularly the people who made the exhibition and with whom I have collaborated. Here are their names: Enver Hadžiomerspahić, Jusuf Hadžifejzović, Radoslav Tadić, from the very organisational core of it; with Edin Numenkadić and Dean Jokanović as background support. I list these names not only to remember them and to speak their names before others, but also to point to what can be inferred with the very mention of these names. These are people who belong to all three of the larger communities that live in Bosnia, people whom I know for a fact who have cooperated and collaborated among and between each other, who have a common vocation and share a devotion to art, and who have no second thoughts whatsoever related to anything national or ethnic connecting or separating them. On the contrary, they believed that it is precisely the fact that they come from different circles that ensures they are not a compact, nationally determined group, which is their advantage, and which makes them qualified to gather around the project of realising one of the last major exhibitions of contemporary art in Yugoslavia, when other fields and disciplines had no interest in such affairs, did not want to finance such affairs, and even did not know how to do such a thing in terms of concept and selection, nor professionally in terms of organisation, as was the case with the second Sarajevo *Documents*, held in 1989.

They themselves were very aware of such characteristics, and occasionally emphasised the fact that only entirely unencumbered by questions of nationality could they have initiated and staged the largest and most spectacular art exhibitions ever in the former Yugoslavia. And they were not doing all this carried away by the ideological slogan that Bosnia is, allegedly, Yugoslavia 'in a nutshell' but primarily for fundamental, culturally-driven reasons: namely, they knew that only a strong and broad Yugoslav art scene, and not some small, local, closed one, might enable them to enter the European art scene. They recognised as paramount inclusion – in the context within which every progressive contemporary art scheme moves, according to which each is measured and evaluated – and cooperation, without which it cannot hope to be an active force. It is in such a context and atmosphere that preparations for the third *Documents* began and were already underway, and Enrico Comi, the critic and editor of the journal *Spazio Umano* (*Human Space*) from Milan, was invited to be the international selector. But in the middle of these efforts to realise such an ambitious scheme the horrible drama of Sarajevo and the subsequent collapse of all modern urban institutions in this dying city began.

Today, I see that perhaps the highest price was paid precisely by those who in that city had thought and lived the widest cultural horizons, those who had nothing national or nationalistic within them, those who were internationalists with European views, those for whom art was simply the only vocation and who had no other ambitions than to deal with art in terms of creativity and organisation. With the exception of all but one person, who lives abroad, all the others from the core of the creators of *Documents* remained in the hell that was Sarajevo the entire time and, despite being of different nationalities, they hadn't, as far as I know, gone their separate ways. And I would say that was because they, as artists and intellectuals, were connected through the most universal ideas and through the deepest feelings and convictions one could possibly have: these are the ideas and feelings about the unity and togetherness within art, on the basis of which the Sarajevo *Documents* events were in fact established in the first place. It sounds almost unreal, but while we were still able to communicate via phone, before they entered the ninth circle of their own inferno, one of the creators of *Documents* asked me whether I would like to join them for the next *Documents*, which would symbolise the resurrection of Sarajevo. Of course I agreed, because I knew I had to respond to his hope and belief in the same way, with the same optimism; but, deep down inside, I feared that it wouldn't be this way, or at least not for a long time. Because everything was too horrible, the consequences for culture would remain for a long time, perhaps irevocably so. All this utter helplessness among small circles of intellectuals is both horrifying and profoundly disappointing, as expressed by one of my Sarajevo friends about *Documents*: namely, that no project in the field of culture could bring the weight of any example that could oppose such a terribly brutal political and everyday life reality. But what is most horrifying is not the awareness of the definitive powerlessness of the individuals and small groups within artistic and intellectual circles; much worse, it is the awareness that some of these intellectuals – at least judging by the titles they have – are to be found among the leaders involved in the conflict; that they were directly involved in initiating, stirring up and justifying the war, and some of them are among those most responsible for all of this evil.

AFTERWORD

On the Other Line
Boris Groys

The quotes by Varvara Stepanova reproduced in this essay on page 377 are excerpted from her essay 'The General Theory of Constuctivism', in Will Bradley, Charles Esche (eds.), *Art and Social Change: A Critical Reader*, Tate Publishing, London 2007, p. 71 and 73.

In the middle of the Second World War, in 1942, Stalin famously said, 'Hitlers come and go, but the German people remains.' However, after the end of Soviet socialism the Soviet people also disappeared. The same happened to the Yugoslav people – it disappeared together with Yugoslav socialism. What remained is a number of small nations that consider the historical period that they spent in the socialist space as traumatic. This period is remembered only as a demonstration of the strength and resilience of these nations that were able to survive and keep intact their cultural identities under the pressure of an antinational, socialist regime. But what about socialism itself? It seems that it does not belong to any organic, historical national identity, since it has a completely artificial, nonorganic, unnatural character. In other words, socialism belongs to the history of modern and contemporary art. And, indeed, we see that

the memory of socialism has found its place primarily in
contemporary art milieus. This book is a good illustration of
that, and at the same time an explanation of why this shift
from the politico-economic space to the art space took place.

In his texts and conversations Ješa Denegri opposes two
basic modes of human existence: destiny and project. To
simplify this opposition, one may say: destiny is how the past
defines our present, whereas the project is the orientation
of the present towards the future. The notion of human
existence as ontologically directed towards the future – as
a project – was made popular by the existential philosophy
of Martin Heidegger and, especially, by Jean-Paul Sartre.
Here it is interesting that, at least in his earlier period,
Heidegger associated the past with a mood: when we want
to act, we always find ourselves being already in a certain
mood that comes from the past. In this sense the expressionist, surrealist mode of art production that makes moods
and affects its main topic should be considered to reflect
the effects of the past on the subjectivity of artists and
spectators. The project presupposes, on the contrary, a break
with the past and its moods. When Denegri speaks about
the Other Line of art, he obviously means artists who took
the decision to use art neither as a representation of the
external world nor as an expression of the internal world of
subjective moods and feelings, but as the construction of
a new, future reality. However, if an artist has formulated a
project directed towards the future and decided to pursue
it, then the following question arises: what guarantees that
this artist will be able to realise the project? It is precisely
at this point that the concept of socialism emerges.

It is possible to imagine that an individual can pursue
their project alone, outside of society and its economic and
political activity. Christian and Buddhist monks who lead
a lonely life of pure contemplation are an example of this.
However, artists do not contemplate: they produce. An individual artistic technique is necessarily dependent on the
general state of technology that is dominant in the society in
which the artist lives. The constructivism that Denegri sees
as belonging to the Other Line is a reflection of this dependence. Thus, in her text 'The General Theory of Constructivism' (1921) Varvara Stepanova wrote, 'Construction of

a painting is based on technical necessity, rejecting the inner spiritual necessity … Subconscious inspiration (a fortuitous phenomenon) is transformed into organised activity.'
The concept of organised activity is crucial here. Art was understood by the constructivist artists like Stepanova and Alexander Rodchenko as the organisation of the relationship between humans and their technology. This organisation is necessary because the advance of technology destroys the traditional place of humans in nature. Thus, the search for a new balance between humans and their technological environment becomes unavoidable. And this search has to be renewed again and again. As Stepanova continued, 'the basic peculiarity of the modern epoch is temporality, transience'. The technique is based on the principle of the ceaseless shift and, thus, requires constant organisational activity by artists to restore the lost balance.

This activity has economic and political dimensions. The technological shifts are effects of planning that are directed towards the future, and affect the most everyday and intimate aspects of human existence. This planning is undertaken by big corporations and state agencies. If individual artists want to create their own projects, they inevitably begin to compete with plans and projects that have already been formulated by much more powerful actors. For individual artistic projects to be realised they need to be recognised by the society in which their artists live. But how can individual artistic projects find recognition by that society?

Under standard capitalist conditions the recognition of particular artworks is regulated by the art market. As an individual producer, the artist is dependent on the decisions of private collectors and/or art institutions to acquire their work. However, the art market cannot support artistic projects. The artworks, as far as they are already produced, belong to the past. The art projects, on the contrary, are directed towards the future – towards giving the future a certain shape. This means that the art market is fundamentally opposed to art that is understood as a project. The capitalist market as such is a medium of destiny, to use Denegri's word. It functions as a competition among different actors in which the fittest wins. But being the fittest means being the best accommodated to the political and economic world as it is. This explains the most obvious characteristic of capitalism: it combines the technological dynamic with the repetitive, stagnating character of human relations. To change these relations, an artistic project that would give a new form to society is needed. It is this desire for a new social form that is common for constructivist artistic projects and socialism. Indeed, socialism means the rejection of competition and market. Instead, a new era of collaboration is begun, with a goal of the realisation of a commonly shared project.

This explains why the upending of the socialist project also entails the dissolution of a community that was its bearer. The national community survives all the political and economic catastrophes because it has a common past – it is based on nativity, on a common natural origin that precedes all the political, economic and social projects, and thus survives their demise. However, the socialist community does not have a common past – it has only a common future. When this future loses its attractiveness, the community dissolves. The same can be said about artistic groups that are built around common artistic projects. When these projects become equivocal, the artistic groups dissolve. Now a question emerges: what happens to the heritage of these groups and, for that matter, to the heritage of socialism as well?

During the period of modernity, the basic metaphysical, religious and ideological question – namely, the question 'what is permanent?' – has become a technical problem of museum collecting and preserving. Museums are constructed in such a way that the particular cultural identities presented in them are distinguished from each other by certain externally identifiable formal characteristics. The local fundamentalist identity seeker and the international tourist in search of cultural differences are therefore internally connected by the same museum-informed gaze. Thus, today, the universalism of modern projects, including socialism, has been replaced by the universal accessibility of local cultures. However, the socialist civilisation was, from the beginning, a modern civilisation. That is why socialist civilisation has left no monuments of its own that are comparable to pre-modern models: no Egyptian pyramids, no Greek temples. The demand for the creation of a particular, proletarian, socialist, formally and aesthetically specific culture, which the Russian post-revolutionary avant-garde formulated with the aim of giving a body to the spectre of communism was, as is well known, rejected by Soviet power. Thus, it is no coincidence that only the constructivist, 'proletarian' Russian art of the earlier post-revolutionary years, and not later Soviet art, is often shown in Western museums. I still remember quite well how the collapse of the socialist regimes – especially in Russia – created expectations in the Western art world of discovering a completely new, exotic, authentic art that had originated in isolation from the West and could therefore offer a real opportunity for Western art collections. The disappointment was great, as it turned out that the official and unofficial art of the former socialist countries did not differ significantly from Western art on an aesthetic level. The hopes of discovering something radically new, as in the case of Japanese or African art at the beginning of the 20th century, were dashed, creating bitterness in Western art milieus.

The critique of museums is widespread, especially in left-oriented cultural circles. Museums are seen as celebrating commodity fetishism and demonstrating the power of the wealthy. It is, of course, true that the museums neutralise original artistic projects by displaying them as artefacts of the past and, thus, denying them the future. However, it is always possible to re-open projects of the past to a new future. The cultural history of Europe is the history of revivals. The Renaissance was a revival of the antique Greek understanding of man and nature inspired by the collections of antique Greek and Roman art. The French Revolution launched a new revival of Roman classicism. Later, William Morris combined a socialist political programme with the revival of pre-Renaissance medieval art practices. And the neo-avant-garde of the 1960s was a revival of the Russian avant-garde, Bauhaus and Dada – a revival that would have been impossible if these avant-garde projects had not been put in museums and, thus, inherited by later generations. The Other Line of which Denegri speaks, is precisely a succession of revivals and re-enactments – of new artistic projects using old artistic projects as their models. In fact, this book itself belongs to this Other Line.

APPENDIX

Index of Names

Written by Branislav Dimitrijević, Vladimir Jerić Vlidi, Aleksandra Mirčić and Jelena Vesić

A

MARINA ABRAMOVIĆ (Belgrade, 1946)
Performance artist whose practice re-examines the abilities, limitations and endurance of the body and mind. Educated at the Academies of Fine Arts in Belgrade and Zagreb, from the 1970s onwards she abandoned painting and began experimenting with ambient soundscapes and conceptual photography. From 1971 to 1976 Abramović was a member of an informal group of six artists who collaborated with the Student Cultural Centre Gallery in Belgrade (not to be confused with the Zagreb Group of Six Artists – see entry below). She presented her first performance, *Rhythm 10*, in 1973 at the Edinburgh Festival, where she also met Joseph Beuys, who would have a great influence on her work. From 1976 she began living and working with the German artist Ulay. Their marriage and collaboration ended in 1988 with the performance *Lovers*, during which they walked to meet each other from opposite ends of the Great Wall of China. In 2010 The Museum of Modern Art (MoMA) in New York organised a retrospective of Abramović's work entitled *The Artist is Present*.

KARPO GODINA AĆIMOVIĆ (Skopje, 1943)
Cinematographer, director, screenwriter and film editor, Aćimović began his cinematographic carrier by filming Želimir Žilnik's *Early Works,* and from 1970s directed a number of short documentaries and experimental films, including *The Gratinated Brains of Pupilija Ferkeverk* (1970) and *Healthy People for Fun* (1971). He later directed a number of feature films including *The Medusa Raft* (1980) and *Artificial Paradise* (1990).

JÓZSEF ÁCS (Bačka Topola, 1914–Novi Sad, 1990)
Painter, art critic and pedagogue, Acz was a key figure in Informel painting in Vojvodina in the 1960s. He was the director of the School of Applied Arts in Novi Sad from 1952 to 1956 and an art critic for the daily newspaper *Magyar Szo*.

BORISLAV ALEKSIĆ (Sarajevo, 1936)
Graphic artist and painter. Aleksić taught at the Academy of Fine Arts in Sarajevo.

DRAGAN ALEKSIĆ (Bunić near Korenica, 1901–Belgrade, 1958)
Poet, writer, journalist and founder of Yugo-Dada. Aleksić was introduced to Dada during his studies in Prague, and on his return to Yugoslavia began collaborating with the magazine *Zenit*. After being expelled from the Zenit circle in 1922 he launched the magazines *Dada Tank* and *Dada Jazz*, and organised several *Dadaist Matinée* actions in Osijek, Vinkovci and Subotica. Aleksić lived in Prague, Vinkovci, Zagreb and Belgrade.

KOSTA ANĐELI (ANGELI) RADOVANI (London, 1916–Zagreb, 2002)
Sculptor, one of the founders of the Zagreb Academy of Applied Arts, and a professor at the Faculty of Fine Arts in Sarajevo. His sculptures represent figural stylisations; the most famous are the *Dunje* (*Quince*) series (1960s–1970s) in which he modelled full and mature nude female forms. He was also engaged with monumental sculpture, producing more than 30 large-scale public pieces.

BRANISLAVA ANĐELKOVIĆ (Belgrade, 1966)
Art historian and curator. Anđelković was the director of the Centre for Contemporary Art (1998–2001) and director of the Museum of Contemporary Art, Belgrade (2001–2013). She lectured at the Belgrade Centre for Women's Studies and published *Introduction to Feminist Theories of Image* (2002). Contesting nationalistic revisions, Anđelković initiated the exhibition *The Yugoslav Art Space*, curated by Ješa Denegri at the Belgrade Museum of Contemporary Art in 2005 as the first museum display of Yugoslav art after the dissolution of the country.

MIHAJLO ARSOVSKI (Skopje, 1937)
Graphic designer and typographer, considered to have a pivotal role in Croatian and Yugoslav graphic design from the late 1960s. In his designs for books, magazines, posters and other printed media and his interior and stage design, Arsovski employs techniques of collage and photomontage and an innovative approach to typography. He is the only Yugoslav graphic designer included in the Thames & Hudson *Encyclopaedia of Graphic Design & Designers* (London 1992).

ANTUN AUGUSTINČIĆ (Klanjec, 1900–Zagreb, 1979)
Sculptor and one of the founders of the Zemlja (Earth) group (1929–1935). Augustinčić was a professor at the Academy of Fine Arts in Zagreb. A much appreciated artist both before and after the Second World War, he designed the most famous figural sculptural portrait of Josip Broz Tito and the first post-war monument in Yugoslavia, the *Monument of Gratitude to the Red Army* (1947) in Batina. His other notable sculptures include the *Peace* monument (1954) that stands in front of the United Nations building in New York City and the *Miner* statue (1936–1939) in front of the International Labour Organization headquarters in Geneva.

AUTOPSIA (Ruma, early 1980s)
Artistic and musical group, an indigenous offshoot of the independent and intermedia subcultural scene formed around punk and the new wave. In Ruma, Autopsia focused on the subject of death. Based in Prague since 1990, the group has published a large number of music and graphic releases.

B

LJUBO BABIĆ (Jastrebarsko, 1890–Zagreb, 1974)
Painter, art historian and professor at the Academy of Fine Arts in Zagreb. Babić took part in the formation of the Independent Group of Croatian Artists. He was the first curator of the Modern Gallery (1919) and after 1947 was the director of the Strossmayer Gallery of Old Masters in Zagreb. He participated in the organisation of the exhibition *Medieval Art in Yugoslavia* in Paris (1950) and in the exhibition *Half a Century of Yugoslav Painting* (1953).

ZDENKA BADOVINAC (Novo Mesto, 1958)
Curator, writer and co-founder of L'Internationale museum confederation. Badovinac was the director of Moderna galerija (Museum of Modern Art, Ljubljana) from 1993 to 2021, where she initiated the first collection of Eastern European art and the 2000+ Arteast Collection, and curated many affiliated exhibitions such as *Body and the East – From the 1960s to the Present* (1998); *7 Sins: Ljubljana-Moscow* (2004, with Victor Misiano and Igor Zabel); *Interrupted Histories* (2006); *The Schengen Women* (2008); and *NSK from Kapital to Capital/Neue Slowenische Kunst – An Event of the Final Decade of Yugoslavia* (2015). With Bojana Piškur, Badovinac re-staged the second *Yugoslav Documents* (Sarajevo, 1989) at the Moderna galerija in Ljubljana in 2017, under the title *The Heritage of 1989/Case Study: The Second Yugoslav Documents Exhibition*.

IVANA BAGO (Mostar, 1979)
Independent art historian, writer and curator. With Antonia Majača, Bago co-founded DeLVe–Institute for Duration, Location and Variables dedicated to examining the intersection between artistic, academic and curatorial practice. She has published essays on Eastern European art, global conceptualisms, post-Yugoslav art and feminism. Her dissertation *Inheriting the Yugoslav Century: Art, History and Generation* (Duke University) deals with the politics of a Yugoslav identity and a Yugoslav aesthetics.

VOJIN BAKIĆ (Bjelovar, 1915–Zagreb, 1992)
Sculptor, one of the most important representatives of post-war modernist abstraction. His work is characterised by innovation and research into the dynamism of form. Bakić used sheets of metal to produce specific light-reflecting and leafy forms. He participated in many of the most prestigious international exhibitions of fine arts (Venice Biennale, documenta in Kassel, São Paulo Biennial). Bakić is one of the most prolific creators of monumental sculpture in Yugoslavia and has built some of the most famous monuments such as the *Monument to Stjepan Filipović* in Valjevo (1960), the *Monument to the Revolution of the Peoples of Slavonia* in Kamenska (1968), the *Memorial Complex on Petrova Gora* (1981) and many more.

NENA BALJKOVIĆ-DIMITRIJEVIĆ (Šibenik, 1950)
Art historian and curator. In 1971 with the artist Braco Dimitrijević she organised the first exhibition of Conceptual art in Yugoslavia, entitled *At the Moment*, in the entrance hall of a residential building in Frankopanska Street, Zagreb. The exhibition was recreated in the Student Cultural Centre Gallery in Belgrade the same year as an exhibition experiment in three phases entitled *At Another Moment*. Baljković-Dimitrijević also organised the first exhibition of the Gorgona group at the Gallery of Contemporary Art in Zagreb in 1977. She subsequently continued to work with Dimitrijević in an international arena.

ALEKSANDER BASSIN (Ljubljana, 1938)
Art critic and curator. Bassin was manager of the City Gallery in Ljubljana where he curated a large number of exhibitions, critiques and studies on contemporary art.

AZRA BEGIĆ (Počitelj, 1931–Sarajevo, 2017)
Art historian, art critic and curator. From 1960, Begić worked as a curator at the National Gallery of Bosnia and Herzegovina, where she was the head of the collection of Yugoslav paintings and ran the Programme Activities Department. Begić researched and wrote numerous essays on art in Bosnia and Herzegovina and curated a number of individual and group exhibitions on Hegedušić, Hozo, Tikveša, Nevestić and others. During the siege of Sarajevo, she was one of the key figures responsible for saving cultural heritage and important art exhibits.

BOŽIDAR (BOŽO) BEK (Đurđevac, 1926–Zagreb, 2000)
Art historian, founder and long-time director of the Gallery of Contemporary Art in Zagreb. During the 1960s Bek organised exhibitions of important international artists in Zagreb (Chagall, Jawlensky, Nolde, Calder, Leger, Dubuffet, Vasarely, Klein, Fontana, Duchamp, Bresson, Munari, Boltanski and Picasso). He is also the founder and *spiritus movens* of the New Tendencies movement and the series of exhibitions of the same name (1961–1973), which brought Zagreb the status of an international cultural centre. He was the initiator and editor-in-chief of the magazine *Bit International*. In his public role Bek remained devoted to the ideas of the Russian avant-garde, and especially to Constructivism. He was the last secretary of the Zagreb branch of the League of Communists of Yugoslavia.

JANEZ BERNIK (Gunclje near Ljubljana, 1933–Ljubljana, 2016)
Influential painter, graphic artist and professor at the Ljubljana Academy of Fine Arts. Bernik was a member of Group 69.

OTO BIHALJI-MERIN (Zemun, 1904–Belgrade, 1993)
Writer, art historian, painter and critic, author of a large number of books on modern, medieval and naive art. Bihalji-Merin studied painting in Belgrade and Berlin, where he joined the German Communist Party. He was also a pilot in the Royal Yugoslav Air Force. With his brother Pavle he founded the publishing house Nolit in Belgrade in 1928. In 1933, he founded the Institute for the Fight Against Fascism in Paris with Arthur

Koestler. He also took part in the Spanish Civil War. After the Second World War Bihalji-Merin lived in Belgrade and was active as an art critic and as one of the leading figures in Yugoslav cultural policy and cultural diplomacy. As one of the members of the international expert commission in charge of the large exhibition *Fifty Years of Modern Art* at the World Expo in Brussels in 1958, his endeavours significantly promoted Yugoslav art.

DUNJA BLAŽEVIĆ (Zagreb, 1944)
Art historian and curator of contemporary art. Blažević ran the Gallery of the Student Cultural Centre in Belgrade from 1971 to 1976, and then was the director of the Student Cultural Centre until 1980. In 1975 she initiated the counter-exhibition on art and self-management entitled *October 75*. With Žarana Papić and Nada Ler-Sofronić Blažević also initiated the Drug-ca Žena (Comrade Woman) conference, the first feminist conference in the non-Western world, held at the Student Cultural Centre in 1978. Since the beginning of the 1980s she has produced *TV Gallery*, a well-known programme dedicated to art and culture on Television Belgrade. In the early 1990s Blažević moved to Paris where she worked as a critic, curator and independent art producer. From 1996 to 2010 she was the director of the Soros Centre for Contemporary Art in Sarajevo.

KOSTA BOGDANOVIĆ (Osijek near Sarajevo, 1930–Belgrade, 2012)
Sculptor and art historian. Bogdanović worked at the Museum of Contemporary Art in Belgrade as a curator (1967–1994) and was the acting director from 1985 to 1987. In 1974 he founded the Centre for Visual Culture and Information at the Museum, and wrote about visual perception and the theory of form. He also taught at art academies in Novi Sad, Sarajevo and Banja Luka. Based on his own research, Bogdanović established a new subject, Visual Culture, at the Sarajevo Academy (taught from 1982) and Theory of Visual Culture at Novi Sad Academy (taught from 1992).

SLAVKO BOGDANOVIĆ (Niš, 1948)
From the late 1960s one of the participants in the Novi Sad neo-avant-garde scene and a member of the conceptual KÔD group. Bogdanović was a member of the editorial board of the magazine *Indeks*. With Miroslav Mandić he initiated and published *L.H.O.O.Q.*, 'an underground magazine for the development of interpersonal relations and the permanent destruction of everything that exists'. Because of his radical views on society and culture Bogdanović was politically persecuted and sentenced to eight months in prison in 1972.

VLADIMIR BONAČIĆ (Novi Sad, 1938–Ittenbach, 1999)
Artist and engineer at the Ruđer Bošković Institute in Zagreb. From 1968, Bonačić started using computers to create art, and presented his kinetic objects for the first time at the New Tendencies exhibition in Zagreb in 1969. He began developing the concept of the Computer Controlled Dynamic Object with the support of UNESCO, where he was an advisor for art and science in 1971. That same year he established the BCD Cybernetic Art Team together with Miro A. Cimerman and Dunja Donassy. From 1972 the group ran the Programme in Art and Science at the Bezalel Academy of Arts and Design in Jerusalem. In 1973, Bonačić became a member of the editorial board of the journal *Leonardo*; he moved to Germany in 1980.

BOGDAN BORČIĆ (Ljubljana, 1926–Slovenj Gradec, 2014)
A graphic artist, painter and professor at the Academy of Fine Arts in Ljubljana, Borčić also studied painting at the Academy under professor Gabrijel Stupica. In 2004 he created a series of images relating to his experience of the concentration camp where he was incarcerated during the Second World War.

BOSCH+BOSCH (Subotica, 1969–1977)
Conceptual art group established in Subotica. It was founded by Slavko Matković with László Szalma, Bálint Szombathy, Edit Basch, István Krekovics, Zoltán Magyar and Slobodan Tomanović. These last four members soon left the group, while László Kerekes, Attila Csernik, Katalin Ladik and Ante Vukov joined. Bosch+Bosch was engaged in Conceptual art, performance, visual poetry, Land art, Mail art and in publishing their *WOW* magazine.

VERA BOŽIČKOVIĆ-POPOVIĆ (Brčko, 1920–Belgrade, 2002)
Painter, member of the Zadar Group, best known for her work within the Belgrade Informel scene. Božičković-Popović made tapestry, and designed costumes for theatre and film.

TOMAŽ BREJC (Ljubljana, 1946)
Art historian and influential art critic. Brejc was the Dean and a professor of art history and theory at the Academy of Fine Arts in Ljubljana. He dealt with different periods of Slovenian modern art, from Impressionism through Existentialism ('dark modernism'), to Minimal and Conceptual art ('reism'). He has written a number of books, curated exhibitions, and is on the editorial boards of the magazines *Sinteze* and *Naši razgledi* among others.

BORIS BUĆAN (Zagreb, 1947–2023)
A painter and graphic designer, Bućan began his career in the late 1970s as part of the conceptual practice of interventions in public space. More recently, he is known for his posters for various cultural events.

JAGODA BUIĆ (Split, 1930–Venice, 2022)
A sculptor who gained international prominence in the 1960s for her monumental tapestries and fibre art installations.

C

JOVAN ČEKIĆ (Belgrade, 1953)
Philosopher, art theorist and artist, and one of the founders of Group 143. Čekić was the editor of *Moment* magazine, editor-in-chief of the *New Moment* magazine for visual culture, and the author and editor of numerous theoretical books. He teaches as the Head of the Department for Digital Art at the Faculty of Media and Communications, Singidunum University, Belgrade.

ALEKSA ČELEBONOVIĆ (Lausanne, 1917–Belgrade, 1987)
A painter and art critic, Čelebonović was a professor at the Faculty of Applied Arts, at the Faculty of Philosophy in Belgrade and at the History of Art Study Group (today the History of Art department). He was a member and secretary of the Association of Fine Artists of Serbia (ULUS) and the founder and president of the Yugoslav section of the International Association of Art Critics (AICA). Čelebonović founded the Yugoslav Triennial of Visual Arts in 1961 and was its first director.

MARKO ČELEBONOVIĆ (Belgrade, 1902–Saint Tropez, 1986)
Painter and professor at the Academy of Fine Arts in Belgrade from 1948 to 1960. Between the two World Wars Čelebonović lived in France, and during the Second World War he was active in the French Resistance movement. His paintings are characterised by his distinctive use of colour and poetic realism to depict intimate bourgeois spaces, interiors and still lives.

STOJAN ĆELIĆ (Bosanski Novi, 1925–Belgrade, 1992)
Modernist painter and graphic artist. Ćelić's imagery developed from the reduction of natural forms and lyrical abstraction to geometric abstraction. He was a member of the December Group and is one of the founders and the first editor of the magazine *Umetnost*. Ćelić was a professor at the Academy of Fine Arts in Belgrade.

AVGUST ČERNIGOJ (Trieste, 1898–Sežana, 1985)
Constructivist artist. In 1924 Černigoj enrolled in the Bauhaus art school in Weimar. For financial reasons his studies were interrupted and he went to Ljubljana, where he met the poet Srečko Kosovel and founded the School of Architecture. He was forced to leave Yugoslavia because of his communist sympathies, and in 1925 he travelled back to Trieste, where he became the central figure of the Constructivist Group and the editor of the avant-garde magazine *Tank* (1927). In the 1930s Černigoj made murals and other commissions, while his work acquired distinctly surrealist features. After the Second World War he explored various artistic directions, from Informel to drip painting, producing paintings, graphics, tapestries, mosaics, stained glass, inlays, photographs, scenography, costumes and more. In the late 1960s he returned to making constructed objects and collages and to his earlier avant-garde positions.

BORA ĆOSIĆ (Zagreb, 1932)
A novelist, essayist and translator, Ćosić was the editor of the magazines *Danas* (1961–1963) and *Rok* (1969–1970) in Belgrade. He wrote a series of novels, including *My Family's Role in the World Revolution* (1969), for which he received the NIN Award. With Branko Vučićević, Ćosić produced the neo-avant-garde book *Mixed Media* (1970), which became a cult classic.

D

RADOMIR DAMNJANOVIĆ DAMNJAN (Mostar, 1936)
Artist working with painting, drawing, graphics, photography, film, video and performance art. During the late 1960s Damnjanović's painting followed the spirit of minimalist abstraction. In the early 1970s he joined the New Art Practices and became increasingly involved in performance. In his later work, which features an expanded range of media, Damnjanović maintained a critical attitude towards the artistic and cultural mainstream.

OSKAR DAVIČO (Šabac, 1909–Belgrade, 1989)
A novelist and poet, he was the youngest and the most famous writer in the Belgrade surrealist scene of the 1930s. Before the Second World War Davičo was both prosecuted for his communist activities and briefly excluded from the Communist Party of Yugoslavia for backing Miroslav Krleža during the Clashes within the Left. He spent the war in partisan units, and immediately afterwards took part in founding the new Yugoslav press agency. He was the editor of *Nova misao*, and later founded and edited the journals *Delo* and *Dalje*. He also translated literature from the French, German and Russian. The only writer to be awarded the *NIN* Literary Award three times, Davičo published more than 30 books of poetry and 10 novels, including *Poem* (1952), *Concrete and Fireflies* (1955) and *Silences* (1963).

RIKO DEBENJAK (Kanal Ob Soči, 1908–Ljubljana, 1987)
Painter and graphic artist. Debenjak was a professor at the Academy of Fine Arts in Ljubljana and a key figure at the Ljubljana School of Graphic Arts.

DECEMBER GROUP (Belgrade, 1955–1960)
The members were Zoran Petrović, Miloš Bajić, Aleksandar Luković, Lazar Vujaklija, Mladen Srbinović, Aleksandar Tomašević, Lazar Vozarević, Miodrag B. Protić, Stojan Ćelić and Dragutin Cigarčić. The December Group brought together modernist painters of various artistic sensibilities, mainly opposed to Socialist Realism and favouring abstraction.

JOVAN DESPOTOVIĆ (Belgrade, 1952)
An art historian and critic, Despotović actively promoted the
Serbian art scene of the 1980s, and in 1983 curated the first
exhibition in Belgrade to introduce the local postmodern scene
at the Museum of Contemporary Art. He was a curator at the
Museum from 1981 to 2001 and its director in 2014–2015.

SLOBODAN BRACO DIMITRIJEVIĆ (Sarajevo, 1948)
Conceptual artist. In his work Dimitrijević considers the usual,
every day, transient and accidental in contrast with the historical,
eternal, mythical and artistic. He began making work in the late
1960s with Goran Trbuljak in the group Pensioner Tihomir
Simčić. Since the 1970s he has exhibited at numerous prestigious
international exhibitions such as documenta 6 in Kassel (1977).

DRAGOSLAV DJORĐEVIĆ (Sarajevo, 1931–Belgrade, 1989)
Art historian and art critic. From 1960 to 1989 Djordević was the
curator of the Collection of Yugoslav Painting after 1945 at the
Museum of Contemporary Art in Belgrade.

JURAJ DOBROVIĆ (Jelsa on Hvar, 1928)
Artist working in sculpture, painting and graphics. The focus of
Dobrović's neo-constructivist practice is the optical relationship
between light and form.

GORAN ĐORĐEVIĆ (Prishtine, 1950)
Artist active from the mid-1970s to the mid-1980s. Until his 1979
attempt to convene an 'International Artists' Strike against the
Art System' Đordević practised analytical conceptualism. Later,
he dedicated himself to copying as a theoretical and practical
means of fighting art with the means of art, and then proclaimed
his artistic career over. Since 1985, Đordević's name has been
linked to a series of anonymous or para-institutional projects
that deal anthropologically with art history and exhibition
policies.

ČEDOMIR DRČA (Odžaci, 1950)
A member of the Novi Sad conceptual group (Ǝ, Drča works
with graphic design and photography.

MIODRAG DADO ĐURIĆ (Cetinje, 1933–Paris, 2010)
Painter who became internationally known for his intense and
expressive style of fantastical painting. From 1956, Đurić lived
and worked in Paris.

DUŠAN DŽAMONJA (Strumica 1928–Zagreb, 2009)
One of the most distinguished and productive modernist
sculptors in Yugoslavia. Džamonja worked mainly in metal and
concrete. He exhibited in the Yugoslav pavilion at the Venice
Biennale in 1960, when he was nominated for the Grand Prix.
Džamonja is particularly known for his monumental sculpture
in urban and architectural environments, the most famous
of which are the *Monument of the Revolution in Podgarić* (1966),
the *Memorial Ossuary to the Fallen Yugoslav Soldiers of the First and
Second World Wars* in Barletta, Italy (1969) and the *Monument to
the Revolution* in Kozara (1973).

E

EXAT 51 (Zagreb, 1951–1956)
Neo-avant-garde, constructivist art group from Zagreb, who
derived their name by abbreviating 'Experimental Atelier' the
year of their launch. The group comprised the designer Bernardo
Bernardi, the architect Zdravko Bregovac, the painter Vlado
Kristl, the painter, graphic artist and designer Ivan Picelj, the
architect Zvonimir Radić, the architect, set designer and painter
Božidar Rašica, the architect and sculptor Vjenceslav Richter,
the painter and sculptor Aleksandar Srnec and the architect

Vladimir Zarahović. EXAT 51 made their first public appearance
through the Manifesto exhibited at the Plenum of the
Association of Fine Artists of Applied Arts of Croatia in Zagreb
on 7 December 1951. Their innovative approach combines
architecture, painting and design.

F

EUGEN FELLER (Split, 1942)
A self-taught painter, Feller was one of the most radical
representatives of Art Informel in modern Yugoslav painting of
the late 1950s together with Ivo Gattin. His Informel paintings
were mostly monochromatic, with dense textures made of
plaster and cement. With his objects from the 1960s constructed
mostly of wood, his work became influenced by Minimal art.
Later he returned to painting exploring primary abstraction.

BRANKO FILO FILIPOVIĆ (Cetinje, 1924–Belgrade, 1997)
Painter. In the 1950s and 1960s Filipović explored the materiality
of painting, producing some of the earliest Yugoslav Informel
pieces, but he considered Informel to be 'more of a manner
of expression than a definitive painting style'. In the 1970s and
1980s Filipović moved towards pure painting, combining
expressive representation with associative abstract landscape
features. He exhibited as the very last representative of SFRY
in the Yugoslav Pavilion at the Venice Biennale in 1990.

G

MLADEN GALIĆ (Lištica, 1934)
Painter, graphic artist, ambient artist and graphic designer.
Galić made abstract serigraphs, and is known for his lumino-
kinetic installations using ultraviolet light and black-and-white
images in the spirit of geometric abstraction.

GRGO GAMULIN (Jelsa, 1910–Zagreb, 1997)
Influential art historian, art critic and writer, professor at the
University of Zagreb and co-founder of the Institute of Art
History. Gamulin founded several journals (*Ars 37*, *The Works of
the Department of Art History*, *The Life of Art*) and published a
number of books and artist monographs.

IVO GATTIN (Split, 1926–Zagreb, 1978)
Painter. Like Eugen Feller, Gattin represents the radical current
of the Zagreb Informel. From 1956 he experimented with various
materials (wax, sand, resin, cement) and processes (for example,
burning materials on his paintings) and incorporated burlap
to create reliefs in irregular shapes. During the 1960s he was
associated with the Gorgona group.

OTON GLIHA (Črnomelj, 1914–Zagreb, 1999)
Painter. Gliha is known for his abstract patterns inspired by
the structure of coastal and island rocks, and especially by the
distinctive dry-stone walls – the *gromača* structures.

GORGONA (Zagreb, 1959–1966)
Neo-avant-garde art group active in Zagreb from 1959 to 1966.
Gorgona's members were the painters Josip Vaništa, Julije
Knifer, Marijan Jevšovar, Đuro Seder; the sculptor Ivan Kožarić;
the architect and painter Miljenko Horvat; the art critics and art
historians Radoslav Putar and Matko Meštrović, and the artist,
curator and art critic Dimitrije Bašičević, who was later better
known by his pseudonym Mangelos. The group never proclaimed
any common principles but worked together in a spontaneous
manner. Gorgona's first public appearance was the launch of
their eponymously titled anti-magazine. Each issue of *Gorgona*
was edited by different artist: Vaništa, Knifer, Jevšovar, Victor

Vasarely, Kožarić, Horvat, Harold Pinter and Dieter Roth. A total of 11 volumes were published.

TOMISLAV TOM GOTOVAC (Sombor, 1937–Zagreb, 2010)
Film director, actor, performer, multimedia and conceptual artist. In the early 1960s Gotovac performed his first Happenings in Yugoslavia and made his first structuralist films. Since the 1970s he has been known for street performances featuring his naked body. Gotovac had a significant influence on contemporary art and alternative film within the Yugoslav scene and beyond. He was obsessed by and devoted to film – 'it is all a movie' was the crucial motto of his entire artistic and life philosophy. In 2005 he changed his name to Antonio G. Lauer.

GROUP 69 (Ljubljana, 1969–late 1970s)
Group 69 was based on 'guild principles that connect many artists of different strengths and profiles'. Its members were Janez Bernik, Jagoda Bujić, Jože Ciuha, Stojan Ćelić, Dušan Džamonja, Dževad Hozo, Andrej Jemec, Adrian Maraž, France Mihalić, Štefan Planinc, Miodrag B. Protić, Vjenceslav Richter, France Rotar, Gabrijel Stupica, Miroslav Šutej, Slavko Tihec, Drago Tršar, Vladimir Veličković and Mehmed Zaimović.

GROUP 143 (Belgrade, 1975–1980)
Conceptual art group connected to the Student Cultural Centre in Belgrade. Its members were Biljana Tomić, Miško Šuvaković, Neša Paripović, Jovan Čekić, Paja Stanković, Maja Savić, Mirko Diliberović, Vladimir Nikolić, Dejan Dizdar, Nada Seferović, Bojana Burić, Stipe Dumić, Momčilo Rajin, Ivan Marošević and Slobodan Šajin. Influenced by the activities of the conceptual international group Art & Language, Group 143 explored the relationship between art and knowledge production as an artists-produced theory. Their main artistic medium was the 'conversation-as-event' that took the form of art seminars and theoretical performances.

GROUP OF SIX ARTISTS (Zagreb, 1975–circa 1982)
This group was formed in Zagreb in 1975 when six artists of the New Art Practices (Boris Demur, Željko Jerman, Vlado Martek, Mladen Stilinović, Sven Stilinović and Fedor Vučemilović) launched the magazine *MAJ 75*, which they continued publishing until 1984, producing 18 issues in total. The artists' collaboration began without a formal group name, so it was given one in 1978 by the curator Marijan Susovski. In the beginning they mainly produced interventions and actions in public space, where day-long events would be created spontaneously and guerrilla tactics were used. In the late 1970s the group registered as the Podroom Working Community of Artists and operated from the basement of the house in Mesnička 12, Zagreb. The initiative would later grow to become the Extended Media Section of the Croatian Society of Fine Artists. The Group of Six Artists was characterised by collaborative work, political provocation, communication with the audience, the use of consumables and critical thinking about the media.

MARINA GRŽINIĆ (Rijeka, 1958)
Philosopher, theorist and artist. Gržinić was the editor at the Student Cultural Centre Gallery in Ljubljana and has worked at the Philosophical Institute of the Slovenian Academy of Sciences and Arts since 1993. Since 2003, she has been a professor at the Academy of Fine Arts in Vienna. Gržinić has made video art since 1982 in collaboration with Aina Schmid. She has written numerous essays and books dealing with the relationships between technology and ideology, biopolitics and necropolitics and decolonialism and transfeminism.

HERMAN GVARDIJANČIČ (Gorenja Vas-Reteče, 1943)
Painter who used the principle of mediation between photography and painting to produce hyperrealistic images. The paintings from Gvardijančič's best-known phase largely comprise monochrome landscapes.

NEDELJKO GVOZDENOVIĆ (Mostar, 1902–Belgrade, 1988)
Painter, professor at the Academy of Fine Arts in Belgrade and member of the Serbian Academy of Sciences and Arts. Known for his intimate approach, Gvozdenović created landscapes, still life, interiors and portraits.

H

PETAR HADŽI BOŠKOV (Skopje, 1928–2015)
Sculptor. Hadži Boškov produced abstract sculptures of reduced forms. He was a professor at the Faculty of Fine Arts in Skopje.

JUSUF HADŽIFEJZOVIĆ (Prijepolje, 1956)
Hadžifejzović is a performance artist known for his installations made using a method he calls 'depotgraphy', which involves collecting stored items from depots and arranging them in exhibitions in order to 'dislocate the already dislocated objects'. He launched the contemporary art scene of Sarajevo in the 1980s and co-founded the *Yugoslav Documents* exhibitions and the Ars Aevi Collection.

ENVER (ENJO) HADŽIOMERSPAHIĆ (Banja Luka, 1946)
Founder and director of the Ars Aevi project in Sarajevo. Hadžiomerspahić was the first director of the Youth Centre in Sarajevo (1969–1972) and one of the founders and the organisational director of the *Yugoslav Documents* exhibitions (1987–1989).

KRSTO HEGEDUŠIĆ (Petrinja, 1901–Zagreb, 1975)
Painter and one of the founders of the Zemlja (Earth) group. Hegedušić founded the School of Peasant Painters in Hlebine in 1950. He was a professor at the Academy of Fine Arts in Zagreb, and from 1950 held his own master class. Hegedušić is considered to be a prominent representative of social and engaged painting. His series of drawings *Podravski motivi* (*Podravina Motifs*, 1933) represent the artist's statement on independent and engaged art, rooted in the geopolitical specificity of the industrially under-developed and oppressed peoples of the periphery. Miroslav Krleža's foreword to the publication of Hegedušić's *Podravina Motifs* is a key text in the analysis of the tendencies of leftist artistic thought within the Yugoslav Art Space. With this text the Clashes within the Left (1928–1952) developed, through which Yugoslav art and aesthetics are presented. Although the new artistic expressions of the 1960s and 1970s were articulated through resistance to the Krleža-Hegedušić tendency dominant in the leftist narrative of post-war Yugoslav art, Hegedušić's master class was also attended by such important protagonists of the New Art Practices as Neša Paripović and Marina Abramović.

VERA HORVAT PINTARIĆ (Sisak, 1926)
Art historian, critic and curator. Horvat Pintarić was a professor at the Faculty of Philosophy, University of Zagreb, where in 1967 she founded the Department of Visual Communications and Design. She developed a specific analytical approach to artistic morphology and wrote critical studies on a variety of topics, from baroque to modern and avant-garde art to comics, posters, television and animated film. Horvat Pintarić explored the relationship between art and ideology (especially in her book *From Kitsch to Eternity*, 1979), and wrote one of the major books on modern art, *Tradition and Modernity* (2009), as well as numerous monographs on such artists as Džamonja, Bakić, Kraljević, Richter, Stupica, Seissl and Wagner. She created a series of educational shows on modern and contemporary art on TV Zagreb.

DŽEVAD HOZO (Užice, 1938)
Graphic artist and professor of graphics at the Academy of
Fine Arts in Sarajevo. Hozo's best-known work connects motifs
from the Bosnian-Herzegovinian cultural tradition with their
contemporary semiotic interpretation, while respecting classic
printmaking techniques.

I

BOŽA ILIĆ (Žitni Potok, 1919–Belgrade, 1993)
An academically trained painter, Ilić was best known for his
Socialist Realist period, and especially for his 1948 painting
Sondiranje terena na Novom Beogradu (*Probing the Terrain in
New Belgrade*).

IRWIN (Ljubljana, 1983–present)
Group of artists, primarily painters, formed in Ljubljana in 1983
and founder in 1984 of the Neue Slowenische Kunst (NSK)
collective with the music group Laibach and the Scipion Nasice
Sisters Theatre group. The founders were Dušan Mandič,
Miran Mohar, Andrej Savski, Roman Uranjek and Borut
Vogelnik. In a purposefully paradoxical artistic and ideological
position of simultaneously looking backwards and forwards,
IRWIN describe their work as based on the 'retro-principle'
or as 'retro-avant-garde'. In addition to installations of paintings
combining the styles and motifs of the historical avant-gardes
with Soviet Socialist Realism and German Nazi-kunst, the
collective has presented such performances as *Black Square on
Red Square* (1992), in which a large square of black cloth was
unfurled on Moscow's Red Square in homage to Kazimir
Malevich and suprematism. More recently IRWIN edited the
book *East Art Map* (2006), which represents the first comprehensive publication on the radical art of Eastern Europe.

ĐORĐE IVAČKOVIĆ (Horgos 1930–Paris 2012)
Painter and avant-garde jazz musician. Ivačković lived and
worked in Paris from 1962 onwards. He is known for his abstract
paintings of wide and free colourful gestures on a white
background inspired by contemporary jazz.

LJUBO IVANČIĆ (Split, 1925–Zagreb, 2003)
Painter and sculptor. From the second half of the 1950s Ivančić
painted under the influence of Informel, using thick layers of
pigment that rise from the surface like a relief, while his imagery
retained its character of figuration charged with existentialist
meaning.

IVAN IVANJI (Zrenjanin, 1929–Weimar, 2024)
Author of many renowned novels. Ivanji was held in the
Auschwitz and Buchenwald concentration camps during 1944
and 1945. From 1982 to 1988 he was the Secretary General of
the Yugoslav Writers' Union. He acted as a personal translator
of German for President Josip Broz Tito and wrote about this
experience in his autobiographical book.

OLJA IVANJICKI (Pančevo, 1931–Belgrade, 2009)
Painter and member of the Mediala group. In her early work
of the 1960s Ivanjicki explored performance and Happenings,
and produced Neo-Dada objects and paintings with Pop art
characteristics. She later turned to commercial painting based
on Renaissance art and national themes.

SANJA IVEKOVIĆ (Zagreb, 1949)
A pioneer of video art, conceptual photomontage, performance
and installation art. Active since the early 1970s, Iveković was
one of the first artists in the Yugoslav Art Space overtly to tackle
feminist themes. Her series of media collages *Double Life* (1975)
and *Bitter Life* (1975–1976) juxtapose advertising imagery with
personal photographs, emphasising the claim of feminism's
second wave that 'the personal is political'. In her seminal
performance *Triangle* (1979) Iveković simulates masturbation on
her balcony during President Tito's ceremonial visit to Zagreb,
provoking the patriarchal constructions of power, and exploring
body politics and spaces of femininity. She co-founded the
Podroom Working Community of Artists (1978–1980) with
Dalibor Martinis.

J

BOŽIDAR JAKAC (Novo Mesto, 1899–Ljubljana, 1989)
Graphic artist, painter, illustrator, also engaged in photography
and film. In 1943, Jakac joined the partisan movement and
promoted cultural and educational activities and graphic art as a
means of anti-fascist and revolutionary struggle. He participated
in the Second AVNOJ session in Jajce in 1943, where he made
one of the best-known portraits of Josip Broz Tito. Later he
served as a professor and the first Dean of the Academy of Fine
and Applied Arts in Ljubljana. Jakac is one of the founders of the
International Biennial of Graphic Arts in Ljubljana.

RICHARD JAKOPIČ (Ljubljana, 1869–1943)
Impressionist painter and art critic, considered to be the
founder of modern painting in Slovenia. Jakopič participated in
the formation of the Slovenian Art Society in 1900 and organised
an exhibition of 80 years of Slovenian painting in 1910. He
exhibited at the First Yugoslav Exhibition in Belgrade in 1904.

OLGA JANČIĆ (Bitola, 1929–Belgrade, 2012)
Modernist sculptor. Jančić won a prize at the first Paris Biennial
in 1959, and participated in the 31st Venice Biennale in 1962.
Her work may be seen as fitting into a specific line of European
modern sculpture characterised by organic forms and
biomorphism.

ANDREJ JEMEC (Ljubljana, 1934)
Painter, graphic artist and art pedagogue. Jemec was a professor
and served twice as the Dean of the Academy of Fine Arts in
Ljubljana.

ZMAGOSLAV ZMAGO JERAJ (Ljubljana, 1937–Ptuj, 2015)
Painter, graphic artist and photographer. Jeraj considered art to
be not a spontaneous aesthetic activity, but 'a project, always
done on purpose', and aimed to overcome the distinction
between mimetic and non-mimetic painting by proclaiming all
painting abstract.

ŽELJKO JERMAN (Zagreb, 1949–Korčula, 2006)
One of the conceptual artists who belonged to the Group of Six
Artists in Zagreb, Jerman experimented with photography using
collage, blurring, photogram, added text, splitting, cutting,
burning and various interventions with photographic chemicals.
His existential rebellion is best summarised in the sentence:
'This is not my world,' which he wrote using a developing
chemical on a large roll of photographic paper and exhibited on
the facade of the Belgrade Student Cultural Centre in 1976.

BORIS JESIH (Škofja Loka, 1943–Ljubljana, 2024)
Painter and graphic artist. Jesih taught at the Faculty of
Education in Ljubljana. His works are classified as Nouveau
Réalisme and hyperrealism.

OLGA JEVRIĆ (Belgrade, 1922–2014)
Modernist sculptor. Jevrić graduated from the Music Academy
and the sculpture department at the Academy of Fine Arts in
Belgrade; she also studied art history. Since her first solo
exhibition entitled *Spatial Compositions* in Belgrade in 1957,

Jevrić's work has stood out from the work of other artists in Serbia for its non-representative research of sculptural form, structure, materials and space. Her participation in the Yugoslav pavilion at the 29th Venice Biennale in 1958 attracted the attention of European critics and brought her widespread acclaim. Jevrić's unique and original approach is characterised by sculptural forms made up of two or more cement masses organised in a unified whole by means of a construction of iron bars. Her objects typically have an abstract plastic structure redolent with expressive, metaphorical characteristics.

MARIJAN JEVŠOVAR (Zagreb, 1922–1998)
Founding member of Gorgona, graphic artist and designer. Through his work on grey and white monochrome surfaces, Jevšovar investigated a process of dissolution that has been described as anti-painting.

BOGOLJUB JOVANOVIĆ (Belgrade, 1924–?)
Painter who began his artistic career in Belgrade in 1953 with two solo exhibitions. In 1954 Jovanović went to Paris, where he made his best-known work, the painting *K55*. Soon afterwards, he moved to New York and withdrew from public appearances.

JOVAN JOCA JOVANOVIĆ (Belgrade, 1940–2022)
Director, screenwriter, editor and film theorist. Jovanović directed some of the provocative feature and documentary films that can be classified as the Black Wave of Yugoslav cinema, such as *Mlad i zdrav kao ruza* (*Young and Healthy as a Rose*, 1971), *Izrazito Ja* (*Distinctly Me*, 1969) and *Colt 15 Gap* (1971).

MILAN JOZIĆ (Belgrade, 1947)
Art historian and photographer. Jozić took the famous photographs of the Belgrade conceptualists at the Student Cultural Centre. He worked at the Library of the Faculty of Fine Arts in Belgrade.

K

ĐORĐE KADIJEVIĆ (Šibenik, 1933)
Art historian, art critic, film director and screenwriter. Kadijević was the first curator of the Gallery of the Youth Centre in Belgrade. He wrote art criticism for the weekly journal *NIN*. Kadijević directed such important films as *Praznik* (*The Feast*, 1967) and *Leptirica* (*The She-Butterfly*, 1973) among others.

DRAGOŠ KALAJIĆ (Belgrade, 1943–2005)
Painter, writer and scriptwriter for TV shows. In Serbia he was known for his influential anti-modernist and radical right-wing ideological views. Kalajić is among the first artists in Yugoslavia whose work could be classified as postmodernist, while his paintings are described as hyperborean realism.

JAGODA KALOPER (Zagreb, 1947–Vienna, 2016)
Artist and actress. Kaloper is known for her roles in Yugoslav and Croatian films of the late 1960s and early 1970s such as Krsto Papic's drama *Lisice* (*Handcuffs*, 1969), and Dušan Makavejev's *WR: Mysteries of the Organism* (1971) which received international acclaim.

HANIFA KAPIDŽIĆ-OSMANAGIĆ (Sarajevo, 1935–2019)
Historian and literary theorist, translator, editor of the magazine *Novi Izraz* and professor at the Faculty of Philosophy in Sarajevo. Kapidžić-Osmanagić wrote about Yugoslav Surrealism and received her PhD for *Le Surréalisme serbe et ses rapports avec le Surréalisme français* (*Serbian Surrealism and its Relations with French Surrealism*) at the University of Dijon, which she published as a book of the same title in Sarajevo in 1966.

MILAN KAŠANIN (Beli Manastir, 1895–Belgrade, 1981)
Art historian, art critic, writer and literary historian. In 1928 he was appointed director of the former Museum of Contemporary Art in Belgrade (not related to the current Museum of Contemporary art which was founded in 1958 and opened in 1965). This museum was merged with the Historical Museum in 1935 to become the Museum of Prince Paul, which Kašanin directed until 1944. He is the author of a number of books on Serbian art.

BORIS KELEMEN (Podravska Slatina, 1930–Zagreb, 1983)
Art historian and curator, one of the organisers of the New Tendencies project in Zagreb. Kelemen was the curator and director of the Gallery of Primitive Art in Zagreb.

TARAS KERMAUNER (Ljubljana, 1930–2008)
Literary historian, critic, philosopher, essayist, playwright and translator. Kermauner belonged to a group of intellectuals and artists known as the Critical Generation. He edited the magazines *Revija 57* and *Perspektive* among others.

JULIJE KNIFER (Osijek, 1924–Paris, 2004)
Painter and founding member of the Gorgona group. Knifer began his research into the possibility of creating an anti-painting in the 1960s, and after a process of relentless reduction he arrived at his signature form of black-and-white meander, which he repeated and elaborated for the rest of his life.

KÔD GROUP (Novi Sad, April 1970–March 1971)
Conceptual art group whose members were Slavko Bogdanović, Janez Kocijančić, Mirko Radojčić, Miroslav Mandić, Slobodan Tišma and Predrag Vranešević. KÔD sought to establish a common artistic, political and moral attitude. The members had all studied literature, determining the character of their work in the fields of visual and concrete poetry. Departing from concrete poetry, they aimed at a synthetic approach to the democratisation and deinstitutionalisation of art. Their work involved Happenings and performances, actions and interventions in public space, film and Land art. They were active in editing and designing the student journal *Index* and contributed to other journals such as *Polja* (*Fields*) and *Új Symposion*. The group had a radical leftist political stance that brought them into conflict with the cultural and political bureaucracy in Novi Sad.

LJILJANA KOLEŠNIK (Slavonski Brod, 1959)
Art historian and researcher, specialised in art and visual culture of the 1950s and 1960s in socialist Yugoslavia and Central Europe. A Senior Research Adviser at the Zagreb Institute of Art History, in 1995 Kolešnik co-founded the Centre for Women's Studies in Zagreb, and in 2010 she initiated the Regional Centre for Art, Culture and New Media. In 2012 she co-curated the exhibition *Socialism and Modernity: Art, Culture, Politics 1950–1974* (Museum of Contemporary Art, Zagreb) and co-edited its catalogue. She has written a number of books including *Between East and West: Croatian Art and Art Criticism in the 1950s* (1999). Kolešnik teaches at universities in Split, Zadar and Zagreb.

VLADIMIR KOPICL (Đeneral Janković, 1949)
Artist, poet, translator, theatre and film critic and member of the group (Ǝ KÔD. Kopicl was the editor of the Youth Forum Art Centre in Novi Sad and actively participated in the Conceptual art scene of the 1970s.

GOJMIR ANTUN KOS (Gorica 1896–Ljubljana 1970)
Painter, professor at the Academy of Fine Arts in Ljubljana and director of the Ljubljana Modern Gallery.

ŽELIMIR KOŠČEVIĆ (Zagreb, 1939)
Art historian, curator and critic. Koščević was a curator at the Museum of Arts and Crafts in Zagreb, and in 1966 became the director of the Gallery of the Zagreb Student Centre. He developed his thinking under the influence of the exhibition practices of EXAT 51, the New Tendencies, Pontus Hultén and Willem Sandberg, and through a dialogue with the new modes of exhibiting introduced by Harald Szeemann and Seth Siegelaub. During the 1960s and 1970s he authored a series of experimental curatorial projects such as the Happening *Hit Parade* (1967), *The Exhibition of Men and Women at the Student Centre Zagreb* (1969), the street action *Draft Decree on the Democratization of the Arts* (1970) and the exhibition *Mail Art/Poštanske pošiljke* in collaboration with Catherine Millet and presented at the 1971 Paris Biennial and the Student Cultural Centre Belgrade in 1972. Koščević was the chief curator of the Gallery of Contemporary Art and an associate professor in Museology at the Group for Art History at the University of Zagreb.

SREČKO KOSOVEL (Sežana, 1904–Tomaj, 1926)
Poet. Kosovel founded the magazine *Konstruktor* with Avgust Černigoj and wrote constructivist poetry.

IVAN KOŽARIĆ (Petrinja, 1921–Zagreb, 2020)
Sculptor, mixed media artist and member of the neo-avant-garde group Gorgona. Kožarić produced public monuments, ready-mades, installations, conceptual proclamations, temporary sculptures, textual works, drawings and paintings that sometimes involved performative elements and continuously explored process, method and form. Although he frequently abandoned his previous research and concepts for new challenges, he remained faithful to the concepts of artistic freedom and artistic autonomy. Kožarić exhibited at numerous major international events, including the Venice Biennale in 1976 and the São Paulo Biennial in 1979. At documenta 11 in Kassel (2002) he presented an installation of 7,200 objects from his studio. His entire studio became part of the permanent collection of the Museum of Contemporary Art in Zagreb. Ješa Denegri has described Kožarić as a 'sculptor, anti-sculptor and non-sculptor in the same person at the same time'.

MIROSLAV KRALJEVIĆ (Gospić, 1885–Zagreb, 1913)
Painter. Kraljević began his education in Vienna and continued at the Academy of Arts in Munich and the Académie de la Grande Chaumière in Paris, becoming one of the founders of modernist painting in Croatia. In Munich Kraljević studied with Oskar Herman, Vladimir Becić and Josip Račić; this group of artists became known as the Munich Circle for their influence on modern art in Croatia.

MIROSLAV KRLEŽA (Zagreb, 1893–1981)
Writer, playwright, poet, essayist, critic and encyclopaedist. Krleža is deemed by many to be the most important writer in the Yugoslav languages. He wrote such novels as *The Return of Philip Latinowicz* (1932), *On the Edge of Reason* (1938), *The Banquet in Blitva* (1938) and *The Banners* (1962), while his dramatic works include the *Glembay Family* trilogy (1932) comprising the plays *Messrs. Glembay*, *In Agony* and *Leda*. He advocated engaged art beyond the Party's dictates and is one of the central figures during the Clashes within the Left on the eve of the Second World War. Krleža founded the magazine *Pečat* (1939) and came into conflict with the Communist Party of Yugoslavia, which at the time had adopted the Soviet canon in art. After the war he was close to President Tito and became one of the most influential figures in Yugoslav cultural policy, especially after the break with the Soviet Union in 1948. In 1950 he founded the Yugoslav Lexicographic Institute, directing it until his death, when the Institute was named after him. Many modernist artists in Yugoslavia constructed and developed themselves in dialogue with or through resistance to Krleža's ideas.

FRANO KRŠINIĆ (Lumbarda on Korčula, 1897–Zagreb, 1982)
Sculptor, one of the founders of the Zemlja (Earth) group and a member of the group Nezavisni (Independents). Kršinić was a professor at the Academy of Fine Arts in Zagreb, where he held a master class after the Second World War. He made sculptures in stone and bronze and is responsible for numerous public monuments, including the largest statue of Josip Broz Tito (erected in Užice in 1961).

ZORAN KRŽIŠNIK (Žirovnica, 1920–Ljubljana, 2008)
Art historian and art critic. Kržišnik was the warden (1947–1957) and then the director (1957–1986) of the Modern Gallery in Ljubljana. In 1955, he organised the 1st International Exhibition of Graphic Arts at the Modern Gallery; it was renamed the International Biennial of Graphic Arts in 1973. Kržišnik focused on cultural policy and international cultural relations. The Ljubljana Biennial became famous for both the importance of its exhibits and for negating the then-dominant Cold War divisions between the East and West, and global divisions into First and Third World countries, thus affirming the official Yugoslav policy of non-alignment. From 1986 to 2000 Kržišnik was the director of the International Centre of Graphic Arts in Lubljana. In 1969, he founded Group 69, aiming to help Yugoslav modernist artists to gain recognition in the art market.

FERDINAND KULMER (Cap Martin, France, 1925–Zagreb, 1998)
Painter. Kulmer's imagery ranges from the abstract and calligraphic in the 1960s and 1970s to figuration with mythological and historical references in the 1980s.

L

LAIBACH (Trbovlje, 1980)
Music and multimedia group founded in Trbovlje in 1980 under the German name for Ljubljana. Since their earliest public appearances, Laibach has been associated with controversy, provoking strong reactions from the political authorities of the former Yugoslavia. Many elements of their artistic and media practice relate to the avant-garde, Nazi-kunst and Socialist Realism. Their process is frequently defined using the terms 'retro-avant-garde' and 'subversive affirmation', a form of excessive ideological identification. In 1984 Laibach initiated the founding of the wider collective Neue Slowenishe Kunst (NSK) with the artists from the IRWIN group and the Scipion Nasice Sisters Theatre group.

VASKO LIPOVAC (Kotor, 1931–Split, 2006)
Painter, sculptor, graphic artist, designer, illustrator and set designer.

STANKO LASIĆ (Karlovac, 1927–Paris, 2017)
Historian and literary theorist. Lasić researched Yugoslav and Croatian cultural and political history, especially the work of Miroslav Krleža, to which he dedicated a large number of studies and books. He wrote and edited the seminal edition *The Conflict on the Literary Left 1928–1952* (1970), dedicated to the various positions and opinions on art and politics of the writers, artists and politicians in Yugoslavia. Lasić lectured at the Faculty of Philosophy in Zagreb until 1976, and from 1978 to 1992 he lectured at the University of Amsterdam.

OTO LOGO (Belgrade, 1931–2016)
Predominantly modernist sculptor. Logo produced figural and abstract sculptures, including public monuments.

ZVONIMIR LONČARIĆ (Zagreb, 1927–2004)
Sculptor and painter. Lončarić worked in the Zagreb cartoon studio as a set designer and illustrator. He was the producer and

art director of numerous animations including $1\times1 = 1$ (1964) and *Escape* (1969).

PETAR LUBARDA (Ljubotinj, 1907–Belgrade, 1974)
Modernist painter inspired by historical themes and motifs, medieval fresco-painting and Montenegrin landscapes. Lubarda's exhibition in Belgrade in 1951 is considered a turning point and the end of the Socialist Realist dogma in art, marking a shift in the official cultural policy to modernism as the definitive guiding paradigm. His expressive and monumental paintings, rooted in tradition and history, were seen as successfully uniting the procedures of modern art and state policies. As a result, Lubarda was chosen for most of Yugoslavia's international artistic representation during the 1950s (Venice, São Paulo, Tokyo, Brussels and more). Later, many of his works became an integral part of the collections of numerous state institutions.

STEVAN LUKETIĆ (Budva, 1925–Zagreb, 2002)
A sculptor who worked with discarded materials, researching the relationships between materials and form. Luketić also produced monumental sculpture.

TANAS LULOVSKI (Želevo, 1940–Skopje, 2006)
A painter whose work is characterised as poetic hyperrealism.

M

MIROSLAV MANDIĆ (Novi Sad, 1949)
Artist and poet. Mandić founded the KÔD group and was one of the key protagonists of the Novi Sad Conceptual art scene. He was sentenced to prison for his artistic and political activities for nine months during 1972–1973. From 1991 to 2001 Mandić carried out a durational performance *The Rose of Wandering*, when he walked the length of the circumference of the globe.

DIMITRIJE BAŠIČEVIĆ MANGELOS (Šid, 1921–Zagreb, 1987)
Art historian, critic, curator and artist. Bašićević is one of the founders of the Gorgona group. During the 1960s he ran the Gallery of Primitive Art in Zagreb, and in the 1970s he directed the Centre for Film, Photography and Television. Bašićević made art from his high school days, but only began to exhibit his 'anti-art' or 'no-art' at the end of the 1960s under the pseudonym Mangelos. His works examining the semiotic and poetic relations and negations of images and words were presented in notebooks, on blackboards and globes, and as interventions in books and magazines. Mangelos's practice first became significant in the context of the New Art Practices, and then gained international recognition in relation to the history of the neo-avant-garde.

IVAN MARTINAC (Split, 1938–2005)
Film director, screenwriter, editor, cameraman, poet, journalist, architect, painter and chess player. Martinac is one of the most respected Croatian filmmakers, producing short experimental and documentary films through amateur cinema clubs in Belgrade and Split from the beginning of the 1960s onwards. Martinac aimed to make 'pure film', for which he invented a distinctive film editing technique, and was a prominent film critic.

DALIBOR MARTINIS (Zagreb, 1947)
One of the pioneers of video art in Yugoslavia, notable for his performances, video and media art and graphic design. Martinis co-founded the Podroom Working Community of Artists (1978–1980) with Sanja Iveković. Their open studio became an alternative space that served as a place of discussion and self-articulation for the artist-protagonists of the New Art Practices.

ADRIANA MARAŽ (Ilirska Bistrica, 1931–2015)
Graphic artist. Maraž worked in a combined graphic technique, with a focus on everyday objects.

ZORAN MARKUŠ (Zemun, 1925–Belgrade, 1996)
Art historian and art critic. He worked in the Federal Committee for Foreign Cultural Relations and as an advisor to the Yugoslav Triennial of Visual Arts. Markuš wrote art criticism for the daily newspapers *Borba* and *Politika*.

MILENKO MATANOVIĆ (Ljubljana, 1947)
Member of the OHO group. Matanović wrote concrete and visual poetry and made paintings and objects from industrial materials and simple objects from natural materials. In 1971, along with the other members of the OHO group, he joined the Šempas Family Art Commune. A year later Matanović moved to Scotland and then to the United States.

GORANKA MATIĆ (Maribor, 1949)
Photographer whose work developed simultaneously in both art photography and photojournalism. Matić is considered to have been a chronicler of the events of the artistic, social and political scene of Belgrade since the 1980s. She was the photographic editor of the weekly journal *Vreme* and the daily newspaper *Politika*, and taught photojournalism at the Faculty of Political Sciences in Belgrade.

DAVOR MATIČEVIĆ (Split, 1945–Zagreb, 1994)
Art historian, curator of the department of Contemporary Art of the Gallery of the City of Zagreb (now the Museum of Contemporary Art). From 1983 Matičević was the head of the Centre for Photography, Film and Television, and from 1991 the Gallery's director. He was involved in art criticism from 1966, publishing articles in the magazines *Polet*, *Studentski list*, *Dizajn*, *Čovjek i prostor*, *Telegram*, *Novine Galerija SC*, *Pitanja* and *Sinteza*. As one of the most important art historians and curators, Matičević influenced the Croatian art scene of the 1970s and 1980s. He represented the contemporary Yugoslav scene at such major international exhibitions such the São Paulo Biennial, the Venice Biennale, IFA Stuttgart and others.

SLAVKO MATKOVIĆ (Subotica, 1948–1994)
Conceptual artist engaged in visual-poetic research, experimental film, interventions in space, performance, bodily actions, Arte Povera, adhesive tape texts, mental sculptures, author's comic-books, literature, poetry and Mail art. Matković was one of the founding members of the Bosch+Bosch group.

MEDIALA (Belgrade, 1957–1966)
Art group founded in 1957 in Belgrade, and launched in 1958 with its first exhibition, *Mediala Research*. Although the name of the group appears to refer to the Middle Ages, it actually combines the word *med* (honey, understood here as elixir or medicine) and the word *ala* (dragon, as a symbol of darkness and destruction). Mediala's founding members were Leonid Šejka, Miro Glavurtić, Olja Ivanjicki and Vladan Radovanović. They were later joined by Siniša Vuković, Svetozar Samurović, Dado Đurić, Milovan Vidak, Predrag Ristić, Milić od Mačve, Vladimir Veličković, Ljuba Popović, Kosta Bradić and others. The group's principles for action were published in 1959 in the only issue of their samizdat journal *List za umetnost* (*Art Magazine*), which was edited by the main ideologist of the group Glavurtić. Characteristic of Mediala was its members' interest in mysticism, the occult and the esoteric. The codex written by Vidak advocates the 'liberation from fear and the desire to revive anachronism' and 'tearing down the Hegelian wall'. Their work is characterised by a resistance to socialist modernism and a belief in the timeless properties of art. Mediala is primarily a painting movement whose members turn to the idealisation of Renaissance, Baroque

and Byzantine art, and paint mainly in the spirit of post-surrealist fiction and metaphysics in an attempt to resist to what they perceived as the alienation of modern art and the destructiveness of modern civilisation. Mediala presented as a group at three exhibitions in Belgrade (1958–1960) and one in Novi Sad (1961). After that, its members mainly acted independently, but the group's ideas became representative of extremes – either very influential or very contested – within the Serbian art scene.

LIDIJA MERENIK (Belgrade, 1958)
Art historian, curator and professor of Modern Art at the Faculty of Philosophy in Belgrade. In her historical research Merenik examined the relationship between art and ideology in socialist Yugoslavia and published the book *Ideological Models: Painting in Serbia 1945–1968* (2001). Merenik was especially active as an art critic and curator within the Belgrade scene of the 1980s and published a series of essays on artists and the book *Belgrade: The 1908s, New Phenomena in Painting and Sculpture 1979–1989* (1994).

IVAN MEŠTROVIĆ (Vrpolje, 1883–South Bend, 1962)
Influential sculptor and architect. One of the founders of the Medulić group in Split, which advocated national art based on folk epics and folklore. A strong advocate of Yugoslav unification, Meštrović was inspired by Serbian myth and history when he conceived his complex sculptural installation, the *Vidovdan Temple* (c. 1906–1913). This state project was never realized in its entirety, but a large number of monumental figures produced as part of it are exhibited in the National Museum in Belgrade. Meštrović created numerous public monuments including the *Monument of Gratitude to France* (1930), the *Victor* monument (1928) at the Kalemegdan Fortress in Belgrade and *Gregory of Nin* (1927) in Split; and the grand sculptural-architectural pieces *Monument to the Unknown Hero on Mount Avala* (1938) and the *Mausoleum of Njegoš* on Mount Lovćen (1974). After the Second World War, he emigrated to the United States and became a US citizen.

MATKO MEŠTROVIĆ (Korčula, 1933)
Historian and theoretician of art and design. From 1956 to 1964 Meštrović worked as an art critic for Radio Zagreb. In 1959 he co-founded the Gorgona group and was active within it until it dissolved in 1966. He was one of the initiators and organizers of the New Tendencies. His art criticism and theory examined the relationship between technology, science, art, design and the media. He was the editor of the magazine *Bit International 4*, published in 1969. From 1970 to 1987 he was an advisor to the director of Radio-Television Zagreb, and from 1987 to 1992 he was the director of the Croatian Institute of Culture. Meštrović worked at the Centre for Industrial Design in Zagreb and for the International Council of Industrial Design Societies (ICSID). He is the author of a number of theoretical books, including *Design Theory and Environmental Problems* (1980).

LJUBOMIR MICIĆ (Sošice near Jastrebarsko, 1895–Kačarevo, 1971)
Avant-garde artist and poet. One of the founders and *spiritus movens* of the avant-garde movement Zenit and the founder of the magazine *Zenit* (1921–1926). Micić was in contact with a wide network of European avant-garde artists, and in 1924 he organised the first exhibition of avant-garde art in Belgrade. After he published his essay 'Zenitism through the Prism of Marxism' in *Zenit* under a pseudonym in 1926, the magazine was banned for its role in 'spreading communist propaganda'. Micić proclaimed Zenit as a 'Balkan Totalizer of a New Life and New Art' and advocated the concepts of the Balkan 'Barbarogenius' and the Balkanization of Europe.

MILORAD BATA MIHAILOVIĆ (Pančevo, 1923–Paris, 2011)
Painter, founding member of the Zadar Group and the Group of Eleven. Mihailović's practice comprises gestural painting close to abstract expressionism and lyrical abstraction. After 1952 he lived and worked alternately in Belgrade and Paris.

VELIZAR VASA MIHIĆ (Otočac, 1933)
Sculptor and painter. Mihić developed new synthetic materials from which he derived his minimalist Colour Field sculptural installations. He has lived Los Angeles since 1960 where he taught at the University of California's department of Design and Media Arts.

JURE MIKUŽ (Ljubljana, 1949)
Art historian, curator and art critic. Mikuž was the curator of the Museum of the Slovenian Revolution, curator and director of the Modern Gallery in Ljubljana and a professor at the University of Ljubljana.

SLOBODAN ERA MILIVOJEVIĆ (Užice, 1944–Belgrade, 2021)
Conceptual artist, member of the informal group of six artists connected to the Belgrade Student Cultural Centre in the 1970s. Milivojević's practice includes performances, actions, situations, events, sessions, photographs, masks, diagrams, chess games and other activities in which the boundaries between art and life disappear. As part of his work he conducted daily 'art sessions', which he described as transformations of an event into a situation that cannot be entirely predicted in advance. For Milivojević, a 'situation is closest to a state of affairs and presents an intersection of a multitude of events'.

MILO MILUNOVIĆ (Cetinje, 1897–Belgrade, 1967)
Painter and professor at the Academy of Fine Arts in Belgrade, where he also led the master class. Through the authority he commanded he secured the transfer of the principles of interwar painting to post-war art.

ISMET MUJEZINOVIĆ (Tuzla, 1907–1984)
Painter and soldier and journalist in the People's Liberation Struggle during the early 1940s. After the National Liberation War, Mujezinović's painting remained attached to themes related to the war and the revolution, resulting in his work being seen as a classic example of Socialist Realism. He is one of the founders of the School of Fine Arts in Sarajevo.

EDO MURTIĆ (Velika Pisanica, 1921–Zagreb, 2005)
Painter. Murtić began his career in the interwar period, when his work moved between colouristic intimacy and realism. He participated in the People's Liberation Struggle of the Second World War by producing posters, slogans and illustrations for bulletins and propaganda leaflets. His most significant works from this period are his illustrations for the poem *Jama* (*The Pit*) by Ivan Goran Kovačić. After the war, his painting evolved towards expressive and lyrical abstraction, and Murtić became one of the most influential modernist painters in Croatia.

ZORAN MUŠIČ (Gorica, 1909–Venice, 2005)
Painter and graphic artist. In addition to such classic genres as landscapes, still life and portraits, Music's most memorable images are his horror scenes from the Dachau concentration camp where he was detained during the Second World War. He lived in Paris for most of his later life.

N

PREDRAG NEŠKOVIĆ (Bijela, 1938)
A painter who began his career in the mid-1960s. Nešković's work incorporates kitsch, trash and artistic amateurism in ironic relation to the media and consumer culture.

VIRGILIJE NEVJESTIĆ (Tomislavgrad, 1935–Paris, 2009)
Graphic artist, painter and poet. Nevjestić lived in Paris from
1968, where he founded l'Académie Virgile in 1987 and taught a
special course in graphics. He also taught at the French Institute
for the Restoration of Works of Art.

DAVID NEZ (Cambridge, Massachusetts, 1949)
Conceptual artist, member of the OHO group and the Šempas
Family Art Commune. Nez made objects, installations and Land
art and is known for his installations of mirrors in the landscape.
In 1972, he left Yugoslavia and returned to the United States.

KOLOMAN NOVAK (Dobrovnik, 1933–Belgrade, 2018)
A neo-constructivist artist who experimented with Kinetic and
Lumino-Kinetic art. In his practice, Novak strove to synthesise
colour, movement, light and sound.

EDIN NUMANKADIĆ (Sarajevo, 1948)
Painter. His practice is understood as inhabiting a space between
Color Field painting and analytical painting. In the mid-1970s
Numankadić co-founded the Sarajevo art group Prostor-Oblik
(Space-Form). After the wars of the 1990s he destroyed all his
pre-war works. Numankadić is one of the founders of the Ars
Aevi collection.

O

OHO GROUP (Ljubljana, 1966–1971)
Conceptual art group comprising Marko Pogačnik, Iztok Geister
Plamen, Marjana Ciglič, Milenko Matanović, Andraž Šalamun,
Tomaž Šalamun, David Nez, Matjaž Hanšek, Naško Križnar,
Vojin Kovač Chubby, Aleš Kermavner, Franci Zagoričnik, Marika
Pogačnik, Zvona Ciglič and Nuša and Srečo Dragan. The group
developed their activities through all types of the New Art
Practices: Conceptual art, performance, Happenings, concrete
and visual poetry, Mail art and experimental film. In 1970, OHO
participated in the exhibition *Information* at the Museum of
Modern Art, New York. They published books through their
OHO Edition.

PETAR OMČIKUS (Sušak, 1926–Belgrade, 2019)
Painter, member of the Zadar Group and the Group of Eleven.
In the 1950s he went to Paris, where he developed his artistic
language, ranging from 'abstract landscape' to a gestural
colouristic figuration in which he discreetly referred to social
and political events. Omčikus later devoted himself mainly
to painting portraits.

DUŠAN OTAŠEVIĆ (Belgrade, 1940)
A painter whose work has had the characteristics of Pop art
since the mid-1960s. Inspired by the craft of storefront signage,
Otašević uses non-painting materials to examine the relationship
between popular culture and art, myths, politics and kitsch.

P

ŽARANA PAPIĆ (Sarajevo, 1949–Belgrade, 2002)
Sociologist and anthropologist, professor at the University of
Belgrade, one of the founders of the feminist movement in
Yugoslavia and co-founder of the Belgrade Centre for Women's
Studies in 1992. With Dunja Blažević and Nada Ler-Sofronić
Papić initiated and led the legendary conference Drug-ca Žena
(Comrade Woman) at the Belgrade Student Cultural Centre in
1978, which was crucial for the development of feminism's
second wave in Yugoslavia and a renewed focus on womens'
issues after the self-abolition of the Anti-Fascist Women's Front
in 1953.

NEŠA PARIPOVIĆ (Belgrade, 1942)
Conceptual artist and member of the informal group of six
artists operating in the early 1970s at the Student Cultural Centre
in Belgrade. Paripović's art is discreet and introverted and is
characterised by a particular sensibility in dealing with ephemeral
and transitory acts in the process of 'becoming art'. In his own
words, 'a work-act reveals its own existence by not having the
constructive character that would make it become a rule,
discipline, message, style – anything other than life itself'. In his
practice Paripović freely traversed different media: painting,
drawing, photography, film, video, text, performance, interventions, installations and more. His film *N.P. 77* (1977), in which
the artist records his journey negotiating Belgrade by stepping
from roof to roof and jumping over obstacles, became one of
the best-known works of the New Art Practices in Yugoslavia.

ZORAN PAVLOVIĆ (Skopje, 1932–Belgrade, 2006)
Painter and art critic. Pavlović was a professor at the Faculty of
Fine Arts in Belgrade. In the early 1960s he painted in the spirit
of Informel before he moved to New Figuration as a means for
commenting on modern society.

BOJANA PEJIĆ (Belgrade, 1948)
Art historian and curator, significant for the articulation of
feminist art histories in an international context with an
emphasis on Yugoslav and Eastern European art. From 1977 to
1991 Pejić worked as one of the curators at the Student Cultural
Centre Gallery in Belgrade. She moved to Germany in 1991,
where she worked as a visiting professor at Humboldt University
in Berlin. Pejić has curated several major international exhibitions
including such seminal curatorial projects as *After the Wall*
(Moderna Museet, Stockholm, 1999) and *Gender Check* (Museum
of Modern Art, Vienna, 2009).

DUŠAN PERČINKOV (Skopje, 1939)
Painter and graphic artist. Perčinkov was a professor at the
Faculty of Fine Arts in Skopje. In his painting he uses objects
and signs as the starting point for a journey to geometric
abstraction through processes of reduction and multiplication.

VLADIMIR PETEK (Zagreb, 1940–2003)
Artist who worked with experimental film and photography.
His first experimental films made in the early 1960s were the
subject of the famous 'Anti-film and Us' debates in Cinema Club
Zagreb, which led to the establishment of the GEFF Festival
of Experimental Film. Petek also founded the FAVIT (Film,
Audiovisual Investigations, Television) festival in Zagreb in 1971.
In his cinematic experiments he applied unconventional editing
processes to leftover and discarded film footage, intervening
directly (for example cutting or painting) on the film stock itself.

ORDAN PETLEVSKI (Prilep, 1930–Zagreb, 1997)
Painter, graphic artist and illustrator. Petlevski won the Grand
Prix at the first Paris Biennial in 1959. Influenced by Informel,
Petlevski's later works on canvas are characterised by intense
colours and thick layers of paint presenting abstracted organic
forms with figurative elements.

MIHAJLO PETROV (Belgrade, 1902–1983)
Painter, graphic artist, illustrator, poet, critic, teacher and active
participant in the avant-garde movement. Petrov mostly collaborated with the magazine *Zenit*, but also with the magazines
Dada Tank and *Út*. He wrote art reviews, published a number of
articles about fine art and made posters and graphics for books.
Petrov was a member of the Oblik (Form) group (1926–1929).
From 1940 to 1951 he was a professor at the Academy of Fine Arts
in Belgrade where he founded the Graphics department. Later
he moved to the Belgrade Academy of Applied Arts, where he
headed the department of Applied Graphics.

PROSTOR-OBLIK GROUP (SPACE-FORM GROUP;
Sarajevo, 1975–mid 1980s)
Group of artists dedicated to 'autonomous plastic thinking'
in painting. The founding members were Ljubomir Perčinlić,
Edin Numankadić, Tomislav Dugonjić and Enes Mundžić.
Other members include Bekir Misirlić, Nikola Njirić, Mustafa
Skopljak and Radoslav Tadić.

MIODRAG B. PROTIĆ (Vrnjačka Banja, 1922–Belgrade, 2014)
Artist, art historian, art theorist, critic and curator. Protić joined
the Belgrade December Group and the Independents group in
the 1950s. One of the most influential figures of cultural life in
post-war Yugoslavia, Protić was an initiator of the founding of
the Modern Gallery, later the Museum of Contemporary Art in
Belgrade, and was the Museum's first director from 1965 to 1980.
His painting is characterised by a reduction and flattening of
object-forms leading to a gradual shift towards pure geometric
abstraction. As the director of the Museum of Contemporary
Art, Protić established modern museological standards in the
institution, and as an art historian and art theorist he laid
the foundations for the periodisation of Yugoslav art of the
20th century through a series of publications that followed the
exhibitions he organised at the Museum. In these books he
presented the most comprehensive review of Yugoslav modern
art from 1920 to 1960 ever published in socialist Yugoslavia. He
classified art according to media (painting, sculpture, graphics)
and stylistic series, namely artistic tendencies and directions.
Protić gathered art historians from all parts of Yugoslavia within
these editions in order to gain the widest possible view on the
entirety of Yugoslav art production.

MARIJA PUŠIĆ (Belgrade, 1926–2004)
Art historian and art critic. Pušić worked as curator of the
Museum of Contemporary Art in Belgrade and became the
director of the Museum from 1980 to 1984.

RADOSLAV PUTAR (Varaždin, 1921–Zagreb, 1994)
Art historian and influential art critic. Putar was one of the
founders of the New Tendencies project. He was also a member
of Gorgona. From 1972 to 1978 he was the director of the
Gallery of the City of Zagreb, and from 1979 to 1983 he was the
director of the Zagreb Museum for Arts and Crafts.

R

JOSIP RAČIĆ (Zagreb, 1885–Paris, 1908)
Painter and one of the founders of modern painting in Croatia.
He studied with Miroslav Kraljević, Oskar Herman and Vladimir
Becić in Munich, where they formed a group known as the
Croatian School, which later became influential in Croatia as the
Munich Circle. Račić committed suicide in Paris in 1908 under
unexplained circumstances.

VANJA RADAUŠ (Vinkovci, 1906–Zagreb, 1975)
Sculptor. Between the two World Wars Radauš exhibited with
the socially engaged Zemlja (Earth) group. During the Second
World War he fought with the partisans, and later became
a professor at the Academy of Fine Arts in Zagreb.

MIRKO RADOJIČIĆ (Bojište near Nevesinje, 1948–Paris, 2004)
Artist and philosopher and a member of the KÔD group.
Radojičić's practice encompasses Conceptual art, photography,
literary and artistic theory and translation. He was one of the
editors of *Index* magazine.

VLADAN RADOVANOVIĆ (Belgrade, 1932–2023)
Intermedia artist and one of the pioneers of electronic music in
Serbia. During the 1950s Radovanović researched tactile art and

was one of the founders of the Mediala group. He participated
in founding the electronic studio within Radio Belgrade,
which he managed from 1972 to 1999. Through his artistic work
Radovanović explored the synthesis of different types of art
and introduced the concept of the 'vocovisual'.

ZORAN RADOVIĆ (Kraljevo, 1940)
Experimental artist. In the early 1960s he worked on a mechanical
and later an electronic ornamentograph. In his experiments
Radović combines the fields of contemporary science and
contemporary art.

RADOMIR RELJIĆ (Skopje, 1938–Belgrade, 2006)
Painter, whose work in the 1960s was classified as New Figuration.
Reljić's paintings are characterised by literary references and
black humour. He was a professor at the Faculty of Fine Arts
in Belgrade.

VUJICA REŠIN TUCIĆ (Melenci, 1941–Novi Sad, 2009)
Poet, conceptual artist and editor of several magazines. Rešin
Tucić introduced elements of film and performance into
renditions of his songs and poems. In 1977, he founded the
neo-avant-garde magazine *Adresa* (*Address*). He published several
collections of poetry and one novel – *The Horrors of the
Underworld* (1991).

VJENCESLAV RICHTER (Donja Drenova, 1917–Zagreb, 2002)
Architect and one of the founders of EXAT 51, engaged in
urbanism, sculpture, graphic design, painting and scenography.
Richter's practice was guided by the idea of the synthesis of the
arts. He participated in founding the Studio of Industrial Design
(1956) and the Centre for Industrial Design (1963) in Zagreb.
He headed the Department of Architecture at the Academy of
Applied Arts in Zagreb. Richter designed the Yugoslav pavilions
at the Brussels EXPO in 1958 and at the Triennial in Milan
in 1965.

MARKO RISTIĆ (Belgrade, 1902–1984)
Editor, publisher of surrealist writings and publications and one
of the most prominent representatives of Belgrade Surrealism.
Ristić collaborated with the Paris surrealists and published
articles in their magazines. He wrote poetry and literary criticism.
Ristić's works combine a mixture of decalcomania processes,
photograms, collages, assemblages, photomontages and more.
During the 1930s he was a prominent protagonist of the Clashes
within the Left and an advocate of the Breton-Trotsky
aesthetic-political position, which was later supported by many
intellectuals and artists of the time, including Miroslav Krleža,
but was also challenged by the Communist Party. After the
Second World War Ristić became one of the main actors in the
cultural policy of the SFRY and the chairman of the Federal
Committee for Foreign Cultural Relations.

FRANCE ROTAR (Ljubljana, 1933–2001)
Sculptor and fervent modernist, recognizable by his sculptures
presenting the reduced shape of a ball or a sphere that opens
and bursts like a ripe fruit.

BRANKO RUŽIĆ (Slavonski Brod, 1919–1997)
Sculptor and professor at the Academy of Fine Arts in Zagreb.
He produced sculptures in wood and other materials with
characteristically rough workmanship, and created several
significant monumental sculptures.

S

ĐURO SEDER (Zagreb, 1927–2022)
Painter and founding member of Gorgona (1959–1966). During this period Seder painted monochrome images made up of thick layers of paint that were influenced by Informel. After 1976 his paintings became figurative with a broader range of colours and expressive gestures.

JOSIP SEISSEL or JO KLEK (Krapina, 1904–Zagreb, 1987)
Painter, architect and urban planner who was active in the Zenit movement and in the constructivist current of the avant-garde. Seissel co-founded the group Traveleri (Travellers) in Zagreb in 1922. Assuming the pseudonym Jo Klek within Zenit, he worked on graphic design, scenography and costume design. He called his painting process PaFaMa (*Papier-Farben-Malerei*, meaning paper-colour-painting). In 1929 Seissel graduated in architecture from the Technical Faculty in Zagreb; during the 1930s he worked in the Department for the Regulation of Zagreb and became the director of the School of Applied Arts. In 1965 he became a professor at the Zagreb Faculty of Architecture. Seissel received the Grand Prix and the Order of the Legion of Honour for his design of the Yugoslav pavilion at the World Exhibition in Paris in 1937.

LJILJANA SIMIĆ (Belgrade, 1937–London, 1993)
Curator of the Museum of Contemporary Art in Belgrade in charge of international cooperation.

MLADEN SRBINOVIĆ (Sušica near Gostivar, 1925–Belgrade, 2009)
Painter, member of the December Group. Srbinović was a professor at the Faculty of Fine Arts in Belgrade. In addition to painting and graphics, he produced illustration, mosaics and tapestry.

DEJAN SRETENOVIĆ (Belgrade, 1962)
Curator, historian and art theorist. In the 1990s he ran the Centre for Contemporary Art in Belgrade and has been the chief curator of the Museum of Contemporary Art in Belgrade since 2001. Sretenović has written numerous articles and books, including a study of Belgrade Surrealism (*The Uproarious Marble*, 2016). At the Belgrade Museum of Contemporary Art he has curated major retrospective exhibitions of artists of the New Art Practices, such as Raša Todosijević, Neša Paripović and Marina Abramović, for which he also wrote the catalogues.

ALEKSANDAR SRNEC (Zagreb, 1924–2010)
Artist known for his distinct constructivist approach. In 1953 Srnec presented his first kinetic object, and from the early 1960s began exhibiting lumino-plastic and lumino-kinetic objects and environments. He is one of the founders of the group EXAT 51 and was also involved in film animation.

LJUBICA SEKA STANIVUK (Livno, 1949–New York, 2013)
Art historian. In the 1970s Stanivuk worked as an organiser at the Student Cultural Centre in Belgrade, and after 1979 was a curator at the Centre for Visual Culture at the Belgrade Museum of Contemporary Art. In 1985 she moved to the United States.

MLADEN STILINOVIĆ (Belgrade, 1947–Pula, 2016)
Artist, member of the Zagreb Group of Six Artists, and one of the most influential representatives of the New Art Practices. Stilinović's life and work have been a significant inspiration for younger generations of artists throughout the Yugoslav art space. In his practice Stilinović critically and ironically examined the relationship between artistic and socio-economic systems, artistic production and ideological speech, work and laziness, language and money. From 1969 to 1976 he made experimental films and ran the Gallery of Extended Media (PM) in Zagreb.

BRANKA STIPANČIĆ (Zagreb, 1953)
Art historian and curator. During the 1980s she was a curator at the Museum of Contemporary Art in Zagreb, and in the 1990s ran the Zagreb Centre for Contemporary Art. Stipančić is the author and editor of a number of editions and monographs of artists and protagonists of the New Art Practices, including Mangelos, Mladen Stilinović, Vlado Martek, Goran Trbuljak, Vlasta Delimar and Goran Petercol among others. From 2004 to 2021 Stipančić has been working with a group of curators to establish the Kontakt Collection in Vienna.

JOSIP STOŠIĆ (Zagreb, 1935–2009)
Poet, art historian and artist. Stošić's multimedia practice encompasses poetry, scripts for short plays, films, animations, installations, objects, concepts, graphics, photography and more.

GABRIJEL STUPICA (Dražgoše, 1913–Ljubljana, 1990)
Painter. Stupica developed a complex painting technique and often used a combination of oil, tempera, graphic, collage and assemblage. He is best known for his large format 'white paintings' in which he surrounded fragile figures with details that subtly point to the relationship between sexuality and death.

IRINA SUBOTIĆ (Belgrade, 1941)
Art historian and curator. Between 1965 and 1978 Subotić was a curator at the Museum of Contemporary Art in Belgrade and from 1979 to 1995 curator at the National Museum in Belgrade. From 1991 to 2002 she taught the history of modern art at the Faculty of Architecture in Belgrade, and since 1995 she has taught at the Academy of Arts in Novi Sad. Subotić has organised numerous exhibitions of Yugoslav art of the 20th century both at home and abroad. Her particular interests include researching avant-garde art and the Zenit movement. She has written numerous books and articles about the art circles around the magazine *Zenit*, the best known being the award-winning monograph *Zenit 1921–1926* (2008, with Vidosava Golubović).

MARIJAN SUSOVSKI (Zagreb, 1943–2003)
Art historian, critic, curator and director of the Zagreb City Gallery. He researched avant-garde art and the New Art Practices, design, video and television. Susovski published art criticism and discussions and wrote forewords in exhibition catalogues. He co-edited the seminal exhibition catalogue *New Art Practices 1966–1978*, Gallery of Contemporary Art, Zagreb, 1978.

BÁLINT SZOMBATHY (Pačir, 1950)
Artist, theorist and critic. Szombathy began his artistic career as a co-founder of the Bosch+Bosch group. His work moves between politics and poetics, aesthetics and ethics. In the mid-1980s he became actively involved in performance. He was the graphic editor of the magazine *Új Symposion* (Novi Sad) and edited the Budapest-based magazine *Magyar Műhely*.

Š

ANDRAŽ ŠALAMUN (Ljubljana, 1947–2024)
Artist and member of the OHO group. After working as a conceptual artist and producing photographic projects, installations and objects in the early 1970s, he returned to abstract painting in the second half of the decade. In the 1980s, Šalamun moved to figuration, developing a new style of painting characterised by raw gestures and abstract colours.

TOMAŽ ŠALAMUN (Zagreb, 1941–Ljubljana, 2014)
Poet, conceptual artist and member of the OHO group. A brother of the artist Andraž Šalamun, Tomaž worked as a professor at the Academy of Fine Arts in Ljubljana and as a curator at the Moderna galerija (Modern Gallery) in Ljubljana.

JUDITA ŠALGO (Novi Sad, 1941–1996)
Writer and poet. From the late 1960s Šalgo was one of the key
figures of the New Art Practices in Novi Sad. She was the editor
of the Youth Forum, the editor of TV Novi Sad and the editor
of the Matica srpska publishing house. In her textual and
performative works, Šalgo dealt with feminist issues and topics,
although she never explicitly declared herself a feminist.

LEONID ŠEJKA (Belgrade, 1932–1970)
Artist, art theorist and one of the founders of the Mediala group.
Šejka represented a specific phenomenon on the Belgrade art
scene of the 1950s and 1960s. He was the first of his contemporaries to realise that an artistic act is possible without an aesthetic
object, and as early as the 1950s he performed various ritual
actions as artistic acts. At the same time, in his painting he used
quotations to refer to the canon of art history, thus heralding
the postmodern era.

THE ŠEMPAS FAMILY ART COMMUNE (1971–1979)
The commune was formed in 1971 when the members of the
OHO group decided to stop working in the art world. The idea
of establishing a community was to live in harmony with nature
in an agricultural-artistic commune. The Šempas Family
represented Yugoslav art at the Venice Biennale in 1978. It
consisted of Bojan Brecelj, Andrej Klančar, Marika Pogačnik,
Ajra Pogačnik, Nike Pogačnik, Ana Pogačnik and Marko
Pogačnik. David Nez and Milenko Matanović from OHO were
part of the commune for its first year. It disbanded in 1979.

LJERKA ŠIBENIK (Zagreb, 1935)
Artist. In 1975 Šibenik co-founded the Nova Gallery in Zagreb,
where she promoted neo-avant-garde artists until 2003. In her
own art, Šibenik created complex structures and ambiences
using synthetic materials and worked on intensely coloured
objects with a minimalist aesthetic.

ILIJA ŠOŠKIĆ (Dečani, 1935)
Member of the first generation of Yugoslav artists who worked in
the spirit of the New Art Practices. Before becoming an artist
Šoškić played sports and was state champion and member of the
SFRY national team in the hammer throw. He studied art at the
Accademia di Belle Arti in Bologna, where he lived from 1969
to 1972 when he moved to Rome. He gained recognition through
his collaboration with the Rome gallery L'Attico, where he
exhibited alongside such Italian artists as Jannis Kounellis, Luigi
Ontani and Michelangelo Pistoletto. Šoškić's artistic practice
includes elements of performance, living images (tableaux
vivants), the art of behaviour, guerrilla art, video, cultural and
political myth, mathematics and the metaphysics of nature.

SAVA ŠUMANOVIĆ (Vinkovci, 1896–Sremska Mitrovica, 1942)
One of the most prominent modernist painters of the interwar
period. In 1920 Šumanović went to Paris to study with André
Lhote, where he adopted modernist principles of image
construction. In Paris again during 1925–1928, he worked in a
post-cubist style, combining constructivist procedures and
a gestural expressive use of colour. From 1930 he lived in Šid,
where he painted landscapes in an expressionistic style,
and a series of bathers known as the *Women of Šid*, which has a
special place in his oeuvre. Šumanović also wrote essays on art.
He was executed with other Serb civilians by the Croatian fascist
Ustaša police in a concentration camp in Sremska Mitrovica
in 1942.

MIROSLAV ŠUTEJ (Duga Resa, 1936–Krapinske Toplice, 2005)
Painter and graphic artist engaged in optical research,
particularly graphics. Šutej created art objects that enabled him
to expand his graphic research into the third dimension.

MIŠKO ŠUVAKOVIĆ (Belgrade, 1954)
Art theoretician. He co-founded the conceptual Group 143
(1975–1980) and the informal artistic and theoretical institution
Community for Space Investigation (1982–1989). Šuvaković is the
dean and a professor at the Faculty of Media and Communications, Singidunum University, Belgrade. He also teaches aesthetics and art theory at the Faculties of Music and Interdisciplinary
Postgraduate Studies at the Belgrade University of the Arts,
and is a lecturer at the Faculty of Architecture there. Šuvaković
is considered to be the most prolific researcher of Yugoslav
and Serbian avant-garde and neo-avant-garde art. He has written
a number of books, including *Impossible Histories: Historical Avant-
Gardes, Neo-Avant-Gardes, and Post-Avant-Gardes in Yugoslavia,
1918–1991*, MIT Press, Cambridge (MA) 2003 (with Dubravka
Djurić).

T

IVAN TABAKOVIĆ (Arad, 1898–Belgrade, 1977)
Painter and ceramicist; co-founder of the Zagreb Zemlja (Earth)
group, as well as the Belgrade groups Dvanaestorica (Group of
Twelve) and Šestorica (Group of Six). With Zemlja, Tabaković
painted in a socially engaged spirit, but he later turned to more
intimate topics. In the 1950s he embarked on new research and
experimented with various themes and with a new stylistic
and poetic repertoire. In his experiments Tabaković introduced
reflections on the image through philosophy and science, and
explored the possibilities for the visualisation of knowledge and
the materialisation of the immaterial. Collage, photographic
interventions and photomontage play an important role in his
work, as presented in his cycles *Hidden Worlds* (1960–1968)
and *Life, Thoughts, Dreams* (1965–1977). Tabaković also taught at
the Belgrade Academy of Fine Arts.

RADOSLAV TADIĆ (Sarajevo, 1946–2013)
Painter, graphic artist and sculptor. Tadić was a professor at
the Academy of Fine Arts in Sarajevo and one of the founders
of the Yugoslav *Documents '89* project.

MARINO TARTALJA (Zagreb, 1894–1984)
Painter active over seven decades, from the 1920s to the 1980s.
Tartalja's work ranges from expressionist and post-Cezanne
painting to a personal language of abstraction that he reached
through a process of reducing his self-portrait. Tartalja is one of
the founders of the Oblik (Form) group (1926–1939). He lived
in Split, Rome, Vienna, Belgrade and Zagreb, and was a professor
at the Academy of Fine Arts in Zagreb.

SLAVKO TIHEC (Maribor, 1928– Ljubljana, 1993)
Sculptor. Tihec was a representative of post-war abstract
modernist sculpture. He researched Kinetic art and also worked
on monumental sculpture.

JASNA TIJARDOVIĆ POPOVIĆ (Split, 1947–Belgrade, 2023)
Art historian active among artists and critics gathered around
the Student Cultural Centre in Belgrade. Tijardović Popović
spent some time in New York in 1974 with the artist Zoran
Popović, following the movement of the community of artists
gathered around Art & Language. From 1975 she was a curator
at the Centre for Visual Culture and Information of the Museum
of Contemporary Art in Belgrade, where she introduced the
discourse of Conceptual art into the museum. Later she became
the curator of the collection of New Media in the same museum.
Tijardović Popović collaborated on the catalogues for the
seminal exhibitions *New Art Practices 1966–1978*, Gallery of
Contemporary Art, Zagreb, 1978 and *New Art in Serbia: Individuals,
Groups, Phenomena*, Museum of Contemporary Art, Belgrade, 1980.

SLAVKO TIMOTIJEVIĆ (Brzohode, 1949)
Art historian and curator. From 1971 to 1974 Timotijević was a member of the Group for Action and Anonymous Attraction (A3). From 1974 to 1998 he was the editor of the Happy Gallery at the Student Cultural Centre in Belgrade, and was the director of the Student Cultural Centre from 2000 to 2005. Timotijević was the editor-in-chief of the contemporary art magazines *Beorama*, launched in 1985, and *Art FAMA* during 2007–2013.

SLOBODAN TIŠMA (Stara Pazova, 1946)
Artist, poet, writer and musician. In the late 1960s Tišma began working at the Novi Sad Youth Forum and at the student newspaper *Index*, where he became an editor. At that time, he was engaged in Conceptual art and poetry, and was one of the founding members of the KÔD group. In the late 1970s and early 1980s Tišma founded the rock bands La Strada and Luna. In the late 1980s he retired from public life and began writing his poetic diary, which was eventually published in 2001. An acclaimed novelist, Tišma won the *NIN* Award for literature in 2012.

RAŠA TODOSIJEVIĆ (Belgrade, 1945)
Artist working in performance, interventions, installations and painting. He was a member of the informal group of six artists connected with the Student Cultural Centre Belgrade during the 1970s. In all the media he uses, Todosijević uncompromisingly expresses his artistic views and is critical of social, economic-political, cultural-artistic and educational systems. His works such as *Was ist Kunst?* (1976–1978) influenced the concept of the retro-avant-garde of the NSK (Neue Slowenische Kunst) group, and has also influenced many contemporary artists.

BILJANA TOMIĆ (Novo Selo, 1940)
Art historian, critic and curator. As the curator of Gallery 212 and the BITEF festival in the late 1960s, Tomić brought together performative and visual art forms, presented concrete poetry, and contributed to the emergence of the New Art Practices scene. She collaborated with the Youth Forum in Novi Sad where she organised numerous programmes promoting the views of the historical and neo-avant-gardes. From 1971 to 1999 Tomić worked as a curator of the Student Cultural Centre Gallery in Belgrade. Her work at the April Meetings' Festival of Expanded Media was key to the internationalisation of the New Art Practices on the Belgrade scene. Throughout her curatorial practice, she has actively participated in the forming of new generations of young artists. Tomić was also a founding member of the conceptual Group 143, and the curator of Real Presence, an international exchange and exhibiting platform aimed at young artists and art students.

IVANA TOMLJENOVIĆ-MELLER (Zagreb, 1906–1988)
Graphic designer, photographer and art pedagogue. Tomljenović-Meller attended the Bauhaus art school in the 1920s and was a member of the German Communist Party. She created posters, photomontage and photographs alongside teaching.

GORAN TRBULJAK (Varaždin, 1948)
Conceptual artist. In his work Trbuljak redefines the status of the artwork and artistic labour in the context of the dematerialisation of artistic practice. Trbuljak radically re-examined the autonomy of art within the museum and gallery system in accordance with the paradigm of art of institutional critique. In 1969, he formed the conceptual project Pensioner Tihomir Simčić with Braco Dimitrijević. Trbuljak also worked as a graphic designer for a number of notable magazines such as *Film*, *Polet* and *Gordogan*, and wrote articles about film, photography and the arts for such popular daily and weekly newspapers as *Globus* and *Slobodna Dalmacija*.

LAZAR TRIFUNOVIĆ (Belgrade, 1929–Paris, 1983)
Art historian, art critic and director of the National Museum in Belgrade (1962–1968). Trifunović was a professor at the University of Belgrade where he founded the Department for the History of Modern Art. He was the most influential art critic in Serbia, known in particular for supporting Informel painting in the 1960s and Scene Painting (*slikarstvo prizora*) in the 1970s. His books include *Serbian Painting, 1990–1950* (1973) and *The Anthology of Art Criticism in Serbia* (1967), and a series of monographs and catalogues on individual artists, including Petar Lubarda, Sreten Stojanović and Mića Popović. Since 1993, the annual Award for Art Criticism in Serbia by the Cultural Centre of Belgrade has been named after him.

U

GERGELY (GERGELJ) URKOM (Skorenovac, 1940)
Conceptual artist and member of the informal group of six artists associated with the Student Cultural Centre in Belgrade. In Urkom's approach to artistic thought and work the idea always precedes the final materialisation, regardless of the medium used. His conceptual work *Six Minutes of the Hour as Recorded by Xerox* (1971) was the first work of the New Art Practices purchased by the Belgrade Museum of Contemporary Art. In 1973, Urkom moved to London, where he taught at the Chelsea College of Art and Design.

V

BERISLAV VALUŠEK (Osijek, 1954)
Art historian, curator and director of the Modern Gallery in Rijeka. He is the founder of the international art event *Ex tempore* (Opatija, 1983) and the Biennial of Mediterranean Youth (Rijeka, 1993).

JOSIP VANIŠTA (Karlovac, 1924–Zagreb, 2018)
Painter, graphic artist and writer. Vaništa was one of the founding members of the Gorgona group, initiated the anti-magazine *Gorgona*, and is considered to be the *spiritus movens* of the group. His painting is characterised by a conceptual reduction that goes beyond such considerations as artistic talent, expression and improvisation. This is manifested in his best-known Gorgonist painting of 1964, the anti-painting *Silver Line on a White Surface*, in which the 'mental' image and the 'perceptive' image coincide, arguably constituting the first conceptual painting in Yugoslav art. Vaništa was a long-time professor at the Faculty of Architecture in Zagreb.

VLADIMIR VELIČKOVIĆ (Belgrade, 1935–Split, 2019)
Painter, one of the members of the Mediala group. His imagery inhabits the realms of the figural and the existential, while themes of corporality, suffering and death pervade his entire oeuvre. Veličković lived in Paris where he was a professor at the Academy of Fine Arts for several decades.

VERBUMPROGRAM (established 1974)
Artistic couple comprising Ratomir Kulić (Ruma, 1948) and Vladimir Mattioni (Ruma, 1943). They have operated as 'more than an individual and less than a group' positioned 'before history and after art' since 1974. Verbumprogram's basic medium is text, alongside which they produce art objects that represent a materialisation of the ideas contained in the text.

EMANUEL VIDOVIĆ (Split, 1870–1953)
Painter of coastal landscapes, intimate spaces and memories. Vidović is one of the founders of the Medulić Society of Croatian Artists.

JADRANKA VINTERHALTER (Zemun, 1948)
Art historian. Vinterhalter worked as a curator at the Centre for Visual Culture at the Museum of Contemporary Art in Belgrade. Since 1984 she has worked at the Museum Documentation Centre in Zagreb and as the editor of the magazine *Informatica Museologica*. Vinterhalter has taught museology at the Academy of Fine Arts in Zagreb since 2007.

LAZAR VOZAREVIĆ (Sremska Mitrovica, 1925–Belgrade, 1968)
Painter. Vozarević exhibited with the group Jedanaestorica (Group of Eleven) and the December Group. The structure of his paintings is based on post-Cubist experience, while the contents are derived from motifs and themes from medieval art and mythology. Vozarević taught at the Academy of Fine Arts in Belgrade.

PEĐA VRANEŠEVIĆ (Novi Sad, 1946–2022)
Musician, artist and member of the KÔD group. Vranešević worked as a film critic at the student newspaper *Index*, and was a film editor at the Youth Forum. He founded the rock band Laboratorija Zvuka (Laboratory of Sound).

BRANKO VUČIĆEVIĆ (Belgrade, 1934–2016)
Screenwriter, writer, translator, film critic and historian of avant-garde art. Vučićević is a key figure of the Belgrade neo-avant-garde and the only associate member of Fluxus from Yugoslavia. An avid advocate of the artistic process of montage, Vučićević wrote the scripts for some of the most important Yugoslav films including *Early Works* (1968), *Innocence Unprotected* (1968), *Pictures from the Life of a Shock Worker* (1972), *The Medusa Raft* (1980) and *Serbian Fine Arts* (2007).

ALEKSANDAR VUČO (Belgrade, 1897–1985)
Writer and one of the founders of the surrealist movement in Belgrade. Vučo was the editor and collaborator of the magazine *Surrealism Here and Now* (1931–1932) and the surrealist almanac *L'Impossible* (1929). He was an active participant in the cultural life of post-war Yugoslavia and wrote several novels, including *The Belgrade Trilogy* which treats the fate of a civic intellectual during the revolution.

LAZAR VUJAKLIJA (Vienna, 1914–Belgrade, 1995)
Self-taught painter and member of the December Group. Vujaklija explored archaic motifs and symbols from the past found in ancient stone sculptures, particularly in the local Bosnian tradition of *stećak* medieval tombstones. His paintings transform these motifs into a universal sign or a decorative ornament, and merge traditional symbolism and artisanship with the reduction and flatness of modernist painting.

DRAGICA VUKADINOVIĆ (Raška, 1949)
Art historian. She worked at the Student Cultural Centre in Belgrade from 1971 to 2012 and led the Documentation Programme. Vukadinović retroactively established the programme archive and database of the Belgrade Student Cultural Centre, starting with the digitisation of materials, and edited its newsletter.

SINIŠA VUKOVIĆ (Kumanovo, 1932–Belgrade, 2011)
Painter and architect, one of the founders and members of the Mediala group. Vuković was a professor at the Faculty of Applied Arts in Belgrade, and wrote art criticism for the *NIN* weekly journal.

ŠIME VULAS (Drvenik Veli, 1932–Zagreb, 2018)
Modernist sculptor. Working mainly in wood, Vulas created sculptures whose motifs are totems, pipe organs, spars and masts. He also produced monumental sculpture, such as *Monument to the Victims of Fascism* (1970), located in the village of Podhum.

W

WHAT, HOW & FOR WHOM/WHW (1999–2024)
Curatorial collective comprising the curators Ivet Ćurlin, Ana Dević, Nataša Ilić and Sabina Sabolović with the designer Dejan Kršić. The collective named themselves after the title of the exhibition they organized in Zagreb in 2000 to mark the 152nd anniversary of the publication of Karl Marx's *Communist Manifesto*. WHW envision their projects as platforms for socially engaged models of cultural production reflecting on social reality. They have initiated numerous investigations into the history of Yugoslavia, socialism and modernism. Their exhibitions and publications include *Vojin Bakić* (Gallery Nova, Zagreb, 2008), *Art Always Has its Consequences* (Zagreb, 2008–2010), *What Keeps Mankind Alive?* (11th Istanbul Biennial, 2009), *Everything we see could also be otherwise (My sweet little lamb)* (Showroom Gallery, London, 2017), *Želimir Žilnik/Shadow Citizens* (Sternberg Press, 2019) and many more. WHW were the collective artistic directors of the Vienna Kunsthalle from 2019 to 2024. They curate the programme of the non-profit city gallery Gallery Nova in Zagreb, and run the international WHW Akademija educational programme.

X

XHEVDET XHAFA (Pejë/Peć, 1934)
Modernist painter. Xhafa's work is characterised by associative and lyrical abstraction with strong expressive gestures. He taught at the Academy of Arts in Priština.

Z

IGOR ZABEL (Ljubljana, 1958–2005)
Theoretician and art historian, writer, art critic and curator. From 1986 until his death Zabel worked as a curator at the Modern Gallery in Ljubljana where he curated numerous major exhibitions, including the 1994 retrospective of the OHO group. Zabel was the coordinator of *Manifesta 3*, European Biennial of Contemporary Art held in Ljubljana in 2000, and a member of the International Board of Manifesta. He co-edited the first six issues of *Manifesta Journal* (with Viktor Misiano), and for several years edited the *M'ars* journal published by the Modern Gallery, and acted as one of the advisors for the 2000+ Arteast Collection. A selection of his essays in English was published posthumously by JRP|Ringier, entitled *Igor Zabel: Contemporary Art Theory* (2013). The Igor Zabel Association for Culture and Theory was founded in 2008 by the Zabel family members and the ERSTE Foundation.

ZADAR GROUP (Zadar, 1947)
Zadar Group formed spontaneously in April 1947 when several students in the class of professor Ivan Tabaković at the Belgrade Academy of Fine Arts abandoned the restrictive dictates of the Academy studios for the coastal city of Zadar where they could enjoy the freedom of being and making outside in a natural environment. The students were Mića Popović, Petar Omčikus, Bata Mihailović, Mileta Andrejević, Vera Božičković, Kosara Bokšan and Ljubinka Jovanović. They were soon joined by friends from beyond the Academy, such as the writer Borislav Mihajlović Mihiz. In relation to Socialist Realism, which was then the official doctrine of art, Zadar Group advocated freedom of creation which influenced a new attitude in Serbian fine art.

MEHMED ZAIMOVIĆ (Tuzla, 1938–Sarajevo, 2011)
Painter and member of Group 69. Approaching painting according to modernist principles, Zaimović often used the arabesque and the symbolism of the Orient in his work.

ZEMLJA GROUP (EARTH GROUP; Zagreb, 1929–1935)
Artists' collective founded on the basis of a manifesto in Zagreb
in 1929, produced by an organised gathering of leftist members
and sympathizers, painters, sculptors and architects. With their
manifesto they aimed to articulate precisely the goals of their
social activities, as summarised in the statement 'art and life are
the same'. Zemlja's members were Antun Augustinčić, Vinko
Grdan, Krsto Hegedučić, Drago Iber, Leo Junek, Frano Kršinić,
Omer Mujadžić, Oton Postružnik, Kamilo Ružička, Ivan
Tabaković, Marijan Detoni, Ivan Generalić, Željko Hededušić,
Fedor Vaić, Vilim Svećnjak, Edo Kovačević, Branka Hegedušić-
Frangeš, Ernest Tomačević, Lavoslav Horvat, Stjepan Planić and
Mladen Kauzlarić.

IGOR ZIDIĆ (Split, 1939)
Art historian, critic and poet. Zidić was the director of the
Modern Gallery in Zagreb from 1989 to 2008. From 2002 to 2014
he was the president of Matica Hrvatska, an important cultural
institution with a mission to promote Croatian identity in the
arts and sciences.

NERMINA ZILDŽO (Sarajevo, 1949)
Art historian. Zildžo was a long-time curator at the National
Gallery of Bosnia and Herzegovina. She teaches at the
International University of Sarajevo (IUS).

ŽELIMIR ŽILNIK (Niš, 1942)
Film and television director and screenwriter. Žilnik has written
the scripts for more than 50 feature and documentary films.
For his low-budget docudramas he hires amateur actors to
portray the lives of poor and marginal groups. In his films Žilnik
reacts directly to contemporary social, political and economic
issues, exposing them to a particular critical analysis. His first
feature film *Early Works* (1968) won the Golden Bear Award at the
Berlin Film Festival.

VILKO ŽILJAK (Sveti Ivan Zelina, 1946)
Informatics and computer engineer. Žiljak worked in the research,
development and application of information, computer and
graphics technology. He is a pioneer in mathematical modelling
and simulation, computer graphics and printing, as well as
computer-aided visual research. Žiljak was a postgraduate studies
professor at the Faculty of Graphic Arts, University of Zagreb.

GORKI ŽUVELA (Našice, 1946–Split, 2017)
Artist and early participant in the New Art Practices. Žuvela
created paintings, objects and spatial installations and graphic
design, and taught at the Arts Academy of the University of Split.

(Ǝ

(Ǝ GROUP (Novi Sad, February–May 1971)
Conceptual art group whose members were Ana Raković,
Čedomir Drča, Vladimir Kopicl and Miša Živanović. (Ǝ's goal
was to explore visual and concrete poetry. They closely
collaborated with and sometimes merged with members of the
KÔD group but because of differences in attitudes, they soon
stopped working together.

(Ǝ KÔD GROUP (Novi Sad, 1971–1972)
(Ǝ KÔD's members were Čedomir Drča, Vladimir Kopicl, Mirko
Radojčić, Ana Raković and Pedja Vranešević. The group was
formed by some of the members of the groups (Ǝ and KÔD as a
temporary compromise solution for their joint participation in
the Paris Biennial in 1971. In 1972, the group presented a thematic
issue of the magazine *Polja* (*Fields*) dedicated to Conceptual art,
in which they published translated texts by Joseph Kosuth,
Catherine Millet, Sol LeWitt and others.

About the Authors

Ješa Denegri (Split, 1936) is an art historian, an art critic and a curator based in Belgrade. He was a curator at the Belgrade Museum of Contemporary Art from its opening in 1965 until 1991, when he became a professor of Modern Art History at the Faculty of Philosophy in Belgrade until his retirement in 2007. Since the early 1960s he has been writing on modern and contemporary visual art and he has become one of the most influential writers and curators of the emerging New Art Practices in Yugoslav art of the 1960s and 1970s. He coined the terms the 'Other Line' and 'Art of the Constructive Approach' in order to formulate an alternative and revised historical genealogy of Yugoslav Art, beginning with the historical avant-gardes of the 1920s (Zenit and Yugo-Dada), and continuing after the Second World War with neo-constructivist and neo-avant-garde groups like EXAT 51 and Gorgona and with the radical artistic positions brought by the New Art Practices of the 1960s and the 1970s. His books include *EXAT 51* (1979), *Abstract Art in Croatia* (1985), *Themes of Serbian Art* (1993–1999), *One Possible History of Modern Art: Belgrade as an International Art Scene 1965–1998* (1998), *Art of the Constructive Approach* (2000–2004, in English), *Contributions to the Other Line* (2003) and *Reasons for the Other Line* (2007). He has written a number of monographs on individual artists and essays for exhibition catalogues, and has curated numerous exhibitions at the Belgrade Museum of Contemporary Art and other locations in Yugoslavia, and at international museums and institutions.

Branislav Dimitrijević (Belgrade, 1967) is a professor of History and Theory of Art at the College of Art and Design in Belgrade. He teaches and writes internationally on the art, cinema and politics of socialist Yugoslavia; on avant-garde art, contemporary art and exhibition histories. His books include *Consumed Socialism – Culture, Consumerism and Social Imagination in Yugoslavia, 1950–1974* (2016), *Dušan Makavejev's Sweet Movie* (2017), *Against Art – Goran Djordjević, 1979–1985* (2014, with J. Vesić and D. Sretenović), *On Normality: Art in Serbia 1989–2001* (2005, with B. Andjelković and D. Sretenović) and, most recently, *Yugoslavia: How and Why?* (2019, with I. Erdei and T. Toroman). Since the mid-1990s he has been active as a contemporary art curator primarily interested in exploring site-specificity and context-specificity.

His curatorial projects include the exhibitions *Good Life* (Geozavod, Belgrade, 2012, with M. Hannula) and *No Network* (2011), the first iteration of the Time Machine Biennial in the nuclear bunker in Konjic, Bosnia and Herzegovina. Dimitrijević has co-initiated various unofficial education programmes including the School for History and Theory of Images, Belgrade, 1999–2003.

Jelena Vesić (Belgrade, 1974) is an independent curator, writer, editor and lecturer. She is active in the field of publishing, research and exhibition practice that intertwine political theory and contemporary art. Vesić co-edited *Prelom – Journal of Images and Politics* (2001–2010, Belgrade) and is co-editor of the *Red Thread Journal* (Istanbul), a member of the editorial board of *ARTMargins* and of the advisory board of *Mezosfera*. Vesić co-curated *Lecture Performance*, Museum of Contemporary Art, Belgrade (2010) and the Kölnischer Kunstverein, Cologne, with Anja Dorn and Kathrin Jentjens. She also curated the collective exhibition project *Political Practices of (Post-)Yugoslav Art*, Museum of History of Yugoslavia, Belgrade (2009), which critically examined art historical concepts and narratives on Yugoslav art after the dissolution of Yugoslavia. Her essay-book *On Neutrality* (with V. Jerić Vlidi and R. O'Reilly) is the sixth volume of the *Non-Aligned Modernity* edition of the Museum of Contemporary Art, Belgrade. Vesić co-edited the fifth issue of *Red Thread Journal* entitled *Alt-Truths and Insta-Realities: The Psychopolitics of Contemporary Right* and the book *Feminist Takes: Early Works by Želimir Žilnik* (with A. Majaca and R. O'Reilly, Sternberg Press, London 2021).

Boris Groys is a Professor in the Faculty of Art and Sciences, New York University, and a Professor of Philosophy and Art History, EGS, Saas Fee (Switzerland). His publications include *An Introduction to Antiphilosophy*, Verso, London/New York 2012; *Under Suspicion: A Phenomenology of Media*, Columbia University Press, New York 2012; *On the New*, Verso, London/New York 2014; *In the Flow*, Verso, London/New York 2016; *Logic of the Collection*, Sternberg Press, London 2021; *Philosophy of Care*, Verso, London/New York 2022.

Imprint

EDITORS
Branislav Dimitrijević and Jelena Vesić

AUTHORS
Ješa Denegri, Branislav Dimitrijević, Jelena Vesić
and Boris Groys

EDITORIAL COORDINATION
Clément Dirié

TRANSLATIONS
Mark Brogan, Dušan Đorđević Mileusnić

ORIGINAL TRANSLATIONS OF DENEGRI'S TEXTS
Vera Andressy, Vilim Crlenjak, Maša Marušić, Novica
Petrović and Gordana Žigić

COPY EDITING
Elizabeth Manchester

PROOFREADING
Jeff Bickert, ARK

TECHNICAL AND INTELLECTUAL SUPPORT
Vladimir Jerić Vlidi

PHOTO EDITING
Julia Jachs

DESIGN CONCEPT
Gavillet & Cie, Geneva

GRAPHIC DESIGN
Current Matters, Paris

PRINTING
Standard Impressa, Lithuania

TYPEFACE
Genath (www.optimo.ch)

PHOTO CREDITS
p. 8: Courtesy Želimir Koščević; p. 18, 100, 365: © Museum of Contemporary Art, Zagreb; p. 40: © Museum of Modern and Contemporary Art Koroška (KGLU), Slovenj Gradec; p. 58: © National Museum Belgrade; p. 78: © Museum of Contemporary Art, Zagreb, and Anja Picelj-Kosak; p. 82: Courtesy Peer Gallery; p. 119t: © Institute of Art History, Photoarchive Branko Balić, inv. no. BB-P-01172; p. 119b: Courtesy Olga Olja Ivanjicki Foundation, Belgrade/Photo: Velisav Tomović; p. 129, 177: © Museum of Contemporary Art, Belgrade / Photo: Bojana Janjić; p. 142: © Museum of Contemporary Art, Skopje; p. 175, 210, 260: © Museum of Contemporary Art, Belgrade; p. 196: Courtesy Lutz Becker; p. 238: from the 1977 Paris Biennial catalogue; p. 276t: © Museum of Contemporary Art of Vojvodina, Novi Sad, and Zaviša Matković; p. 276b: Courtesy Želimir Koščević/ Photo: Petar Dabac; p. 292: Courtesy SKC Archive and the artists/Photo: Milan Jozić; p. 299, 319: Courtesy SKC Archive; p. 305: Courtesy SKC Archive and Zoran Popović; p. 322: © Historical Archives of Belgrade, IAB-2128-K373; p. 354: © Jane Štravs; p. 366: © Museum of Contemporary Art Zagreb and Jadranka Vinterhalter

ACKNOWLEDGMENTS
Museum of Contemporary Art, Belgrade; Museum of Contemporary Art, Zagreb; Museum of Contemporary Art, Ljubljana; Museum of Contemporary Art, Skopje; Museum of Contemporary Art of Vojvodina, Novi Sad; as well as Branislava Anđelković, Ivana Bago, Ješa Denegri, Andrej Dolinka, Dušanka Filipović Popović, Boris Groys, Mira Gacina, Ljubinka Gavran, Andreja Hribernik, Jasna Jakšić, Vladimir Jerić Vlidi, Milan Jozić, Želimir Koščević, Nebojša Milenković, Aleksandra Mirčić, Darinka Pop Mitić, Sabina Povšič, Suzana Spasić, Ana Sladojević, Biljana Tomić, Dragica and Vesna Vesić.

This publication was made possible by the Kontakt Collection which is an independent non-profit art association based in Vienna. Its purpose is the support and promotion of Central, Eastern and South-Eastern European Art.

Printed in Europe

PUBLISHED BY
JRP | Editions
Rue des Bains 39
CH–1205 Geneva
info@jrp-editions.com
www.jrp-editions.com

IN CO-EDITION WITH
Les presses du réel
35, rue Colson
FR–21000 Dijon
info@lespressesdureel.com
www.lespressesdureel.com

WITH
Kontakt Collection
Am Belvedere 1
AT–1010 Vienna
info@kontakt-collection.org
www.kontakt-collection.org

on
k   takt

ISBN 978-3-03764-592-5 (JRP | Editions)
ISBN 978-2-37896-432-0 (Les presses du réel)

Distribution

JRP | Editions publications are available internationally
at selected bookstores and from the following distribution
partners:

GERMANY AND AUSTRIA
Through JRP | Editions
info@jrp-editions.com

FRANCE
Les presses du réel
www.lespressesdureel.com

SWITZERLAND
AVA Verlagsauslieferung AG
www.ava.ch

UK, OTHER EUROPEAN COUNTRIES,
USA, CANADA, ASIA, AND AUSTRALIA
ARTBOOK | D. A. P.
www.artbook.com

For a list of our partner bookshops or for any general
questions, please contact JRP | Editions directly at
info@jrp-editions.com, or visit our homepage
www.jrp-editions.com for further information.

Documents Series 32:
Branislav Dimitrijević
& Jelena Vesić
*The Yugoslav Art Space:
Ješa Denegri in the First Person*

This book is the thirty-second
volume in the Documents series,
dedicated to critics' writings.

The series was founded by
Lionel Bovier and Xavier Douroux.